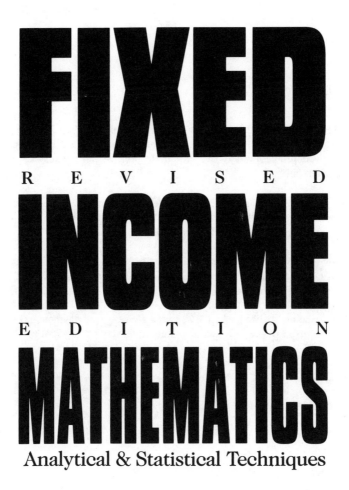

FIXED
R E V I S E D
INCOME
E D I T I O N
MATHEMATICS
Analytical & Statistical Techniques

FRANK J. FABOZZI

PROBUS PUBLISHING COMPANY
Chicago, Illinois
Cambridge, England

ISBN 1-55738-423-1

Printed in the United States of America

BB

1 2 3 4 5 6 7 8 9 0

To my wife, Dessa

Table of Contents

Preface

In recent years, participants in the fixed-income markets have been introduced to new analytical frameworks for evaluating fixed-income securities and new fixed-income portfolio strategies. In discussing fixed-income securities and strategies, we often hear terms such as *duration, effective duration, convexity, negative convexity, option-adjusted spread, total return, PSA, CPR, spot rates, forward rates,* and *delta.* What do these concepts mean? Why are these concepts useful in fixed-income analysis? What are the dangers of using these concepts?

Fixed Income Mathematics not only explains these concepts but also establishes the foundation needed for computation, and describes their limitations and application to fixed-income portfolio management. It begins with the basic elements of the mathematics of finance (the time value of money) and systematically builds on these, taking you through the most state-of-the art methodologies for evaluating fixed-income securities with embedded options, such as callable corporate bonds, and mortgage-backed securities (mortgage pass-through securities, collateralized mortgage obligations, and stripped mortgage-backed securities). The concepts are illustrated with numerical examples and graphs. The material is self-contained and requires only a basic knowledge of elementary algebra.

The second edition of *Fixed Income Mathematics* reflects the advances since 1987. (The first edition was published in 1988 but written in 1987, the difference reflecting the standard delay in publishing a book.) Also included are chapters on the statistical and management science techniques that are often used in fixed-income portfolio management.

Given the expanded coverage in the second edition, the title *Fixed Income Mathematics* does not accurately describe its contents. The subtitle of the book, *Analytical and Statistical Techniques*, is more appropriate.

Many of the chapters in this book are drawn from lectures delivered in my Fixed Income Seminar at the Sloan School of Management at MIT, my conferences, and my presentations to the sales and bond trading personnel at Bear Stearns & Co. and MMAR Group, as well as to other financial institutions and money management firms in the United States, Europe, and Japan.

Differences Between First and Second Editions

The first edition of *Fixed Income Mathematics* was organized in 16 chapters divided into four parts. The second edition delivers 25 chapters divided into six parts. After the time value of money, the second part of the second edition, *Bond Pricing and Return Analysis*, is basically the same as in the first edition, although there is expanded coverage on day count conventions, accrued interest, the yield on floating-rate notes, portfolio yield measures and their limitations, and scenario analysis. At the time the first edition was written, the terms "horizon return" and "total return" were used interchangeably by market participants, and I decided to use the former term in the book. Most market participants now use the term total return, so this is the title for Chapter 8 and the term used throughout the book.

Part III of the second edition, *Bond Price Volatility*, has four chapters compared to three in the second edition. The new chapter presents an expanded discussion and applications of duration. In the first edition, three measures of price volatility (price value of a basis point, yield value of a price change, and duration) were included in one chapter. In this edition, duration is covered in a separate chapter.

Part IV, *The Yield Curve and Its Applications to Pricing and Duration*, is a new two-chapter section. The Treasury yield curve, spot rates, and forward rates are explained and applied to fixed-income valuation in Chapter 13. Chapter 14 then explains how duration measures have been developed to take into account the sensitivity of a portfolio to changes in the shape of the Treasury yield curve.

Part V of the second edition, *Analyzing Bonds With Embedded Options*, applies the analysis in the previous chapters to analyzing bonds with an embedded option. Chapters 15 and 16 are basically the same as Chapters 12 and 13 in the first edition. Two new chapters have been added. Chapter 17 sets forth a model that can be used to value bonds and embedded options. The model is based on the work developed by Andrew Kalotay Associates. Chapter 18 explains the option-adjusted spread technology.

Expanded coverage of mortgage-backed securities is provided in Part VI, *Analyzing Mortgage-Backed Securities*. In the first edition, these securities were covered in two chapters. In the second edition, there are three chapters. The new chapter, Chapter 21, covers the techniques for valuing these securities — the cash flow yield methodology and the option-adjusted spread methodology.

Part VII, *Statistical and Optimization Techniques,* is new to the book. Fixed-income portfolio management increasingly requires statistical analysis and various management science (i.e., operations research) techniques, so coverage of the more important techniques is provided in four new chapters. The techniques covered are probability theory (Chapter 22), Monte Carlo simulation (Chapter 23), regression analysis (Chapter 24), and optimization techniques (Chapter 25).

Acknowledgments

Many people helped me in various ways in this project. Andrew Kalotay and George Williams of Andrew Kalotay Associates assisted in the preparation of Chapter 17, which uses the AKA bond valuation system in the applications. Ron Unz of WallStreet Analytics allowed me to use his CMO system to verify some of my results. David Canuel of Aetna Bond Investors provided the information for the real-world simulation in Chapter 23. Ardavan Nozari of Salomon Brothers Inc. provided the data for one of the regression illustrations in Chapter 24.

Charles Basner of TIPS provided many helpful instructions that I used in developing more efficient spreadsheet programs I wrote for several of the illustrations. His ideas saved me many days of programming. He is also one of the developers of Fabozzi's *Fixed Income Analytics*, which is used for some of the calculations in this book.

Dragomir Krgin of EJV Partners and Jan Mayle of TIPS provided me with information on the day count conventions discussed in Chapter 5. I am grateful to Dragomir for allowing me to reprint an exhibit in Chapter 5 that shows market conventions in major bond markets throughout the world.

I received comments on portions of this book from: John Carlson (Lehman Brothers), Dan Ciola (MMAR Group), Andrew Carron (The First Boston Corporation), Ravi Dattatreya (Sumitomo Bank Capital Markets), Mark Dunetz (The Guardian Life Insurance Company), Frank Jones (The Guardian Life), Matthew Mancuso (Bear Stearns), Edward Murphy (Merchants Mutual Insurance Company), Craig Wood (Olson Research), Sharmin Mossavar-Rahmani (Fidelity Management), Chuck Ramsey (MMAR Group), Dexter Senft (EJV Partners), and Yu Zhu (Merrill Lynch Capital Markets).

I also benefited from conversations with Scott Amero (BlackRock Financial Management), Keith Anderson (BlackRock Financial Management), Anand Bhattacharya (Prudential Securities), Peter Christensen (PaineWebber), Ron Bell (MMAR Group), Jeff Detwiler (Residential Funding Corporation), Gifford Fong (Gifford Fong Associates), Deepak Gulrajani (BARRA), Lakhbir Hayre (Prudential Securities), David Jacob (J.P. Morgan Securities), M. Song Jo (MARR Group), Martin Leibowitz (Salomon Brothers Inc.), Hal Morley (Morley Capital Management), Mark Pitts (Lehman Brothers), Frank Ramirez (MMAR Group), Scott Richard (Miller, Anderson & Sherrerd), Michael Smirlock (Goldman Sachs Asset Management), Ken Spindel (Bear Stearns), C.T. Urban (Norwest Investment Management), Karen Chong-Wulf (Morley Capital Management), and David Yuen (Franklin Management).

Chris Palais and Toni Zuccarini of Drew University edited several drafts of this book, and Pat Peat did the final copyediting.

Frank J. Fabozzi

1

Introduction

Before the 1980s, the analysis of fixed-income securities was relatively simple. In an economic environment that exhibited relatively stable interest rates, investors purchased fixed-income securities intending to hold them to maturity. Yield to maturity could be used as a proxy measure of their relative value. Risk was measured in terms of credit rating. When a fixed-income security was callable, a second measure — yield to call — was used to assess its relative value. For a callable bond, the long-standing rule of thumb for a conservative investor was to select the lower of the yield to maturity and the yield to call as the potential return.

Those days are gone. In today's environment, interest rates fluctuate substantially, and the shape of the yield curve shifts more frequently. Several factors have made the traditional approach to fixed-income analysis of limited value.

First, trading and portfolio strategies that require the sale of a fixed-income security prior to maturity mean that a measure such as the yield to maturity is meaningless. The same holds for the yield to call. And if a fixed-income security is not held to maturity, some measure of risk — to reflect its price volatility as interest rates change — is needed.

Second, investors recognize that the only way to achieve a return equal to the yield to maturity is to reinvest the coupon payments. More specifically, to achieve the yield to maturity that they once thought they had locked in by purchasing a fixed-income security, they must reinvest the coupon payments at an interest rate equal to the yield to maturity. The reduction in anticipated return actually occasioned by reinvesting the coupon payments at an interest rate less than the yield to maturity may not be trivial. The same is true for yield to call.

Third, the plain vanilla bond is being replaced with more complex fixed-income securities as investment bankers continue to design instruments to reduce the cost of debt for their clients. The securitization of mortgages introduces brand new instruments — mortgage pass-through securities, a wide range of collateralized mortgage obligation bond classes, and stripped mortgage-backed securities — that cannot be analyzed using the traditional methodology. Many of these new fixed-income securities have options embedded in them. With the advancement of option theory have come frameworks for analyzing these securities with embedded options.

In their now classic work, *Inside the Yield Book*, Sidney Homer and Martin Leibowitz were the first to demonstrate clearly the limitations of the traditional yield measures (yield to maturity and yield to call).[1] They also document the characteristics of a bond that bear upon its price volatility as interest rates change.

A measure of bond price volatility, popularly known as *duration*, was developed separately as early as 1938 by Frederick Macaulay,[2] in 1945 by Paul Samuelson,[3] in 1946 by Sir John Hicks,[4] and in 1952 by F.M. Redington.[5] However, it was not until 1973 that the link between duration and price volatility was made by Michael Hopewell and George Kaufman.[6] A study by Lawrence Fisher and Roman Weil in 1971 shows the importance of duration for portfolio strategies.[7]

In 1984 a paper written by Stanley Diller with the assistance of his Financial Strategies Group staff when he was employed at Goldman Sachs (particularly Ravi Dattatreya) made two important contributions to our understanding of the price performance

---

[1] Sidney Homer and Martin L. Leibowitz, *Inside the Yield Book* (Englewood Cliffs, N.J.: Prentice-Hall/New York Institute of Finance, 1972), pp. 164-167.

[2] Frederick R. Macaulay, *Some Theoretical Problems Suggested by the Movement of Interest Rates, Bond Yields, and Stock Prices in the United States Since 1865* (New York: National Bureau of Economic Research, 1938).

[3] Paul A. Samuelson, "The Effect of Interest Rate Increases on the Banking System," *American Economic Review* (March 1945), pp. 16-27.

[4] John R. Hicks, *Value and Capital* (Oxford, England: Clarendon Press, 1946).

[5] F. M. Redington, "Review of the Principle of Life Office Valuations," *Journal of the Institute of Actuaries* (1952), pp. 286-340.

[6] Michael Hopewell and George G. Kaufman, "Bond Price Volatility and Years to Maturity," *American Economic Review* (September 1973).

[7] Lawrence Fisher and Roman Weil, "Coping with the Risk of Interest Rate Fluctuations and Returns to Bondholders from Naive and Optimal Strategies," *Journal of Business* (October 1971), pp. 408-431.

of a fixed-income security.[8] First, Diller demonstrates that yield and duration alone are not sufficient to assess the performance of a fixed-income security; a third measure, convexity, is necessary. Second, he links option theory and fixed-income analysis, showing how the embedded option of a fixed-income security will affect the performance of the security. Since then, several works have been published that incorporate and extend the concepts developed by Diller.

There has also come greater recognition that it is not appropriate to value a fixed-income security by using one yield to discount all the cash flows. Instead, a fixed-income security should be viewed as a package of cash flows; each cash flow is effectively a zero-coupon instrument. A 10-year Treasury coupon security, for example, should be thought of as 20 cash flows — 19 semiannual coupons, and a payment equal to the final coupon payment plus the principal. These 20 cash flows should then be viewed as 20 zero-coupon instruments, the first 19 with a maturity value equal to the semiannual coupon payment, and the last with a maturity value equal to the coupon payment plus the principal. The value of each zero-coupon instrument should be determined by discounting the maturity value at an appropriate discount rate derived from the Treasury yield curve (more specifically, from the theoretical Treasury spot rate curve).

Finally, the process of coupon stripping by dealers in the Treasury market, which began in 1982, has forced the price of Treasury securities to their theoretical value. Thus, an understanding of the Treasury yield curve is critical to the valuation of fixed-income securities.

Overview of the Book

The basic foundations of the mathematics of finance are presented in the three chapters of Part I. Chapter 2 explains how to compute the future value of an investment. Chapter 3 shows how to calculate the present value of cash flows to be received (or paid) in the future. The price of any financial asset is the present value of the cash flows expected, so it is essential to have a firm understanding of present value and its characteristics. The yield of any investment is explained in Chapter 4.

Bond pricing and return analysis are the subjects of Part II. Chapter 5 extends the present value concept to the traditional analysis of bonds, showing how their price is determined. Conventional yield measures — yield to maturity and yield to call — which are simply applications of the yield measure reviewed in Chapter 4, are explained in Chapter 6. The potential sources of monetary return by investing in a bond are explained in Chapter 7. The conventional yield measures are then evaluated according to how they account for each of these sources. After highlighting some deficiencies of the conventional yield measures, Chapter 8 describes a better measure of potential return — total

---

[8] Stanley Diller, *Parametric Analysis of Fixed Income Securities* (New York: Financial Strategies Group, Goldman Sachs & Co., June 1984). The paper is reprinted as Chapter 2 in Ravi E. Dattatreya (ed.), *Fixed Income Analytics* (Chicago: Probus Publishing, 1991).

return — that does take into consideration all sources of potential dollar return, even if a bond is expected to be sold prior to the maturity date.

The price volatility of option-free bonds (i.e., bonds without embedded options) is covered in Part III. Price volatility properties of bonds, as well as the characteristics of bonds that affect their price volatility, are illustrated in Chapter 9. Two measures of bond price volatility — price value of a basis point and yield value of a price change — are explained in Chapter 10. The most common measure of price volatility, duration, is the subject of Chapter 11. Chapter 12 demonstrates the role of convexity in explaining the potential price performance of a bond and explains how to calculate convexity.

Part IV brings the Treasury yield curve into the analysis of fixed-income securities. Chapter 13 explains the Treasury yield curve, and then discusses the concept of spot rates and forward rates and how these rates can be determined. The use of spot rates to value fixed-income security is illustrated. Chapter 14 explains how to incorporate the effect of a change in the yield curve on the duration of a portfolio.

The framework developed in Chapters 2 through 14 is then extended in Part V to fixed-income securities with embedded call options. Most non-U.S. Treasury securities traded in the United States have call options embedded in them. Thus, these securities can be viewed as a package of cash flows plus a package of call options. Since the value of the call options affects the value of the security, an understanding of call options and the factors that affect their price is presented in Chapter 15. The price performance and principles of valuing fixed-income securities with embedded call options are presented in Chapter 16. Chapter 17 provides a relatively new model for the valuation of bonds and embedded options. The option-adjusted spread technology is explained in Chapter 18.

Examples of fixed-income securities with embedded call options are mortgage-backed securities (mortgage pass-through securities, collateralized mortgage obligations, and stripped mortgage-backed securities), which depend on the cash flow of mortgage loans. Part VI applies the theory in Part V to the valuation of these securities. Chapter 19 explains determination of the cash flow and the concept of prepayment risk. Chapter 20 provides a brief review of mortgage-backed securities and then illustrates how the current market convention — the PSA benchmark — is used to construct the estimated monthly cash flow of a mortgage pass-through security. Techniques for valuing mortgage-backed securities — cash flow yield and option-adjusted spread — are the subjects of Chapter 21.

The four chapters in Part VII explain the statistical and management science techniques commonly used in fixed-income portfolio management. Chapter 22 reviews basic probability theory and its applications. The concepts explained include expected value, standard deviation (variance), and the normal distribution. This chapter also illustrates the various ways that interest rate volatility is measured by market participants. Monte Carlo simulation is the subject of Chapter 23. Regression analysis, a statistical technique for estimating relationships, is covered in Chapter 24. In the last chapter, Chapter 25, optimization techniques are described.

The guiding objective of this book is to present the mathematics necessary to understand the latest methodologies for evaluating any fixed-income security — those we know about today and those that we will assuredly see in the future — and for understanding the latest trading and portfolio strategies.

I

Time Value of Money

2

Future Value

The notion that money has a time value is one of the most basic concepts in financial analysis. Money has a time value because of the opportunities for investing money at some interest rate. In the three chapters of Section I of this book, we review the three fundamental concepts involved in understanding the time value of money. First, we explain how to determine the future value of an investment. In the next chapter, we explain the procedure for determining how much money must be invested today (called the present value) in order to realize a specific amount in the future. Chapter 3 shows how to compute the yield on any investment.

Future Value of an Investment

Suppose an investor places $1,000 in a bank account and the bank agrees to pay interest of 7% a year. At the end of one year, the account will contain $1,070, that is, $1,000 of the original principal plus $70 of interest. Suppose that the investor decides to let the $1,070 remain in the bank account for another year, and that the bank continues paying interest of 7% a year. The amount in the bank account at the end of the second year will equal $1,144.90, determined as follows:

Principal at beginning of year 2	$1,070.00
Interest for year 2 ($1,070 × .07)	74.90
Total in bank account	$1,144.90

In terms of our original $1,000 investment, the $1,144.90 represents the following:

Original investment at beginning of year 1	$1,000.00
Interest for year 1 ($1,000 × .07)	70.00
Interest for year 2 based on the original investment	70.00
Interest for year 2 earned on the interest from year 1 ($70 × .07)	4.90
Total	$1,144.90

The interest of $4.90 in year 2 above the $70 interest earned on the original principal of $1,000 is interest on interest.

After eight years, the $1,000 investment — if allowed to accumulate tax-free at an annual interest rate of 7% — will be $1,718.19, as shown below:

Beginning of year 1 original investment	$1,000.00
At the end of year 1 ($1,000.00 × 1.07)	$1,070.00
At the end of year 2 ($1,070.00 × 1.07)	$1,144.90
At the end of year 3 ($1,144.90 × 1.07)	$1,225.04
At the end of year 4 ($1,225.04 × 1.07)	$1,310.79
At the end of year 5 ($1,310.79 × 1.07)	$1,402.55
At the end of year 6 ($1,402.55 × 1.07)	$1,500.73
At the end of year 7 ($1,500.73 × 1.07)	$1,605.78
At the end of year 8 ($1,605.78 × 1.07)	$1,718.19

After eight years, $1,000 will grow to $1,718.19 if allowed to accumulate tax-free at an annual interest rate of 7%. We refer to the amount at the end of eight years as the *future value*.

Notice that the total interest at the end of eight years is $718.19. The total interest represents $560 of interest earned on the original principal ($70 × 8) plus $158.19 ($718.19 − $560) earned by the reinvestment of the interest.

Computing the Future Value of an Investment

To compute the amount that $1,000 will grow to at the end of eight years if interest is earned at an annual rate of 7%, $1,000 can be multiplied by 1.07 eight times, as shown below:

$$\$1,000 \, (1.07) \, (1.07) \, (1.07) \, (1.07) \, (1.07) \, (1.07) \, (1.07) \, (1.07)$$

$$= \$1,718.19$$

A shorthand notation for this calculation is

$$\$1,000 \, (1.07)^8 = \$1,718.19.$$

To generalize the formula, suppose $1,000 is invested for N periods at an annual interest rate of i (expressed as a decimal). Then, the future value N years from now can be expressed as follows:

$$\$1,000 \, (1 + i)^N$$

For example, if $1,000 is invested for four years at an annual interest rate of 10% ($i = .10$), then the future value will be $1,464.10:

$$\$1,000 \, (1.10)^4$$
$$= \$1,000 \, (1.4641)$$
$$= \$1,464.10.$$

The expression $(1 + i)^N$ is the amount to which $1 will grow at the end of N years if an annual interest rate of i is earned. This expression is called the *future value of $1*. The future value of $1 multiplied by the original principal yields the future value of the original principal.

For example, we just demonstrated that the future value of $1,000 invested for four years at an annual interest rate of 10% would be $1,464.10. The future value of $1 is $1.4641. Therefore, if instead of $1,000, $50,000 is invested, the future value would be

$$\$50,000 \, (1.4641) = \$73,205.$$

We can generalize the formula for the future value as follows:

$$FV = P \, (1 + i)^N$$

where

$$FV = \text{Future value (\$)};$$
$$P = \text{Original principal (\$)};$$
$$i = \text{Interest rate (in decimal form)};$$
$$N = \text{Number of years.}$$

The following five illustrations show how to apply the future value formula.

Illustration 2-1. A pension fund manager invests $10 million in a financial instrument that promises to pay 8.7% per year for five years. The future value of the $10 million investment is $15,175,665, as shown below:

$$P = \$10,000,000;$$
$$i = .087;$$
$$N = 5$$

$$FV = \$10,000,000 \, (1.087)^5$$
$$= \$10,000,000 \, (1.5175665)$$
$$= \$15,175,665.$$

Illustration 2-2. A life insurance company receives a premium of $10 million, which it invests for five years. The investment promises to pay an annual interest rate of 9.25%. The future value of $10 million at the end of five years is $15,563,500, as shown below:

$$P = \$10,000,000;$$
$$i = .0925;$$
$$N = 5$$

$$FV = \$10,000,000 \ (1.0925)^5$$
$$= \$10,000,000 \ (1.5563500)$$
$$= \$15,563,500.$$

Illustration 2-3. Suppose that a life insurance company has guaranteed a payment of $14 million to a pension fund four years from now. If the life insurance company receives a premium of $11 million and can invest the entire premium for four years at an annual interest rate of 6.5%, will it have sufficient funds from this investment to meet the $14 million obligation?

The future value of the $11 million investment at the end of four years is $14,151,130, as shown below:

$$P = \$11,000,000;$$
$$i = .065;$$
$$N = 4$$

$$FV = \$11,000,000 \ (1.065)^4$$
$$= \$11,000,000 \ (1.2864664)$$
$$= \$14,151,130.$$

Since the future value is expected to be $14,151,130, the life insurance company will have sufficient funds from this investment to satisfy the $14 million obligation to the pension fund.

Illustration 2-4. The portfolio manager of a tax-exempt fund is considering investing $400,000 in an instrument that pays an annual interest rate of 5.7% for four years. At the end of four years, the portfolio manager plans to reinvest the proceeds for three more years and expects that, for the three-year period, an annual interest rate of 7.2% can be earned. The future value of this investment is $615,098, as shown below.

Future value of the $400,000 investment for four years at 5.7%:

$$P = \$400,000;$$
$$i = .057;$$
$$N = 4$$

$$FV = \$400,000 \ (1.057)^4$$
$$= \$400,000 \ (1.248245)$$
$$= \$499,298.$$

Future value of $499,298 reinvested for three years at 7.2%:

$$i = .072;$$
$$N = 3$$
$$FV = \$499,298 \, (1.072)^3$$
$$= \$499,298 \, (1.231925)$$
$$= \$615,098.$$

Illustration 2-5. Suppose that the portfolio manager in the previous illustration has the opportunity to invest the $400,000 for seven years in an instrument that promises to pay an annual interest rate of 6.15%. Is this alternative a more attractive investment than the one analyzed in the previous illustration?

The future value of $400,000 seven years from now at 6.15% is $607,435:

$$P = \$400,000;$$
$$i = .0615;$$
$$N = 7$$

$$FV = \$400,000 \, (1.0615)^7$$
$$= \$400,000 \, (1.518588)$$
$$= \$607,435.$$

Assuming that both investments have the same default risk, the investment in the previous illustration will provide a greater future value at the end of seven years *if* the expectation of the portfolio manager—concerning the annual interest rate at which the rolled-over funds can be reinvested—is realized.

Fractional Periods

In our illustrations, we have computed the future value for whole years. The future value formula, however, is the same if an investment is made for part of a year.

For example, suppose that $100,000 is invested for seven years and three months. Since three months is .25 of one year, N in the future value formula is 7.25. Assuming an annual interest rate of 5%, the future value of $100,000 invested for seven years and three months is $142,437, as shown below:

$$P = \$100,000;$$
$$i = .05;$$
$$N = 7.25$$

$$FV = \$100,000 \, (1.05)^{7.25}$$
$$= \$100,000 \, (1.424369)$$
$$= \$142,437.$$

Compounding More than One Time Per Year

An investment may pay interest more than one time per year. For example, interest may be paid semiannually, quarterly, monthly, weekly, or daily. The future value formula handles interest payments that are made more than once per year by adjusting the annual interest rate and the exponent. The annual interest rate is adjusted by dividing by the number of times that interest is paid per year. The exponent, which represents the number of years, is adjusted by multiplying the number of years by the number of times that interest is paid per year.

Mathematically, we can express the future value when interest is paid m times per year as follows:

$$FV = P (1 + i)^n$$

where

$\quad i = $ *Annual* interest rate divided by m;

$\quad n = $ Number of interest payments ($= N \times m$).

Illustration 2-6. Suppose that a portfolio manager invests $1 million in an investment that promises to pay an annual interest rate of 6.4% for six years. Interest on this investment is paid semiannually. The future value is $1,459,340, as shown below:

$$P = \$1,000,000;$$
$$m = 2;$$
$$i = .032 \ (= .064/2);$$
$$N = 6;$$
$$n = 12 \ (6 \times 2)$$

$$FV = \$1,000,000 \ (1.032)^{12}$$
$$= \$1,000,000 \ (1.459340)$$
$$= \$1,459,340.$$

If interest is paid only once per year, the future value would be $1,450,941 instead of $1,459,340. The higher future value when interest is paid semiannually reflects the more frequent opportunity for reinvesting the interest paid.

Illustration 2-7. Suppose that in the previous illustration, interest is paid quarterly rather than semiannually. The future value is $1,463,690, as shown below:

$$P = \$1,000,000;$$
$$m = 4;$$
$$i = .016 \ (= .064/4);$$
$$N = 6;$$
$$n = 24 \ (6 \times 4)$$

$$FV = \$1,000,000 \ (1.016)^{24}$$
$$= \$1,000,000 \ (1.463690)$$
$$= \$1,463,690.$$

The future value is greater than if interest is paid semiannually.

Future Value of an Ordinary Annuity

Suppose that an investor expects to receive $10,000 a year from some investment for each of the next five years starting one year from now. Each time the investor receives the $10,000 he plans to invest it. Let's assume that the investor can earn an annual interest rate of 6% each time $10,000 is invested. How much money will the investor have at the end of five years?

Our future value formula makes it simple to determine how much each $10,000 investment will grow to. This calculation is shown below, and illustrated graphically in Exhibit 2-1.

Exhibit 2-1

Future Value of an Ordinary Annuity of $10,000 Per Year for 5 Years

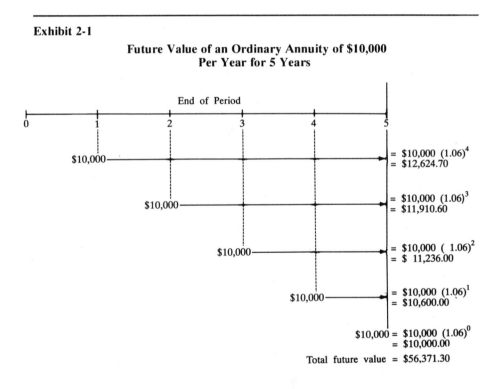

Total future value = $56,371.30

Future value of the first $10,000, received one year from now:

$$P = \$10,000;$$
$$i = .06;$$
$$N = 4.$$

Notice that N is 4 since the first payment of $10,000 will be invested from the beginning of year two (or end of year one) until the end of year five.

$$FV \text{ of first } \$10,000 = \$10,000 \ (1.06)^4$$
$$= \$10,000 \ (1.262470)$$
$$= \$12,624.70$$

Future value of the second $10,000, received two years from now:

$$P = \$10,000$$
$$i = .06;$$
$$N = 3.$$

$$FV \text{ of second } \$10,000 = \$10,000 \ (1.06)^3$$
$$= \$10,000 \ (1.191060)$$
$$= \$11,910.60$$

Future value of the third $10,000, received three years from now:

$$P = \$10,000;$$
$$i = .06;$$
$$N = 2.$$

$$FV \text{ of third } \$10,000 = \$10,000 \ (1.06)^2$$
$$= \$10,000 \ (1.123600)$$
$$= \$11,236.00$$

Future value of the fourth $10,000, received four years from now:

$$P = \$10,000;$$
$$i = .06;$$
$$N = 1.$$

$$FV \text{ of fourth } \$10,000 = \$10,000 \ (1.06)^1$$
$$= \$10,000 \ (1.06)$$
$$= \$10,600.00$$

Future value of the last $10,000, received five years from now:

$$P = \$10,000;$$
$$i = .06;$$
$$N = 0.$$

$$FV \text{ of fifth } \$10,000 = \$10,000 \ (1.06)^0$$
$$= \$10,000 \ (1.00)$$
$$= \$10,000.00$$

Notice that since the last payment is received at the end of the fifth year, it will not be invested. Therefore, its future value will be simply $10,000.

If we total all the future values, we obtain:

Future value of first $10,000	$12,624.70
Future value of second $10,000	11,910.60
Future value of third $10,000	11,236.00
Future value of fourth $10,000	10,600.00
Future value of fifth $10,000	10,000.00
Total future value	$56,371.30

The total future value of $56,371.30 is composed of the five payments of $10,000, or $50,000, plus $6,371.30 of interest earned by investing the $10,000 annual payments.

When the same amount of money is received (or paid) periodically, it is referred to as an *annuity*. When the first receipt (or payment) occurs one period from now, it is referred to as an *ordinary annuity*.

Computing the Future Value of an Annuity

In Chapter 8, you will need to know how to compute the future value of an ordinary annuity. Of course, the procedure we just followed—whereby we computed the future value of each investment—can be used. Fortunately, there is a formula that can be used to speed up this computation. The formula is

$$FV = A \left[\frac{(1 + i)^N - 1}{i} \right]$$

where

A = Amount of the annuity ($);
i = Annual interest rate (in decimal).

The term in the brackets is the *future value of an ordinary annuity of $1 per year*. Multiplying the future value of an ordinary annuity of $1 by the amount of the annuity produces the future value of an ordinary annuity.

For example, in the previous example, in which $10,000 is invested each year for the next five years, starting one year from now, we have:

$A = \$10,000;$
$i = .06;$
$N = 5;$

therefore,

$$FV = \$10,000 \left[\frac{(1.06)^5 - 1}{.06} \right]$$

$$= \$10,000 \left[\frac{1.3382256 - 1}{.06} \right]$$

$$= \$10,000 \, (5.63710)$$

$$= \$56,371.$$

This value agrees with our earlier calculation.

Illustration 2-8. Suppose that a portfolio manager purchases $5 million of par value of a 10-year bond that promises to pay 8% interest per year.[1] The price of the bond is $5 million. The interest payment is made once per year by the issuer; the first annual interest payment will be made one year from now. How much will the portfolio manager have if she (1) holds the bond until it matures 10 years from now and (2) can reinvest the annual interest payments at an annual interest rate of 6.7%?

The amount that the portfolio manager will have at the end of 10 years will be equal to:

(1) The $5 million when the bond matures;

(2) 10 annual interest payments of $400,000 (.08 × $5 million)

(3) The interest earned by investing the annual interest payments.

We can determine the sum of (2) and (3) by applying the formula for the future value of an ordinary annuity. In this illustration, the annuity is $400,000 per year (.08 × $5,000,000). Therefore,

$$A = \$400,000;$$
$$i = .067;$$
$$N = 10$$

$$FV = \$400,000 \left[\frac{(1.067)^{10} - 1}{.067} \right]$$

$$= \$400,000 \left[\frac{1.912688 - 1}{.067} \right]$$

$$= \$400,000 \, [13.62221]$$
$$= \$5,448,884.$$

The future value of the ordinary annuity of $400,000 per year for 10 years invested at 6.7% is $5,448,884. Since $4,000,000 of this future value represents the total annual interest payments made by the issuer and invested by the portfolio manager, $1,448,884 ($5,448,884 − $4,000,000) must be the interest earned by reinvesting the annual interest payments. Therefore, the total amount that the portfolio manager will have at the end of 10 years by making the investment will be:

Par (maturity) value	$5,000,000
Interest payments	4,000,000
Interest on reinvestment of interest payments	1,448,884
Total	$10,448,884

---

[1] Eurodollar bonds, for example, pay coupon interest once per year.

As you will see in Chapter 8, it will be necessary to determine the total future amount at the end of some investment horizon to assess the relative performance of a bond.

Future Value of an Ordinary Annuity when Payments Occur More than Once Per Year

We can easily generalize the future value of an ordinary annuity to handle situations in which payments are made more than one time per year. For example, instead of assuming that an investor receives and then invests $10,000 per year for five years, starting one year from now, suppose that the investor receives $5,000 every six months for five years, starting six months from now.

The general formula for the future value of an ordinary annuity when payments occur m times per year is

$$FV = A \left[\frac{(1 + i)^n - 1}{i} \right]$$

where

A = Amount of the annuity ($);
i = Annual interest rate divided by m (in decimal);
$n = N \times m$.

The value in the brackets is the *future value of an ordinary annuity of $1 per period.*

Illustration 2-9. Let's rework the analysis for the bond in Illustration 2-8 assuming that the interest is paid every six months, and that the first payment is to be received and invested six months from now. The interest payment every six months is $200,000. The future value of the 20 semiannual interest payments of $200,000 to be received plus the interest earned by investing the interest payments is found as follows:

$$A = \$200,000;$$
$$m = 2;$$
$$i = .0335 \ (.067/2);$$
$$n = 20 \ (10 \times 2)$$

$$FV = \$200,000 \left[\frac{(1.0335)^{20} - 1}{.0335} \right]$$

$$= \$200,000 \left[\frac{1.932901 - 1}{.0335} \right]$$

$$= \$200,000 \ [27.84779]$$
$$= \$5,569,558.$$

Since the interest payments are equal to $4,000,000, the interest earned on the interest payments invested is $1,569,558. Because of the more frequent reinvestment of the interest payments received, the interest of $1,569,558 earned by investing the interest payments exceeds the interest earned if interest is paid only one time per year, that is, $1,448,884 (see Illustration 2-8).

The total amount that the portfolio manager will have at the end of 10 years by making the investment will be:

Par (maturity) value	$5,000,000
Interest payments	4,000,000
Interest on reinvestment of interest payments	$1,569,558
Total	$10,569,558

Summary

In this chapter we have explained how to compute the future value of an investment. The formulas that we introduced are summarized in Exhibit 2-2.

Exhibit 2-2

Summary of Formulas for Future Value Computations

(1) Future value of an investment made for N years:

$$FV = P (1 + i)^N,$$

where

FV = Future value ($);
P = Original principal ($);
i = Interest rate (in decimal form);
N = Number of years.

(2) Future value of an investment made for n periods:

$$FV = P (1 + i)^n$$

where

i = *Annual* interest rate divided by m;
n = Number of periods ($=N \times m$);
m = Number of payments per year.

(3) Future value of an ordinary annuity for N years:

$$FV = A \left[\frac{(1 + i)^N - 1}{i} \right],$$

where

A = Amount of the annuity ($);
i = Annual interest rate (in decimal).

(4) Future value of an ordinary annuity for n periods:

$$FV = A \left[\frac{(1 + i)^n - 1}{i} \right],$$

where

A = Amount of the annuity ($);
i = Annual interest rate divided by m (in decimal);
n = Number of periods ($N \times m$);
m = Number of payments per year.

3

Present Value

In the previous chapter, we illustrated how to compute the future value of an investment. In this chapter, we show how to work the process in reverse; that is, given the future value of an investment, we show how to determine the amount of money that must be invested today in order to realize the future value. The amount of money that must be invested today is called the *present value*. Since, as we shall explain later in this chapter, the price of *any* financial instrument is the present value of its expected cash flows, it is necessary to understand present value in order to be able to price a fixed income instrument.

Present Value of a Single Amount to Be Received in the Future

Recall from the previous chapter that the future value of a sum invested for N years can be expressed as

$$FV = P (1 + i)^N,$$

where

FV = Future value ($);
P = Original principal ($);
i = Interest rate (in decimal form);
N = Number of years;
$(1 + i)^N$ = Future value of $1 invested at i for N years.

How do we determine the amount of money that must be invested today, earning an interest rate of i for N years, in order to produce a specific future value? This is done by solving the future value formula for P, the original principal:

$$P = FV \left[\frac{1}{(1 + i)^N} \right] .$$

Instead of using P in the formula, we shall denote the present value as PV. Therefore, the present value formula can be rewritten as

$$PV = FV \left[\frac{1}{(1 + i)^N} \right] .$$

The term in the brackets is equal to the present value of $1; that is, it indicates how much must be set aside today, earning an interest rate of i, in order to have $1 N years from now.

The process of computing the present value is also referred to as *discounting*. Therefore, the present value is sometimes referred to as the *discounted value*, and the interest rate is referred to as the *discount rate*.

The following four illustrations demonstrate how to compute the present value.

Illustration 3-1. A pension fund manager must satisfy a liability of $9 million six years from now. Assuming that an annual interest rate of 7.5% can be earned on any sum invested today, the pension fund manager must invest $5,831,654 today in order to have $9 million six years from now, as shown below:

$$FV = \$9,000,000;$$
$$i = .075;$$
$$N = 6$$

$$PV = \$9,000,000 \left[\frac{1}{(1.075)^6} \right]$$

$$= \$9,000,000 \left[\frac{1}{1.543302} \right]$$

$$= \$9,000,000 \, (.647961)$$

$$= \$5,831,654$$

Illustration 3-2. Suppose now that the pension fund manager could earn 8.3% instead of 7.5%; then the present value of the $9 million to be paid six years from now would be $5,577,912, as shown below:

$$FV = \$9,000,000;$$
$$i = .083;$$
$$N = 6$$

$$PV = \$9,000,000 \left[\frac{1}{(1.083)^6} \right]$$

$$= \$9,000,000 \left[\frac{1}{1.613507} \right]$$

$$= \$9,000,000 \,(.619768)$$
$$= \$5,577,912$$

Illustration 3-3. Suppose a money manager has the opportunity to purchase a financial instrument that promises to pay $800,000 four years from now. The price of the financial instrument is $572,000. Should the money manager invest in this financial instrument if she wants a 7.8% annual interest rate?

To answer this, the money manager must determine the present value of the $800,000 to be received four years from now. The present value is $592,400, as shown below:

$$FV = \$800,000;$$
$$i = .078;$$
$$N = 4$$

$$PV = \$800,000 \left[\frac{1}{(1.078)^4} \right]$$

$$= \$800,000 \left[\frac{1}{1.350439} \right]$$

$$= \$800,000 \,(.740500)$$
$$= \$592,400.$$

As the price of the financial instrument is $572,000, the money manager will realize more than a 7.8% annual interest rate if the financial instrument is purchased and the issuer pays $800,000 four years from now. In the next chapter, we'll show how to compute the annual interest rate that the money manager would realize.

Another way of looking at the problem faced by this money manager is by asking how much the $572,000 would grow to in four years if invested at 7.8%. Using the formula for the future value of an investment, we find that the future value is $772,451, as shown below:

$$P = \$572,000;$$
$$i = .078;$$
$$N = 4$$

$$FV = \$572,000 \ (1.078)^4$$
$$= \$572,000 \ (1.350439)$$
$$= \$772,451.$$

A \$572,000 investment at 7.8% would grow to only \$772,451. Yet, an investment of \$572,000 in the particular financial instrument produces \$800,000 four years from now. Consequently, the financial instrument offers more than a 7.8% annual interest rate. The present value of \$592,400 tells the money manager that as long as she pays no more than \$592,400, an annual interest rate of at least 7.8% will be earned from this investment.

Illustration 3-4. Instead of promising \$800,000 four years from now, suppose that the financial instrument in the previous illustration promises to pay \$800,000 five years from now. Assume that the money manager still wants an annual interest rate of 7.8%. Is the investment still attractive if it is selling for \$572,000?

As shown below, the present value of the \$800,000 five years from now is \$549,536:

$$FV = \$800,000;$$
$$i = .078;$$
$$N = 5$$

$$PV = \$800,000 \left[\frac{1}{(1.078)^5}\right]$$

$$= \$800,000 \left[\frac{1}{1.455733}\right]$$

$$= \$800,000 \ (.686920)$$
$$= \$549,536.$$

Here the present value is less than the price of \$572,000, so the financial instrument offers an annual interest rate that is less than 7.8%.

Present Value for a Fractional Period

If a future value is to be received or paid over a fractional part of a year, the number of years is adjusted accordingly. For example, if \$1,000 is to be received nine years and three months from now and the interest rate is 7%, the present value is determined as follows:

$$FV = \$1,000;$$
$$i = .07;$$
$$N = 9.25 \text{ years (3 months is .25 years)}$$

$$PV = \$1,000 \left[\frac{1}{(1.07)^{9.25}}\right]$$

$$= \$1,000 \left[\frac{1}{1.86982} \right]$$

$$= \$1,000 \, (.53481)$$

$$= \$534.81.$$

Properties of Present Value

There are two properties of present value that you should recognize.

First, for a given future value at a specified time in the future, the higher the interest rate (or discount rate), the lower the present value. To see this, compare the present value in Illustration 3-1 to that in Illustration 3-2. When the annual interest rate increased from 7.5% to 8.3%, the present value of the $9 million needed six years from now decreased from $5,831,654 to $5,577,912. The reason that the present value decreases as the interest rate increases should be easy to understand. The higher the interest rate that can be earned on any sum invested today, the less has to be invested today to realize a specified future value.

The second property of the present value is that for a given interest rate (discount rate), the farther into the future the future value will be received, the lower the present value. This is demonstrated in Illustrations 3-3 and 3-4. When the amount of $800,000 is to be received four years from now, the present value is $592,400; if the $800,000 is to be received five years from now, the present value declines to $549,536. The reason is that the farther into the future a given future value is to be received, the more time there is for interest to accumulate. The result is that fewer dollars have to be invested.

Present Value of a Series of Future Values

In most applications in investment management and asset/liability management, a financial instrument will offer a series of future values, or a financial institution will have multiple liabilities in the future. To determine the present value of a series of future values, the present value of each future value must first be computed. Then, the present values are added to obtain the present value of the series of future values. This procedure is demonstrated in the following three illustrations.

Illustration 3-5. A pension fund manager knows that the following liabilities must be satisfied:

Years from now	Liability
1	$200,000
2	340,000
3	500,000
4	580,000

Suppose that the pension fund manager wants to invest a sum of money that will satisfy this liability stream. Let's assume that any amount that can be invested today can earn an annual interest rate of 8.5%. How much must be invested to satisfy this liability stream?

The answer is the present value of the liability stream. Consequently, the present value of each liability must be calculated and the results totaled, as shown below.

Years from now	Future value of liability	Present value of $1 at 8.5%	Present value of liability
1	$200,000	0.921659	$184,332
2	340,000	0.849455	288,815
3	500,000	0.782908	391,454
4	580,000	0.721574	418,513
		Total present value =	$1,283,114

The present value of $1,283,114 means that if this sum is invested today at an annual interest rate of 8.5%, it will provide sufficient funds to satisfy the liability stream.

For those who must be convinced that this is true, let's look at what would happen if $1,283,114 is invested at 8.5% in a bank account, and at the end of each year enough money is withdrawn from the bank account to satisfy the annual liability.

(1) Year	(2) Amount at beginning of year	(3) Interest at 8.5% [.085 × (2)]	(4) Withdrawn to pay liability	(5) Amount at end of year [(2) + (3) − (4)]
1	$1,283,114	$109,065	$200,000	$1,192,179
2	1,192,179	101,335	340,000	953,514
3	953,514	81,049	500,000	534,563
4	534,563	45,437	580,000	0

As these computations show, the $1,283,114 investment will provide enough money to pay the liability stream. At the end of the fourth year (after the last liability is paid), there is no money left in the account.

Illustration 3-6. An investor is considering the purchase of a financial instrument that promises to make the following payments:

Years from now	Promised payment by issuer
1	$ 100
2	100
3	100
4	100
5	1,100

This financial instrument is selling for $1,243.83. Assume that the investor wants a 6.25% annual interest rate on this investment. Should the investor purchase this investment?

To answer this question, the investor first must compute the present value of the future amounts that are expected to be received, as follows:

Years from now	*Future value of payment*	*Present value of $1 at 6.25%*	*Present value of payment*
1	$ 100	0.9412	$ 94.12
2	100	0.8858	88.58
3	100	0.8337	83.37
4	100	0.7847	78.47
5	1,100	0.7385	812.35
		Total present value =	$1,156.89

The present value of the series of future values promised by the issuer of this financial instrument is less than the price of $1,243.83, so the investor would earn an annual interest rate of less than 6.25%. Thus, the financial instrument is unattractive.

Present Value of an Ordinary Annuity

When the same amount of money is received or paid each year, the series is referred to as an *annuity*. When the first payment is received or paid one year from now, the annuity is called an *ordinary annuity*. When the first payment or receipt is immediate, the annuity is called an *annuity due*. In all the applications discussed in this book, we deal with ordinary annuities.

Of course, one way to compute the present value of an ordinary annuity is to follow the procedure explained in the previous section: compute the present value of each future value and then total the present values. Fortunately, there is a formula that can be employed to compute—in one step—the present value of an ordinary annuity:

$$PV = A \left[\frac{1 - \left[\frac{1}{(1 + i)^N} \right]}{i} \right]$$

where
A = Amount of the annuity ($).

The term in the large brackets is the *present value of an ordinary annuity of $1 for N years.*

Two illustrations will show how to apply this formula.

Illustration 3-7. An investor has the opportunity to purchase a financial instrument that promises to pay $500 a year for the next 20 years, beginning one year from now. The financial instrument is being offered for a price of $5,300. The investor seeks an annual interest rate of 5.5% on this investment. Should the investor purchase this financial instrument?

Since the first payment is to be received one year from now, the financial instrument is offering a 20-year annuity of $500 per year. The present value of this ordinary annuity is calculated as follows:

$$A = \$500;$$
$$i = .055;$$
$$N = 20$$

$$PV = \$500 \left[\frac{1 - \left[\frac{1}{(1.055)^{20}} \right]}{.055} \right]$$

$$= \$500 \left[\frac{1 - \left[\frac{1}{2.917757} \right]}{.055} \right]$$

$$= \$500 \left[\frac{1 - .342729}{.055} \right]$$

$$= \$500 \ (11.950382)$$
$$= \$5,975.19$$

Since the present value of an ordinary annuity of $500 per year when discounted at 5.5% exceeds the price of the financial instrument ($5,300), this financial instrument offers an annual interest rate in excess of 5.5%. Therefore, it is an attractive investment for this investor.

Illustration 3-8. In Illustration 3-6 we computed the present value of a financial instrument that offers $100 a year for four years and $1,100 at the end of the fifth year. This payment series is equivalent to an ordinary annuity of $100 a year for *five* years *plus* a future-value payment of $1,000 five years from now. Viewing the payments of the financial instrument in this way, let's compute the present value.

The present value of an ordinary annuity of $100 per year for five years at an annual interest rate of 6.25% is

$$A = \$100;$$
$$i = .0625;$$
$$N = 5$$

$$PV = \$100 \left[\frac{1 - \left[\frac{1}{(1.0625)^{5}} \right]}{.0625} \right]$$

$$= \$100 \left[\frac{1 - \left[\dfrac{1}{1.354081} \right]}{.0625} \right]$$

$$= \$100 \left[\frac{1 - .738508}{.0625} \right]$$

$$= \$100 \ (4.1838)$$

$$= \$418.38.$$

The present value of the $1,000 to be received five years from now is $738.51, as shown below:

$$FV = \$1,000;$$
$$i = .0625;$$
$$N = 5$$

$$PV = \$1,000 \left[\frac{1}{(1.0625)^5} \right]$$

$$= \$1,000 \left[\frac{1}{1.354081} \right]$$

$$= \$1,000 \ (.738508)$$

$$= \$738.51.$$

The present value of the series offered by this financial instrument is then:

Present value of ordinary annuity of $100 for five years at 6.25%	$ 418.38
Present value of $1,000 five years from now at 6.25%	738.51
Total present value	$1,156.89

This agrees with the computation in Illustration 3-6.

Perpetual Annuity: Special Case

So far we have shown how to compute the present value of an ordinary annuity over a specific time period. Suppose, instead, that the annuity will last forever. This is called a *perpetual annuity*. The formula for a perpetual annuity is[1]

---

[1] The formula is derived from the formula for the present value of an ordinary annuity. As the number of years gets very large, the value of $1/(1 + i)^N$ approaches zero. The numerator in the large brackets is then equal to 1, producing the formula for the present value of a perpetual annuity.

$$PV = \frac{A}{i} \; .$$

Illustration 3-9. An investor can purchase for $1,000 a financial instrument that promises to pay $80 per year forever. The investor wants an annual interest rate of 10% from this investment. Is this investment attractive to the investor?

The present value of the $80 perpetual annuity is equal to $800, as shown below:

$$A = \$80;$$
$$i = .10$$
$$PV = \frac{\$80}{.10}$$
$$= \$800.$$

Since the $1,000 price for the financial instrument is greater than the present value of the perpetual annuity ($800), the investment offers an annual interest rate that is less than 10%; therefore, it is not an attractive investment, given the minimum annual interest rate required by the investor.

Present Value When the Frequency Is More Than Once Per Year

In the computations of present value, we have assumed that the future value is to be received or paid once each year. In practice, the future value may be received or paid more than once per year. In this situation, the formulas for the present value given earlier in this chapter must be modified in two ways. First, the annual interest rate is divided by the frequency per year.[2] For example, if the future values are received or paid semiannually, the annual interest rate is divided by 2; if quarterly, the annual interest rate is divided by 4. Second, the periods when the future value will be received or paid must be adjusted by multiplying the number of years by the frequency per year.

The general formula for the present value of a future sum is

$$PV = FV \left[\frac{1}{(1 + i)^n} \right] \; ,$$

where

i = Periodic interest rate [annual interest rate (in decimal) divided by m];

---

[2] Technically, this is not the proper way for adjusting the annual interest rate. For example, an 8% annual interest rate is not equal to a quarterly interest rate of 2%. However, in the computation of the yield on bonds, the market has adopted a convention that embodies this approach. This will be made clearer in the next two chapters.

n = Number of periods [number of years (N) times m];
m = Frequency of receipt or payment of the future value.

Illustration 3-10. An investor is considering the purchase of a financial instrument that promises to make the following payments every three months (quarterly):

Period (three months)	Promised payments
1	$1,000
2	1,200
3	1,500
4	1,700
5	1,800
6	2,000

If the investor seeks an annual interest rate of 12% from this investment, what is the most that the investor should pay for it?

The most that the investor should pay in order to earn an annual interest rate of at least 12% is the present value of the future payments promised. As shown below, the present value is $8,212.79.

Periods from now	Future value of payment	Present value of $1 at 3.0%*	Present value of payment
1	$1,000	.97087	$ 970.87
2	1,200	.94260	1,131.12
3	1,500	.91514	1,372.71
4	1,700	.88849	1,510.43
5	1,800	.86261	1,552.70
6	2,000	.83748	1,674.96
		Total present value =	$8,212.79

* .12 annual interest rate divided by 4.

When the present value of an ordinary annuity is sought, the general formula is

$$PV = A \left[\frac{1 - \left[\frac{1}{(1 + i)^n} \right]}{i} \right]$$

where

A = Amount of the annuity (in dollars *per period*).

Illustration 3-11. In Illustration 3-6, we computed the present value of the following series of future amounts, assuming an annual interest rate of 6.25%:

Years from now	Promised payment by issuer
1	$ 100
2	100
3	100
4	100
5	1,100

Instead of annual payments, let's assume that the payments are made by the issuer every six months, in the following way:

Six month periods from now	Promised payment by issuer
1	$ 50
2	50
3	50
4	50
5	50
6	50
7	50
8	50
9	50
10	1,050

This is equivalent to an ordinary annuity of $50 per six-month period for 10 six-month periods and $1,000 to be paid 10 six-month periods from now. Notice that the $1,000 is treated on the same time-period basis as the annuity.

The present value of the ordinary annuity, for

$A = \$50$;
$m = 2$ (that is, payments every six months);
$i = .03125$ (.0625 annual interest rate divided by 2);
$n = 10$ (5 years times 2);

is

$$PV = \$50 \left[\frac{1 - \left[\dfrac{1}{(1.03125)^{10}} \right]}{.03125} \right]$$

$$= \$50 \left[\frac{1 - \left[\dfrac{1}{1.360315} \right]}{.03125} \right]$$

$$= \$50 \left[\frac{1 - .735124}{.03125} \right]$$

$$= \$50 \ (8.4760)$$

$$= \$423.80.$$

The present value of the $1,000 to be received after 10 six-month periods, for

$FV = \$1,000$;
$m = 2$ (that is, payments every six months);
$i = .03125$ (.0625 annual interest rate divided by 2);
$n = 10$ (5 years times 2);

is

$$PV = \$1,000 \left[\frac{1}{(1.03125)^{10}} \right]$$

$$= \$1,000 \left[\frac{1}{1.360315} \right]$$

$$= \$1,000 \ (.735124)$$

$$= \$735.12.$$

The present value of the future value series offered by the financial instrument is then:

Present value of ordinary annuity of $50 for 10 six-month periods at .03125	$ 423.80
Present value of $1,000 after 10 six-month periods at .03125%	735.12
Total present value	$1,158.92

Notice that because the payments are made more often, the present value of the future payments has increased from $1,156.89 to $1,158.92.

Illustration 3-12. Suppose a banker agrees to make a $100,000 30-year loan to an individual to purchase a home. Under the terms of the loan, the monthly payments to be made by the individual will all be the same. The annual interest rate that the banker charges for the loan is 12%. How much must the fixed monthly payment be in order for the banker to realize an annual interest rate of 12%?

We can employ the formula for the present value of an ordinary annuity to determine the fixed monthly payment. The banker wants to receive an annuity of some fixed monthly amount such that the present value of that ordinary annuity, at an annual interest rate of 12%, is $100,000. In the formula for the present value of an ordinary annuity, the number of monthly payments is 360 (30 years times 12) and the interest rate is 1% (12% divided by 12). Therefore, we know the following:

$$\$100,000 = A \left[\cfrac{1 - \left[\cfrac{1}{(1.01)^{360}} \right]}{.01} \right]$$

The unknown is A, the monthly annuity or monthly loan payment. We can solve for A as follows:

$$\$100,000 = A \left[\cfrac{1 - \left[\cfrac{1}{35.949641} \right]}{.01} \right]$$

$$= A \left[\cfrac{1 - .0278167}{.01} \right]$$

$$= A \,(97.21833)$$

Solving for A,

$$A = \left[\cfrac{\$100,000}{97.21833} \right] = \$1,028.61.$$

Therefore, the fixed monthly payment must be $\$1,028.61$.

Unequal Discount Rates

Throughout this chapter we have assumed that the same required yield or discount rate should be used to calculate the present value of each payment to be received. This assumption is unwarranted. As we explain in Chapter 13, there is a reason why each payment to be received should be discounted at a unique rate. The present value of a series of payments is then the sum of the present value of each payment where each payment is discounted at a unique rate.

Illustration 3-13. Let's consider Illustration 3-6 where the financial instrument makes the following five payments: $100 for four years and $1,100 in the fifth year. When each payment is discounted at a 6.25% annual interest rate, the total present value is $1,156.89. Suppose, instead, that the required yield for each year is as shown below:

Years from now	Promised payment by issuer	Required yield
1	$100	4.80%
2	100	5.25
3	100	5.50
4	100	6.00
5	1,100	6.25

The present value of each promised payment is shown below. Each payment is discounted at the required yield

Years from now	Promised payment by issuer	Required yield	Present value of $1	Present value of payment
1	100	.0480	.954198	95.4198
2	100	.0525	.902726	90.2725
3	100	.0550	.851614	85.1613
4	100	.0600	.792094	79.2093
5	1,100	.0625	.738508	812.3590

Total = $1,162.4219

The present value of the cash flows is $1,162.42

Pricing Any Financial Instrument

The price of any financial instrument is equal to the present value of the *expected* cash flows from investing in the financial instrument. Determining the price, therefore, requires the following input:

(1) Estimation of the expected cash flows, and

(2) Determination of the appropriate interest rate or discount rate so that the present value of the cash flows can be computed.

The cash flow in any period is simply the difference between the cash inflow and the cash outflow from investing in the financial instrument. The expected cash flows of some financial instruments are simple to compute; for others, the task is not as simple. The determination of the interest rate or discount rate reflects the required yield for financial instruments with *comparable* risk.

Summary

In this chapter we explained how to compute the present value of amounts to be received in the future or payments to be made in the future. A summary of the formulas used in this chapter to compute present values is presented in Exhibit 3-1.

Exhibit 3-1

Summary of Formulas for Computing Present Value

(1) Present value of a future value N years from now:

$$PV = FV \left[\frac{1}{(1 + i)^N} \right] ,$$

where

> PV = Present value ($);
> FV = Future value ($);
> i = Interest rate (in decimal form);
> N = Number of years.

(2) Present value of a future value n periods from now:

$$PV = FV \left[\frac{1}{(1 + i)^n} \right] ,$$

where

> i = Periodic interest rate [annual interest rate (in decimal) divided by m];
> n = Number of periods [number of periods (N) times m];
> m = Frequency of receipt or payment of the future value.

(3) Present value of an ordinary annuity for N years:

$$PV = A \left[\frac{1 - \left[\frac{1}{(1 + i)^N} \right]}{i} \right] ,$$

where

> A = Amount of the annuity ($).

(4) Present value of an ordinary annuity for n periods:

$$PV = A \left[\frac{1 - \left[\frac{1}{(1 + i)^n} \right]}{i} \right] ,$$

where

> A = Amount of the annuity (in dollars) per period;
> i = Periodic interest rate [annual interest rate (in decimal) divided by m].

(5) Present value of a perpetual annuity:

$$PV = \frac{A}{i} .$$

4

Yield
(Internal Rate
of Return)

In the previous chapter we showed how to use present value to determine whether a financial instrument provides a minimum annual interest rate specified by an investor. For example, if the present value of the promised future value payments of some financial instrument selling for $944.14 is $1,039.57, then the investment offers an annual interest rate greater than 9%. But how much greater? What rate of return or yield will the investor earn by buying the financial instrument for $944.14? The purpose of this chapter is to explain how to compute the yield on any investment.

Computing the Yield on Any Investment

The yield on any investment is computed by determining the interest rate that will make the present value of the cash flow from the investment equal to its price. Mathematically, the yield on any investment, y, is the interest rate that will make the following relationship hold:

$$p = \frac{C_1}{(1+y)^1} + \frac{C_2}{(1+y)^2} + \frac{C_3}{(1+y)^3} + \ldots + \frac{C_N}{(1+y)^N}$$

where

p = Price;
C_t = Cash flow in year t;
N = Number of years.

The individual terms summed to yield the price are the present values of the cash flow. The yield calculated from the above relationship is also called the *internal rate of return.*

Alternatively, using the capital Greek letter sigma to denote summation, the above expression can be rewritten as

$$p = \sum_{t=1}^{N} \frac{C_t}{(1+y)^t} .$$

Solving for the yield (y) requires a trial-and-error procedure. The objective is to find the interest rate that will make the present value of the cash flows equal to the price. Exhibit 4-1 explains the trial-and-error procedure. The following two illustrations demonstrate how it is carried out.

Illustration 4-1. A financial instrument offers the following annual payments:

Years from now	Promised annual payments (Cash flow to investor)
1	$2,000
2	2,000
3	2,500
4	4,000

Suppose that the price of this financial instrument is $7,704. What is the yield or internal rate of return offered by this financial instrument?

To compute the yield, we must try different interest rates until we find one that makes the present value of the cash flows equal to $7,704 (its price). Trying an annual interest rate of 10% gives the following present value:

Years from now	Promised annual payments (Cash flow to investor)	Present value of cash flow at 10%
1	$2,000	$1,818
2	2,000	1,652
3	2,500	1,878
4	4,000	2,732
		Total present value = $8,080

Exhibit 4-1

Step-by-Step Summary of Yield Computation
for Any Investment

Objective: Find the interest rate that will make the present value of the cash flow equal to the price of the investment.

Step 1: Select an interest rate.

Step 2: Compute the present value of each cash flow, using the interest rate selected in Step 1.

Step 3: Total the present value of the cash flows found in Step 2.

Step 4: Compare the total present value found in Step 3 with the price of the investment, and:

if the total present value of the cash flows found in Step 3 is equal to the price of the investment, the interest rate selected in Step 1 is the yield.

if the total present value of the cash flows found in Step 3 is more than the price of the investment, the interest rate used is not the yield. Go back to Step 1 and use a higher interest rate.

if the total present value of the cash flows found in Step 3 is less than the price of the investment, the interest rate used is not the yield. Go back to Step 1 and use a lower interest rate.

The present value computed using a 10% interest rate exceeds the price of $7,704, so a higher interest rate must be tried. If a 14% interest rate is tried, the present value is $7,348, as shown below:

Years from now	*Promised annual payments (Cash flow to investor)*	*Present value of cash flow at 14%*
1	$2,000	$1,754
2	2,000	1,538
3	2,500	1,688
4	4,000	2,368
		Total present value = $7,348

At 14%, the present value of the cash flows is less than the $7,704 price of the financial instrument. Therefore, a lower interest rate must be tried. At a 12% interest rate:

Years from now	*Promised annual payments (Cash flow to investor)*	*Present value of cash flow at 12%*
1	$2,000	$1,786
2	2,000	1,594
3	2,500	1,780
4	4,000	2,544
		Total present value = $7,704

The present value of the cash flows is now equal to the price of the financial instrument when a 12% interest rate is used. Therefore, the yield is 12%.

Although the formula for the yield is based on annual cash flows, the formula can be generalized to any number of periodic payments in a year. The generalized formula for determining the yield is

$$p = \frac{C_1}{(1+y)^1} + \frac{C_2}{(1+y)^2} + \frac{C_3}{(1+y)^3} + \ldots + \frac{C_n}{(1+y)^n}$$

where

C_t = Cash flow in period t;
n = Number of periods.

In shorthand notation, this can be expressed as

$$p = \sum_{t=1}^{n} \frac{C_t}{(1+y)^t} \; .$$

Keep in mind that the yield computed is now the yield for the period. That is, if the cash flows are semiannual, the yield is a semiannual yield. If the cash flows are monthly, the yield is a monthly yield. The annual interest rate must be computed by multiplying the yield for the period by the appropriate factor (m).

Illustration 4-2. In Illustration 3-11 of the previous chapter, an investor considered purchasing a financial instrument that promised the following *semiannual* cash flows:

10 payments of $50 every six months
$1,000 10 six-month periods from now

Suppose the price of this financial instrument is $1,243.88. At the 6.5% annual interest rate sought by the investor, the present value of the cash flows is equal to $1,158.92; thus, the financial instrument would not be an attractive investment for this investor. What yield is this financial instrument offering?

The yield can be computed by a trial-and-error procedure, as summarized in the table below:

Annual interest rate	Semi-annual interest rate	Present value of 10 six-month payments of $50*	Present value of $1,000 10 six-month periods from now**	Total present value
6.000%	3.000%	$426.51	$744.09	$1,160.60
5.500	2.750	432.00	762.40	1,194.40
5.000	2.500	437.60	781.20	1,218.80
4.500	2.225	443.31	800.51	1,243.83

* $50 × present value of an ordinary annuity of $1 for 10 periods.
** $1,000 × present value of $1 10 periods from now.

As can be seen from the calculation, when a semiannual interest rate of 2.250% is used to find the present value of the cash flows, the present value is equal to the price of $1,243.83. Hence, 2.250% is the six-month yield. Doubling this yield gives the annual interest rate of 4.5%. This agrees with our earlier conclusion: this financial instrument is unattractive because it offers a yield that is less than the 6.5% annual interest rate required by the investor.

Illustration 4-3. Suppose that the financial instrument analyzed in the previous illustration is selling for $944.14 instead of $1,243.83. What is the yield offered on this financial instrument at this lower price?

The table below shows the calculation of the yield:

Annual interest rate	Semi- annual interest rate	Present value of 10 six-month payments of $50*	Present value of $1,000 10 six-month periods from now**	Total present value
9.000%	4.500%	$395.64	$643.93	$1,039.57
9.500	4.750	390.82	628.72	1,019.54
10.000	5.000	386.09	613.91	1,000.00
10.500	5.250	381.44	599.49	980.93
11.000	5.500	376.88	585.43	962.31
11.500	5.750	372.40	571.74	944.14

* $50 × present value of an ordinary annuity of $1 for 10 periods.
** $1,000 × present value of $1 10 periods from now.

An interest rate of 5.75% equates the present value of the cash flows to the price of the financial instrument; hence, 5.75% is the six-month yield, and 11.50% is the annual interest rate.

Illustration 4-4. A 30-year mortgage for $50,000 is originated today. The mortgage requires that the homeowner (borrower) pay $349.60 each month for 360 months. The manager of a mortgage portfolio has the opportunity to purchase this mortgage today for $43,449. What is the yield offered this series of monthly mortgage payments?

The computations below show that the monthly yield is .75% (.0075):

Annual interest rate	Monthly interest rate	Present value of 360 monthly payments of $349.60*
7.50%	.6250%	$50,000
8.00	.6667	47,643
8.50	.7083	45,469
9.00	.7500	43,449

* $349.60 × present value of an ordinary annuity of $1 for 360 periods.

Since the monthly yield is .7500%, the annual interest rate is 9.0%.

Notice that the annual interest on the mortgage must be 7.50% because it is the monthly yield of .6250% that equates the present value of the monthly payments to the amount borrowed by the homeowner, $50,000.

Illustration 4-5. Issuers of financial instruments must determine the cost of the funds they obtain. The cost of funds, referred to as the *all-in-cost of funds,* is just the interest rate that will equate the present value of the cash payments that the issuer must pay the security holders to the net proceeds received at the time of issuance. That is, the all-in-cost of funds is the internal rate of return.

Suppose that an issuer agrees to make the following payments to security holders every six months:

30 payments every six months of $1 million
$20 million 30 six-month periods from now.

At the time of issuance, the issuer received net proceeds of $19,696,024. The all-in-cost of funds for this issue is 5.10% semiannually, as shown below:

Annual interest rate	Semi-annual interest rate	Present value of 30 six-month payments of $1 million*	Present value of $20 million 30 six-month periods from now**	Total present value
10.000%	5.000%	$15,372,451	$4,627,549	$20,000,000
10.100	5.050	15,285,221	4,561,927	19,847,148
10.200	5.100	15,198,759	4,497,265	19,696,024

* $1 million × present value of an ordinary annuity of $1 for 30 periods.
** $20 million × present value of $1 30 periods from now.

Yield Calculation When There Is Only One Cash Flow

There is a special case when it is unnecessary to go through the time-consuming trial-and-error procedure to determine the yield. This occurs when there is only one cash flow provided by the investment. We'll introduce the formula by means of an illustration.

Illustration 4-6. A financial instrument that can be purchased for $6,805.82 promises to pay $10,000 five years from now. The yield is the interest rate that will make $6,805.82 grow to $10,000 in five years. That is, we are looking for the value of y that will satisfy the following relationship:

$$\$10{,}000 = \$6{,}805.82 \, (1 + y)^5.$$

We can solve this equation as follows. Dividing both sides by $6,805.82:

$$\frac{\$10,000}{\$6,805.82} = (1 + y)^5$$

$$1.46933 = (1 + y)^5.$$

Taking the 5th root of both sides:

$$(1.46933)^{1/5} = (1 + y)$$
$$(1.46933)^{.20} = (1 + y)$$
$$1.0800 = (1 + y).$$

Subtracting 1 from both sides:

$$1.0800 - 1 = y.$$
$$.08 = y.$$

Hence, the yield on this investment is 8%.

It is not necessary to go through all the steps in Illustration 4-6 to compute the yield. The following formula is consistent with those steps:

$$y = (\text{Future value per dollar invested})^{1/n} - 1,$$

where

$n =$ Number of periods until the cash flow will be received;

$$\frac{\text{Future value}}{\text{per dollar invested}} = \frac{\text{Cash flow from investment}}{\text{Amount invested (or price)}}.$$

Illustration 4-7. An investment offers a payment 20 years from now of $84,957. The price of the investment is $20,000. The yield for this investment is 7.50%, as shown below:

$n = 20$

$$\frac{\text{Future value}}{\text{per dollar invested}} = \frac{\$84,957}{\$20,000} = 4.24785$$

$$y = (4.24785)^{1/20} - 1$$
$$= 1.07499 - 1$$
$$= .074999 \text{ or } 7.5\%.$$

Illustration 4-8. In Illustration 2-8, we computed how many dollars would be available to a portfolio manager if he invests $5 million (the par value) in a bond that matures in 10 years and promises to pay an annual interest rate of 8%. The interest is assumed to be paid once per year, and these payments are assumed to be reinvested at an annual interest rate of 6.7%. We calculated that at the end of 10 years, the portfolio manager would have $10,448,884, consisting of $5 million in par value, $4 million in annual interest payments, and the balance, $1,448,884, from interest earned on the reinvestment of the annual interest payments.

The yield on this investment based on the portfolio manager's expectations can be computed by finding the yield that will make a $5 million investment grow to $10,448,884 in 10 years. Since we have reduced the problem to that of an investment that provides the portfolio manager with one cash flow, the yield can be found as follows:

$$n = 10 \, (= N)$$

$$\frac{\text{Future value}}{\text{per dollar invested}} = \frac{\$10,448,884}{\$5,000,000} = 2.08978$$

$$y = (2.08978)^{1/10} - 1$$
$$= 1.07649 - 1$$
$$= .07649 \text{ or } 7.65\%.$$

Annualizing Yields

So far throughout this book, we have annualized interest rates by simply multiplying by the frequency of payments per year. We called the resulting rate the annual interest rate. For example, if we computed a semiannual yield, we annualized it by multiplying by 2. Alternatively, if we had an annual interest rate and wanted to use a semiannual interest rate, we divided by 2.

This single procedure given for computing the annual interest rate, given a periodic (weekly, monthly, quarterly, semiannual, etc.) interest rate is not correct. To see why, suppose that $100 is invested for one year at an annual interest rate of 8%. At the end of one year, the interest is $8. Suppose, instead, that $100 is invested for one year at an annual interest rate of 8%, but interest is paid semiannually at 4% (one-half the annual interest rate). The interest at the end of one year is found by first calculating the future value of $100 at the end of one year:

$$\$100 \, (1.04)^2$$
$$= \$100 \, (1.0816)$$
$$= \$108.16$$

Interest is therefore $8.16 on a $100 investment. The interest rate or yield on the $100 investment is therefore 8.16% ($8.16/$100). The 8.16% is called the *effective annual yield*.

Investors who are familiar with certificates of deposit offered by banks and thrifts should recognize the difference between the annual interest rate and effective annual yield. Typically, both of these interest rates are quoted for a certificate of deposit, the higher interest rate being the effective annual yield.

To obtain the effective annual yield associated with a periodic interest rate, the following formula can be used:

Effective annual yield = $(1 + \text{Periodic interest rate})^m - 1$

where
  m = Frequency of payments per year.

For example, in the previous example, the periodic yield is 4%, and the frequency of payments is twice per year. Therefore,

$$\text{Effective annual yield} = (1.04)^2 - 1$$
$$= 1.0816 - 1$$
$$= .0816 \text{ or } 8.16\%$$

If interest is paid quarterly, then the periodic interest rate is 2% (8%/4), and the effective annual yield is 8.24%, as shown below:

$$\text{Effective annual yield} = (1.02)^4 - 1$$
$$= 1.0824 - 1$$
$$= .0824 \text{ or } 8.24\%$$

We can also determine the periodic interest rate that will produce a given annual interest rate. For example, suppose we want to know what quarterly interest rate would produce an effective annual yield of 12%. The following formula can be used:

$$\text{Periodic interest rate} = (1 + \text{Effective annual yield})^{1/m} - 1.$$

Applying this formula to determine the quarterly interest rate to produce an effective annual yield of 12%, we find:

$$\text{Periodic interest rate} = (1.12)^{1/4} - 1$$
$$= 1.0287 - 1$$
$$= .0287 \text{ or } 2.87\%.$$

Summary

In this chapter we explained how to compute the yield on any investment, given the expected cash flows and the price. The yield is the interest rate that will make the present value of the cash flows equal to the price of the financial instrument. The yield computed in this manner is also called the internal rate of return. We also demonstrated how to compute the effective annual yield of an investment. A summary of the formulas introduced in this chapter is provided in Exhibit 4-2.

Exhibit 4-2

Summary of Yield (Internal Rate of Return) Formulas

(1)   Yield (or internal rate of return) on any investment from which the cash flows are received annually is the interest rate y that will make the following relationship hold:

$$p = \frac{C_1}{(1+y)^1} + \frac{C_2}{(1+y)^2} + \frac{C_3}{(1+y)^3} + \ldots + \frac{C_N}{(1+y)^N}$$

or

$$p = \sum_{t=1}^{N} \frac{C_t}{(1+y)^t} \; .$$

where

p = Price;
C_t = Cash flow in year t;
y = Yield;
N = Number of years.

(2)   Yield (or internal rate of return) on any investment from which the cash flows are received periodically is the interest rate y that will make the following relationship hold:

$$p = \frac{C_1}{(1+y)^1} + \frac{C_2}{(1+y)^2} + \frac{C_3}{(1+y)^3} + \ldots + \frac{C_n}{(1+y)^n}$$

or

$$p = \sum_{t=1}^{n} \frac{C_t}{(1+y)^t} \; .$$

where

C_t = Cash flow in period t;
n = Number of periods.

(3)   Yield (internal rate of return) on an investment in which there is only one cash flow received n periods from now:

y = (Future value per dollar invested)$^{1/n}$ − 1

where

n = Number of periods when cash flow will be received;

$$\frac{\text{Future value}}{\text{per dollar invested}} = \frac{\text{Cash flow from investment}}{\text{Amount invested (or price)}} \; .$$

(4)   Effective annual yield associated with a periodic interest rate:

Effective annual yield $= (1 + \text{Periodic interest rate})^m - 1$

where

$m = $ Frequency of payments per year.

(5) Periodic interest rate consistent with an effective annual yield:

Periodic interest rate $= (1 + \text{Effective annual yield})^{1/m} - 1$

II

Bond Pricing and Return Analysis

5

The Price
of a Bond

In Chapter 3 we explained that the price of any financial instrument is equal to the present value of the expected cash flows. The interest rate or discount rate used to compute the present value depends on the yield offered on comparable securities in the market. In this chapter we explain how to compute the price of a noncallable bond. Call options and the valuation of callable securities are discussed later.

Determining the Cash Flows

The first step in determining the price of a bond is to determine its cash flows. The cash flows of a noncallable bond consist of (1) periodic coupon interest payments to the maturity date, and (2) the par (or maturity) value at maturity. While the periodic coupon payments can be made over any time period during the year (weekly, monthly, quarterly, semiannually, or annually), most bonds issued in the United States pay coupon interest semiannually.

In our illustrations, we shall assume that the coupon interest is paid semiannually. To simplify the analysis, we also assume that the next coupon payment for the bond will be made exactly six months from now. Later in the chapter we generalize the pricing model to allow for a coupon payment that is more or less than six months from now.

Consequently, the cash flows for a noncallable bond consist of an annuity (that is, the fixed coupon interest paid every six months) and the par or maturity value. For example, a 20-year bond with a 9% coupon rate (4.5% each six months) and a par or maturity value of $1,000 has the following cash flows:

$$\text{Semiannual coupon interest} = \$1,000 \times .045$$
$$= \$45;$$
$$\text{Maturity value} = \$1,000.$$

Therefore, there are 40 semiannual cash flows of $45, and a $1,000 cash flow 40 six-month periods from now.

Notice the treatment of the par value. It is *not* treated as if it is received 20 years from now. Instead, it is treated on a consistent basis with the coupon payments, which are semiannual.

Determining the Required Yield

The interest rate or discount rate that an investor wants from investing in a bond is called the *required yield.* The required yield is determined by investigating the yields offered on comparable bonds in the market. By comparable, we mean noncallable bonds of the same credit quality and the same maturity.[1]

The required yield is typically specified as an annual interest rate. When the cash flows are semiannual, the convention is to use one-half the annual interest rate as the periodic interest rate with which to discount the cash flows. As explained at the end of the previous chapter, a periodic interest rate that is one-half the annual yield will produce an effective annual yield that is greater than the annual interest rate.

Pricing a Bond

Given the cash flows of a bond and the required yield, we have all the necessary data to price the bond. The price of a bond is the present value of the cash flows, which can be determined by adding

---

[1] In Chapter 11, we introduce a measure of interest rate risk known as duration. Instead of talking in terms of a bond with the same maturity as being comparable, the analysis can be recast in terms of the same duration.

(1) The present value of the semiannual coupon payments, and

(2) The present value of the par or maturity value.

In general, the price of a bond can be computed using the formula:

$$p = \frac{c}{(1+i)^1} + \frac{c}{(1+i)^2} + \frac{c}{(1+i)^3} + \ldots + \frac{c}{(1+i)^n} + \frac{M}{(1+i)^n} \, ,$$

where

p = Price ($);
c = *Semiannual* coupon payment ($);
i = Periodic interest rate (required yield divided by 2) (in decimal);
n = Number of periods (number of years times 2);
M = Maturity value.

Since the semiannual coupon payments are equivalent to an ordinary annuity, the present value of the coupon payments, that is, the present value of

$$p = \frac{c}{(1+i)^1} + \frac{c}{(1+i)^2} + \frac{c}{(1+i)^3} + \ldots + \frac{c}{(1+i)^n} \, ,$$

can be expressed

$$c \left[\frac{1 - \left[\frac{1}{(1+i)^n} \right]}{i} \right] .$$

This formula is the same as the formula for the present value of an ordinary annuity for n periods introduced in Chapter 3 (see Exhibit 3-1). Instead of using A to represent the annuity, we have used c, the semiannual coupon payment.

Illustration 5-1. Compute the price of a 9% coupon bond with 20 years to maturity and a par value of $1,000 if the required yield is 12%.

The cash flows for this bond are as follows:

(1) 40 semiannual coupon payments of $45 and

(2) $1,000 40 six-month periods from now.

The semiannual or periodic interest rate is 6%.

The present value of the 40 semiannual coupon payments of $45 discounted at 6% is $677.08, as shown below:

$$c = \$45;$$
$$n = 40;$$
$$i = .06.$$

$$\$45 \left[\frac{1 - \left[\frac{1}{(1.06)^{40}} \right]}{.06} \right]$$

$$= \$45 \left[\frac{1 - \left[\frac{1}{10.28572} \right]}{.06} \right]$$

$$= \$45 \left[\frac{1 - .097222}{.06} \right]$$

$$= \$45 \ (15.04630)$$

$$= \$677.08.$$

The present value of the par or maturity value 40 *six-month* periods from now discounted at 6% is $97.22, as shown below:

$$M = \$1,000;$$
$$n = 40;$$
$$i = .06.$$

$$\$1,000 \left[\frac{1}{(1.06)^{40}} \right]$$

$$= \$1,000 \left[\frac{1}{10.28572} \right]$$

$$= \$1,000 \ (.097222)$$

$$= \$97.22.$$

The price of the bond is then equal to the sum of the two present values:

Present value of coupon payments	$677.08
Present value of par (maturity) value	97.22
Price	$774.30

Illustration 5-2. Compute the price of the bond in Illustration 5-1, assuming that the required yield is 7%.

The cash flows are unchanged, but the periodic interest rate is now 3.5% (7%/2).

The present value of the 40 semiannual coupon payments of $45 discounted at 3.5% is $960.98, as shown below:

$$c = \$45;$$
$$n = 40;$$
$$i = .035.$$

$$\$45 \left[\frac{1 - \left[\frac{1}{(1.035)^{40}} \right]}{.035} \right]$$

$$= \$45 \left[\frac{1 - \left[\frac{1}{3.95926} \right]}{.035} \right]$$

$$= \$45 \left[\frac{1 - .252572}{.035} \right]$$

$$= \$45 \ (21.35509)$$

$$= \$960.98.$$

The present value of the par or maturity value of $1,000 40 *six-month periods from now* discounted at 3.5% is $252.57, as shown below:

$$M = \$1,000;$$
$$n = 40;$$
$$i = .035.$$

$$\$1,000 \left[\frac{1}{(1.035)^{40}} \right]$$

$$= \$1,000 \left[\frac{1}{3.95926} \right]$$

$$= \$1,000 \ (.252572)$$

$$= \$252.57.$$

The price of the bond is then equal to the sum of the two present values:

Present value of coupon payments	$960.98
Present value of par (maturity) value	252.57
Price	$1,213.55

Illustration 5-3. Compute the price of the bond in Illustration 5-1, assuming that there are 16 years to maturity rather than 20 years. (Assume that the required yield is still 12%.)

The cash flows for this bond are as follows:

(1) 32 semiannual coupon payments of $45;

(2) $1,000 32 six-month periods from now.

The semiannual or periodic interest rate is 6%.

The present value of the 32 semiannual coupon payments of $45 discounted at 6% is

$$c = \$45;$$
$$n = 32;$$
$$i = .06.$$

$$\$45 \left[\frac{1 - \left[\frac{1}{(1.06)^{32}} \right]}{.06} \right]$$

$$= \$45 \left[\frac{1 - \left[\frac{1}{6.45339} \right]}{.06} \right]$$

$$= \$45 \left[\frac{1 - .154957}{.06} \right]$$

$$= \$45 \, (14.08404)$$
$$= \$633.78.$$

The present value of the par or maturity value 32 *six-month periods from now* discounted at 6% is:

$$M = \$1,000;$$
$$n = 32;$$
$$i = .06.$$

$$\$1,000 \left[\frac{1}{(1.06)^{32}} \right]$$

$$= \$1,000 \left[\frac{1}{6.45339} \right]$$

$$= \$1,000 \, (.154957)$$
$$= \$154.96.$$

The price of the bond is then equal to the sum of the two present values:

Present value of coupon payments	$633.78
Present value of par (maturity) value	154.96
Price	$788.74

Illustration 5-4. Compute the price of a 14-year bond with a 9% coupon rate assuming that the required yield is 7%.

The cash flows for this bond are as follows:

(1) 28 semiannual coupon payments of $45;

(2) $1,000 28 six-month periods from now.

The periodic interest rate is 3.5%.

The present value of the 28 semiannual coupon payments when discounted at 3.5% is

$$c = \$45;$$
$$n = 28;$$
$$i = .035.$$

$$\$45 \left[\frac{1 - \left[\frac{1}{(1.035)^{28}} \right]}{.035} \right]$$

$$= \$45 \left[\frac{1 - \left[\frac{1}{2.62017} \right]}{.035} \right]$$

$$= \$45 \left[\frac{1 - .381655}{.035} \right]$$

$$= \$45 \ (17.66700)$$
$$= \$795.02.$$

The present value of the par or maturity value *28 six-month periods from now* discounted at 3.5% is

$$M = \$1,000;$$
$$n = 32;$$
$$i = .035.$$

$$\$1,000 \left[\frac{1}{(1.035)^{28}} \right]$$

$$= \$1,000 \left[\frac{1}{2.62017} \right]$$

$$= \$1,000 \ (.381654)$$
$$= \$381.65.$$

The price of the bond is then equal to the sum of the two present values:

Present value of coupon payments	$795.02
Present value of par (maturity) value	381.65
Price	$1,176.67

Relationship Between Required Yield and Price at a Given Time

The price of a bond changes in the direction opposite from the change in the required yield. The reason is that the price of the bond is the present value of the cash flows. As the required yield increases, the present value of the cash flows decreases; hence, the price decreases. The opposite is true when the required yield decreases: the present value of the cash flows increases and, therefore, the price of the bond increases.

We can see this by comparing the price of the 20-year, 9% coupon bond that we priced in Illustrations 5-1 and 5-2. When the required yield is 12%, the price of the bond is $774.30. If, instead, the required yield is 7%, the price of the bond is $1,213.55. Exhibit 5-1 shows the price of the bond for required yields from 5% to 14% for the 20-year, 9% coupon bond.

Exhibit 5-1

Price/Yield Relationship for a 20-Year, 9% Coupon Bond

Required yield (%)	Present value of 40 coupon payments*	Present value of par value in 40 periods**	Price of bond
5	$1,129.62	$372.43	$1,502.05
6	1,040.16	306.56	1,346.72
7	960.98	252.57	1,213.55
8	890.67	208.29	1,098.96
9	828.07	171.93	1,000.00
10	772.16	142.05	914.21
11	722.08	117.46	839.54
12	677.08	97.22	774.30
13	636.55	80.54	717.09
14	599.93	66.78	666.71

*   Computed as follows:

$$\$45 \left[\frac{1 - \left[\frac{1}{(1+i)^{40}} \right]}{i} \right],$$

where i is one-half the required yield.

**   Computed as follows:

$$\$1,000 \left[\frac{1}{(1+i)^{40}} \right],$$

where i is one-half the required yield.

If we graph the price/yield relationship for any noncallable bond, we will find it has the "bowed" shape shown in Exhibit 5-2. This shape is referred to as *convex*. The convexity of the price/yield relationship has important implications for the investment properties of a bond. In Chapter 12 we examine this relationship more closely.

Exhibit 5-2

Price/Yield Relationship

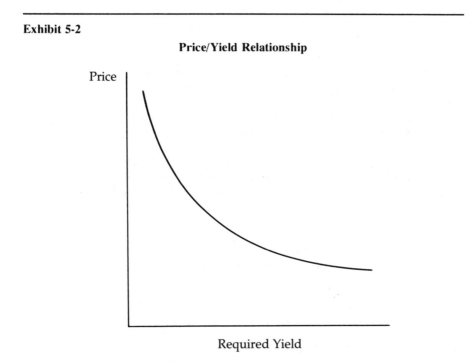

Required Yield

Relationships Among Coupon Rate, Required Yield, and Price

For a bond issue, the coupon rate and the term to maturity are fixed. Consequently, as yields in the marketplace change, the only variable that can change to compensate for the new yield required in the market is the price of the bond. As we saw in the previous section, as the required yield increases (decreases), the price of the bond decreases (increases).

Generally, a bond coupon rate at issue is set at approximately the prevailing yield in the market.[2] The price of the bond will then be approximately equal to its par value.

---

[2] The exception is an original-issue deep-discount bond such as a zero-coupon bond. We'll discuss zero-coupon bonds later in this chapter.

For example, in Exhibit 5-1, we see that when the required yield is equal to the coupon rate, the price of the bond is its par value ($1,000). Consequently, we have the following properties:

When the coupon rate equals the required yield, then the price equals the par value.

When the price equals the par value, then the coupon rate equals the required yield.

When yields in the marketplace rise above the coupon rate at *a particular time,* the price of the bond has to adjust so that the investor can realize additional interest income. This adjustment happens when the bond's price falls below the par value. The difference between the par value and the price is a capital gain, and represents a form of interest income to the investor to compensate for the coupon rate being lower than the required yield.

When a bond sells below its par value, it is said to be selling at a *discount.* We can see this in Exhibit 5-1. When the required yield is greater than the coupon rate of 9%, the price of the bond is always less than the par value ($1,000). Consequently, we have the following properties:

When the coupon rate is less than the required yield, then the price is less than the par value.

When the price is less than the par value, then the coupon rate is less than the required yield.

Finally, when the required yield in the market is below the coupon rate, the bond must sell above its par value. This occurs because investors who would have the opportunity to purchase the bond at par would be getting a coupon rate in excess of what the market would require. Because its yield is attractive, investors would bid up the price of the bond to a price that offers the required yield in the market.

A bond whose price is above its par value is said to be selling at a *premium.* Exhibit 5-1 shows that for a required yield less than the coupon rate of 9%, the price of the bond is higher than its par value. Consequently, we have the following properties:

When the coupon rate is higher than the required yield, then the price is higher than the par value.

When the price is higher than the par value, then the coupon rate is higher than the required yield.

Time Path of a Bond

If the required yield is unchanged between the time the bond is purchased and the maturity date, what will happen to the price of the bond? For a bond selling at par value, the coupon rate is equal to the required yield. As the bond moves closer to maturity, the bond will continue to sell at par value. Thus, the price of a bond selling at par will remain at par as the bond moves toward the maturity date.

The price of a bond will *not* remain constant for a bond selling at a premium or a discount. This can be seen for a discount bond by comparing the price found in Illustration 5-1 to that found in Illustration 5-3. In both illustrations the bond has a 9% coupon rate, and required yield is 12%. In Illustration 5-1, the maturity of the bond is 20 years, while in Illustration 5-3 the maturity is 16 years. With 20 years to maturity, the price of the bond is $774.30. Four years later, when the bond has 16 years remaining to maturity, the price of the bond increases to $788.74. For all discount bonds the following is true: as a bond moves toward maturity, its price will increase if *the required yield* does not change.

Exhibit 5-3 shows the price of the 20-year, 9% coupon bond as it moves toward maturity, assuming that the required yield remains at 12%. The price of the bond is decomposed into the present value of the coupon payments and the present value of the par value. Notice that as the bond moves toward maturity, there are fewer coupon payments to be received by the bondholder. The present value of the coupon payments decreases. Since the maturity date is closer, however, the present value of the par value increases. The increase in the present value of the par value is greater than the decline in the present value of the coupon payments, resulting in a price increase. Exhibit 5-4 graphs the time path of a bond selling at a discount.

For a bond selling at a premium, the price of the bond declines as it moves toward maturity. Illustrations 5-2 and 5-4 show this property for a 9% coupon bond for which the

---

Exhibit 5-3

Time Path of the Price of a Discount Bond: 20-Year, 9% Coupon, 12% Required Yield

Years remaining to maturity	Present value of coupon payments of $45 at 6%	Present value of par value at 6%	Price of bond
20	$677.08	$ 97.22	$ 774.30
18	657.94	122.74	780.68
16	633.78	154.96	788.74
14	603.28	195.63	798.91
12	564.77	256.98	811.75
10	516.15	311.80	827.95
8	454.77	393.65	848.42
6	377.27	496.97	874.24
4	279.44	627.41	906.85
2	155.93	792.09	948.02
1	82.50	890.00	972.50
0	0.00	1,000.00	1,000.00

Exhibit 5-4

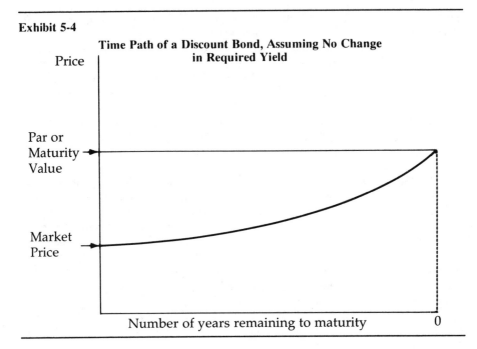

Time Path of a Discount Bond, Assuming No Change in Required Yield

required yield is 7%. When the bond has 20 years to maturity, its price is $1,213.55. Six years later, when the bond has 14 years remaining to maturity, the price of the bond declines to $1,176.67.

The time path of the 20-year, 9% coupon bond selling to yield 7% is shown in Exhibit 5-5. As the bond moves toward maturity, the present value of the coupon payments decreases, and the present value of the par value increases. Unlike a bond selling at a discount, the increase in the present value of the par value is not sufficient to offset the decline in the present value of the coupon payments. As a result, the price of a bond selling at a premium decreases over time if the required yield does not change. A graphical depiction of the time path of any premium bond is presented in Exhibit 5-6.

Analysis of Bond Price Changes

A money manager will be concerned with investigating the expected performance of a bond over an investment horizon, given certain assumptions about the future direction of interest rates. We'll demonstrate how this is done in Chapter 8. Doing so requires that we know how to analyze the way a bond's price will change under a specified set of assumptions.

The price of a bond can change for one or more of the following three reasons:

(1) A change in the required yield due to changes in the credit quality of the issuer;

Exhibit 5-5

Time Path of the Price of a Premium Bond: 20-Year, 9% Coupon, 7% Required Yield

Years remaining to maturity	Present value of coupon payments of $45 at 3.5%	Present value of par value at 3.5%	Price of bond
20	$960.98	$252.57	$1,213.55
18	913.07	289.83	1,202.90
16	858.10	332.59	1,190.69
14	795.02	381.65	1,176.67
12	722.63	437.96	1,160.59
10	639.56	502.57	1,142.13
8	544.24	576.71	1,120.95
6	434.85	661.78	1,096.63
4	309.33	759.41	1,068.74
2	165.29	871.44	1,036.73
1	85.49	933.51	1,019.00
0	0.00	1,000.00	1,000.00

Exhibit 5-6

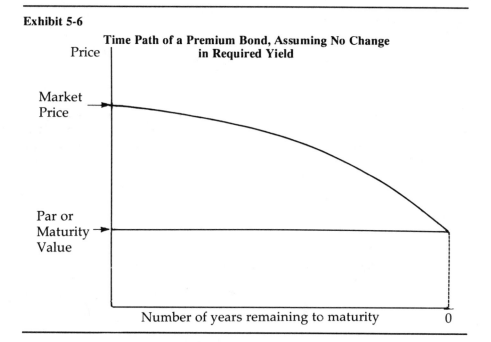

Time Path of a Premium Bond, Assuming No Change in Required Yield

Price

Market Price

Par or Maturity Value

Number of years remaining to maturity   0

(2) A change in the maturity of the bond as it moves toward maturity without any change in the required yield (that is, the time path of the bond);

(3) A change in the required yield due to a change in the yield on comparable bonds (that is, a change in the yield required by the market).

Predicting the change in an issue's credit quality before that change is recognized by the market is one of the challenges of investment management. For purposes of our illustrations below, let's suppose that the issue's credit quality is unchanged, so that we can focus on the last two reasons.

It is informative to separate the effect of the change in price due to the time path of a bond from that of the change due to a change in the required yield. The next two illustrations show how this is done.

Illustration 5-5. Suppose that a money manager purchases a 20-year, 9% coupon bond at a price of $774.30 to yield 12%. The money manager expects to hold this bond for four years, at which time the money manager believes that the required yield on comparable 16-year bonds will be 8%. On the basis of these expectations, we can investigate what will happen to the price of the bond four years from now.

After this bond is held for four years, it becomes a 16-year bond. If the required yield for a 16-year bond is 8%, the price of the bond four years from now will be $1,089.37.[3] The price of this bond is therefore expected to increase by $315.07 ($1,089.37 – $744.30). Not all of the price change, however, is due to the decline in market yield. If the required yield remains at 12%, the price of the bond in four years will have increased to $788.74, an increase of $14.44 ($788.74 – $744.30). Therefore, we can decompose the expected price change after four years as follows:

Price change due to the time path of a discount bond	$ 14.44
Price change due to the change in the required yield	300.63
Total price change	$315.07

Illustration 5-6. Suppose that a money manager is considering the purchase of a 20-year, 9% coupon bond selling at $1,213.55 to yield 7%. If the money manager purchases this bond, she expects to hold it for six years, at which time she expects that the required yield on 14-year bonds may be 11%. What would be the price performance of this bond based on the money manager's expectations?

---

[3] The price is determined as follows:

Present value of 32 coupon payments at 4%	$804.31
Present value of par (maturity) value at 4%	285.06
Price	$1,089.37

The price of a 14-year, 9% coupon bond if an 11% required yield is assumed is $858.79.[4] If the required yield remained at 7%, however, the price of a 14-year bond with a coupon rate of 9% would be $1,176.67 (see Exhibit 5-5). The price change can be broken down as follows:

Price change due to the time path of a discount bond	– $ 36.88
Price change due to the change in the required yield	– 317.88
Total price change	– $354.76

The Price of a Zero-Coupon Bond

So far we have determined the price of coupon-bearing bonds. There are bonds that do not make any periodic coupon payments. Instead, the investor realizes interest by the amount of the difference between the maturity value and the purchase price.

The pricing of a zero-coupon bond is no different from the pricing of a coupon bond: its price is the present value of the expected cash flows. In the case of a zero-coupon bond, the only cash flow is the maturity value. Therefore, the formula for the price of a zero-coupon bond that matures N years from now is

$$p = M \left[\frac{1}{(1 + i)^n} \right] ,$$

where

p = Price;
M = Maturity value;
i = Periodic interest rate (annual interest rate/2);
$n = 2 \times N$, where
N = Number of years.

Pay particular attention to the number of periods used in the pricing of a zero-coupon bond. Although an issue may mature in N years, the number of six-month periods is used in the exponent, and the periodic interest rate is the required yield divided by 2. The reason is that the pricing of a zero-coupon bond must be made consistent with the pricing of a coupon bond. Recall that with a coupon bond the present value of the par or maturity value is computed using twice the number of years to maturity. Therefore, we handle the maturity value for the zero-coupon bond the same way.

---

[4] The price is determined as follows:

Present value of 28 coupon payments at 5.5%	$635.47
Present value of par (maturity) value at 5.5%	223.32
Price	$858.79

Illustration 5-7. Compute the price of a zero-coupon bond that matures 10 years from now if the maturity value is $1,000 and the required yield is 8.6%.

The price is determined as follows:

$$M = \$1,000;$$
$$i = .043 \ (.086/2);$$
$$N = 10;$$
$$n = 20 \ (2 \times 10);$$

$$p = \$1,000 \left[\frac{1}{(1.043)^{20}} \right]$$

$$= \$1,000 \left[\frac{1}{2.321059} \right]$$

$$= \$1,000 \ (.43083)$$

$$= \$430.83.$$

Illustration 5-8. Compute the price of a seven-year, zero-coupon bond with a maturity value of $100,000 if the required yield is 9.8%.

The price is $51,185.06, as shown below:

$$M = \$100,000;$$
$$i = .049 \ (.098/2);$$
$$N = 7;$$
$$n = 14 \ (2 \times 7);$$

$$p = \$100,000 \left[\frac{1}{(1.049)^{14}} \right]$$

$$= \$100,000 \left[\frac{1}{1.953695} \right]$$

$$= \$100,000 \ (.5118506)$$

$$= \$51,185.06.$$

Price Quotations

In all but our last illustration, we have assumed that the maturity or par value of the bond is $1,000. A bond can have a maturity or par value of any amount. Consequently, traders quote bond prices as a percentage of par value.

A bond selling at par is quoted as 100, meaning 100% of its par value. A bond selling at a discount will be selling for less than 100; a bond selling at a premium will be selling for more than 100. The following examples illustrate how a price quote is converted into a dollar price.

Price quote (1)	Converted to a decimal (2) [=(1)/100]	Par value (3)	Dollar price (4) = [(2)×(3)]
95	.9500000	$1,000	$950.00
95 1/2	.9550000	100,000	95,500.00
98 1/4	.9825000	5,000	4,912.50
80 1/8	.8012500	10,000	8,012.50
74 1/32	.7403125	1,000,000	740,312.50
100	1.0000000	10,000	10,000.00
103	1.0300000	1,000	1,030.00
106 3/4	1.0675000	500,000	533,750.00
108 3/8	1.0837500	25,000	27,093.75
111 11/32	1.1134375	100,000	111,343.75

For some securities a unique market convention has been adopted for quoting prices. For example, for Treasury notes and bonds, a quote of "95-5," "95.5," or "95:05" means 95% plus 5/32, the number following the hyphen, decimal, or colon representing the number of 32nds. So for a $100,000 par value Treasury note or bond, a quote of 95-5 or 95.5 or 95:05 indicates a dollar price of $95,156.25, as shown below:

$$95 \frac{5}{32} \% = 95.15625\% = .9515625;$$

then

$$\$100,000 \times .9515625 = \$95,156.25.$$

Corporate and municipal bonds are frequently quoted in eighths rather than 32nds.

Determining the Price When the Settlement Date Falls Between Coupon Periods

Our illustrations have assumed that the next coupon payment is six months away. This means that settlement occurs on the day after a coupon date. Typically, an investor purchases a bond between coupon dates, so that the next coupon payment is less than six months away. To compute the price, we have to answer three questions:

(1) How many days are there until the next coupon payment?

(2) How should we determine the present value of cash flows received over fractional periods?

(3) How much must the buyer compensate the seller for the coupon interest earned by the seller for the fraction of the period that the bond was held?

The first question is the "day-count" question. The second is the "compounding" question. The last question asks how accrued interest is determined.

Day Count Conventions

Market conventions for the number of days in a coupon period and the number of days in a year differ by type of bond issuer (i.e., government, government-related entity, local government, and corporate) and by country. The following notation is typically used to denote a day count convention:

Number of days in a month/Number of days in a year

In practice, there are six day count conventions:[5]

(1) Actual/actual (in period)

(2) Actual/365

(3) Actual/365 (366 in leap year)

(4) Actual/360

(5) 30/360

(6) 30E/360

In calculation of the actual number of days, only one of the two bracketing dates in question is included. For example, the actual number of days between August 20 and August 24 is four days.

The last two day count conventions, 30/360 and 30E/360, require some explanation. We use the notation following to explain them:

Let

$$D1/M1/Y1 = \text{the day (D1), month (M1),}$$
$$\text{and year (Y1) of the first date}$$

$$D2/M2/Y2 = \text{the day (D2), month (M2),}$$
$$\text{and year (Y2) of the second date}$$

30/360 day count: The number of days between two dates assumes 30-day months, according to the following rules for the number of days between the dates D1/M1/Y1 and D2/M2/Y2:

■ if D1 is 31, change to 30.

■ if D2 is 31 and D1 is 30 or 31, change D2 to 30; otherwise leave at 31.

■ then, the number of days between the two dates is:

$$(Y2 - Y1) \times 360 + (M2 - M1) \times 30 + (D2 - D1)$$

---

[5] Dragomir Krgin, *Price/Yield Calculations for Periodic Payment Fixed Income Securities,* undated manuscript, p. 16.

For example, there are 29 days between May 1 and May 30 and 30 days between May 1 and May 31.

30E/360 day count: The number of days between two dates assumes 30-day months, according to the following rules for the number of days between dates D1/M1/Y1 and D2/M2/Y2:

■ if D1 is 31, change D1 to 30.

■ if D2 is 31, change D2 to 30.

■ then, the number of days between the two dates is:

$$(Y2 - Y1) \times 360 + (M2 - M1) \times 30 + (D2 - D1).$$

Just as in the 30/360 day count convention, the number of days between May 1 and May 30 is 29 days. However, unlike the previous day count convention, the number of days between May 1 and May 31 is not 30 days but 29 days. This is because D2 in this case is 31, and therefore D2 is changed to 30.

The various day count conventions in major bond markets throughout the world, as well as the frequency of coupon payments, are listed in Exhibit 5-7.

Application to U.S. Treasury Bonds: In the U.S. Treasury coupon securities market, the day count convention used is to determine the actual number of days between two dates and the actual number of days in a year. This is referred to as the "actual/actual" day count convention. For example, consider a Treasury bond whose previous coupon payment was March 1 and whose next coupon payment is on September 1. Suppose this bond is purchased with a settlement date of July 17th. The actual number of days between July 17 (the settlement date) and September 1 (the date of the next coupon payment) is 46 days, as shown below:

July 17 to July 31	14 days
August	31 days
September 1	1 day
	46 days

The number of days in the coupon period is the actual number of days between March 1 and September 1, which is 184 days.

Application to Federal Agency, Corporate, and Municipal Securities: In contrast to the "actual/actual" day count convention for coupon-bearing Treasury securities, for corporate and municipal bonds and agency securities, the day count convention is "30/360." That is, each month is assumed to have 30 days and each year 360 days. For example, suppose that the security in our previous example is not a coupon-bearing Treasury security but instead either a coupon-bearing corporate bond, municipal bond, or agency security. The number of days between July 17 and September 1 is as shown below:

Exhibit 5-7

Coupon Frequency, Day Count Conventions, and Ex-Dividend Trading Practices in Major Bond Markets Throughout the World

Market	Coupon Payments	Day Count	Ex-Dividend Trading
U.S. Government	Semiannual	Actual/Actual (In Period)	N
U.S. Corporate	Semiannual	30/360	N
U.S. Government Agency	Annual	30/360	N
	Semiannual		N
	Quarterly		N
U.S. Municipal	Semiannual	30/360	N
U.K. Government	Semiannual	Actual/365	Y
Australian Government	Semiannual	Actual/Actual (In Period)	Y
New Zealand Government	Semiannual	Actual/Actual (In Period)	Y
Canadian Government	Semiannual	Actual/Actual (In Period)	N
German Government	Annual	30E/360	Y
Swiss Government	Annual	30E/360	N
Dutch Government	Annual	30E/360	Y
Eurobond	Annual	30E/360	N
Italian Government	Annual	30E/360	N
French Government	Annual	Actual/Actual (In Period)	N
Danish Government	Annual	30E/360	Y
Swedish Government	Annual	30E/360	Y
Spanish Government	Semiannual	Actual/Actual (In Period)	N
Belgian Government	Annual	30E/360	N
Irish Government	Annual	Actual/365	Y
Austrian Government	Annual	30E/365	Y
Norwegian Government	Annual	Actual/365	Y

Source: Dragomir Krgin, *Price/Yield Calculations for Periodic Payment Fixed Income Securities*, undated manuscript, Appendix A, p. 18.

July 17 to July 31	13 days
August	30 days
September 1	1 day
	44 days

Basic financial calendars provide the day count between settlement and the next coupon payment. Most money managers, however, use software programs that will furnish this information.

Compounding

Once the number of days between the settlement date and the next coupon date is determined, the present value formula must be modified to take into account that the cash flows will not be received six months (one full period) from now. The "street" convention is to compute the price as follows:

(1) Determine the number of days in the coupon period.

(2) Compute the ratio:

$$w = \frac{\text{Number of days between settlement and next coupon payment}}{\text{Number of days in the coupon period}}.$$

For a corporate bond, municipal bond, or agency security, the number of days in the coupon period will be 180, since a year is assumed to have 360 days. For a coupon-bearing Treasury security, the number of days is the actual number of days. The number of days in the coupon period is called the *basis*.

(3) For a bond with n coupon payments remaining to maturity, the price is:

$$p = \frac{c}{(1 + i)^w} + \frac{c}{(1 + i)^{1 + w}} + \frac{c}{(1 + i)^{2 + w}} + \ldots$$
$$+ \frac{c}{(1 + i)^{n - 1 + w}} + \frac{M}{(1 + i)^{n - 1 + w}}$$

where

p = Price ($);
c = *Semiannual* coupon payment ($);
i = Periodic interest rate (required yield divided by 2) (in decimal);
n = Number of coupon payments remaining;
M = Maturity value.

The period (exponent) in the formula for determining the present value can be expressed generally as $t - 1 + w$. For example, for the first cash flow, the period is $1 - 1 + w$, or simply w. For the second cash flow it is $2 - 1 + w$, or simply $1 + w$. If the bond has 20 coupon payments remaining, the period is $20 - 1 + w$, or simply $19 + w$.

Illustration 5-9. Suppose that a corporate bond with a coupon rate of 10% maturing March 1, 1999, is purchased with a settlement date of July 17, 1993. What would the price of this bond be if it is priced to yield 6.5%?

The next coupon payment will be made on September 1, 1993. Since the bond is a corporate bond, the 30/360 day count convention is that there are 44 days between the settlement date and the next coupon date. The number of days in the coupon payment is 180 days. Therefore,

$$w = \frac{44}{180} = .24444.$$

The number of coupon payments remaining, n, is 12. The semiannual interest rate is 3.25% (6.5%/2). Calculation of the price is shown in Exhibit 5-8.

Exhibit 5-8

Calculation of Full (Dirty) Price When a Bond Is Purchased Between Coupon Payments

Period	Cash flow per $100 of par	Present value of $1 at 3.25%	Present value of cash flow
0.24444	$5.00	$0.992212	4.961060
1.24444	5.00	0.960980	4.804902
2.24444	5.00	0.930731	4.653658
3.24444	5.00	0.901435	4.507175
4.24444	5.00	0.873060	4.365303
5.24444	5.00	0.845579	4.227896
6.24444	5.00	0.818963	4.094815
7.24444	5.00	0.793184	3.965922
8.24444	5.00	0.768217	3.841087
9.24444	5.00	0.744036	3.720181
10.24444	5.00	0.720616	3.603081
11.24444	105.00	0.697933	73.283000
		Total	$120.028100

The price of this corporate bond is $120.0281. The price calculated in this way is called the *full price* or *dirty price* because it reflects the portion of the coupon interest that the buyer will receive but that the seller has earned.

Accrued Interest

The buyer must compensate the seller for the portion of the next coupon interest payment the seller has earned but will not receive from the issuer because the issuer will send the next coupon payment to the buyer. This amount is called *accrued interest.* Interest accrues on a bond from and including the date of the previous coupon up to but *excluding* a date called the *value date.* The value date is usually, but not always, the same as the settlement date. Unlike the settlement date, the value date is not constrained to fall on a business day.[6]

---

[6] The term "value date" is not used consistently across markets — the definition in the text is that used by the Association of International Bond Dealers (AIBD). In some markets the interest accrues up to and *including* a date that is called the value date. The "dated date" is the date from which accrued interest is calculated on a newly issued security.

Calculation of accrued interest assumes the coupon payment takes place on the scheduled date, even if in practice it will be delayed because the scheduled date is a nonbusiness day. In the formulas below we use the settlement date rather than the value date.

The accrued interest is calculated as follows:

$$AI = c \left[\frac{\text{Number of days from last coupon payment to settlement date}}{\text{Number of days in coupon period}} \right],$$

where

AI = Accrued interest (\$);

c = Semiannual coupon payment (\$).

Accrued interest is not computed for all bonds. No accrued interest is computed for bonds in default and income bonds. A bond that trades without accrued interest is said to be traded "flat."

Illustration 5-10. Let's continue with the hypothetical corporate bond in Illustration 5-9. Since the number of days between settlement (July 17, 1993) and the next coupon payment (September 1, 1993) is 44 days and the number of days in the coupon period is 180, the number of days from the last coupon payment date (March 1, 1993) to the settlement date is 136 (180 – 44). The accrued interest per \$100 of par value is

$$AI - \$5 \left(\frac{136}{180} \right) = \$3.777778.$$

Illustration 5-11. If the bond in the previous illustration were a Treasury bond rather than a corporate, the accrued interest would be computed as follows. The number of days in the coupon period is based on the actual number of days. Between March 1 and September 1 the actual number of days is 184. The actual number of days between March 1 and July 17 is 138. Accrued interest per \$100 of par value is then

$$AI = \$5 \left(\frac{138}{184} \right) = \$3.75.$$

Cum-dividend and ex-dividend trading: When the buyer receives the next coupon, the bond is said to be traded *cum-dividend* (or *cum-coupon*), and the buyer pays the seller accrued interest. If the buyer forgos the next coupon, the bond is said to be traded *ex-dividend* (or *ex-coupon*), and the seller pays the buyer accrued interest. In some markets (the U.S. is one) bonds are always traded cum-dividend. In other markets, bonds are traded ex-dividend for a certain period before the coupon date. The last column in Exhibit 5-7 shows the practices in major bond markets throughout the world.

Price Buyer Pays and Price Quotes

The full or dirty price includes the accrued interest that the seller is entitled to receive. For example, in the calculation of the full price in Exhibit 5-8, the next coupon payment of $5 is included as part of the cash flow. The *clean price* or *flat price* is the dirty price of the bond minus the accrued interest; that is,

Clean price = Dirty price − Accrued interest

The price that the buyer pays the seller is the dirty price. It is important to note that in calculation of the dirty price, the next coupon payment is a discounted value, but in calculation of accrued interest it is an undiscounted value. Because of this market practice, if a bond is selling at par and the settlement date is not a coupon date, the yield will be slightly less than the coupon rate. Only when the settlement date and coupon date coincide is the yield equal to the coupon rate for a bond selling at par.

In the U.S. market, the convention is to quote a bond's clean or flat price. The buyer, however, pays the seller the dirty price. In some non-U.S. markets, the dirty price is quoted.

Summary

In this chapter we have shown how to determine the price of a noncallable bond. The price is simply the present value of the bond's expected cash flows, where the discount rate is equal to the yield offered on comparable bonds. For a noncallable bond, the cash flows are the coupon payments and the par value or maturity value. For a zero-coupon bond, there are no coupon payments: the price is equal to the present value of the maturity value, where the number of periods used to compute the present value is double the number of years. Exhibit 5-9 summarizes the pricing formulas presented in this chapter.

The higher (lower) the required yield, the lower (higher) the price of a bond. Therefore, a bond's price changes in the direction opposite from the change in the required yield. When the coupon rate is equal to the required yield, the bond will sell at its par value. When the coupon rate is less (higher) than the required yield, the bond will sell for less (more) than its par value. A bond selling below (above) its par value is said to be selling at a discount (premium).

Over time, the price of a bond will change. Assuming the credit quality of the issuer is unchanged, the price change can be broken down into an amount attributed to a change in the required yield and an amount attributed to the time path of the bond.

When a bond is purchased between coupon payments, the buyer must pay the seller accrued interest. To calculate the accrued interest, the following must be determined: number of days between the previous coupon payment and the next coupon payment, and present value of the coupons. The conventions for determining these vary by market sector and from country to country. The payment made by the buyer to the seller is called the dirty price. The price quoted in the U.S. is the clean price or flat price, which is equal to the dirty price minus the accrued interest.

Exhibit 5-9

Summary of Pricing Formulas

(1)   Price of a noncallable bond when next coupon payment is six months away:

$$p = \frac{c}{(1+i)^1} + \frac{c}{(1+i)^2} + \frac{c}{(1+i)^3} + \ldots + \frac{c}{(1+i)^n} + \frac{M}{(1+i)^n}$$

where

p = Price (\$);
c = *Semiannual* coupon payment (\$);
i = Periodic interest rate (required yield divided by 2) (in decimal);
n = Number of periods (number of years times 2);
M = Maturity value.

(2)   Present value of the coupon payments:

$$c \; \frac{1 - \left[\dfrac{1}{(1+i)^n}\right]}{i}$$

(3)   Price of a zero-coupon bond:

$$p = M \left[\frac{1}{(1+i)^n}\right]$$

where

$n = 2 \times N$, where
N = Number of years.

(4)   Price of a bond purchased between coupon payments with n coupon payments remaining:

$$p = \frac{c}{(1+i)^w} + \frac{c}{(1+i)^{1+w}} + \frac{c}{(1+i)^{2+w}} + \ldots$$

$$+ \frac{c}{(1+i)^{n-1+w}} + \frac{M}{(1+i)^{n-1+w}}$$

where

i = Periodic interest rate (required yield divided by 2) (in decimal);

$$w = \frac{\text{Number of days between settlement and next coupon payment}}{\text{Number of days in the coupon period}} \; ;$$

Exhibit 5-9 continued.

n = Number of coupon payments remaining.

(5)   Accrued interest

$$AI = c \left[\frac{\text{Number of days from last coupon payment to settlement date}}{\text{Number of days in the coupon period}} \right],$$

where

AI = Accrued interest ($);

(6)   Dirty price = Full price = Present value of the bond's cash flows

(7)   Clean price = Flat price = Dirty price − Accrued interest

6

Conventional Yield Measures for Bonds

In the previous chapter, we explained how to compute the price of a bond, given the required yield. In this chapter, we show how to compute various yield measures for a bond, given its price. We focus largely on three conventional yield measures commonly quoted by dealers and traders: (1) current yield, (2) yield to maturity, and (3) yield to call. While these yield measures are commonly used by bond market participants, their usefulness in assessing the relative value of a bond over some specified investment horizon is questionable. In the next chapter we evaluate these yield measures; in Chapter 8 we suggest a yield measure that is more useful for determining the potential return by investing in a bond.

Current Yield

The current yield relates the *annual* coupon interest to the market price. The formula for the current yield is

$$\text{Current yield} = \frac{\text{Annual dollar coupon interest}}{\text{Price}}.$$

Illustration 6-1. The current yield for an 18-year, 6% coupon bond selling for $700.89 is 8.56%, as shown below:

$$\text{Annual dollar coupon interest} = \$1,000 \times .06$$
$$= \$60;$$

$$\text{Current yield} = \frac{\$60}{\$700.89} = .0856 \text{ or } 8.56\%.$$

Illustration 6-2. The current yield for a 19-year, 11% coupon bond selling for $1,233.64 is 8.92%, as shown below:

$$\text{Annual dollar coupon interest} = \$1,000 \times .11$$
$$= \$110$$

$$\text{Current yield} = \frac{\$110}{\$1,233.64} = .0892 \text{ or } 8.92\%.$$

The current yield considers only the coupon interest and no other source of return that will affect an investor's yield. For example, in Illustration 6-1, no consideration is given to the capital gain that the investor will realize when the bond matures; in Illustration 6-2, no recognition is given to the capital loss that the investor will realize when the bond matures.

Yield to Maturity

In Chapter 4 we explained how to compute the yield or internal rate of return on any investment. The yield is the interest rate that will make the present value of the cash flows equal to the price (or initial investment). The yield to maturity is computed in the same way as the yield; the cash flows are those that the investor would realize by holding the bond to maturity. For a semiannual-pay bond whose next coupon payment will be received six months from now, the yield to maturity is computed by solving the following relationship for y:

$$p = \frac{c}{(1+y)^1} + \frac{c}{(1+y)^2} + \frac{c}{(1+y)^3} + \ldots + \frac{c}{(1+y)^n} + \frac{M}{(1+y)^n}$$

where

$p =$ Price ($);
$c = $ *Semiannual* coupon interest ($);
$y =$ One-half the yield to maturity;
$n =$ Number of periods (number of years × 2);
$M =$ Maturity value ($).

For a semiannual-pay bond, doubling the interest rate or discount rate (y) gives the yield to maturity.

Using the Greek letter sigma to denote summation, we can express this relationship as follows:

$$p = \sum_{t=1}^{n} \frac{c}{(1+y)^t} + \frac{M}{(1+y)^n} \; .$$

The yield to maturity considers not only the current coupon income but any capital gain or loss that the investor will realize by *holding the bond to maturity*. The yield to maturity also considers the timing of the cash flows.

Recall from Chapter 4 that computation of the yield requires a trial-and-error procedure. The next two illustrations show how to compute the yield to maturity for a bond.

Illustration 6-3. In Illustration 6-1 we computed the current yield for an 18-year, 6% coupon bond selling for $700.89. The maturity or par value for this bond is $1,000. The yield to maturity for this bond is 9.5%, as shown below:

Cash flows for the bond:

(1) 36 coupon payments of $30 every six months; and

(2) $1,000 36 six-month periods from now.

To get y, different interest rates must be tried until one is found that makes the present value of the cash flows equal to the price of $700.89. Since the coupon rate on the bond is 6% and the bond is selling at a discount, the yield must be greater than 6%. Exhibit 6-1 shows the present value of the cash flows of the bond for periodic interest rates from 3.25% to 4.75% (corresponding to annual interest rates from 6.50% to 9.50%, respectively). As can be seen from this exhibit, at the interest rate of 4.75%, the present value of the cash flows is $700.89. Therefore, y is 4.75%, and the yield to maturity is 9.50%.

Illustration 6-4. In Illustration 6-2 we computed the current yield for a 19-year, 11% coupon bond selling for $1,233.64. The maturity or par value for this bond is $1,000. The yield to maturity for this bond is 8.50%, as shown below:

Cash flows for the bond:

(1) 38 coupon payments of $55 every six months; and

(2) $1,000 38 six-month periods from now.

Exhibit 6-1

Computation of Yield to Maturity for an 18-Year, 6% Coupon Bond Selling at $700.89

Objective: Find—by trial and error—the semiannual interest rate that will make the present value of the following cash flows equal to $700.89:

36 coupon payments of $30 every six months;
$1,000 36 six-month periods from now.

Annual interest rate	Semi-annual rate	Present value of 36 payments of $30 *	Present value of $1,000 36 periods from now **	Present value of cash flows
6.50%	3.25%	$631.20	$316.20	$947.40
7.00	3.50	608.71	289.83	898.54
7.50	3.75	587.42	265.72	853.14
8.00	4.00	567.25	243.67	810.92
8.50	4.25	548.12	223.49	771.61
9.00	4.50	529.98	205.03	735.01
9.50	4.75	512.76	188.13	700.89

*
$$\$30 \left[\frac{1 - \left[\frac{1}{(1 + \text{Semiannual interest rate})^{36}} \right]}{\text{Semiannual interest rate}} \right].$$

**
$$\$1,000 \left[\frac{1}{(1 + \text{Semiannual interest rate})^{36}} \right].$$

We are looking for the interest rate y that will make the present value of the cash flows equal to $1,233.64 (the price of the bond). Since the bond is selling at a premium and the coupon rate is 11%, the yield must be less than 11%. Exhibit 6-2 shows the present value of the cash flows of the bond for periodic interest rates from 3.00% to 4.25% (corresponding to annual interest rates from 6.0% to 8.50%, respectively). The present value of the cash flows is equal to the price when a 4.25% interest rate is used. The value for y is therefore 4.25%. Doubling 4.25% produces the yield to maturity of 8.50%.

Yield to Maturity for a Zero-Coupon Bond

In Chapter 4 we explained that when there is only one cash flow, it is much easier to compute the yield on an investment. A zero-coupon bond is characterized by a single cash flow resulting from the investment. Consequently, the following formula, presented in

Exhibit 6-2

Computation of Yield to Maturity for a 19-Year, 11% Coupon Bond Selling at $1,233.64

Objective: Find—by trial and error—the semiannual interest rate that will make the present value of the following cash flows equal to $1,233.64:

38 coupon payments of $55 every six months;
$1,000 38 six-month periods from now.

Annual interest rate	Semi-annual rate	Present value of 38 payments of $55 *	Present value of $1,000 38 periods from now **	Present value of cash flows
6.00%	3.00%	$1,237.09	$325.23	$1,562.32
6.50	3.25	1,190.36	296.60	1,486.96
7.00	3.50	1,146.26	270.56	1,416.82
7.50	3.75	1,104.60	246.86	1,351.46
8.00	4.00	1,065.23	225.29	1,290.52
8.50	4.25	1,028.00	205.64	1,233.64

*
$$\$55 \left[\frac{1 - \left[\frac{1}{(1 + \text{Semiannual interest rate})^{38}} \right]}{\text{Semiannual interest rate}} \right]$$

**
$$\$1,000 \left[\frac{1}{(1 + \text{Semiannual interest rate})^{38}} \right]$$

Chapter 4 (Exhibit 4-2), can be applied to compute the yield to maturity for a zero-coupon bond:

$$y = (\text{Future value per dollar invested})^{1/n} - 1$$

where

y = One-half the yield to maturity;

$$\text{Future value per dollar invested} = \frac{\text{Maturity value}}{\text{Price}} .$$

Once again, doubling y gives the yield to maturity. *Remember that the number of periods used in the formula is double the number of years.*

Illustration 6-5. The yield to maturity for a zero-coupon bond selling for $274.78 with a maturity value of $1,000, maturing in 15 years, is 8.8%, as computed below:

Future value per dollar invested = $\dfrac{\$1,000.00}{\$274.78}$

$n = 30\ (15 \times 2)$;

$$y = (3.639275)^{1/30} - 1$$
$$= (3.639275)^{.033333} - 1$$
$$= 1.044 - 1$$
$$= .044 \text{ or } 4.4\%.$$

Doubling 4.4% gives the yield to maturity of 8.8%.

Computing the Yield to Maturity When the Settlement Date Falls Between Coupon Payments

In the last chapter we explained how to determine the price that the buyer pays the seller when a bond is purchased between coupon payments. The amount paid is the dirty or full price. The yield to maturity for a bond when settlement falls between coupon dates is the interest rate that will make the present value of the cash flows equal to the dirty price. That is, for a semiannual-pay bond with n coupon payments remaining, we must solve the following relationship for y:

$$tp = \frac{c}{(1+y)^{w}} + \frac{c}{(1+y)^{1+w}} + \frac{c}{(1+y)^{2+w}} + \ldots +$$

$$\frac{c}{(1+y)^{n-1+w}} + \frac{M}{(1+y)^{n-1+w}} ,$$

where

tp = Dirty price ($);

c = *Semiannual* coupon payment ($);

y = One-half the yield to maturity;

$w = \dfrac{\text{Number of days between settlement and the next coupon payment}}{\text{Number of days in the coupon period}}$;

n = Number of coupon payments remaining;

M = Maturity value.

Doubling y gives the yield to maturity.

Using the Greek letter sigma to denote summation, the formula can be expressed as follows:

$$tp = \sum_{t=1}^{n} \frac{c}{(1+y)^{t-1+w}} + \frac{M}{(1+y)^{n-1+w}} .$$

Illustration 6-6: Suppose that a 10% coupon corporate bond maturing on March 1, 1999, has a dirty price of $118.778. The settlement date is July 17, 1993. The cash flows for this bond per $100 of par value, and the corresponding periods they will be received, are:

Period	Cash flow
.24444 through 10.2444	$5.00
11.24444	$105.00

The semiannual interest rate that will make the present value of the cash flows equal to the dirty price payment of $118.778 is 3.3735%. Doubling the semiannual interest rate gives a yield to maturity of 6.747%.

Illustration 6-7. If the bond in Illustration 6-6 is a Treasury bond rather than a corporate, the cash flows for the bond would be as follows:

Number of days from settlement to next coupon payment = 46;
Number of days in coupon period = 184;

$$w = \frac{46}{184} = .25 \ .$$

The cash flows for this bond per $100 of par value and the corresponding periods they will be received are as follows:

Period	Cash flow
.25 through 10.25	$5.00
11.25	$105.00

Suppose the dirty price is $118.75. The interest rate that will make the present value of the cash flows equal to $118.75 is 3.374%. The yield to maturity is then 6.748%.

Relationships Among Coupon Rate, Current Yield, and Yield to Maturity

These relationships pertain among coupon rate, current yield, and yield to maturity:

Bond selling at	Relationship
Par	Coupon rate = Current yield = Yield to maturity
Discount	Coupon rate < Current yield < Yield to maturity
Premium	Coupon rate > Current yield > Yield to maturity

The relationships for discount and premium bonds can be verified from the illustrations presented earlier in this chapter.

Problem with the Annualizing Procedure

As we pointed out in Chapter 4, multiplying a semiannual interest rate by 2 will produce an underestimate of the effective annual yield. The proper way to annualize the semiannual yield is by applying the following formula presented in Chapter 4 (see Exhibit 4-2):

$$\text{Effective annual yield} = (1 + \text{Periodic interest rate})^k - 1,$$

where

k = Number of payments per year.

For a semiannual-pay bond, the formula can be modified as follows:

$$\text{Effective annual yield} = (1 + \text{Semiannual interest rate})^2 - 1$$

or

$$\text{Effective annual yield} = (1 + y)^2 - 1.$$

For example, in Illustration 6-3, the semiannual interest rate is 4.75%, and the effective annual yield is 9.73%, as shown below:

$$
\begin{aligned}
\text{Effective annual yield} &= (1.0475)^2 - 1 \\
&= 1.0973 - 1 \\
&= .0973 \text{ or } 9.73\%.
\end{aligned}
$$

Although the proper way to annualize a semiannual interest rate is given in the formula above, the convention adopted in the bond market is to double the semiannual interest rate. The yield to maturity computed in this manner—doubling the semiannual yield—is called a *bond equivalent yield.* In fact, this convention is carried over to yield calculations for other types of fixed income securities.[1]

Comparing Yield to Maturity on Annual-Pay and Semiannual-Pay Bonds

While Treasury, corporate, and municipal bonds issued in the United States are semiannual-pay bonds, Eurodollar fixed rate bonds are annual-pay bonds. The yield to maturity on an annual-pay security such as a Eurodollar fixed rate bond is just the interest rate that will make the present value of the annual cash flows equal to the dirty price. To convert the yield to maturity of an annual-pay bond to a yield to maturity on a bond equivalent basis, the following formula should be used:

$$
\begin{aligned}
&\text{Yield to maturity on a bond equivalent basis} \\
&= 2\left[(1 + \text{Yield to maturity})^{1/2} - 1\right].
\end{aligned}
$$

---

[1] For example, in Chapter 19, we discuss the yield calculation for mortgage pass-through securities. The periodic interest rate is computed on a monthly basis. To compute an annual yield, the practice is first to compute an effective semiannual yield as follows:

$$\text{Effective semiannual yield} = (1 + \text{Monthly interest rate})^6 - 1.$$

Then the effective semiannual yield is doubled.

Illustration 6-8. Suppose the yield to maturity on a Eurodollar fixed rate bond is 9%. The yield to maturity for this bond on a bond equivalent basis is

$$2\left[(1.09)^{1/2} - 1\right]$$
$$= 2(1.0440 - 1)$$
$$= .088 \text{ or } 8.8\%.$$

Notice that the yield to maturity on a bond equivalent basis will be less than the yield to maturity computed for an annual-pay bond.

Yield to Call

For a callable bond, investors also compute another yield (or internal rate of return) measure, the *yield to call*. The cash flows for computing the yield to call are those that would result if the issue were called on its first call date. The yield to call is the interest rate that will make the present value of the cash flows if the bond is held to the first call date equal to the price of the bond (or dirty price).

Mathematically, the yield to call for a bond on which the next coupon payment will be due six months from now can be expressed as follows:

$$p = \frac{c}{(1+y)^1} + \frac{c}{(1+y)^2} + \frac{c}{(1+y)^3} + \ldots + \frac{c}{(1+y)^{n*}} + \frac{CP}{(1+y)^{n*}},$$

where

p = Price (\$);
c = *Semiannual* coupon interest (\$);
y = One-half the yield to call;
$n*$ = Number of periods until first call date (number of years $\times$ 2);
CP = Call price (\$).

For a semiannual-pay bond, doubling the interest rate (y) gives the yield to call.

Alternatively, this relationship can be expressed as follows:

$$p = \sum_{t=1}^{n*} \frac{c}{(1+y)^t} + \frac{CP}{(1+y)^{n*}}.$$

The next two illustrations show how the yield to call is computed.

Illustration 6-9. In Illustrations 6-1 and 6-3 we computed the current yield and yield to maturity for an 18-year, 6% coupon bond selling for \$700.89. Suppose that this bond is callable in five years at \$1,030. The cash flows for this bond if it is called in five years are:

(1) 10 coupon payments of \$30 every six months; and

(2) \$1,030 in 10 six-month periods from now.

Exhibit 6-3

Computation of Yield to Call for an 18-Year, 6% Coupon Bond, Callable in 5 Years at $1,030, Selling at $700.89

Objective: Find—by trial and error—the semiannual interest rate that will make the present value of the following cash flows equal to $700.89:

10 coupon payments of $30 every six months;
$1,030 10 six-month periods from now.

Annual interest rate	Semi-annual rate	Present value of 10 payments of $30 *	Present value of $1,030 10 periods from now **	Present value of cash flows
11.20%	5.60%	$225.05	$597.31	$822.36
11.70	5.85	222.38	583.35	805.73
12.20	6.10	219.76	569.75	789.51
12.70	6.35	217.19	556.50	773.69
13.20	6.60	214.66	543.58	758.24
13.70	6.85	212.18	531.00	743.18
14.20	7.10	209.74	518.73	728.47
14.70	7.35	207.34	506.78	714.12
15.20	7.60	204.99	495.12	700.11

*
$$\$30 \left[\frac{1 - \left[\frac{1}{(1 + \text{Semiannual interest rate})^{10}} \right]}{\text{Semiannual interest rate}} \right].$$

**
$$\$1,030 \left[\frac{1}{(1 + \text{Semiannual interest rate})^{10}} \right].$$

The value for y that we seek is the one that will make the present values of the cash flows equal to $700.89. From Exhibit 6-3 it can be seen that when y is 7.6%, the present value of the cash flows is $700.11, which is close enough to $700.89 for our purposes. Therefore, the yield to call on a bond equivalent basis is 15.2% (double the periodic interest rate of 7.6%).

Illustration 6-10. In Illustrations 6-2 and 6-4 we computed the current yield and yield to maturity for a 19-year, 11% coupon bond selling for $1,233.64. Suppose that this bond is callable in six years at $1,055. If the bond is called on the first call date, the cash flows for this bond would be:

(1) 12 coupon payments of $55 every six months; and

(2) $1,055 in 12 six-month periods from now.

Exhibit 6-4 shows the present value of the cash flows for several interest rates. The interest rate that equates the present value of the cash flows to the price of $1,233.64 is approximately 3.55%. Therefore, the yield to call on a bond equivalent basis is 7.1%.

Exhibit 6-4

Computation of Yield to Call for a 19-Year, 11% Coupon Bond, Callable in 6 Years at $1,055, Selling at $1,233.64

Objective: Find—by trial and error—the semiannual interest rate that will make the present value of the following cash flows equal to $1,233.64:

12 coupon payments of $55 every six months;
$1,055 12 six-month periods from now.

Annual interest rate	Semi-annual rate	Present value of 12 payments of $55 *	Present value of $1,055 12 periods from now **	Present value of cash flows
5.10%	2.55%	$562.47	$779.87	$1,342.34
5.60	2.80	554.06	757.42	1,311.48
6.10	3.05	545.84	735.66	1,281.50
6.60	3.30	537.79	714.58	1,252.37
7.10	3.55	529.92	694.15	1,224.07
7.60	3.80	522.22	674.35	1,196.57

*
$$\$55 \left[\frac{1 - \left[\frac{1}{(1 + \text{Semiannual interest rate})^{12}} \right]}{\text{Semiannual interest rate}} \right].$$

**
$$\$1,055 \left[\frac{1}{(1 + \text{Semiannual interest rate})^{12}} \right].$$

Yield to Worst

The yield to call measure uses as the call date the first call date. However, a callable bond has a call schedule with the call price varying for each possible call date. Some practitioners calculate a *yield to worst*. This is the minimum of all the yields calculated for all possible call dates and the yield to maturity. For example, suppose there are only four possible calls dates for a callable bond; that a yield to call assuming each possible call date is 6%, 6.2%, 5.8%, and 5.7%; and that the yield to maturity is 7.5%. Then the yield to worst is the minimum of these values, 5.7% in our example.

Portfolio Yield

There are two conventions that have been adopted by practitioners to calculate a portfolio yield: (1) weighted average portfolio yield and (2) internal rate of return.

Weighted Average Portfolio Yield

Probably the most common — and most flawed — method for calculating a portfolio yield is to calculate the weighted average of the yield of all the securities in the portfolio. The yield is weighted by the proportion of the portfolio that a security makes up. In general, if we let:

w_i = Market value of security i relative to the total market value of the portfolio;
y_i = Yield on security i;
K = Number of securities in the portfolio;

then, the weighted average portfolio yield is

$$w_1 y_1 + w_2 y_2 + w_3 y_3 + \ldots + w_K y_K$$

Illustration 6-11. Consider the following three-bond portfolio:

Bond	Coupon rate	Maturity (years)	Par value	Market value	Yield to maturity
A	7.0%	5	$10,000,000	$ 9,209,000	9.0%
B	10.5	7	20,000,000	20,000,000	10.5
C	6.0	3	30,000,000	28,050,000	8.5

In this illustration, the total market value of the portfolio is $57,259,000, K is equal to 3, and

w_1 = 9,209,000/57,259,000 = .161 y_1 = .090
w_2 = 20,000,000/57,259,000 = .349 y_2 = .105
w_3 = 28,050,000/57,259,000 = .490 y_3 = .085

The weighted average portfolio yield is then:

$$.161 (.090) + .349 (.105) + .490 (.085) = .0928 = 9.28\%$$

While it is the most commonly used measure of portfolio yield, the average yield measure provides little insight into the potential yield of a portfolio. To see this, consider a portfolio consisting of only two bonds: a six-month bond offering a yield to maturity of 11%, and a 30-year bond offering a yield to maturity of 8%. Suppose that 99% of the portfolio is invested in the six-month bond and 1% in the 30-year bond. The weighted average yield for this portfolio would be 10.97%. But what does this yield mean? How can it be used within any asset/liability framework? The portfolio is basically a six-month portfolio even though it has a 30-year bond. Would a manager of a depository institution feel confident offering a two-year CD with a yield of 9%? This would suggest a spread of 197 basis points above the yield on the portfolio, based on the weighted average portfolio yield. This would be an imprudent policy because the yield on this portfolio over the next two years will depend on interest rates six months from now.

Portfolio Internal Rate of Return

Another measure used to calculate a portfolio yield is the internal rate of the portfolio's cash flow. It is computed by first determining the cash flows for all the securities in the portfolio, and then finding the interest rate that will make the present value of the cash flows equal to the market value of the portfolio.[2]

Illustration 6-12: To illustrate how to calculate a portfolio's internal rate of return, we will use the three bonds in Illustration 6-11. To simplify the illustration, it is assumed that the coupon payment date is the same for each bond.

The portfolio's total market value is $57,259,000. The cash flows for each bond in the portfolio and for the whole portfolio are given below:

Period cash flow received	Bond A	Bond B	Bond C	Portfolio
1	$350,000	$1,050,000	$900,000	$2,300,000
2	350,000	1,050,000	900,000	2,300,000
3	350,000	1,050,000	900,000	2,300,000
4	350,000	1,050,000	900,000	2,300,000
5	350,000	1,050,000	900,000	2,300,000
6	350,000	1,050,000	30,900,000	32,300,000
7	350,000	1,050,000	—	1,400,000
8	350,000	1,050,000	—	1,400,000
9	350,000	1,050,000	—	1,400,000
10	10,350,000	1,050,000	—	11,400,000
11	—	1,050,000	—	1,050,000
12	—	1,050,000	—	1,050,000
13	—	1,050,000	—	1,050,000
14	—	21,050,000	—	21,050,000

To determine the yield (internal rate of return) for this three-bond portfolio, the interest rate that makes the present value of the cash flows shown in the last column of the table above equal to $57,259,000 (the total market value of the portfolio) must be found. If an interest rate of 4.77% is used, the present value of the cash flows will equal $57,259,000. Doubling 4.77% gives 9.54%, which is the yield on the portfolio on a bond equivalent basis.

---

[2] In Chapter 11 we discuss the concept of duration. A good approximation to the yield for a portfolio can be obtained by using duration to weight the yield to maturity of the individual bonds in the portfolio.

The portfolio internal rate of return, while superior to the weighted average portfolio yield, suffers from the same problems as yield measures in general, discussed in subsequent chapters.

Yield Measure for Floating-Rate Securities

The coupon rate for a floating-rate security changes periodically according to some predetermined index (such as LIBOR or a Treasury rate). Since the value for the benchmark in the future is not known, it is not possible to determine the cash flows. This means that a yield to maturity cannot be calculated.

A conventional measure used to estimate the potential return for a floating-rate security is the security's *effective margin*. This measure estimates the average spread or margin over the underlying index that the investor can expect to earn over the life of the security. The procedure for calculating the effective margin is as follows:

(1) Determine the cash flows assuming that the index rate does not change over the life of the security.

(2) Select a margin (spread).

(3) Discount the cash flows found in (1) by the current index rate plus the margin selected in (2).

(4) Compare the present value of the cash flows as calculated in (3) to the price. If the present value is equal to the security's price, the effective margin is the margin assumed in (2). If the present value is not equal to the security's price, go back to (2) and try a different margin.

For a security selling at par, the effective margin is simply the spread over the index.

Illustration 6-13: To illustrate the calculation, suppose that a six-year floating-rate security selling for $99.3098 pays a rate based on some interest rate index plus 80 basis points. The coupon rate is reset every six months. Assume that the current interest rate for the index is 10%.

Exhibit 6-5 shows calculation of the effective margin for this security. The second column shows the current interest rate for the index. The third column sets forth the cash flows for the security. The cash flow for the first 11 periods is equal to one-half the current interest rate index (5%) plus the semiannual spread of 40 basis points multiplied by 100. In the twelfth six-month period, the cash flow is 5.4 plus the maturity value of 100. The top row of the last five columns shows the assumed margin. The rows below the assumed margin show the present value of each cash flow. The last row gives the total present value of the cash flows.

For the five assumed yield spreads, the present value is equal to the price of the floating-rate security (99.3098) when the assumed margin is 96 basis points. Therefore, the effective margin on a semiannual basis is 48 basis points and 96 basis points on an annual basis. (Notice that the effective margin is 80 basis points, the same as the spread over the index, when the security is selling at par.)

Exhibit 6-5

Calculation of the Effective Margin for a Floating-Rate Security

Floating-rate security: Maturity = 6 years
Coupon rate = index + 80 basis points
Reset every six months

Present value of cash flow:

Period	Index	Cash flow*	Assumed annual yield spread (in b.p.)				
			80	84	88	96	100
1	10%	5.4	5.1233	5.1224	5.1214	5.1195	5.1185
2	10	5.4	4.8609	4.8590	4.8572	4.8535	4.8516
3	10	5.4	4.6118	4.6092	4.6066	4.6013	4.5987
4	10	5.4	4.3755	4.3722	4.3689	4.3623	4.3590
5	10	5.4	4.1514	4.1474	4.1435	4.1356	4.1317
6	10	5.4	3.9387	3.9342	3.9297	3.9208	3.9163
7	10	5.4	3.7369	3.7319	3.7270	3.7171	3.7122
8	10	5.4	3.5454	3.5401	3.5347	3.5240	3.5186
9	10	5.4	3.3638	3.3580	3.3523	3.3409	3.3352
10	10	5.4	3.1914	3.1854	3.1794	3.1673	3.1613
11	10	5.4	3.0279	3.0216	3.0153	3.0028	2.9965
12	10	105.4	56.0729	55.9454	55.8182	55.5647	55.4385
Present value			100.0000	99.8269	99.6541	99.3098	99.1381

* For periods 1-11: Cash flow = 100 (Index + Assumed margin) (.5)
  For period 12: Cash flow = 100 (Index + Assumed margin) (.5) + 100

There are two drawbacks of the effective margin as a measure of the potential return from investing in a floating-rate security. First, the measure assumes that the index will not change over the life of the security. Second, if the floating-rate security has a cap or floor, this is not taken into consideration.

Summary

In this chapter we have explained three conventional yield measures: (1) current yield, (2) yield to maturity, and (3) yield to call. Exhibit 6-6 summarizes the formulas presented in this chapter to calculate these yield measures. The shortcomings of these measures for evaluating the potential return from owning a bond are explained in the next chapter.

Exhibit 6-6

Summary of Formulas for Conventional Yield Measures

(1)   Current yield:

$$\text{Current yield} = \frac{\text{Annual dollar coupon interest}}{\text{Price}}$$

(2)   Yield to maturity for a bond with a coupon payment due six months from now — solve for y:

$$p = \frac{c}{(1+y)^1} + \frac{c}{(1+y)^2} + \frac{c}{(1+y)^3} + \ldots + \frac{c}{(1+y)^n} + \frac{M}{(1+y)^n}$$

or

$$p = \sum_{t=1}^{n} \frac{c}{(1+y)^t} + \frac{M}{(1+y)^n} \quad,$$

where

   p = Price;
   c = *Semiannual* coupon interest ($);
   y = One-half the yield to maturity;
   n = Number of periods (number of years $\times$ 2);
   M = Maturity value ($).

For a semiannual-pay bond,

$$\text{Yield to maturity} = 2 \text{ times } y.$$

(3)   Yield to maturity for a zero-coupon bond:

$$y = (\text{Future value per dollar invested})^{1/n} - 1,$$

where

   y = One-half the yield to maturity;

$$\text{Future value per dollar invested} = \frac{\text{Maturity value}}{\text{Price}}$$

$$\text{Yield to maturity} = 2 \text{ times } y.$$

(4)   Yield to maturity when the settlement date is between coupon payments — solve for y:

$$tp = \frac{c}{(1+y)^w} + \frac{c}{(1+y)^{1+w}} + \frac{c}{(1+y)^{2+w}} + \ldots +$$

$$\frac{c}{(1+y)^{n-1+w}} + \frac{M}{(1+y)^{n-1+w}} \quad,$$

or

$$tp = \sum_{t=1}^{n} \frac{c}{(1+y)^{t-1+w}} + \frac{M}{(1+y)^{n-1+w}} \; ,$$

where

tp = Dirty price (\$);
c = *Semiannual* coupon payment (\$);
y = One-half the yield to maturity;

$$w = \frac{\text{Number of days between settlement and the next coupon payment}}{\text{Number of days in the coupon period}} \; ;$$

n = Number of coupon payments remaining;
M = Maturity value.

Yield to maturity = 2 times y.

(5)   Yield to call—solve for y:

$$p = \frac{c}{(1+y)^1} + \frac{c}{(1+y)^2} + \frac{c}{(1+y)^3} + \ldots + \frac{c}{(1+y)^{n*}} + \frac{CP}{(1+y)^{n*}}$$

or

$$p = \sum_{t=1}^{n*} \frac{c}{(1+y)^t} + \frac{CP}{(1+y)^{n*}} \; ,$$

where

p = Price (\$);
c = *Semiannual* coupon interest (\$);
y = One-half the yield to call;
$n*$ = Number of periods until first call date (number of years × 2);
CP = Call price (\$).

For a semiannual-pay bond,

Yield to call = 2 times y.

(6)   Yield to worst:

Lowest of (yield to maturity; all possible yields to call).

(7)   Weighted average portfolio yield:

$$w_1 y_1 + w_2 y_2 + w_3 y_3 + \ldots + w_K y_K$$

Exhibit 6-6 continued.

where

w_i = Market value of security i relative to the total
market value of the portfolio;

y_i = Yield on security i;

K = Number of securities in the portfolio.

7

Potential Sources
of Dollar Return

To make an intelligent decision about the attractiveness of a bond, an investor must be able to measure the potential yield from owning it. This requires an understanding of the potential sources of dollar return from investing in a bond and then converting the total dollar return from all sources into a yield measure that can be used to compare different bonds.

   The purpose of this chapter is threefold: (1) to explain the potential sources of dollar return; (2) to examine the characteristics of a bond that affect its dollar return; and (3) to analyze whether the conventional measures of yield discussed in Chapter 6 appropriately account for the potential sources of dollar return. In the next chapter, we present a measure of yield that is more useful to an investor in evaluating the relative value of bonds.

Potential Sources of Dollar Return

The dollar return a bond investor expects to receive takes the form of the periodic interest payments made by the issuer (that is, the coupon interest payments) and any capital appreciation realized when the bond is sold. For example, suppose that an investor buys a 20-year, 7% coupon bond with a par value of $1,000 for $816. Holding this bond until it matures, the investor will receive 40 coupon interest payments of $35, one every six months; then at the end of 20 years he will receive $1,000 for the bond he purchased for $816. This will result in a capital gain of $184. In other words, an investor who buys this bond and holds it to maturity expects a return in the form of 40 semiannual coupon interest payments of $35 and a capital gain of $184.

There is, however, another potential source for a bond's dollar return that may not be recognized by many investors. That source is the interest income that can be realized by reinvesting the coupon interest payments. For example, an investor receiving the first $35 coupon interest payment from the bond issuer must do something with that money. If the money is invested in another instrument for the next 19.5 years, this reinvestment will add to the return from holding the bond. This is also true for the second coupon interest payment of $35, which can be invested for 19 years; and so on for subsequent coupon interest payments. This potential source of return is referred to as the *interest-on-interest* component of a bond's dollar return. In fact, for certain bonds, the interest-on-interest component can represent more than 80% of a bond's potential dollar return.

Conventional Measures and the Three Potential Sources of a Bond's Dollar Return

To summarize, an investor who purchases a bond can expect to receive a dollar return from one or more of the following sources:

(1) The periodic interest payments made by the issuer (that is, the coupon interest payments),

(2) any capital gain (or capital loss, which reduces the dollar return) when the bond matures or is sold, and

(3) Income from reinvestment of the periodic interest payments (the interest-on-interest component).

Any measure of a bond's potential yield should consider all these three potential sources of return. Do the three conventional bond measures (current yield, yield to maturity, and yield to call) take into account these three potential sources of return?

Current yield considers only the coupon interest payments. No consideration is given to any capital gain (or loss) or interest on interest.

Yield to maturity takes into account coupon interest and any capital gain (or loss). It also considers the interest-on-interest component, although implicit in this computation is an assumption that the coupon payments can be reinvested at the computed yield to maturity. The yield to maturity, therefore, is a *promised* yield. That is, the promised yield to maturity will be realized if (1) the bond is held to maturity, and (2) the coupon interest payments are reinvested at the yield to maturity. If either (1) or (2) does not occur, the actual yield realized by an investor will be greater than or less than the yield to maturity.

For example, for our 20-year, 7% coupon bond selling at $816, the yield to maturity is 9%. Thus, if an investor buys this bond, holds it to maturity and reinvests each semiannual coupon payment at 9% until the maturity date, the promised yield to maturity of 9% at the time of the purchase will be realized. We'll demonstrate this in the next section.

Although the yield to maturity does consider the interest-on-interest component of a bond's potential dollar return, the assumption that the coupon interest payments can be reinvested at the yield to maturity is not very realistic. For example, in 1981 an investor could have purchased a long-term investment grade coupon bond offering a yield to maturity of 16%. To realize that promised yield, each coupon payment had to be reinvested at a rate of interest equal to 16%. In recent years, however, yields on investment grade bonds have been nowhere near this rate. Thus, it is unlikely that a 16% yield would be realized by the investor holding the bond to maturity.

The yield to call also takes into account all three potential sources of return. In this case, the assumption is that the coupon payments can be reinvested at the yield to call. This yield measure therefore suffers from the same drawback concerning the reinvestment rate of the coupon interest payments.

Computation of the Interest-on-Interest Component of a Bond's Dollar Return

The interest-on-interest component can represent a substantial portion of a bond's potential return. In this section we explain how to determine the contribution of the interest-on-interest component.

The portion of the potential total dollar return from coupon interest and interest on interest can be computed by using the formula for the future value of an annuity (see Exhibit 2-2 of Chapter 2):

$$FV = A \left[\frac{(1 + i)^n - 1}{i} \right]$$

where

A = Amount of the annuity ($);
i = Annual interest rate divided by m (in decimal);
m = Number of payments per year;
n = Number of periods.

For purposes of computing the coupon interest and interest on interest for a bond paying interest semiannually,

A = *Semiannual* coupon interest ($);
i = *Semiannual* reinvestment rate (in decimal);
m = 2;
n = Double the number of years to maturity.

Letting

$$c = Semiannual \text{ coupon interest (\$)}$$

and

$$r = Semiannual \text{ reinvestment rate (in decimal),}$$

we can rewrite the formula for the future value of an annuity for computing the coupon interest plus interest on interest, as

$$\begin{matrix} \text{Coupon interest} \\ \text{plus} \\ \text{interest on interest} \end{matrix} = c \left[\frac{(1+r)^n - 1}{r} \right] .$$

The total coupon interest is found by multiplying the semiannual coupon interest by the number of periods; that is,

$$\text{Total coupon interest} = n \times c.$$

The interest-on-interest component is then the difference between the coupon interest plus interest on interest and the total coupon interest. Mathematically, this can be expressed as

$$\text{Interest on interest} = c \left[\frac{(1+r)^n - 1}{r} \right] - n \times c .$$

The reinvestment rate assumed for the yield to maturity is the yield to maturity.

The three illustrations that follow demonstrate the application of these formulas, as well as the importance of the interest-on-interest component as a source of potential return from a bond.

Illustration 7-1. Suppose that an investor is considering purchasing a seven-year issue selling at par ($1,000) and having a coupon rate of 9%. Since this bond is selling at par, the yield to maturity is 9%.

Remember that a yield to maturity of 9% as conventionally computed means a 4.5% semiannual yield.[1] If an investor is promised a yield of 4.5% for 14 six-month periods (seven years) on a $1,000 investment, the amount at the end of 14 six-month periods would be[2]

$$\$1,000 \ (1.045)^{14} = \$1,852.$$

Since the investment is $1,000, the total dollar return that the investor expects is $852.

---

[1] See Chapter 6.

[2] This is just an application of the future value of $1 formula, see Chapter 2.

Let's look at the total dollar return from holding this bond to maturity. The total dollar return comes from two sources:

(1) Coupon interest of $45 every six months for seven years; and

(2) Interest earned from reinvesting the semiannual coupon interest payments at 4.5%.

Since the bond is selling at par, no capital gain will be realized by holding the bond to maturity.

For this bond:

$$c = \$45;$$
$$m = 2;$$
$$r = .045 \ (= .09/2);$$
$$n = 14 \ (= 7 \times 2)$$

$$\begin{array}{c} \text{Coupon interest} \\ \text{plus} \\ \text{interest on interest} \end{array} = \$45 \left[\frac{(1.045)^{14} - 1}{.045} \right]$$

$$= \$45 \left[\frac{1.8519 - 1}{.045} \right]$$

$$= \$45 \ (18.9321)$$

$$= \$852.$$

Notice that the total dollar return for this bond is the same as the return that we computed for an investment of $1,000 for 14 six-month periods at 4.5%.

The total coupon interest is 14 × $45 = $630.

The interest-on-interest component is then $222, as shown below:

$$\text{Interest on interest} = \$45 \left[\frac{(1.045)^{14} - 1}{.045} \right] - 14 \ (\$45)$$

$$= \$852 - \$630$$

$$= \$222.$$

Interest on interest as a percentage of total dollar return is

$$\frac{\$222}{\$852} = 26\%.$$

For this seven-year, 9% coupon bond selling at par to offer a yield to maturity of 9%, 26% of this bond's total dollar return must come from reinvesting the coupon payments at a simple annual interest rate of 9%.

Illustration 7-2. Suppose that an investor is considering a 20-year, 7% coupon bond selling for $816. The yield to maturity for this bond is 9%.

First, let's consider how much the total dollar return should be for an investment of $816 for 40 six-month periods if the semiannual yield is 4.5%. The total future amount would be $4,746, because

$$\$816 \, (1.045)^{40} = \$4,746$$

Since the investment is $816, the total dollar return should be $3,930.

Now let's look at the $816 investment in the bond. The total dollar return from holding this bond to maturity comes from all three sources:

(1) Coupon interest of $35 every six months for 20 years;

(2) Interest earned from reinvesting the semiannual coupon interest payments at 4.5%; and

(3) A capital gain of $184 (= $1,000 − $816).

For this bond;

$$c = \$35;$$
$$m = 2;$$
$$r = .045 \, (= .09/2);$$
$$n = 40 \, (= 20 \times 2).$$

$$\begin{matrix} \text{Coupon interest} \\ \text{plus} \\ \text{interest on interest} \end{matrix} = \$35 \left[\frac{(1.045)^{40} - 1}{.045} \right]$$

$$= \$35 \left[\frac{5.8164 - 1}{.045} \right]$$

$$= \$35 \, (107.031)$$

$$= \$3,746.$$

The total coupon interest is 40 × $35 = $1,400.

The interest-on-interest component is then $2,346, as shown by the following calculation:

$$\text{Interest on interest} = \$35 \left[\frac{(1.045)^{40} - 1}{.045} \right] - 40 \, (\$35)$$

$$= \$3,746 - \$1,400$$

$$= \$2,346.$$

The total dollar return is then:

Total coupon interest	$1,400
Interest on interest	2,346
Capital gain	184
Total	$3,930

Once again, the total dollar return is the same as the return that would be expected from investing $816 for 40 six-month periods at 4.5%.

The percentage breakdown of the total dollar return is

Total coupon interest	35%
Interest on interest	60%
Capital gain	5%

Hence, for this bond, the interest-on-interest component must represent 60% of total dollar return if the investor is to realize a 9% yield to maturity.

Illustration 7-3. The two previous illustrations have shown the computation of the interest-on-interest component for a bond selling at par (Illustration 7-1) and a bond selling at a discount (Illustration 7-2), both with a yield to maturity of 9%. Now let's consider a bond selling at a premium with a yield to maturity of 9%. Suppose an investor is considering a 12% coupon bond with 25 years to maturity selling for $1,296. The yield to maturity is 9%.

The total dollar return from holding this bond to maturity is composed of

(1) Coupon interest of $60 every six months for 25 years;

(2) Interest earned from reinvesting the semiannual coupon interest payments at 4.5%; and

(3) A capital loss of $296 (= $1,000 − $1,296)

For this premium bond:

$$c = \$60;$$
$$m = 2;$$
$$r = .045 \ (= .09/2);$$
$$n = 50 \ (= 25 \times 2)$$

$$\begin{matrix} \text{Coupon interest} \\ \text{plus} \\ \text{interest on interest} \end{matrix} = \$60 \left[\frac{(1.045)^{50} - 1}{.045} \right]$$

$$= \$60 \left[\frac{9.0326 - 1}{.045} \right]$$

$$= \$60 \ (178.503)$$
$$= \$10,710.$$

The total coupon interest is 50 × $60 = $3,000.

The interest-on-interest component is then $7,710, as shown below:

$$\text{Interest on interest} = \$60 \left[\frac{(1.045)^{50} - 1}{.045} \right] - 50 \ (\$60)$$

$$= \$10,710 - \$3,000$$
$$= \$7,710.$$

The total dollar return is then

Total coupon interest	$3,000
Interest on interest	7,710
Capital loss	(296)
Total	$10,414

The percentage breakdown of the total dollar return is

Total coupon interest	29%
Interest on interest	74%
Capital loss	-3%

For this long-term bond selling at a premium, the interest on interest represents 74% of the total dollar return necessary to produce a 9% yield to maturity.

To see that the total dollar return from investing in this bond agrees with an investment of $1,296 for 50 six-month periods at 4.5%, the future value is

$$\$1,296 \ (1.045)^{50} = \$11,706.$$

Subtracting from the future value the investment of $1,296 gives the total dollar return of $10,410. (The difference between $10,414 and $10,410 is due to rounding.)

Bond Characteristics That Affect the Importance of the Interest-on-Interest Component

There are two characteristics of a bond that determine the importance of the interest-on-interest component: maturity and coupon.

The Effect of Maturity

For a given yield to maturity and a given coupon rate, the longer the maturity of a bond, the greater the interest-on-interest component as a percentage of the total dollar return. The following three illustrations demonstrate this characteristic.

Illustration 7-4. Consider a 20-year, 9% coupon bond selling at par for a yield to maturity of 9%. Using the formulas presented in the previous section, the total dollar return would be $4,816, broken down as follows:

Total coupon interest	$1,800
Interest on interest	3,016
Total	$4,816

Comparing this bond with the seven-year, 9% coupon bond selling at 9% in Illustration 7-1, we find:

	Total dollar return		% dollar return	
	7-year	20-year	7-year	20-year
Total coupon interest	$630	$1,800	74%	37%
Interest on interest	222	3,016	26	63
Total	$852	$4,816	100%	100%

The interest-on-interest component is 26% of the total dollar return on the seven-year bond but 63% of the total dollar return for the 20-year bond.

Illustration 7-5. Consider a five-year, 7% coupon bond selling for $921, thereby offering a yield to maturity of 9%. The breakdown of the total dollar return is:

Total coupon interest	$350
Interest on interest	80
Capital gain	79
Total	$509

A comparison of this bond with the 20-year, 7% coupon bond analyzed in Illustration 7-2 is given below:

	Total dollar return		% dollar return	
	5-year	20-year	5-year	20-year
Total coupon interest	$350	$1,400	69%	35%
Interest on interest	80	2,346	16	60
Capital gain	79	184	15	5
Total	$509	$3,930	100%	100%

Only 16% of the bond's total dollar return needed to produce a 9% yield to maturity comes from the reinvestment of coupon interest for the five-year bond, compared to 60% for the 20-year bond.

Illustration 7-6. For a seven-year, 12% coupon bond selling at $1,153 with a yield to maturity of 9%, the total dollar return is as follows:

Total coupon interest	$840
Interest on interest	296
Capital loss	(153)
Total	$983

In Illustration 7-3, the total dollar return breakdown for a 25-year, 12% coupon bond priced to give a yield to maturity of 9% was computed. A comparison of the bond in this illustration with the one in Illustration 7-3 is given below:

	Total dollar return		% dollar return	
	7-year	*25-year*	*7-year*	*25-year*
Total coupon interest	$840	$3,000	85%	29%
Interest on interest	296	7,710	30	74
Capital loss	(153)	(296)	−5	−3
Total	$983	$10,414	100%	100%

For the longer-term bond, the interest-on-interest component is 74% of the potential total dollar return, compared with 30% for the seven-year bond.

The Effect of Coupon Rate

For a given maturity and a given yield to maturity, the higher the coupon rate, the more dependent the bond's total dollar return necessary to produce some yield to maturity is on the reinvestment of coupon interest. This means that holding maturity and yield to maturity constant, premium bonds will be more dependent on the interest-on-interest component than bonds selling at par. Discount bonds will be less dependent on the interest-on-interest component than bonds selling at par. These statements are verified in the illustrations below.

Illustration 7-7. Let's compare the total dollar return breakdown of the 20-year, 9% coupon bond selling at par to offer a yield to maturity of 9% (Illustration 7-4) with a 20-year, 5% coupon bond selling at $632 to offer a yield to maturity of 9%. The breakdown of the total dollar return and the percentage return for each bond, which demonstrates that a lower coupon (discount) bond is less dependent on the interest-on-interest component than the higher coupon (par) bond, is summarized below:

	Total dollar return		% dollar return	
	5% coupon (discount)	*9% coupon (par)*	*5% coupon (discount)*	*9% coupon (par)*
Total coupon interest	$1,000	$1,800	33%	37%
Interest on interest	1,676	3,016	55	63
Capital gain	368	0	12	0
Total	$3,044	$4,816	100%	100%

Illustration 7-8. Comparison of a seven-year, 9% coupon bond selling at par to offer a yield to maturity of 9% with a seven-year, 14% coupon bond selling at $1,256 to offer a yield to maturity of 9%, summarized below, shows that a bond selling at par is less dependent on the reinvestment of coupon interest than a premium bond:

	Total dollar return		% dollar return	
	9% coupon (par)	14% coupon (premium)	9% coupon (par)	14% coupon (premium)
Total coupon interest	$630	$980	74%	92%
Interest on interest	222	345	26	32
Capital gain	0	(256)	0	–24
Total	$852	$1,069	100%	100%

Zero-coupon bonds. For zero-coupon bonds, none of the bond's total dollar return is made up of interest on interest. The reason, of course, is that no coupon interest is paid.

Summary and Investment Implications

In this chapter we have explained the three potential sources of dollar return from investing in a bond: (1) coupon interest, (2) interest on interest, and (3) capital gain (or loss). The shortcomings of the three conventional yield measures with respect to each of these sources are explained. The yield to maturity considers all three sources, but it assumes that all coupon interest can be reinvested at the yield to maturity. The yield to call assumes that the coupon interest can be reinvested at the yield to call.

The formulas for computing the interest-on-interest component are presented and applied. The formulas are summarized in Exhibit 7-1. For some bonds, particularly high-coupon, long-term bonds, the interest-on-interest component can be well in excess of 80% of the total dollar return necessary to generate the promised yield to maturity. The longer the term of a coupon bond, all other factors constant, the greater is the interest-on-interest component needed to realize the promised yield to maturity. Lower-coupon bonds, all other factors constant, are less dependent on the reinvestment of coupon interest than higher-coupon bonds. For zero-coupon bonds, none of the bond's total dollar return necessary to generate the yield to maturity at the time of purchase is dependent on the reinvestment of coupon interest.

This chapter has focused on bonds that pay interest semiannually. The same principles apply to fixed income instruments with more frequent cash flow payments, such as mortgage-backed securities. The interest-on-interest component becomes even more important for such securities.

Exhibit 7-1

Summary of Formulas for Computing the Interest-on-Interest Components of a Bond's Total Dollar Return

(1)   Coupon interest plus interest on interest:

$$\begin{matrix} \text{Coupon interest} \\ \text{plus} \\ \text{interest on interest} \end{matrix} = c \left[\frac{(1 + r)^n - 1}{r} \right] .$$

where

      c = Semiannual coupon interest (\$);
      r = Semiannual reinvestment rate (in decimal);
      n = Number of periods to maturity.

The reinvestment rate assumed for the yield to maturity is the yield to maturity.

(2)   Total coupon interest:

    Total coupon interest = $n \times c$.

(3)   Interest on interest:

$$\text{Interest on interest} = c \left[\frac{(1 + r)^n - 1}{r} \right] - n \times c.$$

8

Total Return

In the previous chapter, we explained the three potential sources of dollar return from investing in a bond. We also demonstrated the importance of the interest-on-interest component as a source of dollar return. In this chapter, we present a yield measure that is more meaningful than the commonly used yield to maturity and yield to call for assessing the attractiveness of a bond in a portfolio. This yield measure is called the *total return*.[1]

---

[1] Bond market participants also refer to this yield measure as horizon return, or realized compound yield. The term realized compound yield was first used by Sidney Homer and Martin Leibowitz in *Inside the Yield Book* (Prentice-Hall/New York Institute of Finance, 1972).

Another Look at the Drawbacks of the Yield to Maturity and Yield to Call

Yield to Maturity

In the previous chapter, we explained that the yield to maturity is a *promised* yield. The promised yield assumes:

(1) The bond is held to maturity, and

(2) All coupon interest payments are reinvested at the yield to maturity.

We focused on the second assumption in the previous chapter, where we showed that the interest-on-interest component for a bond may constitute a substantial portion of the bond's promised total dollar return. Failure to reinvest the coupon interest payments at a rate of interest at least equal to the yield to maturity will produce a yield less than the yield to maturity. This risk is called *reinvestment risk.*

Rather than assume that the coupon interest payments are reinvested at a rate of interest equal to the yield to maturity, nothing prevents an investor from making an explicit assumption about the reinvestment rate on the basis of different expectations. The total return is a measure of yield that incorporates an explicit assumption about the reinvestment rate.

Let's take a careful look now at the first assumption. An investor need not hold a bond until maturity. Suppose, for example, that an investor who has a five-year investment horizon is considering four bonds:

Bond	Coupon	Maturity	Yield to Maturity
A	5%	3 years	9.0%
B	6%	20 years	8.6%
C	11%	15 years	9.2%
D	8%	5 years	8.0%

Assuming that all four bonds are of the same credit quality, which one is the most attractive to this investor? An investor who selects bond C because it offers the highest yield to maturity is failing to recognize that the bond must be sold after five years at a price that will depend on the yield required in the market for 10-year, 11% coupon bonds at the time. Hence, there could be a capital gain or capital loss that will make the return higher or lower than the yield to maturity promised now. Moreover, the higher coupon on bond C relative to the other three bonds means that more of this bond's return will be dependent on reinvestment of coupon interest payments.

Bond A offers the second highest yield to maturity. On the surface, it seems to be particularly attractive because it eliminates the problem in the bond C purchase of realizing a possible capital loss when the bond must be sold prior to the maturity date. Moreover, the reinvestment risk seems to be less than for the other three bonds because the coupon rate is the lowest. The investor would not be eliminating the reinvestment risk, however, because after three years the proceeds received at maturity must be reinvested for two more years. The yield that the investor will realize then will depend on the interest rates three years from now, when the investor must reinvest the proceeds.

Which is the best bond? The yield to maturity doesn't seem to be helping us answer this question. The answer depends on the expectations of the investor. Specifically, it depends on the interest rate at which the coupon interest payments can be reinvested until the end of the investor's investment horizon. Also, for bonds with a maturity greater than the investment horizon, it depends on the investor's expectations about interest rates at the end of the investment horizon. Consequently, any of these bonds could be the best investment vehicle on the basis of some reinvestment rate and some future interest rate at the end of the investment horizon. The total return measure takes these expectations into account.

Yield to Call

The yield to call is subject to the same problems as the yield to maturity. First, it assumes that the bond will be held until the first call date. Second, it assumes that the coupon interest payments will be reinvested at the yield to call. If an investor's investment horizon is shorter than the time to the first call date, there remains the potential of having to sell the bond below its acquisition cost. If, on the other hand, the investment horizon is longer than the time to the first call date, there is the problem of reinvesting the proceeds when the bond is called until the end of the investment horizon. Consequently, the yield to call doesn't tell us very much. The total return, however, can accommodate the analysis of callable bonds.

Computing the Total Return for a Bond Held to Maturity

The idea underlying the total return is simple. The objective is to compute the total future amount that will result from an investment. The total return is the interest rate that will make the initial investment in the bond grow to the computed total future amount. To illustrate the computation, we first show how the total return is computed, assuming a bond is held to the maturity date.

For an assumed reinvestment rate, the dollar return that will be available at maturity can be computed from the coupon interest payments and the interest-on-interest component. In the previous chapter we explained how to do this. In addition, at maturity the investor will receive the par value. The total return is then the interest rate that will make the amount invested in the bond (that is, the current market price plus accrued interest) equal to the total future amount available at the maturity date.

More formally, the steps for computing the total return for a bond *held to maturity* are as follows:

Step 1. Compute the total future amount that will be received from the investment. This is the sum of the amount that will be received from the coupon payments, interest on interest based on the coupon payments and the assumed reinvestment rate, and the par value. The coupon payments plus the interest on interest can be computed using the formula presented in the previous chapter:

$$\begin{array}{c} \text{Coupon interest} \\ \text{plus} \\ \text{interest on interest} \end{array} = c \left[\frac{(1 + r)^n - 1}{r} \right]$$

where

$c = $ *Semiannual* coupon interest ($);

$r = $ *Semiannual* reinvestment rate;

$n = $ Number of periods to maturity.

In the case of the yield to maturity, the reinvestment rate is assumed to be one-half the yield to maturity. In computing the total return, the reinvestment rate is set equal to one-half the simple annual interest that the investor assumes can be earned by reinvesting the coupon interest payments.

Notice that the total future amount is different from the total dollar return that we have used in showing the importance of the interest-on-interest component in the previous chapter. The total dollar return includes only the capital gain (or capital loss if there is one), not the entire par value, which is used to compute the total future amount. That is,

Total dollar return = Total future amount − Price of bond

Step 2. To obtain the semiannual total return, use the following formula:

$$\left[\frac{\text{Total future amount}}{\text{Price of bond}} \right]^{1/n} - 1.$$

This formula is an application of the yield discussed in Chapter 4 for an investment that has only one cash flow.

Step 3. Since interest is assumed to be paid semiannually, double the interest rate found in Step 3. The resulting interest rate is the total return on a bond equivalent basis. The total return can also be computed by compounding the semiannual rate as follows:

$$(1 + \text{Semiannual total return})^2 - 1.$$

The total return calculated in this manner is said to be on an *effective rate basis.*

The four illustrations that follow show how to compute the total return for a bond held to maturity.

Illustration 8-1. The total return for a seven-year, 9% coupon bond selling at par, assuming a reinvestment rate of 5% (simple annual interest rate), is 8.1%, as shown in Exhibit 8-1. Since this bond is selling at par, its yield to maturity is 9%, yet its total return is only 8.1%. The total return is less than the yield to maturity because the coupon interest payments are assumed to be reinvested at 5% rather than 9%.

Illustration 8-2. The computation of the total return for the bond in the previous illustration, assuming a reinvestment rate of 9%, is shown in Exhibit 8-2. The total return is 9%. In this case, the total return is equal to the yield to maturity because the coupon interest payments are assumed to be reinvested at 9%.

Exhibit 8-1

Computation of the Total Return for a Seven-Year, 9% Bond Selling at Par and Held to Maturity: Reinvestment Rate = 5%

Step 1. The total future amount from this bond includes:

(1) Coupon interest of $45 every six months for seven years,

(2) Interest earned from reinvesting the semiannual coupon interest payments at 2.5% (one-half the assumed annual reinvestment rate), and

(3) The par value of $1,000.

The coupon interest plus interest on interest can be found as follows:

$$c = \$45;$$
$$m = 2;$$
$$r = .025 \ (=.05/2);$$
$$n = 14 \ (= 7 \times 2)$$

$$\begin{array}{c}\text{Coupon interest}\\ \text{plus}\\ \text{interest on interest}\end{array} = \$45 \left[\frac{(1.025)^{14} - 1}{.025}\right]$$

$$= \$45 \left[\frac{1.4130 - 1}{.025}\right]$$

$$= \$45 \ (16.5189)$$

$$= \$743.35.$$

Total future amount:

Coupon interest plus interest on interest	= $ 743.35
Par value	= 1,000.00
Total	$1,743.35

Step 2. Compute the following:

$$\left[\frac{\$1,743.35}{\$1,000.00}\right]^{1/14} - 1$$

$$= (1.74335)^{.07143} - 1$$
$$= 1.0405 - 1$$
$$= .0405 \text{ or } 4.05\%.$$

Step 3. Doubling 4.05% gives a total return of 8.1%.

Exhibit 8-2

Computation of the Total Return for a Seven-Year, 9% Bond Selling at Par and Held to Maturity: Reinvestment Rate = 9%

Step 1. The total future amount for this bond includes:

(1) Coupon interest of $45 every six months for seven years,

(2) Interest earned from reinvesting the semiannual coupon interest payments at 4.5% (one-half the assumed annual reinvestment rate), and

(3) The par value of $1,000.

The coupon interest plus interest on interest can be found as follows:

$$c = \$45;$$
$$m = 2;$$
$$r = .045 \ (=.09/2);$$
$$n = 14 \ (= 7 \times 2)$$

$$\begin{matrix} \text{Coupon interest} \\ \text{plus} \\ \text{interest on interest} \end{matrix} = \$45 \left[\frac{(1.045)^{14} - 1}{.045} \right]$$

$$= \$45 \left[\frac{1.8519 - 1}{.045} \right]$$

$$= \$45 \ (18.9321)$$

$$= \$851.94.$$

Total future amount:

Coupon interest plus interest on interest	= $ 851.94
Par value	= 1,000.00
Total	$1,851.94

Step 2. Compute the following:

$$\left[\frac{\$1,851.94}{\$1,000.00} \right]^{1/14} - 1$$
$$= (1.85194)^{.07143} - 1$$
$$= 1.0450 - 1$$
$$= .0450 \text{ or } 4.50\%$$

Step 3. Doubling 4.50% gives a total return of 9.0%.

Illustration 8-3. The total return for a 20-year, 7% coupon bond selling for $816, assuming a reinvestment rate of 6% (simple annual interest rate), is 7.62%, as shown in Exhibit 8-3. The yield to maturity is 9%. The total return is less than the yield to maturity because the coupon interest payments are assumed to be reinvested at 6% rather than 9%.

Exhibit 8-3

**Computation of the Total Return for a 20-Year, 7% Bond
Selling for $816 and Held to Maturity:
Reinvestment Rate = 6%**

Step 1. The total future amount from this bond includes:

    (1) Coupon interest of $35 every six months for 20 years,

    (2) Interest earned from reinvesting the semiannual coupon interest payments at 3% (one-half the assumed annual reinvestment rate), and

    (3) The par value of $1,000.

The coupon interest plus interest on interest can be found as follows:

$$c = \$35;$$
$$m = 2;$$
$$r = .03 \ (= .06/2);$$
$$n = 40 \ (= 20 \times 2)$$

$$\begin{array}{c} \text{Coupon interest} \\ \text{plus} \\ \text{interest on interest} \end{array} = \$35 \left[\frac{(1.03)^{40} - 1}{.03} \right]$$

$$= \$35 \left[\frac{3.2620 - 1}{.03} \right]$$

$$= \$35 \ (74.4013)$$

$$= \$2,639.04.$$

Total future amount:

Coupon interest plus interest on interest	= $2,639.04
Par value	= <u> 1,000.00</u>
Total	$3,639.04

Step 2. Compute the following:

Exhibit 8-3 continued.

$$\left[\frac{\$3,639.04}{\$816} \right]^{1/40} - 1$$

$$= (4.45961)^{.025} - 1$$
$$= 1.0381 - 1$$
$$= .0381 \text{ or } 3.81\%$$

Step 3. Doubling 3.81% gives a total return of 7.62%

Illustration 8-4. The total return for the bond in the previous illustration is 10.04% if the reinvestment rate is 11%. The computations are shown in Exhibit 8-4. Since the reinvestment rate is greater than the yield to maturity, the total return is greater than the yield to maturity of 9%.

Exhibit 8-4

Computation of the Total Return for a 20-Year, 7% Bond Selling for $816 and Held to Maturity: Reinvestment Rate = 11%

Step 1. The total future amount from this bond includes:

(1) Coupon interest of $35 every six months for 20 years,

(2) Interest earned from reinvesting the semiannual coupon interest payments at 5.5% (one-half the assumed annual reinvestment rate), and

(3) The par value of $1,000.

The coupon interest plus interest on interest can be found as follows:

$$c = \$35;$$
$$m = 2;$$
$$r = .055 \ (= .11/2);$$
$$n = 40 \ (= 20 \times 2)$$

$$\begin{array}{l} \text{Coupon interest} \\ \text{plus} \\ \text{interest on interest} \end{array} = \$35 \left[\frac{(1.055)^{40} - 1}{.055} \right]$$

$$= \$35 \left[\frac{8.5133 - 1}{.055} \right]$$

$$= \$35 \ (136.6056)$$

$$= \$4,781.20.$$

Exhibit 8-4 continued

Total future amount:

Coupon interest plus interest on interest	= $4,781.20
Par value	= $\underline{1,000.00}$
Total	$5,781.20

Step 2. Compute the following:

$$\left[\frac{\$5,781.20}{\$816} \right]^{1/40} - 1$$
$$= (7.08480)^{.025} - 1$$
$$= 1.0502 - 1$$
$$= .0502 \text{ or } 5.02\%.$$

Step 3. Doubling 5.02% gives a total return of 10.04%.

Computing the Total Return for a Bond to Be Sold Prior to Maturity

The total return as calculated above suffers from the same problem as the yield to maturity in that it assumes holding the bond until maturity. Fortunately, it is quite simple to modify the calculation of the total return to determine the potential yield from holding it until the end of a predetermined investment horizon. We need make only one adjustment to the three steps given above to calculate the total return.

In Step 1, the total future amount is calculated on the basis of (1) the coupon interest payments until the end of the investment horizon, (2) the interest on interest from reinvesting the coupon interest payments until the end of the investment horizon, and (3) the expected price of the bond at the end of the investment horizon.

How does one know the expected price of the bond at the end of the investment horizon? The expected price depends on the investor's expectations about what interest rates will be at the end of the investment horizon. Given the expected yield that the bond will be selling for at the end of the investment horizon and the remaining time to maturity of the bond, the expected price can easily be determined from the formula for the price of a bond given in Chapter 5 (see Exhibit 5-7):

$$p = \frac{c}{(1+i)^1} + \frac{c}{(1+i)^2} + \frac{c}{(1+i)^3} + \ldots + \frac{c}{(1+i)^n} + \frac{M}{(1+i)^n}$$

where

> p = Price ($);
> c = *Semiannual* coupon payment ($);
> i = *Semiannual* required yield (in decimal);
> n = Number of periods (number of years times 2);
> M = Maturity value.

In applying this formula, it is important to remember that n is the number of periods remaining to maturity *at the end of the investment horizon.* For example, if the investment horizon is five years and the number of years to maturity at the present time is 20 years, there would remain 15 years to maturity at the end of the investment horizon. In this case, n would be 30.

The present value of the coupon interest payments in the price formula can be computed using the formula (see Chapter 5, Exhibit 5-7):

$$c \left[\frac{1 - \left[\frac{1}{(1 + i)^n} \right]}{i} \right]$$

Illustration 8-5. Suppose that an investor with a five-year investment horizon is considering purchasing a seven-year, 9% coupon bond selling at par. The investor expects that the coupon interest payments can be reinvested at an annual interest rate of 9.4% and that at the end of the investment horizon two-year bonds will be selling to offer a yield to maturity of 11.2%. As shown in Exhibit 8-5, the total return for this bond is 8.54%. The yield to maturity for this bond is 9%.

Exhibit 8-5

**Computation of the Total Return for a Seven-Year,
9% Bond Selling at Par and Held for Five Years:
Reinvestment Rate = 9.4%**

Step 1. The total future amount from this bond includes:

(1) Coupon interest of $45 every six months for five years (the investment horizon),

(2) Interest earned from reinvesting the semiannual coupon interest payments at 4.7% (one-half the assumed annual reinvestment rate) until the end of the investment horizon, and

(3) The expected price of the bond at the end of five years.

The coupon interest plus interest on interest can be found as follows:

Exhibit 8-5 continued.

$$c = \$45;$$
$$m = 2;$$
$$r = .047 \ (= .094/2);$$
$$n = 10 \ (= 5 \times 2)$$

$$\begin{array}{l} \text{Coupon interest} \\ \qquad \text{plus} \\ \text{interest on interest} \end{array} = \$45 \left[\frac{(1.047)^{10} - 1}{.047} \right]$$

$$= \$45 \left[\frac{1.5830 - 1}{.047} \right]$$

$$= \$45 \ (12.4032)$$
$$= \$558.14.$$

The expected price of the bond five years from now is determined as follows:

(a) Present value of coupon interest payments, assuming the required yield to maturity at the end of the investment horizon is 11.2%:

$$c = \$45;$$
$$i = .056 \ (= .112/2);$$
$$n = 4 \ (= \text{remaining years to maturity} \times 2)$$

$$PV = \$45 \left[\frac{1 - \left[\frac{1}{(1.056)^4} \right]}{.056} \right]$$

$$= \$45 \left[\frac{1 - .8042}{.056} \right]$$

$$= \$45 \ (3.4964)$$
$$= \$157.34$$

(b) Present value of the maturity value:

$$\frac{\$1,000}{(1.056)^4} = \$804.16$$

$$\text{Expected price} = \$157.34 + \$804.16$$
$$= \$961.50$$

Total future amount:

Coupon interest plus interest on interest	= $558.14
Expected price	= 961.50
Total	$1,519.64

Exhibit 8-5 continued.

Step 2. Compute the following:

$$\left[\frac{\$1,519.64}{\$1,000.00}\right]^{1/10} - 1$$

$$= (1.51964)^{.10} - 1$$

$$= 1.0427 - 1$$

$$= .0427 \text{ or } 4.27\%$$

Step 3. Doubling 4.27% gives a total return of 8.54%.

Illustration 8-6. Suppose that an investor with a three-year investment horizon is considering purchasing a 20-year, 8% coupon bond for $828.40. The investor expects that the coupon interest payments can be reinvested at an annual interest rate of 6% and that at the end of the investment horizon 17-year bonds will be selling to offer a yield to maturity of 7%. The total return for this bond is 17.16%. (The computations are shown in Exhibit 8-6.) The yield to maturity for this bond is 10%.

Exhibit 8-6

Computation of the Total Return for a 20-Year, 8% Bond
Selling for $828.40 and Held for Three Years:
Reinvestment Rate = 6%

Step 1. The total future amount from this bond includes:

(1) Coupon interest of $40 every six months for three years (the investment horizon),

(2) Interest earned from reinvesting the semiannual coupon interest payments at 3% (one-half the assumed annual reinvestment rate), and

(3) The expected price of the bond at the end of three years.

The coupon interest plus interest on interest can be found as follows:

$$c = \$40;$$
$$m = 2;$$
$$r = .03 \ (= .06/2);$$
$$n = 6 \ (= 3 \times 2)$$

Exhibit 8-6 continued.

$$\begin{array}{c} \text{Coupon interest} \\ \text{plus} \\ \text{interest on interest} \end{array} = \$40 \left[\frac{(1.03)^6 - 1}{.03} \right]$$

$$= \$45 \left[\frac{1.1941 - 1}{.03} \right]$$

$$= \$40 \ (6.4684)$$

$$= \$258.74.$$

The expected price of the bond three years from now is determined as follows:

(a) Present value of coupon interest payments, assuming the required yield to maturity at the end of the investment horizon is 7%:

$$c = \$40;$$
$$i = .035 \ (= .07/2);$$
$$n = 34 \ (= \text{Remaining years to maturity} \times 2)$$

$$PV = \$40 \left[\frac{1 - \left[\frac{1}{(1.035)^{34}} \right]}{.035} \right]$$

$$= \$40 \left[\frac{1 - .3105}{.035} \right]$$

$$= \$40 \ (19.7007)$$

$$= \$788.03$$

(b) Present value of the maturity value:

$$\frac{\$1,000}{(1.035)^{34}} = \$310.48$$

$$\text{Expected price} = \$788.03 + \$310.48$$
$$= \$1,098.51$$

Total future amount:

Coupon interest plus interest on interest	=\$ 258.74
Expected price	= 1,098.51
Total	\$1,357.25

Step 2. Compute the following:

Exhibit 8-6 continued.

$$\left[\frac{\$1,357.25}{\$828.40}\right]^{1/6} - 1$$
$$= (1.63840)^{.16667} - 1$$
$$= 1.0858 - 1$$
$$= .0858 \text{ or } 8.58\%$$

Step 3. Doubling 8.58% gives a total return of 17.16%.

Illustration 8-7. Suppose that an investor has a six-year investment horizon. The investor is considering a 13-year, 9% coupon bond selling at par. The investor's expectations are as follows:

(1) The first four semiannual coupon payments can be reinvested from the time of receipt to the end of the investment horizon at an annual interest rate of 8%,

(2) The last eight semiannual coupon payments can be reinvested from the time of receipt to the end of the investment horizon at a 10% annual interest rate, and

(3) The required yield to maturity on seven-year bonds at the end of the investment horizon is 10.6%.

Based on these three assumptions, the total return is 8.14%. The calculations are shown in Exhibit 8-7.

Exhibit 8-7

Computation of the Total Return for a 13-Year, 9% Bond Selling at Par and Held for Six Years: Two Different Reinvestment Rates

Step 1. The total future amount from this bond includes:

(1) Coupon interest of $45 every six months for six years (the investment horizon),

(2) Interest earned from reinvesting the first four semiannual coupon interest payments at 4% (one-half the assumed annual reinvestment rate) until the end of the investment horizon,

(3) Interest earned from reinvesting the last eight semiannual coupon interest payments at 5% (one-half the assumed annual reinvestment rate) until the end of the reinvestment horizon, and

(4) The expected price of the bond at the end of six years.

The coupon interest plus interest on interest for the first four coupon payments can be found as follows:

Exhibit 8-7 continued.

$$c = \$45;$$
$$m = 2;$$
$$r = .04 \ (= .08/2);$$
$$n = 4$$

$$\begin{array}{c} \text{Coupon interest} \\ \text{plus} \\ \text{interest on interest} \end{array} = \$45 \left[\frac{(1.04)^4 - 1}{.04} \right]$$

$$= \$45 \left[\frac{1.1699 - 1}{.04} \right]$$

$$= \$45 \ (4.2465)$$
$$= \$191.09.$$

This gives the coupon interest plus interest on interest as of the end of the second year (four periods). Reinvesting at 4% until the end of the investment horizon, four years or eight six-month periods later, $191.09 will grow to

$$\$191.09 \ (1.04)^8 = \$261.52$$

The coupon interest plus interest on interest for the last eight coupon payments can be found as follows:

$$c = \$45;$$
$$m = 2;$$
$$r = .05 \ (= .10/2);$$
$$n = 8$$

$$\begin{array}{c} \text{Coupon interest} \\ \text{plus} \\ \text{interest on interest} \end{array} = \$45 \left[\frac{(1.05)^8 - 1}{.05} \right]$$

$$= \$45 \left[\frac{1.47746 - 1}{.05} \right]$$

$$= \$45 \ (9.5491)$$
$$= \$429.71.$$

The coupon interest and interest on interest from all 12 coupon interest payments is $691.23 ($261.52 + $429.71).

The expected price of the bond six years from now is determined as follows:

(a) Present value of coupon interest payments, assuming the required yield to maturity at the end of the investment horizon is 10.6%:

$$c = \$45;$$
$$i = .053 \ (= .106/2);$$
$$n = 14 \ (= \text{Remaining years to maturity} \times 2)$$

Exhibit 8-7 continued.

$$PV = \$45 \left[\frac{1 - \left[\frac{1}{(1.053)^{14}} \right]}{.053} \right]$$

$$= \$45 \left[\frac{1 - .4853}{.053} \right]$$

$$= \$45 \,(9.7115)$$

$$= \$437.02$$

(b) Present value of the maturity value:

$$\frac{\$1,000}{(1.053)^{14}} = \$485.29$$

$$\text{Expected price} = \$437.02 + \$485.29$$
$$= \$922.31$$

Total future amount:

Coupon interest plus interest on interest	= $691.23
Expected price	= 922.31
Total	$1,613.54

Step 2. Compute the following:

$$\left[\frac{\$1,613.54}{\$1,000.00} \right]^{1/12} - 1$$

$$= (1.613.54)^{.08333} - 1$$

$$= 1.0407 - 1$$

$$= .0407 \text{ or } 4.07\%$$

Step 3. Doubling 4.07% gives a total return of 8.14%.

Analyzing Callable Bonds with the Total Return

The total return can be used to assess the potential return from holding a callable bond. If the first call date falls within the investment horizon, the proceeds from the coupon interest payments plus the interest on interest and the proceeds from calling the issue (the call price) will be available at the first call date. These proceeds can then be reinvested until the end of the investment horizon. Given the total future amount at the end of the investment horizon, the total return can then be computed. The next illustration shows how this is done.

Illustration 8-8. An investor is considering bond C, which we presented earlier in this chapter: 11% coupon, 15 years to maturity and 9.2% yield to maturity. The price for this bond is $1,144.88. Suppose that this bond is callable in three years at $1,055. The yield to call for this bond is 7.48%. Since the yield to call is less than the yield to maturity, this investor might use the 7.48% to assess the relative attractiveness of this bond. However, suppose that this investor's investment horizon is five years (a period extending beyond the first call date but shorter than the maturity of the bond). Also assume that this investor believes that any proceeds can be reinvested at a 6% annual interest rate (3% semiannually).

Exhibit 8-8 shows the computation of the total return on the assumption that the bond is called in three years. The total return is 6.66%. This investor's reinvestment assumption and the investment horizon make this the appropriate yield to use in assessing the attractiveness of this bond compared to other bonds that are purchase candidates.

Exhibit 8-8

Computation of the Total Return for a 15-Year, 11% Bond Selling for $1,144.88, Callable in Three Years at $1,055 and Held for Three Years: Reinvestment Rate = 6%

Step 1. The total future amount from this bond includes:

(1) Coupon interest of $55 every six months for three years (to the first call date),

(2) Interest earned from reinvesting the first six semiannual coupon interest payments at 3% (one-half the assumed annual reinvestment rate) until the first call date, and

(3) Proceeds from reinvesting the call price plus (1) and (2) above for two years at 3% until the end of the investment horizon.

The coupon interest plus interest on interest for the first six coupon payments can be found as follows:

$$c = \$55;$$
$$m = 2;$$
$$r = .03 \ (= .06/2);$$
$$n = 6$$

$$\begin{array}{c} \text{Coupon interest} \\ \text{plus} \\ \text{interest on interest} \end{array} = \$55 \left[\frac{(1.03)^6 - 1}{.03} \right]$$

$$= \$55 \left[\frac{1.1941 - 1}{.03} \right]$$

$$= \$55 \ (6.4683)$$

$$= \$355.76.$$

Exhibit 8-8 continued.

This gives the coupon interest plus interest on interest as of the end of the third year (six periods) when the bond is called. Adding the call price of $1,055 gives the total proceeds that must be reinvested at 3% until the end of the investment horizon, for two years or four periods.

$$\text{Proceeds to be reinvested} = \$355.76 + \$1,055$$
$$= \$1,410.76.$$

Reinvesting $1,410.76 for four periods at 3%:

$$\$1,410.76 \, (1.03)^4 = \$1,587.82$$

Therefore, the total future amount is $1,587.82.

Step 2. Compute the following:

$$\left[\frac{\$1,587.82}{\$1,144.88} \right]^{1/10}$$
$$= (1.38689)^{.10} - 1$$
$$= 1.0304 - 1$$
$$= .0333 \text{ or } 3.33\%$$

Step 3. Doubling 3.33% gives a total return of 6.66%.

Comparing Coupon and Zero-Coupon Bonds: The Break-Even Reinvestment Rate

As we have emphasized throughout this chapter, assessing the relative value of two bonds on the basis of yield to maturity may provide misleading conclusions. A manager of a tax-exempt portfolio who intends to hold a bond until maturity has the advantage of an analytical framework to assess the relative value of a zero-coupon bond and a coupon bond. We present it by using an illustration.

Suppose that the manager of a tax-exempt portfolio is considering two five-year bonds: (1) a 12% bond selling at par ($100), and (2) a zero-coupon bond selling at $57.99 (per $100 par value). Suppose also that the bonds have the same quality rating and that the portfolio manager plans to hold either bond until maturity.

The yield to maturity for the zero-coupon bond is 11.2%, which, since it requires no reinvestment of coupon payments, means that the total return will be 11.2%. While the total return for the 12% coupon bond is 12%, that return will depend on the rate at which the coupon payments can be reinvested. We can determine the reinvestment rate that will produce the same total future amount from both investments. This rate is called the *break-even reinvestment rate*.

Suppose instead of investing $100 in the 12% coupon bond, an investor purchases the zero-coupon bond. The semiannual yield to maturity is 5.6%; therefore, $100 invested in the zero-coupon bond will grow to $172.44 at the end of 10 periods (five years):

$$\$100 \ (1.056)^{10} = \$172.44.$$

An investor will be indifferent between the choice of the zero-coupon bond and the 12% coupon bond if the latter produces a total future amount of $172.44. The total future amount from holding a bond to maturity will be equal to the sum of (1) the coupon payments, (2) the maturity value, and (3) the interest on interest from reinvesting the coupon payments. For the 12% coupon bond, the investor knows for certain that for each $100 invested, the following future amounts will be received:

$$\text{Coupon payments } (10 \times \$6) = \$60.00$$
$$\text{Maturity value} = 100.00$$

That is, $160 will be received with certainty. For the 12% coupon bond to generate $172.44, interest on interest must equal $12.44 ($172.44 – $160.00). Alternatively, this means that the coupon interest plus the interest on interest must equal $72.44.

Recall that the formula for the coupon interest plus interest on interest is equal to:

$$c \left[\frac{(1 + r)^n - 1}{r} \right]$$

where

    c = Semiannual interest payment;
    r = Semiannual reinvestment rate;
    n = Number of semiannual coupon payments.

In our illustration, the investor knows the semiannual coupon interest payment is $6 and that the resulting figure should be equal to $72.44. Substituting, we have

$$\$74.44 = \$6 \left[\frac{(1 + r)^{10} - 1}{r} \right].$$

Solving this equation for r gives a semiannual break-even reinvestment rate of approximately 4%. The break-even reinvestment rate is 8%. Therefore, if the portfolio manager believes at least an 8% reinvestment rate can be realized, the 12% coupon bond will provide more future dollars than the zero-coupon bond. If the reinvestment rate is expected to be less than 8%, then the zero-coupon bond is a better investment, as it will provide a higher total return.

The analysis assumes that the portfolio manager could invest all the coupon payments at a tax-free rate. If taxes on the coupon payments must be paid, the analysis must take this into consideration.

Scenario Analysis

Because the total return depends on the reinvestment rate and the yield at the end of the investment horizon, portfolio managers assess performance over a wide range of scenarios for these two variables. This approach is referred to as *scenario analysis*.

Illustration 8-9. Suppose a portfolio manager is considering the purchase of bond A, a 20-year, 9% noncallable bond selling at $109.896 per $100 of par value. The yield to maturity for this bond is 8%. Assume also that the portfolio manager's investment horizon is three years and that the portfolio manager believes the reinvestment rate range can vary from 3% to 6.5% and the yield at the end of the investment horizon from 5% to 12%.

The top panel of Exhibit 8-9 shows the total future dollars at the end of three years under various scenarios. The bottom panel shows the total return (based on the effective annualizing of the six-month total return). The portfolio manager knows that the maximum and minimum total return will be 14.64% and −.2%, respectively, and the scenarios under which each will be realized. If the portfolio manager faces three-year liabilities guaranteeing, say, 6%, the major consideration is scenarios that will produce a three-year total return of less than 6%. These scenarios can be determined from Exhibit 8-9.

Illustration 8-10. Suppose that the same portfolio manager owns bond B, a 14-year noncallable bond with a coupon rate of 7.25% and a current price of $94.553 per $100 par value. The yield to maturity is 7.9%. Exhibit 8-10 reports the total future dollars and total return over a three-year investment horizon under the same scenarios as Exhibit 8-9. A portfolio manager considering swapping from bond B to bond A would compare the relative performance of the two bonds as reported in Exhibits 8-9 and 8-10. Exhibit 8-11 shows the difference between the performance of the two bonds in basis points. This comparative analysis assumes that the two bonds are of the same investment quality and ignores the financial accounting and tax consequences associated with the disposal of bond B to acquire bond A.

Exhibit 8-9

Scenario Analysis for Bond A

Bond A: 9% coupon, 20-year noncallable bond
Price: $109.896   Yield to maturity: 8.00%
Investment horizon: 3 years

				Yield at end of horizon				
	5.00%	6.00%	7.00%	8.00%	9.00%	10.00%	11.00%	12.00%
				Horizon price				
	145.448	131.698	119.701	109.206	100.000	91.9035	84.763	78.4478

Reinv.				*Total future dollars*				
rate	5.00%	6.00%	7.00%	8.00%	9.00%	10.00%	11.00%	12.00%
3.0%	173.481	159.731	147.734	137.239	128.033	119.937	112.796	106.481
3.5%	173.657	159.907	147.910	137.415	128.209	120.113	112.972	106.657
4.0%	173.834	160.084	148.087	137.592	128.387	120.290	113.150	106.834
4.5%	174.013	160.263	148.266	137.771	128.565	120.469	113.328	107.013
5.0%	174.192	160.443	148.445	137.950	128.745	120.648	113.508	107.193
5.5%	174.373	160.623	148.626	138.131	128.926	120.829	113.689	107.374
6.0%	174.555	160.806	148.809	138.313	129.108	121.011	113.871	107.556
6.5%	174.739	160.989	148.992	138.497	129.291	121.195	114.054	107.739

Reinv.				*Total return (effective rate)*				
rate	5.00%	6.00%	7.00%	8.00%	9.00%	10.00%	11.00%	12.00%
3.0%	16.44	13.28	10.37	7.69	5.22	2.96	0.87	−1.05
3.5%	16.48	13.32	10.41	7.73	5.27	3.01	0.92	−0.99
4.0%	16.52	13.36	10.45	7.78	5.32	3.06	0.98	−0.94
4.5%	16.56	13.40	10.50	7.83	5.37	3.11	1.03	−0.88
5.0%	16.60	13.44	10.54	7.87	5.42	3.16	1.08	−0.83
5.5%	16.64	13.49	10.59	7.92	5.47	3.21	1.14	−0.77
6.0%	16.68	13.53	10.63	7.97	5.52	3.26	1.19	−0.72
6.5%	16.72	13.57	10.68	8.02	5.57	3.32	1.25	−0.66

Exhibit 8-10

Scenario Analysis for Bond B

Bond B: 7.25% coupon, 14-year noncallable bond
Price: $94.553   Yield to maturity: 7.90%
Investment horizon: 3 years

			Yield at end of horizon					
	5.00%	6.00%	7.00%	8.00%	9.00%	10.00%	11.00%	12.00%
			Horizon price					
	118.861	109.961	101.896	94.5808	87.9386	81.9009	76.4066	71.4012

Reinv. rate				Total future dollars				
	5.00%	6.00%	7.00%	8.00%	9.00%	10.00%	11.00%	12.00%
3.0%	141.443	132.543	124.478	117.163	110.521	104.483	98.989	93.983
3.5%	141.585	132.685	124.620	117.305	110.663	104.625	99.131	94.125
4.0%	141.728	132.828	124.763	117.448	110.806	104.768	99.273	94.268
4.5%	141.872	132.971	124.907	117.592	110.949	104.912	99.417	94.412
5.0%	142.017	133.116	125.051	117.736	111.094	105.056	99.562	94.557
5.5%	142.162	133.262	125.197	117.882	111.240	105.202	99.708	94.703
6.0%	142.309	133.409	125.344	118.029	111.387	105.349	99.855	94.849
6.5%	142.457	133.556	125.492	118.176	111.534	105.497	100.002	94.997

Reinv. rate				Total return (effective rate)				
	5.00%	6.00%	7.00%	8.00%	9.00%	10.00%	11.00%	12.00%
3.0%	14.37	11.92	9.60	7.41	5.34	3.38	1.54	−0.20
3.5%	14.41	11.96	9.64	7.45	5.38	3.43	1.59	−0.15
4.0%	14.44	12.00	9.68	7.50	5.43	3.48	1.64	−0.10
4.5%	14.48	12.04	9.72	7.54	5.48	3.53	1.69	−0.05
5.0%	14.52	12.08	9.77	7.58	5.52	3.57	1.74	0.00
5.5%	14.56	12.12	9.81	7.63	5.57	3.62	1.79	0.05
6.0%	14.60	12.16	9.85	7.67	5.61	3.67	1.84	0.10
6.5%	14.64	12.20	9.90	7.72	5.66	3.72	1.89	0.16

Exhibit 8-11

Scenario Analysis Showing the Relative Performance of
Bonds A and B

Total return for Bond A – Total return for Bond B
in basis points

Reinv.				Yield at end of horizon				
rate	5.00%	6.00%	7.00%	8.00%	9.00%	10.00%	11.00%	12.00%
3.0%	207	136	77	28	–12	–43	–67	–85
3.5%	207	136	77	28	–11	–42	–66	–84
4.0%	207	136	77	28	–11	–42	–66	–84
4.5%	207	136	77	29	–11	–42	–66	–83
5.0%	207	137	78	29	–10	–41	–65	–83
5.5%	208	137	78	29	–10	–41	–65	–82
6.0%	208	137	78	30	–10	–41	–64	–82
6.5%	208	137	78	30	–9	–40	–64	–81

Summary and Implications

In this chapter we have presented an alternative yield measure, the total return, that investors can use to assess the relative attractiveness of bonds over some investment horizon. The total return takes into consideration the investor's –1 investment horizon, –2 expected reinvestment rate over the investment horizon, and –3 expected yield for the bond at the end of the investment horizon. We show how multiple reinvestment rates can be incorporated into the analysis and how callable bonds can be evaluated using the total return framework.

The total return is applicable as well to evaluating mortgage-backed securities and floating-rate securities. The total return can handle the situation where a taxable bond is included in a taxable portfolio so that only a portion of the coupon interest payments can be reinvested. This permits a comparison of taxable and tax-exempt bonds in a taxable portfolio, which is more meaningful than the common procedure of multiplying the taxable yield by one minus the marginal tax rate. The evaluation of a bond swap, the sale of a bond in a portfolio for another bond, should be conducted using the total return framework.

One objection to the total return is that it requires the investor to make assumptions about reinvestment rates and future yields, as well as to think in terms of an investment horizon. It is more convenient for some to simply use a meaningless measure such as the yield to maturity or yield to call. If an investor is managing money, however, expectations are part of the game. It is not difficult to use the total return framework to analyze the performance of a bond assuming different interest rate scenarios and investment horizons. This is called scenario analysis.

III

Bond Price Volatility

9

Price Volatility of Option-Free Bonds

To implement effective portfolio trading and risk-control strategies, it is necessary to understand the price volatility characteristics of bonds. The four chapters in this section of the book focus on bond price volatility. In this chapter, general price volatility properties of option-free bonds are discussed, as well as bond characteristics that determine price volatility.

A Closer Look at the Price/Yield Relationship for Option-Free Bonds

In Chapter 2 we demonstrated a fundamental principle of all option-free bonds (a bond that does not have an embedded option): *the price of a bond changes in the opposite direction of the change in the required yield for the bond.* This principle follows from the fact that the price of an option-free bond is equal to the present value of its expected cash flows. An increase (decrease) in the required return decreases (increases) the present value of its expected cash flows, and therefore, the bond's price.

Exhibit 9-1 illustrates this property for 12 hypothetical bonds: three bonds with the same coupon rate but different maturities (5, 15, and 30 years), and four bonds with the same maturity but different coupon rates (0%, 8%, 10%, and 14%). These 12 bonds are used in this and the following three chapters to demonstrate the bond price volatility of option-free bonds and measures of bond price volatility.

For each bond in Exhibit 9-1 the price of the bond (with par equal to 100) is shown for 13 yield levels. The top panel shows the price for yield levels from 10% to 13%; the bottom panel, the price for yield levels from 7% to 10%.

If the price/yield relationship for any of the 12 bonds in Exhibit 9-1 is graphed, the shape of the graph would be as shown in Exhibit 9-2. As the required yield rises, the price of the option-free bond declines. However, the relationship is not linear (that is, it is not a straight line). The price/yield relationship for all option-free bonds takes this nonlinear shape, referred to as *convex*.

While all option-free bonds will have the convex shape shown in Exhibit 9-2, the curvature of every option-free bond will be different. As we will see in this chapter and the following three, it is this convex shape that holds the key to assessing the performance of a bond and a portfolio of bonds.

It is important to keep in mind that the price/yield relationship that we have discussed refers to an instantaneous change in the yield. As we explained in Chapter 2, assuming no change in the perceived credit risk of the issuer as a bond moves toward maturity, there are two factors that influence the price of any option-free bond. First, the bond's price will change as the required yield changes, as we know. Second, for discount and premium bonds the bond's price will change even if yields remain the same. In particular, the price of a discount bond will increase as it moves toward maturity, reaching par value at the maturity date; for a premium bond, the bond's price will decrease as it moves closer to maturity, finally declining to the par value at the maturity date.

The Price Volatility Characteristics of Option-Free Bonds

To investigate bond price volatility in terms of percentage price change, let's assume that the prevailing yield in the market is 10% for all 12 bonds. The dollar price change per $100 of par value for various changes in yield is shown in Exhibit 9-3. Exhibit 9-4 shows the corresponding percentage change in each bond's price. The percentage price change shown in Exhibit 9-4 is found by dividing the dollar price change in Exhibit 9-3 by the price of the bond at a 10% yield, as shown in Exhibit 9-1.

For example, consider the 8%, 15-year bond. The price for this bond if the required yield is 10% is $84.63. If the required yield increases 100 basis points to 11%, the price of this bond would fall to $78.20. The dollar price change per $100 of par value is − $6.43, as shown in Exhibit 9-3. The percentage price change is then:

$$\frac{\$78.20 - \$84.63}{\$84.63} = -.076 \text{ or } -7.60\%.$$

This is shown in Exhibit 9-4.

Exhibit 9-1

Price/Yield Relationship for 12 Hypothetical Bonds

Coupon	Term		Yield level						
		10.00%	10.01%	10.10%	10.50%	11.00%	12.00%	13.00%
.00%	5	$ 61.39	$ 61.36	$ 61.10	$ 59.95	$ 58.54	$ 55.84	$ 53.27
.00%	15	23.14	23.10	22.81	21.54	20.06	17.41	15.12
.00%	30	5.35	5.34	5.20	4.64	4.03	3.03	2.29
8.00%	5	92.28	92.24	91.91	90.46	88.69	85.28	82.03
8.00%	15	84.63	84.56	83.95	81.32	78.20	72.47	67.35
8.00%	30	81.07	80.99	80.29	77.30	73.83	67.68	62.42
10.00%	5	100.00	99.96	99.61	98.09	96.23	92.64	89.22
10.00%	15	100.00	99.92	99.24	96.26	92.73	86.24	80.41
10.00%	30	100.00	99.91	99.06	95.46	91.28	83.84	77.45
14.00%	5	115.44	115.40	115.02	113.35	111.31	107.36	103.59
14.00%	15	130.74	130.65	129.81	126.15	121.80	113.76	106.53
14.00%	30	137.86	137.73	136.60	131.79	126.17	116.16	107.52

Exhibit 9-1 continued.

Coupon	Term	Yield level						
		10.00%	9.99%	9.90%	9.50%	9.00%	8.00%	7.00%
.00%	5	$ 61.39	$ 61.42	$ 61.68	$ 62.87	$ 64.39	$ 67.56	$ 70.89
.00%	15	23.14	23.17	23.47	24.85	26.70	30.83	35.63
.00%	30	5.35	5.37	5.51	6.18	7.13	9.51	12.69
8.00%	5	92.28	92.32	92.65	94.14	96.04	100.00	104.16
8.00%	15	84.63	84.70	85.31	88.13	91.86	100.00	109.20
8.00%	30	81.07	81.15	81.87	85.19	89.68	100.00	112.47
10.00%	5	100.00	100.04	100.39	101.95	103.96	108.11	112.47
10.00%	15	100.00	100.08	100.77	103.96	108.14	117.29	127.57
10.00%	30	100.00	100.09	100.95	104.94	110.32	122.62	137.42
14.00%	5	115.44	115.49	115.87	117.59	119.78	124.33	129.11
14.00%	15	130.74	130.84	131.69	135.60	140.72	151.88	164.37
14.00%	30	137.86	137.99	139.13	144.44	151.60	167.87	187.31

Exhibit 9-2

Shape of Price/Yield Relationship for an
Option-Free Bond

An examination of Exhibits 9-3 and 9-4 reveals the following four properties about price volatility of option-free bonds.

Property 1. Price volatility is not the same for all bonds. Although the prices of all option-free bonds move in the opposite direction of the change in yield, for a given change in the yield, the price change is not the same for all bonds. A natural question is what characteristics of a bond determine its price volatility. We'll focus on this question in the next section.

Property 2. Price volatility is approximately symmetric for small yield changes. F o r very small changes in yield, the percentage price change for a given bond is roughly the same, whether the yield increases or decreases. For example, look at the top panel of both Exhibits 9-3 and 9-4. For a 10-basis-point change in the required yield, the 10%, 30-year bond's price would decrease by $0.94 per $100 of par value or 0.94% of the initial price. Now in the bottom panel of the two exhibits, note that the 10%, 30-year bond's price would increase by $0.95 per $100 of par value or 0.95% of the initial price for a 10-basis-point decrease in the required yield.

Property 3. Price volatility is not symmetric for large yield changes. For large changes in yield, the percentage price change is not the same for an increase in yield as it is for a decrease in yield. Once again, look at the 10%, 30-year coupon bond. Note that if the required yield increases by 300 basis points (from 10% to 13%), the price decline per

Exhibit 9-3

Dollar Price Change per $100 of Par Value as Yield Changes for 12 Hypothetical Bonds

		Change in basis points from 10%					
		1	10	50	100	200	300
		New yield level					
Coupon	Term	10.01%	10.10%	10.50%	11.00%	12.00%	13.00%
.00%	5	$ −.03	$ −.26	$ −1.15	$ −1.41	$ −2.70	$ −2.57
.00%	15	−.03	−.33	−1.59	−3.07	−5.73	−8.02
.00%	30	−.02	−.15	−.71	−1.33	−2.32	−3.07
8.00%	5	−.04	−.37	−1.81	−3.58	−7.00	−10.25
8.00%	15	−.07	−.68	−3.31	−6.43	−12.16	−17.27
8.00%	30	−.08	−.78	−3.78	−7.25	−13.39	−18.65
10.00%	5	−.04	−.39	−1.91	−3.77	−7.36	−10.78
10.00%	15	−.08	−.76	−3.74	−7.27	−13.76	−19.59
10.00%	30	−.09	−.94	−4.54	−8.72	−16.16	−22.55
14.00%	5	−.04	−.42	−2.09	−4.14	−8.08	−11.85
14.00%	15	−.09	−.94	−4.59	−8.94	−16.98	−24.22
14.00%	30	−.13	−1.25	−6.07	−11.68	−21.70	−30.34

Exhibit 9-3 continued.

		Change in basis points from 10%					
		−1	−10	−50	−100	−200	−300
		New yield level					
Coupon	Term	9.99%	9.90%	9.50%	9.00%	8.00%	7.00%
.00%	5	$ .03	$ .29	$ 1.48	$ 3.00	$ 6.17	$ 9.50
.00%	15	.03	.33	1.72	3.56	7.69	12.49
.00%	30	.02	.16	.82	1.78	4.15	7.34
8.00%	5	.04	.37	1.86	3.77	7.72	11.88
8.00%	15	.07	.69	3.51	7.23	15.37	24.57
8.00%	30	.08	.79	4.12	8.61	18.93	31.40
10.00%	5	.04	.39	1.95	3.96	8.11	12.47
10.00%	15	.08	.77	3.96	8.14	17.29	27.59
10.00%	30	.09	.95	4.94	10.32	22.62	37.42
14.00%	5	.04	.42	2.14	4.34	8.89	13.66
14.00%	15	.09	.95	4.85	9.98	21.13	33.63
14.00%	30	.13	1.27	6.58	13.74	30.01	49.45

Exhibit 9-4

Percentage Price Change as Yield Changes for 12 Hypothetical Bonds

		Change in basis points from 10%					
		1	10	50	100	200	300
		New yield level					
Coupon	Term	10.01%	10.10%	10.50%	11.00%	12.00%	13.00%
.00%	5	-.05%	-.47%	-2.35%	-4.64%	-9.04%	-13.22%
.00%	15	-.14	-1.42	-6.89	-13.28	-24.75	-34.66
.00%	30	-.29	-2.82	-13.30	-24.80	-43.38	-57.30
8.00%	5	-.04	-.40	-1.97	-3.88	-7.58	-11.11
8.00%	15	-.08	-.80	-3.91	-7.60	-14.37	-20.41
8.00%	30	-.10	-.96	-4.66	-8.94	-16.52	-23.01
10.00%	5	-.04	-.39	-1.91	-3.77	-7.36	-10.78
10.00%	15	-.08	-.76	-3.74	-7.27	-13.76	-19.59
10.00%	30	-.09	-.94	-4.54	-8.72	-16.16	-22.55
14.00%	5	-.04	-.37	-1.81	-3.58	-7.00	-10.26
14.00%	15	-.07	-.72	-3.51	-6.84	-12.99	-18.52
14.00%	30	-.09	-.91	-4.40	-8.48	-15.74	-22.01

Exhibit 9-4 continued.

				Change in basis points from 10%			
		−1	−10	−50	−100	−200	−300
				New yield level			
Coupon	Term	9.99%	9.90%	9.50%	9.00%	8.00%	7.00%
.00%	5	.05%	.48%	2.41%	4.89%	10.04%	15.48%
.00%	15	.14	1.44	7.41	15.40	33.25	53.98
.00%	30	.29	2.90	15.38	33.16	77.57	137.10
8.00%	5	.04	.40	2.02	4.08	8.37	12.87
8.00%	15	.08	.81	4.14	8.54	18.16	29.03
8.00%	30	.10	.98	5.08	10.62	23.35	38.73
10.00%	5	.04	.39	1.95	3.96	8.11	12.47
10.00%	15	.08	.77	3.96	8.14	17.29	27.59
10.00%	30	.09	.95	4.94	10.32	22.62	37.42
14.00%	5	.04	.37	1.86	3.76	7.70	11.84
14.00%	15	.07	.73	3.71	7.63	16.16	25.72
14.00%	30	.09	.92	4.78	9.96	21.77	35.87

$100 of par value would be $22.55 or 22.55% of the initial price; for a 300-basis-point decrease in the yield, the price increase per $100 of par value would be $37.42 or 37.42% of the initial price.

Property 4. Price increases are greater than price decreases. For a given change in yield, the price increase is greater than the price decrease. This can be seen in Exhibits 9-3 and 9-4 by comparing the upper panel (which shows price volatility for increases in yield) to the lower panel (which shows price volatility for decreases in yield). For each bond, the price change is larger in the lower panel than in the upper panel for a given change in yield.

The reason for this property lies in the convex shape of the price/yield relationship. This is illustrated graphically in Exhibit 9-5. Suppose the initial required yield is Y in Exhibit 9-5. The corresponding initial price is P. Consider large equal basis point changes in the initial yield. Y_1 and Y_2 indicate the lower and higher yields, respectively; the corresponding prices are denoted P_1 and P_2. The vertical distance from the yield axis to the price/yield relationship represents the price. The distance between P_1 and P measures the price increase if the yield decreases; the distance between P and P_2 measures the price decrease if the yield increases. The diagram clarifies that the price increase will be greater than the price decrease for an equal change in basis points.

This will always be true when the curve is convex, and because all option-free bonds have a convex price/yield relationship, this property will always hold for option-free bonds. Exhibit 9-6 shows a less convex price/yield relationship than shown in Exhibit

Exhibit 9-5

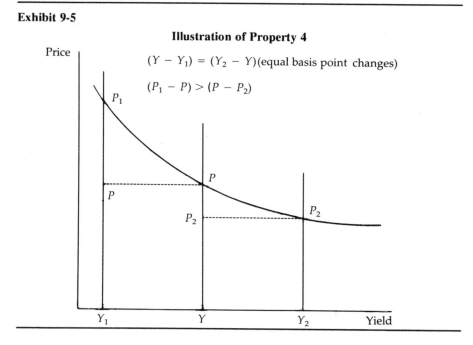

Illustration of Property 4

$(Y - Y_1) = (Y_2 - Y)$(equal basis point changes)

$(P_1 - P) > (P - P_2)$

Exhibit 9-6

The Impact of Less Convexity on Property 4

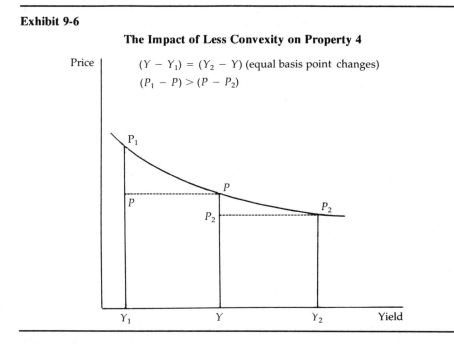

$$(Y - Y_1) = (Y_2 - Y) \text{ (equal basis point changes)}$$
$$(P_1 - P) > (P - P_2)$$

9-5. While the property still holds, the price gain when the yield falls is not that much greater than the price loss for an equal basis point increase in the yield.

An implication of Property 4 is that if an investor owns a bond (that is, is long a bond), the price appreciation that will be realized if the yield decreases is greater than the capital loss that will be realized if the yield rises by the same number of basis points. For an investor who is short a bond, the reverse is true: the potential capital loss is greater than the potential capital gain if the yield changes by a given number of basis points.

Characteristics of a Bond That Affect Its Price Volatility

Property 1 states that price volatility is not the same for each bond. There are two characteristics of an option-free bond that determine its price volatility: coupon and term to maturity.

Characteristic 1. Price volatility is greater, the lower the coupon rate.[1] For a given term to maturity and initial yield, the price volatility of a bond is greater the lower the coupon rate. This characteristic can be seen by comparing the 0%, 8%, 10%, and 14%

---

[1] This property does not necessarily hold for long-term deep discount *coupon* bonds.

coupon bonds with the same maturity. For example, if the yield for all the 30-year bonds is 10% and the yield rises to 12% (i.e., a 200-basis-point increase), the 0% coupon bond will fall by 43.38% while the 14%, 30-year bond will fall by a smaller percentage, 15.74%.[2]

The investment implication is that bonds selling at a deep discount will have greater price volatility than bonds selling near or above par. Zero-coupon bonds will have the greatest price volatility for a given maturity.

Characteristic 2. Price volatility increases with maturity. For a given coupon rate and initial yield, the longer the term to maturity the greater the price volatility. This can be seen in Exhibit 9-4 by comparing the 5-year bonds to the 30-year bonds with the same coupon. For example, if the yield increases 200 basis points from 10% to 12%, the 10%, 30-year bond's price will fall by 16.16%, while that of the 5-year bond will fall by only 7.36%.

The investment implication is that an investor expecting interest rates to fall, all other factors constant, should hold bonds with long maturities in the portfolio. To reduce a portfolio's price volatility in anticipation of a rise in interest rates, bonds with short maturities should be held in the portfolio.

The Effect of the Yield Level on Price Volatility

So far, we have described how the characteristics of a bond affect its price volatility. But we cannot ignore the fact that credit considerations cause different bonds to trade at different yields, even if they have the same coupon and maturity. How, then, holding other factors constant, does the yield to maturity affect a bond's price volatility? As it turns out, the higher the yield to maturity that a bond trades at, the lower the price volatility.

To see this, compare a 10%, 15-year bond trading at various yield levels as shown in Exhibit 9-7. The first column shows the yield level each bond is trading at and the second column the initial price. The third column indicates the bond's price if yields change by 100 basis points. The fourth and fifth columns show the dollar price change and the percentage price change, respectively. As can be seen from these last two columns, the higher the initial yield, the less the price volatility.

---

[2] Notice that while the percentage price change is greater, the lower the coupon rate, the dollar price change is smaller, the lower the coupon rate.

Exhibit 9-7

Price Change for a 100-Basis-Point Change in Yield for 10%, 15-Year Bonds Trading at Different Yield Levels

Yield level	Initial price	New price*	Price decline	Percent decline
7%	$127.57	$117.29	$10.28	8.1%
8	117.29	108.14	9.15	7.8
9	108.14	100.00	8.14	7.5
10	100.00	92.73	7.27	7.3
11	92.73	86.24	6.49	7.0
12	86.24	80.41	5.83	6.8
13	80.41	75.18	5.23	6.5

* as a result of a 100-basis-point increase in yield.

This can also be seen in Exhibit 9-8. When the yield level is high (Y_H in the exhibit), a given change in yield will not produce as large a change in the price of a bond as when the yield level is low (Y_L in the exhibit).

An implication of this is that, for a given change in yields, price volatility is greater when yield levels in the market are high, and price volatility is lower when yield levels

Exhibit 9-8

The Effect of the Yield Level on Price Volatility

$$(Y_H'-Y_H) = (Y_H-Y_H'')=(Y_L'-Y_L) =(Y_L-Y_L'')$$
$$(P_H-P_H')<(P_L-P_L') \text{ and}$$
$$(P_H-P_H'')<(P_L-P_L'')$$

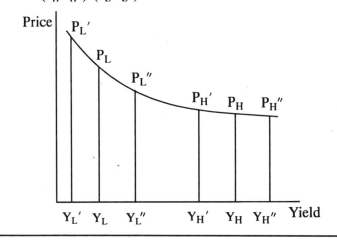

are low. For example, in the early 1980s when yields on long-term Treasury bonds were in the neighborhood of 14%, a yield change of 10 basis points produced a greater price change than in 1992 when long-term Treasury yields were 7.5%. Also, another implication is that high-yield bonds (more popularly referred to as "junk" bonds) will have less price volatility for a given change in yield than Treasury bonds because the former trade at a higher yield level than the latter.

Summary

In this chapter we have discussed the price volatility properties of option-free bonds. Four properties of bond price volatility are demonstrated, and two characteristics that affect bond price volatility (coupon rate and maturity) are illustrated. The yield level affects price volatility. The lower the yield level, all other factors constant, the greater the price volatility for a given change in yield.

What market participants would like to have is a measure that can be used to quantify the price volatility of a bond. For example, suppose a portfolio manager expects that interest rates will fall and is considering purchasing one of the following two bonds: (1) Bond A, 7%, 22-year bond selling to yield 8%, and (2) Bond B, a zero-coupon, 15-year bond selling to yield 8.40%. With interest rates expected to decline, the portfolio manager will want to purchase the bond that offers the greater price volatility. Which has higher price volatility? On the one hand, Bond B has a lower coupon than Bond A, so it would seem that Bond B has a greater price volatility. On the other hand, Bond A has a longer maturity than Bond B, so it would seem that Bond A has more price volatility. Complicating this further is the fact that the two bonds are trading at different yield levels. In fact, none of the three factors (coupon rate, maturity, or yield) is equal for the two bonds. The purpose of the next two chapters is to discuss measures of bond price volatility appropriate for such a situation. One of the things we do know is that any measure of price volatility should take into consideration the three factors that affect price volatility: coupon rate, maturity, and yield level.

10

Price Volatility Measures: PVBP and YV of a Price Change

Portfolio managers, arbitrageurs, hedgers, and traders need to have a way to measure a bond's price volatility in order to implement strategies. The three measures commonly used are (1) price value of a basis point, (2) yield value of a price change, and (3) duration. The first two measures are the subject of this chapter; duration is discussed in the next chapter.

Price Value of a Basis Point

The *price value of a basis point,* also referred to as the *dollar value of a basis point* or *DV01,* is the change in the price of the bond if the yield changes by one basis point. Note that this measure of price volatility indicates *dollar* price volatility as opposed to price volatility as a *percentage* of the initial price. The price value of a basis point is expressed as the absolute value of the change in price.

Property 2 of the price/yield relationship explained in the previous chapter states that for small changes in yield, price volatility is the same, regardless of the direction of the change in yield. Therefore, it does not make any difference if we increase or decrease the yield by one basis point to compute the price value of a basis point.

We will show how to calculate the price value of a basis point using the 12 bonds in Exhibit 9-1 of the previous chapter. For each bond, the initial price, the price after increasing the yield by one basis point (from 10.00% to 10.01%), and the price value of a basis point per $100 of par value (the difference between the two prices) are shown in the top panel of Exhibit 10-1. Similarly, if we decrease the yield by one basis point, from 10.00% to 9.99%, we would find approximately the same price value of a basis point for the 12 bonds, as shown in the bottom panel of Exhibit 10-1.

Exhibits 10-2A and 10-2B show graphically what happens to the price value of a basis point at different yields. Notice that the price value of a basis point is smaller, the higher the initial yield. The investment implication is that at higher yields, dollar price volatility is less. Also notice that the larger the price value of a basis point, the greater the convexity. This can be seen by comparing the price value of a basis point in Exhibit 10-2A to that in Exhibit 10-2B, in which the curve is less convex.

The Price Value of More Than One Basis Point

In implementing a strategy, some investors will calculate the price value of a change of more than one basis point. The principle of calculating the price value of any number of basis points is the same. The price value of x basis points is found by computing the difference between the initial price and the price if the yield is changed by x basis points. For example, the price value per $100 of par value for several values of x for the 10% coupon, 15-year bond is found as follows if the yield is increased:

Change (x, in basis points)	Initial price (10% yield)	Price at 10% + x yield	Price value of x basis points
10	100.00	99.2357	.7643
50	100.00	96.2640	3.7360
100	100.00	92.7331	7.2669

For small changes in yield (such as 10 basis points), the price value of x basis points is roughly that found by multiplying the price value of one basis point by x. For example, the price value of 10 basis points computed by multiplying the price value of a basis point, namely, .08, by 10 gives .80, which is very close to the price value of 10 basis

Exhibit 10-1

Computation of the Price Value of a Basis Point

Bond Coupon	Term (years)	Price @10.00%	Price @10.01%	Price value of a basis point*
.00%	5	61.3913	61.3621	.0292
.00%	15	23.1377	23.1047	.0330
.00%	30	5.3536	5.3383	.0153
8.00%	5	92.2783	92.2415	.0367
8.00%	15	84.6275	84.5595	.0681
8.00%	30	81.0707	80.9920	.0787
10.00%	5	100.0000	99.9614	.0386
10.00%	15	100.0000	99.9232	.0768
10.00%	30	100.0000	99.9054	.0946
14.00%	5	115.4435	115.4011	.0423
14.00%	15	130.7449	130.6506	.0943
14.00%	30	137.8586	137.7323	.1263

Bond Coupon	Term (years)	Price @10.00%	Price @9.99%	Price value of a basis point
.00%	5	61.3913	61.4206	.0292
.00%	15	23.1377	23.1708	.0331
.00%	30	5.3536	5.3689	.0153
8.00%	5	92.2783	92.3150	.0367
8.00%	15	84.6275	84.6957	.0681
8.00%	30	81.0707	81.1496	.0788
10.00%	5	100.0000	100.0386	.0386
10.00%	15	100.0000	100.0769	.0769
10.00%	30	100.0000	100.0947	.0947
14.00%	5	115.4435	115.4858	.0424
14.00%	15	130.7449	130.8393	.0944
14.00%	30	137.8586	137.9851	.1265

* Absolute value per $100 of par value

Exhibit 10-2

Graphical Illustration of the Price Value of a Basis Point

A.

B.

points computed above. In fact, the approximation is much better than indicated here because we computed the price value of a basis point to only two decimal places.

For a decrease in the yield, the price value of an *x*-basis-point change per $100 of par value is:

Change (x, in basis points)	Initial price (10% yield)	Price at 10% − x yield	Price value of x basis points
10	100.00	100.7730	.7730
50	100.00	103.9551	3.9551
100	100.00	108.1444	8.1444

Once again, note the approximate symmetry of the price change for small changes (10 basis points) in yield (Property 2 of the price/yield relationship). For larger changes in yield, however, there will be a difference between the price value of an *x*-basis-point movement, depending on whether the yield is increased or decreased. Many investors who use the price value of a large basis point movement in implementing a strategy will compute the average of the two price values. For example, the price value of 100 basis points would be approximated by averaging 7.2669 and 8.1444 to give 7.7057.

Application of Price Value of a Basis Point to Portfolio and Dealer Position

Suppose that a portfolio manager wants to know the price value of a basis point for a portfolio. Let's assume the following portfolio, comprised of three of our hypothetical bonds, all priced to yield 10%:

Bond	Par amount owned	Price
10%, 5-year	$4 million	$4,000,000
8%, 15-year	5 million	4,231,375
14%, 30-year	1 million	1,378,586

The price of a basis point per $100 of par value for each of these bonds, assuming an increase of 1 basis point, is:

Bond	Par amount owned	Price value for:	
		$100 par	Amount owned
10%, 5-year	$4 million	$.0386	$1,544
8%, 15-year	$5 million	.0681	3,405
14%, 30-year	$1 million	.1263	1,263

Thus, the portfolio's exposure to a one-basis-point movement is $6,212, that is, $1,544 + $3,405 + $1,263.

The same analysis can be used to determine the exposure of a bond dealer's inventory.

Price Change Versus Percentage Change

So far we have dealt with the dollar price change. If we want to know the percentage price change, we can find it by dividing the price value of a basis point by the initial price. That is,

$$\text{Percentage price change} = \frac{\text{Price value of a basis point}}{\text{Initial price}}$$

Application to Hedging

To hedge a portfolio or bond position, a portfolio manager or trader wants to take an opposite position in a cash market security (or securities) or in a derivative instrument (option or futures contract) so that any loss in the position held is offset by a gain in the opposite position. To do so, the *dollar* price volatility of the position used to hedge must equal the *dollar* price volatility of the position to be hedged. That is, the objective in hedging is

Dollar price change in position to be hedged
= Dollar price change of hedging vehicle.

The hedger encounters two problems. First, for a given change in yield, the dollar price volatility of the bond to be hedged will not necessarily be equal to the dollar price volatility of the hedging vehicle. For example, if yields change by 50 basis points, the price of the bond to be hedged may change by X, while the price of the hedging vehicle may change by more or less than X. The second problem is that factors that result in a change in the yield of a given number of basis points for the bond to be hedged may not result in a change of the same number of basis points for the hedging vehicle. That is, if yields change by x basis points for the bond to be hedged, the yield for the hedging vehicle may change by more or less than x basis points.

Consequently, a portfolio manager or trader attempting to hedge a $10 million long position in some bond will not necessarily take a $10 million short position in the vehicle used for hedging because the relative dollar price volatility of the two positions will not necessarily be the same. The hedger would have to consider the relative dollar price volatility of the two positions in constructing the hedge. As a result, the objective in hedging can be restated as follows:

Dollar price change of bond to be hedged =
Dollar price change of hedging vehicle

$$\times \frac{\text{Dollar price volatility of bond be hedged}}{\text{Dollar price volatility of hedging vehicle}}.$$

The last ratio is commonly referred to as the *hedge ratio*. The hedge ratio can be computed from the price value of a basis point by the following formula:

$$\frac{\text{Price value of a basis point for bond to be hedged}}{\text{Price value of a basis point for hedging vehicle}}$$

$$\times \; \frac{\text{Change in yield for bond to be hedged}}{\text{Change in yield for hedging vehicle}} \; .$$

The first ratio shows the price change for the bond to be hedged relative to the price change for the hedging vehicle, both based on a yield change of one basis point. The second ratio indicates the relative change in the yield of the two instruments. This ratio is commonly referred to as the *yield beta* and is estimated using the statistical technique of regression analysis, which is described in Chapter 24. Therefore, the hedge ratio can be rewritten as

$$\frac{\text{Price value of a basis point for bond to be hedged}}{\text{Price value of a basis point for hedging vehicle}} \times \text{Yield beta.}$$

To illustrate this relationship, we'll look at how to hedge a $10 million long position in a 15-year, 8% coupon bond selling to yield 10% with a 10% coupon bond with the same maturity and selling at the same yield. The following information is known:

Bond to be hedged = 15-year, 8% bond selling to yield 10%;
Hedging vehicle = 15-year, 10% bond selling to yield 10%;

For bond to be hedged,
Price value of a basis point per $100 of par = 0.0681

For hedging vehicle,
Price value of a basis point per $100 of par = 0.0768.

For this illustration, we shall assume that the yield beta is 1. The hedge ratio is then

$$\frac{0.0681}{0.0768} \times 1 = .8867.$$

The hedge ratio of .8867 means that for every $1 of par value of the 15-year, 8% coupon bond to be hedged, the hedger should short $.8867 of $1 par of the hedging vehicle. Since this illustration involves a long position of $10 million of the 15-year, 8% coupon bond, a short position of $8.867 million of the 15-year, 10% bond should be taken.

To demonstrate that this hedge ratio will result in equal dollar price changes for the bond to be hedged and the hedging vehicle, suppose interest rates rise by 10 basis points. The price of the bond to be hedged will decline from 84.6275 per $100 of par to 83.9505, resulting in a loss for the $10 million position of $67,700. The short position, however, will gain. The price of the 15-year, 10% coupon bond will decline from 100 per $100 of par to 99.2357, resulting in a gain of $67,770 for the $8.867 million position. The gain is almost identical to the loss.

Yield Value of a Price Change

Some investors use another measure of the dollar price volatility of a bond: the change in the yield for a specified price change. This is found by first calculating the bond's yield if the bond's price is increased by, say, X dollars. Then the difference between the initial yield and the new yield is the yield value of the X-dollar price change.

The smaller the yield value of an X-dollar price change, the greater the *dollar* price volatility. This is because it would take a larger X-dollar price movement to change the yield a specified number of basis points. This is illustrated graphically in Exhibit 10-3.

Exhibit 10-3

Graphical Illustration of Yield Value of X Price Change

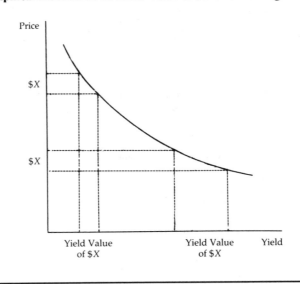

Yield Value of a 32nd for Treasury Securities

Treasury notes and bonds are quoted in 32nds of a percentage point of par. Consequently, investors in this market compute the yield value of a 32nd. The yield value of a 32nd for three 10% coupon bonds selling to yield 10% is computed below.

Decreasing the price by a 32nd:

Bond	Initial price – one 32nd	Yield at new price	Initial yield	Yield value of a 32nd
10%, 5-year	99.96875	.1000810	.10000	.0000810
10%, 15-year	99.96875	.1000407	.10000	.0000407
10%, 30-year	99.96875	.1000330	.10000	.0000330

Increasing the price by a 32nd:

Bond	Initial price + one 32nd	Yield at new price	Initial yield	Yield value of a 32nd
10%, 5-year	100.03125	.0999190	.10000	.0000810
10%, 15-year	100.03125	.0999593	.10000	.0000407
10%, 30-year	100.03125	.0999670	.10000	.0000330

Notice that the yield value of a 32nd for the 30-year bond is lower than for the five-year bond. This agrees with our earlier statement that the lower the yield value of an $X price change, the greater the dollar price volatility.

Yield Value of an 8th for Corporate and Municipal Securities

Corporate bonds and municipal bonds are traded in 8ths of a percentage point. Consequently, investors in these markets frequently compute the yield value of an 8th. The calculation of the yield value of an 8th for the three 10% coupon bonds selling to yield 10% is shown below.

Decreasing the price by an 8th:

Bond	Initial price − one 8th	Yield at new price	Initial yield	Yield value of an 8th
10%, 5-year	99.875	.10032	.10000	.00032
10%, 15-year	99.875	.10016	.10000	.00016
10%, 30-year	99.875	.10013	.10000	.00013

Increasing the price by an 8th:

Bond	Initial price + one 8th	Yield at new price	Initial yield	Yield value of an 8th
10%, 5-year	100.125	.09968	.10000	.00032
10%, 15-year	100.125	.09984	.10000	.00016
10%, 30-year	100.125	.09987	.10000	.00013

Application to Hedging

The hedge ratio can be rewritten as follows using the yield value of a price change:

$$\frac{\text{Yield value of a price change for hedging vehicle}}{\text{Yield value of a price change for bond to be hedged}} \times \text{Yield beta.}$$

Summary

There are three commonly used measures of price volatility: price value of a basis point, yield value of a price change, and duration. Our focus in this chapter has been on the first two measures.

The price value of basis point (also called the dollar value of a basis point or DV01) is a measure of the dollar price change of a bond when the yield changes by one basis point. The yield value of a price change indicates how the yield will change if the price is changed by a certain amount. Those dealing with Treasury securities compute the yield value of a price change of one 32nd; for corporate and municipal securities, the yield of a price change of one 8th is computed.

These two measures can be used in hedging applications to calculate the appropriate hedge ratio. The principles can be extended to weighting trades so that a strategy employed will not be affected by yield changes.

11

Price Volatility Measures: Duration

In this chapter we discuss the third measure of bond price volatility: duration. We illustrate some applications of duration in portfolio strategies and discuss its limitations.

Macaulay Duration

In 1938, Frederick Macaulay constructed a measure that he could use as a proxy for the length of time a bond investment was outstanding.[1] He referred to this number as the *duration* of a bond and defined it as a weighted average term-to-maturity of the bond's

---

[1] Frederick Macaulay, *Some Theoretical Problems Suggested by the Movements of Interest Rates, Bond Yields and Stock Prices in the United States Since 1865* (National Bureau of Economic Research, 1938).

157

cash flows. The weights in this weighted average are the present value of each cash flow as a percent of the present value of all the bond's cash flows (i.e., the weights are the present value of each cash flow as a percent of the bond's price). As we will see, Macaulay's measure is linked to the price volatility of a bond. First, let's look at how this measure, referred to as *Macaulay duration*, is computed.

Computing Macaulay Duration

Mathematically, Macaulay duration is computed as follows:

$$\text{Macaulay duration (in periods)} =$$

$$\frac{(1)\,PVCF_1 + (2)\,PVCF_2 + (3)\,PVCF_3 + \ldots + (n)\,PVCF_n}{PVTCF}$$

where

$PVCF_t$ = The present value of the cash flow in period t discounted at the prevailing period yield (in the case of a semiannual-pay bond, one-half the yield to maturity);

t = The period when the cash flow is expected to be received ($t = 1, \ldots, n$);

n = Number of periods until maturity (specifically, number of years to maturity times k, rounded down to the nearest whole number);[2]

k = Number of periods, or payments, per year (i.e., $k = 2$ for semiannual-pay bonds, $k = 12$ for monthly pay bonds);

$PVTCF$ = Total present value of the cash flow of the bond, where the present value is determined using the prevailing yield to maturity.

For an *option-free bond* with semiannual payments, the cash flow for periods 1 to $n - 1$ is one-half the annual coupon interest. The cash flow in period n is the semiannual coupon interest plus the maturity value. Since the bond's price is equal to its cash flow discounted at the prevailing yield to maturity, $PVTCF$ is the current market price *plus* accrued interest.

The formula for Macaulay duration gives a value in terms of periods. Dividing by the number of payments per year converts Macaulay duration to years. That is,

$$\text{Macaulay duration (in years)} = \frac{\text{Macaulay duration (in periods)}}{k} .$$

---

[2] For example, if there are 5.2 years to maturity for a semiannual-pay bond (i.e., $k = 2$), then:

$n = 5.2 \times 2$

$\quad = 10.4$

Rounding down to the nearest whole number gives a value of 10 for n.

Exhibits 11-1 and 11-2 show the calculation of Macaulay duration for two of our hypothetical bonds (the 10%, five-year bond and the 14%, five-year bond), assuming each bond is selling to yield 10%. The Macaulay duration in years for our 12 hypothetical bonds is given below:

Bond	*Macaulay duration (years)*
0%, 5-year	5.00
0%, 15-year	15.00
0%, 30-year	30.00
8%, 5-year	4.18
8%, 15-year	8.45
8%, 30-year	10.20
10%, 5-year	4.05
10%, 15-year	8.07
10%, 30-year	9.94
14%, 5-year	3.85
14%, 15-year	7.58
14%, 30-year	9.63

Note in this summary that the Macaulay duration of a coupon bond is less than its maturity. It should be obvious from the formula that the Macaulay duration of a zero-coupon bond is equal to its maturity. The lower the coupon, generally the greater the duration of the bond.[3]

Notice the consistency between the properties of bond price volatility that we discussed earlier and the properties of duration. We showed that, all other factors constant, the greater the maturity, the greater the price volatility. A property of duration is that, all other factors constant, the greater the maturity, the greater the duration. We also showed that the lower the coupon rate, all other factors constant, the greater the bond price volatility. As we just noted, generally the lower the coupon rate, the greater the duration. It appears that duration is telling us something about bond price volatility.

---

[3] This property does not necessarily hold for some long maturity deep discount coupon bonds, as explained below.

Exhibit 11-1

Calculation of Macaulay Duration and Modified Duration
for a 10%, 5-year Bond Selling to Yield 10%

Coupon rate = 10.00%;
Maturity (years) = 5;
Initial yield = 10.00%

Period (t)	Cash flow*	Present value of $1 at 5%	Present value of cash flow (PVCF)	t × PVCF
1	$5.00	0.952380	4.761905	4.761905
2	5.00	0.907029	4.535147	9.070295
3	5.00	0.863837	4.319188	12.957563
4	5.00	0.822702	4.113512	16.454049
5	5.00	0.783526	3.917631	19.588154
6	5.00	0.746215	3.731077	22.386461
7	5.00	0.710681	3.553407	24.873846
8	5.00	0.676839	3.384197	27.073574
9	5.00	0.644608	3.223045	29.007401
10	105.00	0.613913	64.460892	644.608920
Total			100.000000	810.782168

*   Cash flow per $100 of par value

$$\frac{\text{Macaulay duration}}{\text{(in half years)}} = \frac{810.782168}{100.000000} = 8.11$$

$$\frac{\text{Macaulay duration}}{\text{(in years)}} = \frac{8.11}{2} = 4.05$$

$$\frac{\text{Modified duration}}{\text{(in years)}} = \frac{4.05}{1.0500} = 3.86$$

Exhibit 11-2

Calculation of Macaulay Duration and Modified Duration
for a 14%, 5-year Bond Selling to Yield 10%

Coupon rate = 14.00%;
Maturity (years) = 5;
Initial yield = 10.00%

Period (t)	Cash flow*	Present value of $1 at 5%	Present value of cash flow (PVCF)	t × PVCF
1	$7.00	0.952380	6.666667	6.666667
2	7.00	0.907029	6.349206	12.698412
3	7.00	0.863837	6.046863	18.140589
4	7.00	0.822702	5.758917	23.035669
5	7.00	0.783526	5.484683	27.423415
6	7.00	0.746215	5.223508	31.341046
7	7.00	0.710681	4.974769	34.823385
8	7.00	0.676839	4.737876	37.903004
9	7.00	0.644608	4.512262	40.610361
10	107.00	0.613913	65.688718	656.887180
Total			115.443470	889.529728

*   Cash flow per $100 of par value.

$$\frac{\text{Macaulay duration}}{\text{(in half years)}} = \frac{889.529728}{115.443470} = 7.71$$

$$\frac{\text{Macaulay duration}}{\text{(in years)}} = \frac{7.71}{2} = 3.85$$

$$\frac{\text{Modified duration}}{\text{(in years)}} = \frac{3.85}{1.0500} = 3.67$$

Short-cut Formulas for Macaulay Duration

Mathematically, Macaulay duration for a semiannual-pay bond can be shown to be equivalent to:[4]

Macaulay duration (in six-month periods) =

$$\left[\frac{1+y}{y}\right] H + \left[\frac{y-c}{y}\right] n (1 - H) \ ,$$

where

y = One-half the yield;

H = Ratio of the present value of the annuity of the semiannual coupon payments to the price of the bond;

c = One-half the annual coupon *rate*.

From Chapter 3, the present value of the semiannual coupon payments is:

$$100 c \left[\frac{1 - \left[\frac{1}{(1 + y)^n}\right]}{y}\right] .$$

Illustration 11-1. We can use the formula above to calculate Macaulay duration for the 14% coupon bond with five years to maturity, selling to yield 10%, by inserting the values:

$$y = .05 \ (.10/2);$$
$$c = .07 \ (.14/2);$$
$$n = 10 \ (5 \times 2).$$

The price of this bond is 115.44 (see Exhibit 9-1 of Chapter 9). The present value of the coupon payments is:

$$\$100 \ (.07) \left[\frac{1 - \left[\frac{1}{(1.05)^{10}}\right]}{.05}\right] .$$

$$= \$7 \left[\frac{1 - .613913}{.05}\right]$$

$$= \$54.05.$$

Then,

$$H = \frac{\$54.05}{\$115.44} = .4682$$

---

[4] The mathematical proof is given in Frank J. Fabozzi, *Bond Markets, Analysis and Strategies* (Englewood Cliffs, NJ: Prentice-Hall, 1993, 2nd ed), pp. 70-71.

and

Macaulay duration (in six-month periods) =

$$\frac{1.05}{.05}(.4682) + \left[\frac{.05 - .07}{.05}\right](10)(1 - .4682)$$

$$= 21(.4682) + (-.40)(10)(.5318)$$
$$= 9.8322 - 2.1272$$
$$= 7.705.$$

Dividing by 2 to give Macaulay duration in years, we have 3.85. Notice that this agrees with the Macaulay duration calculated for this bond in Exhibit 11-2.

When a bond is selling at par, c is equal to y. The formula for Macaulay duration then reduces to

Macaulay duration for a bond selling at par (in six-month periods)

$$= \left[\frac{1+y}{y}\right]H.$$

Illustration 11-2. In the formula for the Macaulay duration for a bond selling at par, the numbers needed to calculate Macaulay duration for the 10% coupon bond with five years to maturity selling to yield 10% are

$$y = .05 \ (.10/2);$$
$$c = .05 \ (.10/2);$$
$$n = 10 \ (5 \times 2).$$

The present value of the coupon payments is:

$$\$100(.05)\left[\frac{1 - \left[\frac{1}{(1.05)^{10}}\right]}{.05}\right].$$

$$= \$5\left[\frac{1 - .613913}{.05}\right]$$

$$= \$38.61.$$

Then,

$$H = \frac{\$38.61}{\$100} = .3861$$

and

Macaulay duration (in six-month periods) =

$$= \frac{1.05}{.05}(.3861)$$

$$= 21(.3861)$$
$$= 8.1081.$$

Dividing by 2 gives 4.05, the Macaulay duration in years. This result agrees with the calculation of Macaulay duration in Exhibit 11-1.

For a zero-coupon bond, the present value of the coupon payments is obviously zero, thus H is zero. The Macaulay duration for a zero-coupon bond in six-month periods is

$$\left[\frac{1+y}{y}\right] H + \left[\frac{y-c}{y}\right] n\,(1-H)\;,$$

$$= \left[\frac{1+y}{y}\right] 0 + \left[\frac{y-0}{y}\right] n\,(1-0)\;,$$

$$= 0 + \left[\frac{y}{y}\right] n$$

$$= n.$$

Thus we see that the Macaulay duration of a zero-coupon bond in periods is just the number of six-month periods. Dividing by 2 gives the term of the bond in years.

Link Between Duration and Bond Price Volatility

Now that we know how to compute Macaulay duration, how do we interpret it? Some investors continue to think of duration in the context in which it was developed by Macaulay — as a measure of the length of time a bond investment is outstanding. Forget it! The significance and interpretation of Macaulay duration lie in its link to bond price volatility.

The link between bond price volatility and Macaulay duration can be shown to be as follows:[5]

Approximate percentage change in price =

$$-\left[\frac{1}{(1+y)}\right] \times \text{Macaulay duration} \times \text{Yield change,}$$

where y = One-half the yield to maturity.

Generally, the first two terms are combined, and the resulting measure is called *modified duration;* that is,

$$\text{Modified duration} = \frac{\text{Macaulay duration}}{(1+y)}\;.$$

---

[5] Mathematically, this relationship is derived from the first term of a Taylor series of the price function.

The relationship can then be expressed as

Approximate percentage change in price =
− Modified duration × Yield change.

Illustration 11-3. Consider the 8%, 15-year bond selling at 84.63 to yield 10%. The Macaulay duration for this bond is 8.45. Modified duration is 8.05:

$$\text{Modified duration} = \frac{8.45}{(1.05)} = 8.05$$

If the yield increases instantaneously from 10.00% to 10.10%, a yield change of +0.0010, the *approximate* percentage change in price is

$$- 8.05 \times (+.0010) = -.00805 = -.81\%.$$

Exhibit 9-4 in Chapter 9 shows that the actual percentage change in price is –0.80%. Similarly, if the yield decreases instantaneously from 10.00% to 9.90% (a 10-basis-point decrease), the approximate percentage change in price would be +0.81%. Exhibit 9-4 shows that the actual percentage price change would be +0.80%. This example illustrates that for small changes in yield, modified duration provides a good approximation of percentage change in price.

Illustration 11-4. Instead of a small change in yield, let's assume that yields increase by 300 basis points, from 10% to 13% (a yield change of +.03). The approximate percentage change in price estimated using modified duration would be:

$$- 8.05 \times (+.03) = - .2415 = 24.15\%$$

How good is this approximation? As can be seen from Exhibit 9-4 in Chapter 9, the actual percentage change in price is only –20.41%. Moreover, if the yield decreases by 300 basis points, from 10% to 7%, the approximate percentage change in price based on duration would be +24.15%, compared to an actual percentage change in price of +29.03%. Thus, not only is the approximation off, but we can see that modified duration estimates a symmetric percentage change in price, which, as we pointed out in Chapter 9, is not a property of the price/yield relationship for bonds.

Exhibit 11-3 shows the estimated percentage change in price using modified duration for our 12 hypothetical bonds. The difference between the actual percentage price change, as reported in Exhibit 9-4, and the estimated percentage change in price using modified duration, as reported in Exhibit 11-3, is shown in Exhibit 11-4. The property that we just illustrated — that modified duration gives a good estimate of the percentage price change for small changes in yield but a poor estimate for large changes — can be seen in Exhibit 11-4. The percentage price change not explained by modified duration increases, the greater the change in yield. For some bonds, however, the approximation is in error by less than others. For example, for the 14%, 30-year bond, the unexplained percentage price change for a 300-basis-point increase is 5.5%, while for the zero-coupon bond of the same maturity it is 28.41%.

Exhibit 11–3

Percentage Change in Price Estimated Using Modified Duration

			Yield change (in basis points) from 10%					
			1	10	50	100	200	300
					New yield level			
Coupon	Term (years)	Modified duration (years)	10.01%	10.10%	10.50%	11.00%	12.00%	13.00%
.00%	5	4.76	-.05%	-.48%	-2.38%	-4.76%	-9.52%	-14.28%
.00%	15	14.29	-.14	-1.43	-7.15	-14.29	-28.58	-42.87
.00%	30	28.57	-.29	-2.86	-14.29	-28.57	-57.14	-85.71
8.00%	5	3.98	-.04	-.40	-1.99	-3.98	-7.96	-11.94
8.00%	15	8.05	-.08	-.81	-4.03	-8.05	-16.10	-24.15
8.00%	30	9.72	-.10	-.97	-4.86	-9.72	-19.44	-29.16
10.00%	5	3.86	-.04	-.39	-1.93	-3.86	-7.72	-11.58
10.00%	15	7.69	-.08	-.77	-3.85	-7.69	-15.38	-23.07
10.00%	30	9.46	-.09	-.95	-4.73	-9.46	-18.92	-28.38
14.00%	5	3.67	-.04	-.37	-1.84	-3.67	-7.34	-11.01
14.00%	15	7.22	-.07	-.72	-3.61	-7.22	-14.44	-21.66
14.00%	30	9.17	-.09	-.92	-4.59	-9.17	-18.34	-27.51

Exhibit 11-3 continued.

Coupon	Term (years)	Modified duration (years)	Yield change (in basis points) from 10%					
			−1	−10	−50	−100	−200	−300
			New yield level					
			9.99%	9.90%	9.50%	9.00%	8.00%	7.00%
.00%	5	4.76	.05%	.48%	2.38%	4.76%	9.52%	14.28%
.00%	15	14.29	.14	1.43	7.15	14.29	28.58	42.87
.00%	30	28.57	.29	2.86	14.29	28.57	57.14	85.71
8.00%	5	3.98	.04	.40	1.99	3.98	7.96	11.94
8.00%	15	8.05	.08	.81	4.03	8.05	16.10	24.15
8.00%	30	9.72	.10	.97	4.86	9.72	19.44	29.16
10.00%	5	3.86	.04	.39	1.93	3.86	7.72	11.58
10.00%	15	7.69	.08	.77	3.85	7.69	15.38	23.07
10.00%	30	9.46	.09	.95	4.73	9.46	18.92	28.38
14.00%	5	3.67	.04	.37	1.84	3.67	7.34	11.01
14.00%	15	7.22	.07	.72	3.61	7.22	14.44	21.66
14.00%	30	9.17	.09	.92	4.59	9.17	18.34	27.51

Exhibit 11-4

Percentage Price Change Not Explained by Modified Duration

Coupon	Term (years)	Modified duration (years)	Yield change (in basis points) from 10% — New yield level					
			1	10	50	100	200	300
			10.01%	10.10%	10.50%	11.00%	12.00%	13.00%
.00%	5	4.76	.00%	.00%	.03%	.12%	.48%	1.06%
.00%	15	14.29	.00	.01	.26	1.01	3.83	8.21
.00%	30	28.57	.00	.04	.99	3.77	13.76	28.41
8.00%	5	3.98	.00	.00	.02	.10	.38	.83
8.00%	15	8.05	.00	.00	.12	.45	1.73	3.74
8.00%	30	9.72	.00	.01	.20	.78	2.92	6.15
10.00%	5	3.86	.00	.00	.02	.09	.36	.80
10.00%	15	7.69	.00	.00	.11	.42	1.62	3.48
10.00%	30	9.46	.00	.01	.19	.74	2.76	5.83
14.00%	5	3.67	.00	.00	.02	.09	.34	.75
14.00%	15	7.22	.00	.00	.10	.38	1.45	3.14
14.00%	30	9.17	.00	.01	.18	.69	2.60	5.50

Exhibit 11-4 continued.

Coupon	Term (years)	Modified duration (years)	−1 9.99%	−10 9.90%	−50 9.50%	−100 9.00%	−200 8.00%	−300 7.00%
					New yield level			
.00%	5	4.76	.00%	.00%	.03%	.13%	.52%	1.20%
.00%	15	14.29	.00	.01	.27	1.11	4.67	11.11
.00%	30	28.57	.00	.04	1.09	4.59	20.43	51.39
8.00%	5	3.98	.00	.00	.03	.10	.41	.93
8.00%	15	8.05	.00	.00	.12	.49	2.06	4.88
8.00%	30	9.72	.00	.01	.22	.90	3.91	9.57
10.00%	5	3.86	.00	.00	.02	.10	.39	.89
10.00%	15	7.69	.00	.00	.11	.45	1.91	4.52
10.00%	30	9.46	.00	.01	.21	.86	3.70	9.04
14.00%	5	3.67	.00	.00	.02	.09	.36	.83
14.00%	15	7.22	.00	.00	.10	.41	1.72	4.06
14.00%	30	9.17	.00	.01	.19	.79	3.43	8.36

Yield change (in basis points) from 10%

The reason that modified duration provides a good approximation for small changes in yield but a poor approximation for large changes in yield lies in the convex shape of the price/yield relationship. This point is examined fully in the next chapter.

Modified Duration as a Measure of Percentage Price Change Per 100-Basis-Point Yield Change

For a 100-basis-point change in yield, the percentage change in the bond's price is

$$\text{Modified duration} \times (.01).$$

For example, if the modified duration is 6, the approximate percentage change in the bond's price for a 100-basis-point change in yield is

$$6 \times (.01) = .06 \text{ or } 6\%.$$

Thus, a bond with a modified duration of 6 would change by approximately 6% for a 100-basis-point (1%) change in yield. Similarly, a bond with a modified duration of X would change by approximately $X\%$ for a 100-basis-point change in yield. For this reason, some investors refer to modified duration as the percentage price change of a bond per 100-basis-point change in yield. So, for example, a bond with a modified duration of 5.4 will change by approximately 5.4% for a 100-basis-point change in yield. For a 50-basis-point change in yield, the percentage price change would then be half of 5.4%, or 2.7%. For a 10-basis-point change in yield, the percentage price change would be one-tenth of 5.4%, or .54%.

Dollar Duration

The modified duration of a bond can be used to approximate the percentage change in the price of the bond per basis point change. Given the initial price of the bond and the approximate percentage change in price based on modified duration, the dollar price change can be computed. Alternatively, the dollar price change per $100 of par value can be computed as follows:

$$\text{Approximate dollar price change} =$$
$$- (\text{Modified duration}) \times (\text{Initial price}) \times (\text{Yield change}).$$

The product of modified duration and the initial price is called *dollar duration*; that is,

$$\text{Dollar duration} = \text{Modified duration} \times \text{Initial price}.$$

Therefore,

$$\text{Approximate dollar price change} =$$
$$- (\text{Dollar duration}) \times (\text{Yield change}).$$

For example, suppose that the yield for the 8%, 15-year bond selling to yield 10% (price equal to $84.6275) increases by one basis point; then the approximate price change is as follows:

$$\text{Dollar duration} = \text{Modified duration} \times \text{Initial price}$$
$$= 8.05 \times \$84.6275$$
$$= \$681.25$$

$$\text{Approximate dollar price change} = -681.25 \times .0001$$
$$= .0681$$

It should be noted that there is no standard terminology used for dollar duration. More specifically, some market participants refer to "dollar duration" when they mean the "dollar duration of a basis point." In our example, the dollar duration would then be .0681, since this is the dollar duration of one basis point. The dollar duration of a basis point is equivalent to the price value of a basis point that we discussed in the previous chapter. Some market participants refer to the dollar duration in terms of the dollar duration of 100 basis points. In our example, the dollar duration would then be 6.81.

How good an estimate of the dollar price change is given by dollar duration? For small changes in yield, it will be good, as we saw in Illustration 11-3, where modified duration is used to estimate the percentage price change. For large changes in yield, the approximation is not as good. Recall from Illustration 11-4 that when the yield increases by 300 basis points, the estimated percentage decline in price is greater than the actual decline in price. This means that the estimated dollar price decline will be greater than the actual price decline, so that the estimated new price is less than the actual price at a higher yield. Also in Illustration 11-4, the estimated percentage price increase is less than the actual price increase when yield declines by 300 basis points. The actual price increase, therefore, is underestimated using modified duration, and the estimated price at a lower yield will be less than the actual price. Thus, whether the yield rises or falls by a large number of basis points, modified duration and dollar duration will underestimate what the new price will be. A graphical explanation for this fact is given in the next chapter.

Portfolio Duration

A portfolio's modified duration can be obtained by calculating the weighted average of the modified duration of the bonds in the portfolio. The weight is the proportion of the portfolio that a security comprises. Mathematically, a portfolio's modified duration can be calculated as follows:

$$w_1 D_1 + w_2 D_2 + w_3 D_3 + \ldots + w_K D_K$$

where
w_i = Market value of bond i/market value of the portfolio;
D_i = Modified duration of bond i;
K = Number of bonds in the portfolio.

To illustrate this calculation, consider the three-bond portfolio used in the previous chapter to demonstrate how to calculate the price value of a basis point for a portfolio:

Bond	Par amount owned	Price
10%, 5-year	$4 million	$4,000,000
8%, 15-year	5 million	4,231,375
14%, 30-year	1 million	1,378,586

This illustration assumes that the next coupon payment for each bond is six months from now. The market value for the portfolio is $9,609,961. The market price per $100 value of each bond, its yield to maturity, and its modified duration are as follows:

Bond	Price	Yield to Maturity	Modified duration
10%, 5-year	100.0000	10%	3.861
8%, 15-year	84.6275	10%	8.047
14%, 30-year	137.8590	10%	9.168

In this illustration, K is equal to 3, and:

$w_1 = 4,000,000/9,609,961 = .416$ $D_1 = 3.861$
$w_2 = 4,231,375/9,609,961 = .440$ $D_2 = 8.047$
$w_3 = 1,378,586/9,609,961 = .144$ $D_3 = 9.168$

The portfolio's modified duration is:

$$.416 \,(3.861) + .440 \,(8.047) + .144 \,(9.168) = 6.47$$

A portfolio modified duration of 6.47 means that for a 100-basis-point change in the yield for *all* three bonds, the market value of the portfolio will change by approximately 6.47%. But keep in mind that the yield on all three bonds must change by 100 basis points for the modified duration measure to be useful. This is a critical assumption and its importance can not be overemphasized. We shall return to this point in Chapter 14.

In the previous chapter, we calculated the price value of a basis point for this three-bond portfolio and found it to be $6,212. Since the dollar duration for a one-basis-point change in yield will be the same as the price value of a basis point, let's see if this is true when we use our dollar duration formula. The dollar duration for the portfolio is:

Portfolio dollar duration =

Portfolio modified duration × Initial portfolio market value

= 6.47 × 9,609,961

= 62,176,447

The approximate dollar price change of the portfolio per one-basis- point change in yield is found by multiplying the portfolio dollar duration by .0001; that is:

Approximate dollar price change of portfolio per
one-basis-point change in yield

= 62,176,447 × .0001 = 6,218

This agrees with our calculation for the price value of a basis point (the difference of $6 is due to rounding).

Portfolio Duration for a Global Portfolio

Many global money managers calculate a portfolio duration for a portfolio consisting of bonds with cash flows denominated in several currencies. For example, a U.S. portfolio manager who has a portfolio of U.S. Treasury securities denominated in U.S. dollars, German government bonds denominated in deutschemarks, Japanese government bonds denominated in yen, and French government bonds denominated in francs might calculate a Macaulay duration and a modified duration for the portfolio. The question is what does a portfolio modified duration in such cases mean?

Since modified duration is a measure of the percentage price volatility of a bond to changes in yield, what yield is modified duration measuring price sensitivity to? U.S. yields, German yields, Japanese yields, or French yields? There is no answer to this question. Using the modified duration measure as discussed thus far in this chapter for a global portfolio is of questionable value.

Approximating Duration

Since modified duration is a measure of the price sensitivity of a bond to interest rate changes, it can be approximated by simply changing yields by a small amount up and down, and then looking at how the price changes. More specifically, the modified duration can be approximated using the formula:

$$= \frac{P_- - P_+}{(P_0)(y_+ - y_-)}$$

where
    P_- = *Price if yield is decreased by* x basis points;
    P_+ = Price if yield is increased by x basis points;
    P_0 = Initial price (per $100 of par value);
    y_+ = Initial yield plus x basis points;
    y_- = Initial yield minus x basis points.

To illustrate this formula for approximating modified duration, consider a 20-year, 7% coupon bond selling at $74.26 to yield 10%. Suppose we evaluate the price changes for a 20-basis-point change up and down. Then,

    P_- = 75.64
    P_+ = 72.92
    P_0 = 74.26
    y_+ = .102
    y_- = .098

then substituting into the formula:

$$\frac{75.64 - 72.92}{(74.26)\,(.102 - .098)} = 9.16$$

The modified duration for this bond calculated using the formula presented earlier is 9.18.

Effective Duration

The approximation formula above is important when we analyze bonds that are not option-free in later chapters; that is, when the bonds are putable or callable. Modified duration is not a good measure of the price sensitivity of such bonds to yield changes because it assumes that yield changes will not change the expected cash flows of a bond. For example, when a bond is callable, a decline in market yields may change the expected cash flows of the bond since it may increase the likelihood that the bond is called. In the case of mortgage-backed securities – the subject of Part VI of this book – a change in market yields will change prepayments of borrowers.

In such instances where the cash flow is interest-rate sensitive (interest-rate dependent), the price sensitivity of a bond to yield changes must take into consideration how yield changes affect the expected cash flows and, in turn, the price of a bond. A duration measure that does allow for changes in cash flows as yields change is called an *effective duration*. The formula we gave above for approximating the modified duration is the formula that is used to calculate the effective duration of a bond. We shall see how this formula is used for bonds with interest-rate sensitive cash flows in later chapters.

Applications

Using Dollar Duration to Compute the Hedge Ratio

Modified duration is related to percentage price volatility. As explained in the previous chapter, in hedging we are interested in dollar price changes. Consequently, to compute the hedge ratio using duration, dollar duration should be used, not modified duration. The hedge ratio is computed from dollar duration as follows:

$$\frac{\text{Dollar duration for bond be hedged}}{\text{Dollar duration for hedging vehicle}} \times \text{Yield beta.}$$

Recall that the dollar duration per basis point per $100 of par value is the same as the price value of a basis point. Therefore, dollar duration will produce the same hedge ratio as the price value of a basis point.

Role of Duration in Immunization Strategies

In Chapter 7, we explained that the return that is realized by investing in a coupon security will depend on the interest rate earned on the reinvestment of the coupon payments. When interest rates rise, interest on interest from the reinvestment of the coupon payments will be higher, but if the investment horizon is shorter than the maturity of the bond, a loss will be realized upon the sale of the bond. The reverse is true if interest rates fall: price appreciation will be realized when the bond is sold, but interest on interest from reinvesting the coupon payments will be lower. Because of these two risks, the investor cannot be assured of locking in the yield at the time of purchase.

Because the interest rate risk and reinvestment risk offset each other, however, is it possible to select a bond or bond portfolio that will lock in the yield at the time of purchase regardless of interest rate changes in the future? That is, is it possible to *immunize* the bond or bond portfolio against interest rate changes? Fortunately, under certain circumstances, it is. This can be accomplished by constructing a portfolio so that its Macaulay duration is equal to the length of the investment horizon. Thus, a portfolio manager with an investment horizon of five years who wants to lock in a return over that time period should select a portfolio with a Macaulay duration of five years. This is demonstrated using an example.

Suppose a portfolio manager knows that a liability of $17,183,033 must be paid in 5.5 years. Also suppose that interest rates are currently 12.5% on a bond equivalent basis. The present value of the $17,183,033 liability 5.5 years from now assuming interest can be earned at a rate of 6.25% per six-month period is $8,820,262. Thus, if the portfolio manager invested $8,820,262 at the current rate of 6.25% per six-month period for the next 11 six-month periods, the accumulated value would be sufficient to satisfy the liability.

Suppose the portfolio manager buys $8,820,262 par value of a bond selling at par with a 12.5% yield to maturity that matures in 5.5 years. The Macaulay duration for this bond is 4.14 years, which is shorter than the length of the investment horizon. Will the portfolio manager be assured of realizing the target yield of 12.5% or, equivalently, a target accumulated value of $17,183,033? As we explained in Chapter 6, the portfolio manager will realize a 12.5% yield only if the coupon interest payments can be reinvested at 6.25% every six months. That is, the accumulated value will depend on the reinvestment rate.

To illustrate this, suppose that immediately after investing the $8,820,262 in the 12.5% coupon, 5.5-year maturity bond, yields in the market change and stay at the new level for the remainder of the 5.5 years. Exhibit 11-5 illustrates what happens at the end of 5.5 years. The first column shows the new yield. The second column shows the total coupon interest payments. The third column gives the interest on interest over the entire 5.5 years if the coupon interest payments are reinvested at the new yield shown in the first column. The price of the bond at the end of 5.5 years, shown in the fourth column, is the par value. The fifth column is the accumulated value from all three sources: coupon interest, interest on interest, and price of bond. The total return is shown in the last column.

When yields do not change, so that the coupon payments can be reinvested at 12.5% (6.25% every six months), the target accumulated value will be achieved by the portfolio manager. If market yields rise, an accumulated value (total return) higher than the target accumulated value (target yield) will be achieved, because the coupon interest payments can be reinvested at a rate higher than the initial yield to maturity. Contrast this circumstance with what happens when the yield declines. The accumulated value (total return) will be less than the target accumulated value (target yield). *Therefore, investing*

Exhibit 11–5

Accumulated Value and Total Return:
5.5-year, 12.5% Coupon Bond Selling to Yield 12.5%

Investment horizon (years)	5.5
Coupon rate	12.5%
Maturity (years)	5.50
Yield to maturity	12.5%
Price	100.00000
Par value purchased	$8,820,262
Purchase price	$8,820,262
Target accumulated value	$17,183,033

New yield	Coupon	Interest on interest	Over 5.5 years Price of bond	Accumulated value	Total return
16.0%	$6,063,930	$3,112,167	$8,820,262	$17,996,360	13.40%
15.5	6,063,930	2,990,716	8,820,262	17,874,908	13.26
14.5	6,063,930	2,753,177	8,820,262	17,637,369	13.00
14.0	6,063,930	2,637,037	8,820,262	17,521,230	12.88
13.5	6,063,930	2,522,618	8,820,262	17,406,810	12.75

Exhibit 11–5 continued.

Over 5.5 years

New yield	Coupon	Interest on interest	Price of bond	Accumulated value	Total return
13.0	6,063,930	2,409,894	8,820,262	17,294,086	12.62
12.5	6,063,930	2,298,840	8,820,262	17,183,033	12.50
12.0	6,063,930	2,189,433	8,820,262	17,073,625	12.38
11.5	6,063,930	2,081,648	8,820,262	16,965,840	12.25
11.0	6,063,930	1,975,462	8,820,262	16,859,654	12.13
10.5	6,063,930	1,870,852	8,820,262	16,755,044	12.01
10.0	6,063,930	1,767,794	8,820,262	16,651,986	11.89
9.5	6,063,930	1,666,266	8,820,262	16,550,458	11.78
9.0	6,063,930	1,566,246	8,820,262	16,450,438	11.66
8.5	6,063,930	1,476,712	8,820,262	16,351,904	11.54
8.0	6,063,930	1,370,642	8,820,262	16,254,834	11.43
7.5	6,063,930	1,275,014	8,820,262	16,159,206	11.32
7.0	6,063,930	1,180,808	8,820,262	16,065,000	11.20
6.5	6,063,930	1,088,003	8,820,262	15,972,195	11.09
6.0	6,063,930	996,577	8,820,262	15,880,769	10.98
5.5	6,063,930	906,511	8,820,262	15,790,703	10.87
5.0	6,063,930	817,785	8,820,262	15,701,977	10.77

in a coupon bond with a yield to maturity equal to the target yield and a maturity equal to the investment horizon does not assure that the target accumulated value will be achieved.

Suppose that instead of investing in a bond maturing in 5.5 years, the portfolio manager invests in a 15-year bond with a coupon rate of 12.5% and selling at par to yield 12.5%. The Macaulay duration for this bond is 7.12 years, which is longer than the 5.5-year investment horizon. The accumulated value and total return if the market yield changes immediately after the bond is purchased and remains at the new yield are presented in Exhibit 11-6. The fourth column in Exhibit 11-6 is the market price of a 12.5% coupon, 9.5-year bond (since 5.5 years have passed), assuming that the market yield is as shown in the first column. If the market yield increases, the portfolio will fail to achieve the target accumulated value; the opposite is true if the market yield decreases – the accumulated value (total return) will exceed the target accumulated value (target yield).

The reason for this result can be seen in Exhibit 11-7, which summarizes the change in interest on interest and the change in price resulting from a change in the market yield. For example, if the market yield rises instantaneously by 200 basis points, from 12.5% to 14.5%, interest on interest will be $454,336 greater; the market price of the bond, however, will decrease by $894,781. The net effect is that the accumulated value will be $440,445 less than the target accumulated value. The reverse is true if the market yield decreases: the change in the price of the bond will more than offset the decline in the interest on interest, resulting in an accumulated value that exceeds the target accumulated value. Exhibit 11-7 clearly demonstrates the trade-off between interest rate (or price) risk and reinvestment risk.

Consider an 8-year, 10.125% coupon bond selling at 88.20262 to yield 12.5%, which has a Macaulay duration of 5.5 years. Suppose $10,000,000 of par value of this bond is purchased for $8,820,262. For this bond, Exhibit 11-8 provides the same information as Exhibits 11-5 and 11-6. Looking at the last two columns, we see that the accumulated value and the total return are never less than the target accumulated value and the target yield. Thus, the target accumulated value is assured regardless of what happens to the market yield. Exhibit 11-9 shows why. When the market yield rises, the change in the interest on interest more than offsets the decline in price. On the other hand, when the market yield declines, the increase in price exceeds the decline in interest on interest.

Notice that the last bond, which assures that the target accumulated value will be achieved regardless of what happens to the market yield, has a Macaulay duration equal to the length of the investment horizon. This is the key. To immunize a portfolio's target accumulated value (target yield) against a change in the market yield, a portfolio manager must invest in a bond (or a bond portfolio) such that (1) the Macaulay duration is equal to the investment horizon,[6] and (2) the present value of the cash flow from the bond (or bond portfolio) equals the present value of the liability.

---

[6] This is equivalent to equating the modified duration of the portfolio to the modified duration of the investment horizon. This is because the Macaulay duration of the liability is the length of the investment horizon and dividing by one plus one-half the yield to maturity gives a

Exhibit 11-6

Accumulated Value and Total Return:
15-year, 12.5% Coupon Bond Selling to Yield 12.5%

Investment horizon (years)	5.5
Coupon rate	12.5%
Maturity (years)	15
Yield to maturity	12.5%
Price	100.00000
Par value purchased	$8,820,262
Purchase price	$8,820,262
Target accumulated value	$17,183,033

		Over 5.5 years		
New yield	Coupon	Interest on interest	Price of bond	Accumulated value	Total return
16.0%	$6,063,930	$3,112,167	$7,337,902	$16,514,000	11.73%
15.5	6,063,930	2,990,716	7,526,488	16,581,134	11.81
14.5	6,063,930	2,753,177	7,925,481	16,742,587	12.00
14.0	6,063,930	2,637,037	8,136,542	16,837,510	12.11
13.5	6,063,930	2,522,618	8,355,777	16,942,325	12.23

Exhibit 11-6 continued.

			Over 5.5 years		
New yield	Coupon	Interest on interest	Price of bond	Accumulated value	Total return
13.0	6,063,930	2,409,894	8,583,555	17,057,379	12.36
12.5	6,063,930	2,298,840	8,820,262	17,183,033	12.50
12.0	6,063,930	2,189,433	9,066,306	17,319,669	12.65
11.5	6,063,930	2,081,648	9,322,113	17,467,691	12.82
11.0	6,063,930	1,975,462	9,588,131	17,627,523	12.99
10.5	6,063,930	1,870,852	9,864,831	17,799,613	13.18
10.0	6,063,930	1,767,794	10,152,708	17,984,432	13.38
9.5	6,063,930	1,666,266	10,452,281	18,182,477	13.59
9.0	6,063,930	1,566,246	10,764,095	18,394,271	13.82
8.5	6,063,930	1,467,712	11,088,723	18,620,366	14.06
8.0	6,063,930	1,370,642	11,426,770	18,861,342	14.31
7.5	6,063,930	1,275,014	11,778,867	19,117,812	14.57
7.0	6,063,930	1,180,808	12,145,682	19,390,420	14.85
6.5	6,063,930	1,088,003	12,527,914	19,679,847	15.14
6.0	6,063,930	996,577	12,926,301	19,986,808	15.44
5.5	6,063,930	906,511	13,341,617	20,312,058	15.76
5.0	6,063,930	817,785	13,774,677	20,656,393	16.09

Exhibit 11-7

Change in Interest on Interest and Price Due
to Interest Rate Change:
15-Year, 12.5% Coupon Bond Selling to Yield 12.5%

New yield	Change in interest on interest	Change in price	Total change in accumulated value
16.0%	$813,327	−$1,482,360	−$669,033
15.5	691,875	−1,293,774	−601,898
14.5	454,336	−894,781	−440,445
14.0	338,197	−683,720	−345,523
13.5	223,778	−464,485	−240,707
13.0	111,054	−236,707	−125,654
12.5	0	0	0
12.0	−109,407	246,044	136,636
11.5	−217,192	501,851	284,659
11.0	−323,378	767,869	444,491
10.5	−427,989	1,044,569	616,581
10.0	−531,046	1,332,446	801,400
9.5	−632,574	1,632,019	999,445
9.0	−732,594	1,943,833	1,211,239
8.5	−831,128	2,268,461	1,437,333
8.0	−928,198	2,606,508	1,678,309
7.5	−1,023,826	2,958,605	1,934,779
7.0	−1,118,032	3,325,420	2,207,388
6.5	−1,210,838	3,707,652	2,496,814
6.0	−1,302,263	4,106,039	2,803,776
5.5	−1,392,329	4,521,355	3,129,026
5.0	−1,481,055	4,954,415	3,473,360

Exhibit 11–8

Accumulated Value and Total Return:
8-year, 10.125% Coupon Bond Selling to Yield 12.5%

Investment horizon (years)	5.5
Coupon rate	10.125%
Maturity (years)	8
Yield to maturity	12.5%
Price	88.20262
Par value purchased	$10,000,000
Purchase price	$8,820,262
Target accumulated value	$17,183,033

Over 5.5 years

New yield	Coupon	Interest on interest	Price of bond	Accumulated value	Total return
16.0%	$5,568,750	$2,858,028	$8,827,141	$17,253,919	12.58%
15.5	5,568,750	2,746,494	8,919,852	17,235,096	12.56
14.5	5,568,750	2,528,352	9,109,054	17,206,156	12.53
14.0	5,568,750	2,421,697	9,205,587	17,196,034	12.51
13.5	5,568,750	2,316,621	9,303,435	17,188,807	12.51

Exhibit 11–8 continued.

Over 5.5 years

New yield	Coupon	Interest on interest	Price of bond	Accumulated value	Total return
13.0	5,568,750	2,213,102	9,402,621	17,184,473	12.50
12.5	5,568,750	2,111,117	9,503,166	17,183,033	12.50
12.0	5,568,750	2,010,644	9,605,091	17,184,485	12.50
11.5	5,568,750	1,911,661	9,708,420	17,188,831	12.51
11.0	5,568,750	1,814,146	9,813,175	17,196,071	12.51
10.5	5,568,750	1,718,078	9,919,380	17,206,208	12.53
10.0	5,568,750	1,623,436	10,027,059	17,219,245	12.54
9.5	5,568,750	1,530,199	10,136,236	17,235,185	12.56
9.0	5,568,750	1,438,347	10,246,936	17,254,033	12.58
8.5	5,568,750	1,347,859	10,359,184	17,275,793	12.60
8.0	5,568,750	1,258,715	10,473,006	17,300,472	12.63
7.5	5,568,750	1,170,897	10,588,428	17,328,075	12.66
7.0	5,568,750	1,084,383	10,705,477	17,358,610	12.70
6.5	5,568,750	999,156	10,824,180	17,392,086	12.73
6.0	5,568,750	915,197	10,944,565	17,428,511	12.77
5.5	5,568,750	832,486	11,066,660	17,467,895	12.82
5.0	5,568,750	751,005	11,190,494	17,510,248	12.86

Exhibit 11-9

Change in Interest on Interest and Price Due
to Interest Rate Change:
8-Year, 10.125% Coupon Bond Selling to Yield 12.5%

New yield	Change in interest on interest	Change in price	Total change in accumulated value
16.0%	$746,911	-$676,024	$70,887
15.5	635,377	-583,314	52,063
14.5	417,235	-394,112	23,123
14.0	310,580	-297,579	13,001
13.5	205,504	-199,730	5,774
13.0	101,985	-100,544	1,441
12.5	0	0	0
12.0	-100,473	101,925	1,452
11.5	-199,456	205,254	5,798
11.0	-296,971	310,010	13,038
10.5	-393,039	416,215	23,176
10.0	-487,681	523,894	36,212
9.5	-580,918	633,071	52,153
9.0	-672,770	743,771	71,000
8.5	-763,258	856,019	92,760
8.0	-852,402	969,841	117,439
7.5	-940,221	1,085,263	145,042
7.0	-1,026,734	1,202,311	175,578
6.5	-1,111,961	1,321,014	209,053
6.0	-1,195,921	1,441,399	245,478
5.5	-1,278,632	1,563,494	284,862
5.0	-1,360,112	1,687,328	327,216

In this example, we assumed a one-time instantaneous change in the market yield. In practice, the market yield will fluctuate over the investment horizon. As a result, the Macaulay duration of the portfolio will change as the market yield changes. In addition, the Macaulay duration will change with the passage of time. In the face of changing market yields, a manager can still immunize a portfolio by rebalancing it so that the Macaulay duration of the portfolio is equal to the remainder of the investment horizon. For example, if the investment horizon is initially 5.5 years, the initial portfolio should have a Macaulay duration of 5.5 years. After six months, the remaining investment horizon is five years. The Macaulay duration then will probably be different from five years. Thus the portfolio must be rebalanced so that its Macaulay duration is equal to five years. Six months later, the portfolio must be rebalanced so that its Macaulay duration is equal to 4.5 years, etc.

Constructing a portfolio so that its Macaulay duration is equal to the investment horizon will assure that the target yield will be realized only if the yields on all bonds change by the same amount. For example, if short-term yields fall but long-term yields rise, then the offsetting of interest rate risk and reinvestment risk by matching duration will not work. A decline in short-term yields will reduce reinvestment income, while a rise in long-term rates will result in a capital loss of bonds with a maturity greater than the investment horizon. This risk of failing to immunize can be reduced, however.[7]

Duration of an Interest Rate Swap

An interest rate swap is an agreement whereby two parties (called counterparties) agree to exchange periodic interest payments. The dollar amount of the interest payments exchanged is based on some predetermined dollar principal, which is called the *notional principal amount*. The dollar amount each counterparty pays to the other is the agreed-upon periodic interest rate times the notional principal amount. The only dollars that are exchanged between the parties are the interest payments, not the notional principal amount. In the most common type of swap, one party agrees to pay the other party fixed interest payments at designated dates for the life of the contract. This party is referred to as the *fixed-rate payer*. The other party agrees to make interest rate payments that float with some reference rate and is referred to as the *floating-rate payer*.

For example, suppose that for the next five years party X agrees to pay party Y 10% per year, while party Y agrees to pay party X six-month LIBOR. Party X is a fixed-rate payer/floating-rate receiver, while party Y is a floating-rate payer/fixed-rate receiver. Assume that the notional principal amount is $50 million, and that payments are exchanged every six months for the next five years. This means that every six months, party

---

[7] See H. Gifford Fong and Oldrich Vasicek, "A Risk Minimizing Strategy for Multiple Liability Immunization," *Journal of Finance* (December 1984), pp. 1541-1546. For a less technical description, see: H. Gifford Fong and Frank J. Fabozzi, *Fixed Income Portfolio Management* (Homewood, Ill.: Dow Jones-Irwin, 1985), pp. 133-136.

X (the fixed-rate payer/floating-rate receiver) will pay party Y \$2.5 million (10% times \$50 million divided by 2). The amount that party Y (the floating-rate payer/fixed-rate receiver) will pay party X will be six-month LIBOR times \$50 million divided by 2. For example, if six-month LIBOR is 7%, party Y will pay party X \$1.75 million (7% times \$50 million divided by 2). Note that we divide by two because one-half year's interest is being paid.

Interest rate benchmarks commonly used for the floating rate in an interest rate swap are those on various money market instruments: Treasury bills, London Interbank Offered Rate (LIBOR), commercial paper, bankers acceptance, certificates of deposit, federal funds rate, and prime rate.

One way to interpret an interest rate swap position is as a package of cash flows from buying and selling cash market instruments. To understand why, consider the following. Suppose that an investor enters into the following transaction:

- buys a \$50 million par of a five-year floating-rate bond that pays six-month LIBOR every six months

- finances the purchase of the five-year floating-rate bond by borrowing \$50 million for five years with the following terms: 10% annual interest rate paid every six months.

The cash flow of this transaction is presented in Exhibit 11-10. The second column of the exhibit sets out the cash flow from purchasing the five-year floating-rate bond. There is a \$50 million cash outlay and then cash inflows. The amount of the cash inflows is uncertain because they depend on future LIBOR. The third column shows the cash flow from borrowing \$50 million on a fixed-rate basis. The last column shows the net cash flow from the entire transaction. As can be seen in the last column, there is no initial cash flow (no cash inflow or cash outlay). In all 10 six-month periods the net position results in a cash inflow of LIBOR and a cash outlay of \$2.5 million. This net position, however, is identical to the position of a fixed-rate payer/floating-rate receiver.

It can be seen from the net cash flow in Exhibit 11-10 that a fixed-rate payer has a cash market position that is equivalent to a long position in a floating-rate bond and borrowing the funds to purchase the floating-rate bond on a fixed-rate basis. But the borrowing can be viewed as issuing a fixed-rate bond, or equivalently, being short a fixed-rate bond. Consequently, the position of a fixed-rate payer can be viewed as being long a floating-rate bond and short a fixed-rate bond.

What about the position of a floating-rate payer? It can be easily demonstrated that the position of a floating-rate payer is equivalent to purchasing a fixed-rate bond and financing that purchase at a floating rate, with the floating rate being the reference interest rate for the swap. That is, the position of a floating-rate payer is equivalent to a long position in a fixed-rate bond and a short position in a floating-rate bond.

As with any fixed-income contract, the dollar value of a swap will change as interest rates change. Duration is a measure of the sensitivity of a bond's price to a change in interest rates. From the perspective of the party who pays floating and receives fixed, the position can be viewed as follows:

long a fixed-rate bond + short a floating-rate bond

Exhibit 11-10

Cash Flow for the Purchase of a Five-Year Floating-Rate Bond Financed by Borrowing on a Fixed-Rate Basis

Transaction: Purchase for $50 million a five-year floating-rate bond: floating rate = LIBOR, semiannual pay

                        Borrow $50 million for five years: fixed rate = 10%, semiannual payments

Cash flow (in millions of dollars) from:

Six-month period	Floating-rate bond	Borrowing cost	Net
0	−$ 50	+$50.0	$0
1	+(LIBOR$_1$/2) × 50	− 2.5	+(LIBOR$_1$/2) × 50 − 2.5
2	+(LIBOR$_2$/2) × 50	− 2.5	+(LIBOR$_2$/2) × 50 − 2.5
3	+(LIBOR$_3$/2) × 50	− 2.5	+(LIBOR$_3$/2) × 50 − 2.5
4	+(LIBOR$_4$/2) × 50	− 2.5	+(LIBOR$_4$/2) × 50 − 2.5
5	+(LIBOR$_5$/2) × 50	− 2.5	+(LIBOR$_5$/2) × 50 − 2.5
6	+(LIBOR$_6$/2) × 50	− 2.5	+(LIBOR$_6$/2) × 50 − 2.5
7	+(LIBOR$_7$/2) × 50	− 2.5	+(LIBOR$_7$/2) × 50 − 2.5
8	+(LIBOR$_8$/2) × 50	− 2.5	+(LIBOR$_8$/2) × 50 − 2.5
9	+(LIBOR$_9$/2) × 50	− 2.5	+(LIBOR$_9$/2) × 50 − 2.5
10	+(LIBOR$_{10}$/2) × 50 + 50	− 52.5	+(LIBOR$_{10}$/2) × 50 − 2.5

Note: The subscript for LIBOR indicates the six-month LIBOR as per the terms of the floating-rate bond at time *t*.

This means that the duration of an interest rate swap from the perspective of a floating-rate payer is just the difference between the duration of the two bond positions that make up the swap. That is,

Duration of a swap =

      Duration of a fixed-rate bond − Duration of a floating-rate bond

Most of the interest rate sensitivity of a swap will result from the duration of the fixed-rate bond since the duration of the floating-rate bond will be small. It will always be less than the length of time to the next reset date. Therefore, the duration of a floating-rate bond for which the coupon rate resets every six months will be less than six months. The duration of a floating-rate bond is smaller, the closer the swap is to its reset date.

Summary

In this chapter we have discussed a popular measure of price volatility called duration. Macaulay duration is related to price volatility and is commonly used as some measure of the weighted average life of a bond. Modified duration is the approximate percentage price change of a bond for a 100-basis-point change in interest rates. Dollar duration is a measure of the dollar price change of a bond to changes in interest rates; for a one-basis-point change in yield, dollar duration is equal to the price value of a basis point.

A portfolio's modified duration is found by computing the weighted average modified duration of all the bonds in the portfolio, where a particular bond's weight is the market value of the bond relative to the market value of the portfolio.

There are several problems with duration as a measure of the sensitivity of a bond or a portfolio to changes in yield:

(1) Duration does a good job of estimating the sensitivity of a bond or portfolio to small changes in yield only. This is due to the convex shape of the price/yield relationship.

(2) A portfolio's duration is a good measure of price sensitivity only if the yields of all bonds in the portfolio change by the same amount.

(3) For a portfolio consisting of bonds denominated in multiple currencies, modified duration as conventionally calculated does not provide insight into the price sensitivity of the portfolio.

(4) For bonds with interest-rate sensitive cash flows, modified duration is inappropriate since it assumes that cash flows will not change as yields change. A more appropriate measure in such instances is effective duration.

In the next chapter, we will take a look at the first problem. In Chapter 14, we will look at the second problem. Finally, when we look at bonds with embedded options, we will focus on the last problem.

There are several applications of duration: determining the hedge ratio, immunizing a portfolio against interest rate changes, and determining the duration of an interest rate swap.

12

Price Volatility Measures: Convexity

We're now ready to tie together the price/yield relationship and several of the properties about the bond price volatility that we discussed in previous chapters. Recall that the shape of the price/yield relationship is convex. It is the convex shape that gives rise to the properties.[1]

---

[1] The formulas shown in this chapter are presented without proof. For a mathematical derivation of the formulas, see Chapter 4 of Frank J. Fabozzi, *Bond Markets, Analysis and Strategies* (Englewood Cliffs, NJ: Prentice-Hall, 1993, 2nd ed).

Exhibit 12-1

Tangent to Price/Yield Relationship

Estimating Price with Duration: A Graphical Depiction

In the previous chapter, we explained how duration (modified or dollar) can be used to estimate price change when yield changes. In Exhibit 12-1, a line is drawn tangent to the curve depicting the price/yield relationship at point y^*.[2] The tangent line shows the rate of change of price with respect to a change in interest rates at that point (yield). Consequently, the tangent line is directly related to the dollar duration of the bond.[3]

How can the tangent line be used to approximate the new price if yield changes? If we draw a vertical line from any yield (on the horizontal axis), as we do in Exhibit 12-2,

---

[2] In nontechnical terms, a tangent line is defined as a line that touches the price/yield relationship at the point y^* and does not touch the price/yield relationship at any other point.

[3] Technically, the slope of the tangent line is the change in price for a change in yield, sometimes referred to as dP/dy, a term adopted from calculus because the slope is the first derivative of the price function for a bond. The modified duration would be the slope of the tangent line if the price/yield relationship is drawn with the natural logarithm of the bond's price, rather than price, on the vertical axis. To simplify the discussion below, we shall refer to the slope of the tangent line as the dollar duration.

Exhibit 12-2

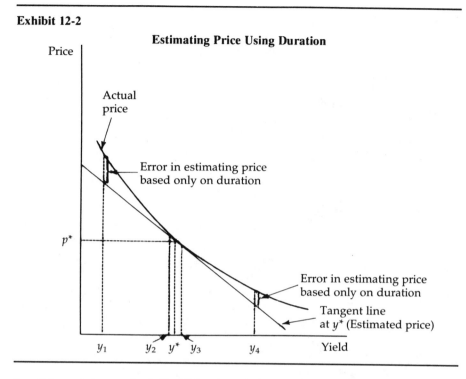

Estimating Price Using Duration

the distance between the horizontal axis and the tangent line represents the price as estimated using duration. Notice that the approximation will always underestimate the actual price at the new yield. This agrees with what we illustrated in the previous chapter: duration leads to an underestimate of the new price.

For small changes in yield, the tangent line gives a satisfactory estimate of the actual price. However, the farther we move from the initial yield, y^*, the worse the approximation. It should be apparent that the accuracy of the approximation from using duration (the tangent line) depends on the convexity of the price/yield relationship for the bond. Exhibit 12-3 shows the convexity of two hypothetical bonds. Both have the same duration at y^*; but Bond A has less convexity than Bond B. As a result, the duration-based approximation of the price is better for Bond A than Bond B.

Measuring Convexity

Exhibit 12-3 indicates that how well we can approximate the new price will depend on the convexity of a bond. In this section, we give a formula for measuring the convexity of a bond. In the next section, we show how the price change due to convexity can be estimated.

Exhibit 12-3

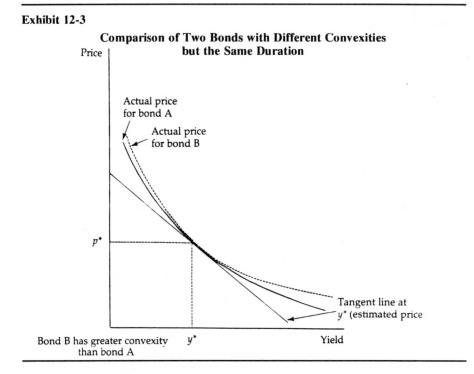

The convexity of an option-free bond is measured as follows:[4]

Convexity (in periods) =

$$\frac{1(2)\,PVCF_1 + 2(3)\,PVCF_2 + 3(4)\,PVCF_3 + \ldots + n(n+1)\,PVCF_n}{(1+y)^2 \times PVTCF}$$

where

PVCF$_t$ = Present value of the cash flow in period t discounted at the prevailing period yield (in the case of a semiannual-pay bond, one-half the yield to maturity);

t = Period when the cash flow is expected to be received ($t = 1, \ldots, n$);

n = Number of periods until maturity;

PVTCF = Total present value of the cash flow of the bond where the present value is determined using the prevailing yield to maturity.

---

[4] Sometimes this formula is used to approximate convexity (in periods):

$$\frac{(1)^2\,PVCF_1 + (2)^2\,PVCF_2 + (3)^2\,PVCF_3 + \ldots + (n)^2\,PVCF_n}{(1+y)^2 \times PVTCF}$$

For a zero-coupon bond, the convexity in periods reduces to

$$\text{Convexity for a zero--coupon bond (in periods)} = \frac{n(n+1)}{(1+y)^2}$$

To convert a bond's convexity from periods to years, the following formula is used:

$$\text{Convexity (in years)} = \frac{\text{Convexity (in periods)}}{k^2},$$

where

    k = Number of payments per year (i.e., k = 2 for semiannual-pay bonds, k = 12 for monthly pay bonds).

For an option-free bond, the convexity measure will always be positive.

Exhibits 12-4 and 12-5 summarize the calculation of convexity for two of the hypothetical bonds (the 8%, five-year bond and the 14%, five-year bond) whose Macaulay durations are calculated in Exhibits 11-1 and 11-2 of Chapter 11, respectively, assuming each bond is selling to yield 10%. For the five-year, zero-coupon bond, the convexity is

$$\text{Convexity for a zero--coupon bond (in periods)} = \frac{n(n+1)}{(1+y)^2}$$

since n = 10 (number of periods) and y is .05;

$$\text{Convexity} = \frac{10(10+1)}{(1.05)^2} = 24.94.$$

The convexities in years for the 12 hypothetical bonds we examined in the previous chapters are:

Coupon	*Maturity*	*Convexity*
.00%	5	24.94
.00	15	210.88
.00	30	829.94
8.00	5	19.58
8.00	15	94.36
8.00	30	167.56
10.00	5	18.74
10.00	15	87.62
10.00	30	158.70
14.00	5	17.44
14.00	15	78.90
14.00	30	148.28

What do these convexity numbers mean? How can they be used? We will answer these questions in the sections that follow.

Exhibit 12-4

Worksheet for Computation of Convexity for Five-Year, 8% Coupon Bond Selling to Yield 10%

Coupon rate	=	8%
Term (years)	=	5
Initial yield	=	10%
Price	=	92.27826

Period (t)	Cash flow	PVCF	t(t + 1)	PVCF × t(t + 1)
1	$4.00	$3.8095	2	$7.6190
2	4.00	3.6281	6	22.7687
3	4.00	3.4554	12	41.4642
4	4.00	3.2908	20	65.8162
5	4.00	3.1341	30	94.0231
6	4.00	2.9849	42	125.3642
7	4.00	2.8427	56	159.1926
8	4.00	2.7074	72	194.9297
9	4.00	2.5784	90	232.0592
10	104.00	63.8470	110	7,023.1676
			Total	$7,965.4046

$$\text{Convexity (in half years)} = \frac{7,965.4046}{(1.05)^2\,92.27826} = 78.2942$$

$$\text{Convexity (in years)} = \frac{78.2942}{2^2} = 19.58$$

Exhibit 12-5

Worksheet for Computation of Convexity for Five-Year, 14% Coupon Bond Selling to Yield 10%

Coupon rate	=	14%
Term (years)	=	5
Initial yield	=	10%
Price	=	115.4434

Period (t)	Cash flow	PVCF	t(t + 1)	PVCF × t(t + 1)
1	$7.00	$6.6667	2	$13.333
2	7.00	6.3492	6	38.0952
3	7.00	6.0469	12	72.5624
4	7.00	5.7589	20	115.1783
5	7.00	5.4847	30	164.5405
6	7.00	5.2235	42	219.3873
7	7.00	4.9748	56	278.5871
8	7.00	4.7379	72	341.1270
9	7.00	4.5123	90	406.1036
10	107.00	65.6887	110	7,225.7590
			Total	$8,874.6738

$$\text{Convexity (in half years)} = \frac{8,874.6738}{(1.05)^2 \, 115.4434} = 69.7276$$

$$\text{Convexity (in years)} = \frac{69.7276}{2^2} = 17.44$$

Percentage Price Change Due to Convexity

Modified duration provides a first approximation to the percentage change in price. Convexity provides a second approximation, based on the following relationship:

Approximate percentage change in price due to convexity =
$$(.5) \times \text{Convexity} \times (\text{Yield change})^2.$$

Since the convexity measure is always positive, the approximate percentage change in price due to convexity is positive for either an increase or a decrease in yield.

Illustration 12-1. Consider the 8%, 15-year bond selling to yield 10%. If the yield increases from 10% to 13% (a 300-basis-point or .03 yield change), then the percentage price change due to convexity is

$$(.5) \times 94.36 \times (.03)^2 \times 100 = .0425 = 4.25\%.$$

If the yield decreases by 300 basis points, from 10% to 7%, the percentage price change due to convexity is 4.25%.

Exhibit 12-6 shows the percentage price change due to convexity for various changes in yield for each of the 12 hypothetical bonds.

Percentage Price Change Due to Duration and Convexity

The approximate percentage change in price resulting from both duration and convexity is found by simply adding the two estimates.

Illustration 12-2. For the 8%, 15-year bond selling to yield 10%, if yields change from 10% to 13%, we have:

Price change based on	Approx. % price change
Duration	−24.15
Convexity	+ 4.25
Total	−19.90

The actual percentage change in price would be −20.41%.

For a decrease of 300 basis points, from 10% to 7%:

Price change based on	Approx. % price change
Duration	+24.15
Convexity	+ 4.25
Total	28.40

The actual percentage price change would be +29.03%.

Exhibit 12–6

Percentage Price Change Due to Convexity

Coupon	Term (years)	Convexity	Change (in basis points)					
			1	10	50	100	200	300
0%	5	24.94	.00%	.00%	.03%	.12%	.50%	1.12%
0	15	210.88	.00	.01	.26	1.05	4.22	9.49
0	30	829.94	.00	.04	1.04	4.15	16.60	37.35
8	5	19.58	.00	.00	.02	.10	.39	.88
8	15	94.36	.00	.00	.12	.47	1.89	4.25
8	30	167.56	.00	.01	.21	.84	3.35	7.54
10	5	18.74	.00	.00	.02	.09	.37	.84
10	15	87.62	.00	.00	.11	.44	1.75	3.94
10	30	158.70	.00	.01	.20	.79	3.17	7.14
14	5	17.44	.00	.00	.02	.09	.35	.78
14	15	78.90	.00	.00	.10	.39	1.58	3.55
14	30	148.28	.00	.01	.19	.74	2.97	6.67

Consequently, for large yield movements, a better approximation for bond price volatility is obtained by combining duration and convexity.

Exhibit 12-7 shows the percentage price changes due to both duration and convexity for our 12 hypothetical bonds. The percentage price change not explained by duration and convexity is shown in Exhibit 12-8. As can be seen from this exhibit, most of the change in price is explained by using duration and convexity.

Dollar Convexity

In the previous chapter, we explained that dollar duration can be obtained by multiplying modified duration by the initial price. Dollar convexity can be obtained by multiplying convexity by the initial price:

$$\text{Dollar convexity} = \text{Convexity} \times \text{Initial price}.$$

To determine the dollar price change, the following formula is used:

$$\text{Dollar price change due to convexity} = (.5) \times \text{Dollar convexity} \times (\text{Yield change})^2.$$

Illustration 12-3. For the 8%, 15-year bond selling to yield 10%, the dollar convexity per $100 of par value is

$$94.36 \times \$84.63 = \$7,985.69.$$

The dollar price change per $100 of par value for a 100-basis-point change is

$$(.5) \times \$7,985.69 \times (.01)^2 = \$.399.$$

Thus, for a 100-basis-point change, the price of the bond will change by approximately $.40 per $100 par value.

For a 200-basis-point change, the dollar price change per $100 of par value is

$$(.5) \times \$7,985.69 \times (.02)^2 = \$1.597.$$

For a 200-basis-point change, the dollar price change is approximately $1.60 per $100 of par value—quadruple the $.40 for a 100-basis-point change. Consequently, unlike dollar duration in which the dollar price change due to duration is proportionate to the change in yield—doubling the yield change from 100 basis points to 200 basis points, for example, doubles the dollar price change due to duration—the dollar price change due to convexity changes more than proportionately.

Convexity as a Measure of the Change in Dollar Duration

The tangent line in Exhibit 12-1 is a measure of the dollar duration of the price/yield relationship at point y^*. The steeper the tangent line, the greater the dollar duration; the flatter the line, the lower the dollar duration.

Exhibit 12-7

Estimated Percentage Price Change Using Duration and Convexity

		Yield change (in basis points) from 10%					
		1	10	50	100	200	300
		New yield level					
Coupon	Term (years)	10.01%	10.10%	10.50%	11.00%	12.00%	13.00%
0%	5	-.05%	-.47%	-2.35%	-4.64%	-9.02%	-13.16%
0	15	-.14	-1.42	-6.88	-13.24	-24.36	-33.38
0	30	-.29	-2.82	-13.25	-24.42	-40.54	-48.36
8	5	-.04	-.40	-1.97	-3.88	-7.57	-11.06
8	15	-.08	-.80	-3.91	-7.58	-14.21	-19.90
8	30	-.10	-.96	-4.65	-8.88	-16.09	-21.62
10	5	-.04	-.39	-1.91	-3.77	-7.35	-10.74
10	15	-.08	-.76	-3.74	-7.25	-13.63	-19.13
10	30	-.09	-.94	-4.53	-8.67	-15.75	-21.24
14	5	-.04	-.37	-1.81	-3.58	-6.99	-10.23
14	15	-.07	-.72	-3.51	-6.83	-12.86	-18.11
14	30	-.09	-.91	-4.40	-8.43	-15.37	-20.84

Exhibit 12-7 continued.

Coupon	Term (years)	Yield change (in basis points) from 10%					
		-1	-10	-50	-100	-200	-300
		New yield level					
		9.99%	9.90%	9.50%	9.00%	8.00%	7.00%
0%	5	.05%	.48%	2.41%	4.88%	10.02%	15.40%
0	15	.14	1.44	7.41	15.34	32.80	52.36
0	30	.29	2.90	15.32	32.72	73.74	123.06
8	5	.04	.40	2.01	4.08	8.35	12.82
8	15	.08	.81	4.14	8.52	17.99	28.40
8	30	.10	.98	5.07	10.56	22.79	36.70
10	5	.04	.39	1.95	3.95	8.09	12.42
10	15	.08	.77	3.95	8.13	17.13	27.01
10	30	.09	.95	4.93	10.25	22.09	35.52
14	5	.04	.37	1.86	3.76	7.69	11.79
14	15	.07	.73	3.71	7.61	16.02	25.21
14	30	.09	.92	4.77	9.91	21.31	34.18

Exhibit 12–8

Estimated Percentage Price Change Not Explained by Using Both Duration and Convexity

Coupon	Term (years)	Yield change (in basis points) from 10%					
		1	*10*	*50*	*100*	*200*	*300*
		New yield level					
		10.01%	10.10%	10.50%	11.00%	12.00%	13.00%
0%	5	.00%	.00%	.00%	.00%	-.02%	-.07%
0	15	.00	.00	.00	-.05	-.39	-1.28
0	30	.00	.00	-.05	-.38	-2.83	-8.94
8	5	.00	.00	.00	.00	-.02	-.05
8	15	.00	.00	.00	-.02	-.15	-.51
8	30	.00	.00	-.01	-.06	-.43	-1.39
10	5	.00	.00	.00	.00	-.01	-.05
10	15	.00	.00	.00	-.01	-.14	-.46
10	30	.00	.00	-.01	-.06	-.42	-1.31
14	5	.00	.00	.00	.00	-.01	-.04
14	15	.00	.00	.00	-.02	-.13	-.41
14	30	.00	.00	-.01	-.05	-.36	-1.17

Exhibit 12-8 continued.

		Yield change (in basis points) from 10%					
		−1	−10	−50	−100	−200	−300
				New yield level			
Coupon	Term (years)	9.99%	9.90%	9.50%	9.00%	8.00%	7.00%
0%	5	.00%	.00%	.00%	.00%	.02%	.07%
0	15	.00	.00	.00	.05	.46	1.62
0	30	.00	.00	.05	.44	3.83	14.05
8	5	.00	.00	.00	.00	.02	.05
8	15	.00	.00	.00	.02	.18	.64
8	30	.00	.00	.01	.06	.56	2.03
10	5	.00	.00	.00	.00	.02	.05
10	15	.00	.00	.00	.02	.16	.58
10	30	.00	.00	.01	.07	.53	1.90
14	5	.00	.00	.00	.00	.01	.04
14	15	.00	.00	.00	.02	.14	.51
14	30	.00	.00	.01	.05	.46	1.69

Exhibit 12-9 graphically depicts what happens to the dollar duration as the yield changes. Notice that for an option-free bond, as the yield declines below y^*, the dollar duration increases; as the yield increases above y^*, the dollar duration decreases. This is true for all option-free bonds: *the dollar duration increases as the yield decreases and decreases as the yield increases.* Exhibit 12-10 shows the dollar durations for our 12 hypothetical bonds for various yields and confirms our graphical illustration.

Exhibit 12-9

Dollar Duration at Different Yields

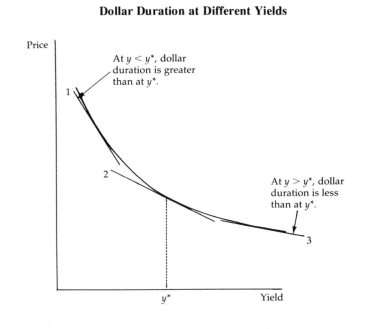

Why is this property of an option-free bond attractive? As the yield declines, an investor who is long a bond would want its price to increase as much as possible — hence, an investor wants dollar duration to increase. The opposite is true if the yield increases. An investor wants the dollar duration to decline when the yield increases. For this reason, investors commonly refer to the shape of the price/yield relationship for an option-free bond as having "positive" convexity, "positive" indicating that it is a good attribute of a bond. It is because of positive convexity that we observed the property in Chapter 9 that the increase in price will be greater than the decrease in price for a given change in yield. In Chapter 16, we'll discuss bonds that have "negative" convexity, which means that dollar duration does not change in the desired direction.

Exhibit 12-11 is the same as Exhibit 12-3, which shows the price/yield relationship of two bonds, A and B, with different convexities. Bond B has greater convexity than Bond A, while both have the same duration. Bond B is preferred over Bond A because it

Exhibit 12-10

Dollar Duration Per 100 Basis Points Per $100 Par Value

Coupon	Term			Yield level				
		4%	6%	8%	10%	12%	14%	16%
0%	5	$4.02	$3.61	$3.25	$2.92	$2.63	$2.38	$2.14
0	15	8.12	6.00	4.45	3.31	2.46	1.84	1.38
0	30	8.96	4.94	2.74	1.53	.86	.48	.27
8	5	5.14	4.65	4.21	3.82	3.47	3.16	2.87
8	15	14.72	11.45	8.98	7.10	5.67	4.57	3.71
8	30	26.48	17.34	11.75	8.24	5.98	4.48	3.46
10	5	5.42	4.91	4.45	4.04	3.68	3.35	3.06
10	15	16.37	12.81	10.11	8.05	6.47	5.25	4.30
10	30	30.86	20.44	14.00	9.92	7.26	5.48	4.26
14	5	5.97	5.43	4.93	4.49	4.10	3.74	3.42
14	15	19.67	15.53	12.38	9.95	8.07	6.61	5.46
14	30	39.61	26.64	18.50	13.27	9.82	7.48	5.85

Exhibit 12-11

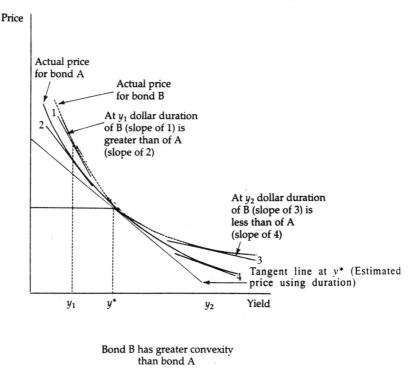

Dollar Duration for Different Convexitites

Price

Actual price
for bond A

Actual price
for bond B

At y_1 dollar duration
of B (slope of 1) is
greater than of A
(slope of 2)

1

2

At y_2 dollar duration
of B (slope of 3) is
less than of A
(slope of 4)

3

4 Tangent line at y^* (Estimated
price using duration)

y_1 y^* y_2 Yield

Bond B has greater convexity
than bond A

provides a higher bond price regardless of how yield changes — greater price appreciation
if yield declines, and smaller price loss if yield increases. Notice that the steepness of
Bond B is greater than that of Bond A at yields below y^*. This means that the dollar
duration of Bond B is greater than Bond A if the yield decreases. Thus, the investor
realizes greater price appreciation from Bond B than from Bond A. Look at what happens
if the yield increases above y^*. The tangent line is flatter for Bond B than for Bond A,
indicating a lower dollar duration for Bond B than for Bond A. The investor in Bond B
realizes a smaller price decline that the investor in Bond A.

Exhibit 12-12 shows for each of our 12 hypothetical bonds the percentage change
in dollar duration per 100 basis points per $100 par value, assuming an initial yield of
10%. This exhibit is constructed from the dollar durations in Exhibit 12-10. Also shown
is the convexity for each bond at a 10% yield. Notice that the change in dollar duration is
greater, the higher the convexity. *Convexity measures the rate of change of dollar duration for a bond.*

Exhibit 12-12

Percentage Change in Dollar Duration Per 100 Basis Points Per $100 Par Value

Assumption: Initial yield = 10%
Convexity computed at 10% yield

Coupon	Term (years)	Convexity	Yield level					
			4%	6%	8%	12%	14%	16%
0%	5	24.94	37.6%	23.6%	11.1%	−9.9%	−18.7%	−26.6%
0	15	210.88	145.6	81.5	34.5	−25.5	−44.3	−58.2
0	30	829.94	486.1	223.2	79.3	−43.9	−68.4	−82.1
8	5	19.58	34.5	21.7	10.2	−9.2	−17.4	−24.8
8	15	94.36	107.2	61.2	26.4	−20.2	−35.7	−47.7
8	30	167.56	221.4	110.5	42.6	−27.4	−45.6	−58.0
10	5	18.74	33.9	21.3	10.1	−9.0	−17.1	−24.4
10	15	87.62	103.3	59.1	25.6	−19.6	−34.8	−46.6
10	30	158.70	211.2	106.1	41.2	−26.8	−44.7	−57.1
14	5	17.44	33.0	20.8	9.8	−8.8	−16.7	−23.9
14	15	78.90	97.6	56.1	24.4	−18.9	−33.6	−45.1
14	30	148.28	198.5	100.7	39.4	−26.0	−43.6	−55.9

Summary of Properties of Convexity

The convexity properties of all option-free bonds are summarized below.

Property 1. As the yield increases (decreases) the dollar duration of a bond decreases (increases). We demonstrated this in the previous section.

Property 2. For a given yield and maturity, the lower the coupon, the greater the convexity of a bond. This can be seen from the computed convexity of our 12 hypothetical bonds. An implication of this property is that for two bonds with the same maturity, a zero-coupon bond has greater convexity than a coupon bond.

Property 3. For a given yield and modified duration, the lower the coupon, the smaller the convexity. The investment implication of this property is that zero-coupon bonds have the lowest convexity for a given modified duration.

To see this, consider three bonds:

Coupon	Maturity (years)	Yield to maturity	Modified duration (years)	Convexity
11.625%	10.00	10%	6.05	50.48
5.500	8.00	10	6.02	44.87
zero	6.33	10	6.03	39.24

Notice that all three bonds are selling to yield 10% and have a modified duration of approximately six years.[5] The convexity of the bonds decreases as the coupon rate decreases.

Property 4. The convexity of a bond increases at an increasing rate as duration increases. This is depicted in Exhibit 12-13. Doubling duration, for example, will more than double convexity.

Value of Convexity

Look again at Exhibit 12-3, where Bonds A and B have the same duration but different convexities. We stated that Bond B would be preferred to Bond A because both have the same price (same yield) and the same duration, but Bond B has greater convexity than Bond A. Thus, it offers better price performance if yield changes.

Generally, the market will take the greater convexity of Bond B compared to Bond A into account in pricing the two bonds. That is, the market prices convexity. Consequently, while there may be times when a situation such as depicted in Exhibit 12-3 may exist, generally the market will require investors to "pay up" (accept a lower yield) for the greater convexity offered by Bond B.

---

[5] A six-year, zero-coupon bond has a Macaulay duration equal to its maturity. It has a modified duration that is less than six years.

Exhibit 12-13

**Property 4: Relationship Between
Duration and Convexity**

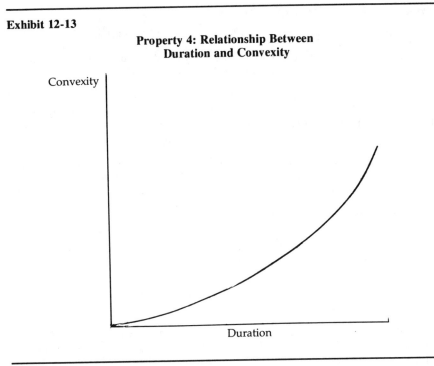

How much should the market want investors to pay for convexity? Look again at Exhibit 12-3. Notice that if investors expect that yields will change by very little—that is, they expect low interest rate volatility—the advantage of owning Bond B over Bond A is insignificant because the two bonds will offer approximately the same price performance for small changes in yield. Thus, investors should not be willing to pay much for convexity. In fact, if the market is pricing convexity high, which means that Bond A will be offering a higher yield than Bond B, then investors with expectations of low interest rate volatility would probably be willing to "sell convexity"—sell Bond B if they own it, and buy Bond A. In contrast, if investors expect substantial interest rate volatility, Bond B would probably sell at a much lower yield than Bond A.

Illustration 12-4. To see how two portfolios with the same dollar duration but with different convexities can perform differently, consider the three bonds shown in Exhibit 12-14 and the following two portfolios.[6] One portfolio consists of only Bond C, the 10-year bond and shall be referred to as the "bullet portfolio." A second portfolio consists of

---

[6] This illustration is adapted from Ravi E. Dattatreya and Frank J. Fabozzi, *Active Total Return Management of Fixed Income Portfolios* (Chicago: Probus Publishing, 1989).

50.2% of Bond A and 49.8% of Bond B; this portfolio shall be referred to as the "barbell portfolio." The dollar duration per 100-basis-point change in yield of the bullet portfolio is 6.43409. Recall from Chapter 11 that dollar duration is a measure of the dollar price sensitivity of a bond or a portfolio. As shown in Exhibit 12-14, the dollar duration per 100-basis-point change in yield of the barbell — which is just the weighted average of the dollar duration of the two bonds — is the same as the bullet portfolio. In fact, the barbell portfolio was designed to produce this result. The dollar convexity of the two portfolios, shown in Exhibit 12-14, is not equal. The dollar convexity of the bullet portfolio is less than that of the barbell portfolio.

The "yield" for the two portfolios is not the same. The yield (yield to maturity) for the bullet is simply the yield to maturity of Bond C, 9.25%. The traditional yield calcula-tion for the barbell portfolio, which is found by taking a weighted average of the yield to maturity of the two bonds included in the portfolio, is 8.998%. This would suggest that the "yield" of the bullet portfolio is 25.2 basis points greater than the barbell portfolio. Alternatively, a cash flow yield can be approximated for the barbell portfolio by calculat-ing the dollar duration market weighted yield of the portfolio. As shown in Exhibit 12-14, the cash flow yield of the barbell portfolio is 9.187%, suggesting that the "yield" of the bullet portfolio is 6.3 basis points greater than the barbell portfolio. Thus, both portfolios have the same dollar duration but, using either yield measure, the yield of the bullet portfolio is greater than the yield of the barbell portfolio. However, the dollar convexity of the barbell portfolio is greater than that of the bullet portfolio. The difference in the two yields is sometimes referred to as the "cost of convexity."

Exhibit 12-15 shows the difference in the total return over a six-month investment horizon for the two portfolios, assuming that the yields for all three bonds change by the same number of basis points shown in the first column.[7] The total return reported in the second column of Exhibit 12-15 is:

Bullet portfolio's total return − Barbell portfolio's total return

Thus, a positive sign in the second column means that the bullet portfolio outperformed the barbell portfolio, while a negative sign means that the barbell portfolio outperformed the bullet portfolio.

Which portfolio is the better investment alternative if the yields of all three bonds change by the same amount *and* the investment horizon is six months? The answer depends on the amount by which yields change. Notice in the second column that if yields change by less than 100 basis points, the bullet portfolio will outperform the barbell portfolio. The reverse is true if yields change by more than 100 basis points.

The key point here is that looking at measures such as yield (yield to maturity or some type of portfolio yield measure), duration, or convexity tells us little about perform-ance over some investment horizon because performance depends on the magnitude of the

---

[7] Note that no assumption is needed for the reinvestment rate since the three bonds shown in Exhibit 12-14 are assumed to be trading right after a coupon payment has been made and therefore there is no accrued interest.

Exhibit 12-14

Barbell-Bullet Analysis

Bond	Coupon	Maturity (years)	Price plus accrued	Yield	Dollar duration*	Dollar convexity*
		Three bonds used in analysis				
A	8.50%	5	100	8.50%	4.00544	19.8164
B	9.50	20	100	9.50	8.88151	124.1702
C	9.25	10	100	9.25	6.43409	55.4506

Bullet: Bond C
Barbell: Bonds A and B
Composition of barbell: 50.2% of Bond A; 49.8% of Bond B

Dollar duration of barbell =
$.502 \times 4.00544 + .498 \times 8.88151 = 6.434$
Average yield of barbell =
$.502 \times 8.50 + .498 \times 9.5 = 8.998$

Yield pickup = Yield on bullet – Cash flow yield of barbell
$= 9.25 - 9.187 = .063$, or 6.3 basis points

Cash flow yield of barbell[†] =

$$\frac{(8.5 \times .502 \times 4.00544) + (9.5 \times .498 \times 8.88151)}{6.434} = 9.187$$

Analysis based on duration, convexity, and average yield

Dollar convexity of barbell =
$.502 \times 19.8164 + .498 \times 124.1702 = 71.7846$

Yield pickup = Yield on bullet – Average yield of barbell
$= 9.25 - 8.998 = .252$, or 25.2 basis points
Convexity giveup = Convexity of barbell – Convexity of bullet
$= 71.7846 - 55.4506 = 16.334$

---

* Per 100 basis point change in yield
† The calculation shown is actually a dollar-duration-weighted yield, a very close approximation to cash flow yield.

Exhibit 12-15

Relative Performance of Bullet Portfolio and Barbell Portfolio
Over A Six-Month Investment Horizon

Yield Change	Difference in total return	Yield Change	Difference in total return
−5.000	−7.19	.250	.24
−4.750	−6.28	.500	.21
−4.500	−5.44	.750	.16
−4.250	−4.68	1.000	.09
−4.000	−4.00	1.250	.01
−3.750	−3.38	1.500	−.08
−3.500	−2.82	1.750	−.19
−3.250	−2.32	2.000	−.31
−3.000	−1.88	2.250	.44
−2.750	−1.49	2.500	−.58
−2.500	−1.15	2.750	−.73
−2.250	−.85	3.000	−.88
−2.000	−.59	3.250	−1.05
−1.750	−.38	3.500	−1.21
−1.500	−.20	3.750	−1.39
−1.250	−.05	4.000	−1.57
−1.000	.06	4.250	−1.75
−.750	.15	4.500	−1.93
−.500	.21	4.750	−2.12
−.250	.24	5.000	−2.31
.000	.25		

* Performance is based on the difference in total return over the six-month investment horizon. Specifically:

Bullet portfolio's total return − Barbell portfolio's total return

Therefore a negative value means that the barbell portfolio outperformed the bullet portfolio.

change in yields. Moreover, as we shall see in Chapter 14, the relative performance will also depend on the relative change in yields of each bond.

Approximating Convexity: Effective Convexity

In the previous chapter, a formula for approximating modified duration was given. The corresponding formula to approximate convexity is given below:

$$= \frac{P_+ + P_- - 2\,(P_0)}{(P_0)\,[0.5\,(y_+ - y_-)]^2}$$

where

P_+ = Price if yield is increased by × basis points;

P_- = Price if yield is decreased by × basis points;

P_0 = Initial price (per \$100 of par value);

y_+ = Initial yield plus × basis points;

y_- = Initial yield minus × basis points.

For example, consider the 20-year, 7% coupon bond selling at 74.26 to yield 10% that we used in the previous chapter to illustrate how to approximate modified duration. Suppose we evaluate the price changes for a 20-basis-point change up and down. Then,

P_+ = 72.92

P_- = 75.64

P_0 = 74.26

y_+ = .102

y_- = .098

Substituting these values in the formula:

$$\frac{72.92 + 75.64 - 2\,(74.26)}{(74.26)[.5\,(.102 - .0982)]^2} = 134.66$$

The convexity is equal to 132.08. The approximated convexity (134.66) has proven itself to be a good approximation of convexity (132.08).

Effective Convexity

Just as in the case of modified duration, the convexity measure discussed in this chapter does not take into consideration how the cash flows may change if yield changes. In later chapters, we can use the formula above to calculate the convexity of a bond when there are interest-rate sensitive cash flows. When the formula above is used in this way, the resulting convexity is called an *effective convexity* because it allows the cash flow to change as yields change.

Summary

In this chapter, we have presented a graphical explanation of how duration is used to approximate the change in price when yield changes. We showed why duration will underestimate the new price and why the error in estimating price becomes greater for large yield changes. The explanation lies in the convex shape of the price/yield relationship for an option-free bond. We then introduced a convexity measure for an option-free bond to provide a formula that links the convexity measure to price change.

The convexity of a bond will determine its price performance when yield changes. For two bonds with the same duration and the same yield to maturity, the bond with the greater convexity will be the more attractive. Typically, convexity does not come without a cost, however. The cost is the yield give-up necessary to improve convexity. Just how much investors should be willing to pay for better convexity depends on their expectations about the volatility of future interest rates. The greater the expected volatility, the more investors should be willing to pay for convexity. Trades that hold duration constant and improve convexity may enhance return over some specified holding period if the movement in yield is sufficient to offset the cost of obtaining the better convexity.

IV

The Yield Curve and Its Applications to Pricing and Duration

13

The Yield Curve, Spot Rate Curve, and Forward Rates

Our discussion so far relies on several critical assumptions in determining the price of a bond and in using duration. In particular, the pricing of a bond has assumed that all cash flows are discounted at the same yield. With regard to duration, we have assumed that the yield on all bonds in a portfolio changes by the same number of basis points. These assumptions are unwarranted for reasons to be explained in this and the next chapter. The yield curve should be considered in the analysis of bonds. In this chapter, we explain what the yield curve is and describe two important derivatives of the yield curve: spot rates and forward rates. We then illustrate how the yield curve and its derivatives are used in bond analysis.

A Bond Is a Package of Zero-Coupon Instruments

Modern financial theory tells us that a "bond is not a bond." Well, if it is not a bond, what is it? A bond should be viewed as a package of cash flows, with each cash flow viewed as a zero-coupon instrument, with the maturity date the date that the cash flow will be paid, and the maturity value equal to the cash flow. This means that a 30-year, 8% coupon Treasury bond with a par value of $100,000 should be viewed as a package of 60 zero-coupon instruments: 59 zero-coupon instruments maturing every six months for the next 29.5 years, with a maturity value equal to the semiannual coupon of $4,000, and one zero-coupon instrument that matures 30 years from now, with a maturity value equal to $104,000 (the semiannual coupon plus $100,000).

If a bond is viewed as a package of zero-coupon instruments, how then should a bond be priced? The price of a bond is the total value of the price of all the zero-coupon instruments. The value of each zero-coupon instrument is determined in turn by discounting its maturity value at a rate that is unique to that zero-coupon instrument. But what is the yield that should be used to value each zero-coupon instrument? The minimum yield is the yield that the U.S. Treasury would have to pay if it issued a zero-coupon bond with the maturity of the cash flow analyzed.

Of course, the U.S. Treasury does not issue zero-coupon bonds. While there are stripped Treasury securities created by dealers, the yield offered on these securities is not the same as what the U.S. Treasury would have to pay if it issued zero-coupon bonds; stripped Treasuries have less liquidity. Fortunately, we can use arbitrage arguments to calculate from the yield curve theoretical zero-coupon rates that the Treasury would have to pay.

The Yield Curve

The graphical depiction of the relationship between the yield to maturity on securities of the same credit risk and different maturity is called the *yield curve*. The yield curve is constructed from the maturity and observed yield of Treasury securities because Treasuries reflect the pure effect of maturity alone on yield, given that market participants do not perceive government securities to have any credit risk. When market participants refer to the "yield curve," they usually mean the Treasury yield curve. This is also true in the bond markets of other countries; the reference is to risk-free government securities.

Exhibit 13-1 shows four yield curves that have been observed in the U.S. Treasury market (and occur in other major government bond markets). In the yield curve in panel a, the yield increases with maturity. This shape is commonly referred to as an *upward sloping* or *normal yield curve*. The yield curve in panel b is a *downward sloping* or an *inverted yield curve*, because yield decreases with maturity. In a *humped yield curve*, depicted in panel c of the exhibit, the yield curve initially is upward sloping, but after a certain maturity it becomes downward sloping. Finally, a *flat yield curve* is one where the yield is the same regardless of the maturity. A flat yield curve is shown in panel d.

Exhibit 13-1

Four Hypothetical Yield Curves

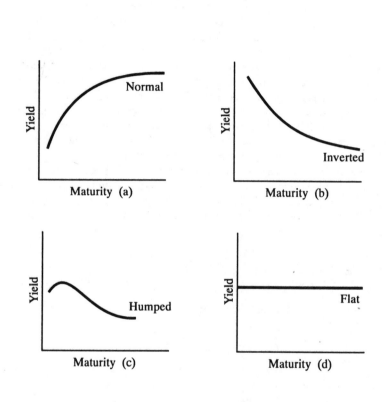

Several theories have been proposed to explain the shape of the yield curve, although discussion of these theories is beyond the scope of this book.[1] Analysis of the yield curve in this chapter is based on what is called the *pure expectations theory of interest rates*. According to the pure expectations theory, the only factor that affects the shape of the yield curve is market expectations about future interest rates.

---

[1] The interested reader is referred to Chapter 9 of Frank J. Fabozzi, *Bond Markets, Analysis and Strategies* (Englewood Cliffs, NJ: Prentice Hall, 1992) for a discussion of these theories.

The Spot Rate Curve

The Treasury yield curve shows the relationship between the yield on Treasury securities (Treasury bills and coupon securities) and maturity. According to the pure expectations theory and arbitrage arguments, we can determine the theoretical relationship between the yield on zero-coupon Treasury securities and maturity. This relationship is called the *Treasury spot rate curve*. The yield on a zero-coupon instrument is called a *spot rate*.

To illustrate how to construct a theoretical spot rate curve from the yield offered on Treasury securities, we use the 20 hypothetical Treasury securities shown in Exhibit 13-2.

The basic principle is that the value of a Treasury coupon security should be equal to the value of a package of zero-coupon Treasury securities. Consider first the six-month Treasury bill in Exhibit 13-2. Because a Treasury bill is a zero-coupon instrument, its yield of 8% is equal to the spot rate. Similarly, for the one-year Treasury, the yield of 8.3% is the one-year spot rate. Given these two spot rates, we can compute the spot rate for a 1.5-year zero-coupon Treasury. The value or price of a 1.5-year zero-coupon Treasury should equal the present value of the three cash flows from the 1.5-year coupon Treasury, where the yield used for discounting is the spot rate corresponding to the cash flow. Using $100 as par, the cash flow for the 1.5-year coupon Treasury is as follows:

0.5 year	$.085 \times \$100 \times .5$	= $4.25
1.0 year	$.085 \times \$100 \times .5$	= $4.25
1.5 years	$.085 \times \$100 \times .5 + 100$	= $104.25

The present value of the cash flow is then:

$$\frac{4.25}{(1 + y_1)^1} + \frac{4.25}{(1 + y_2)^2} + \frac{104.25}{(1 + y_3)^3}$$

where

y_1 = One-half the six-month theoretical spot rate
y_2 = One-half the one-year theoretical spot rate
y_3 = One-half the 1.5-year theoretical spot rate

Because the six-month spot rate and one-year spot rate are 8.0% and 8.3%, respectively, then

$$y_1 = .04 \text{ and } y_2 = .0415$$

Therefore the present value of the 1.5-year coupon Treasury security is:

$$\frac{4.25}{(1.0400)^1} + \frac{4.25}{(1.0415)^2} + \frac{104.25}{(1 + y_3)^3}$$

As the price of the 1.5-year coupon Treasury security is $99.45, the following relationship must hold:

$$99.45 = \frac{4.25}{(1.0400)^1} + \frac{4.25}{(1.0415)^2} + \frac{104.25}{(1 + y_3)^3}$$

Exhibit 13-2

Maturity and Yield to Maturity for 20 Hypothetical Treasury Securities

Maturity	Coupon	Yield to Maturity	Price
.50	.0000	.080	96.15
1.00	.0000	.830	92.19
1.50	.0850	.089	99.45
2.00	.0900	.092	99.64
2.50	.1100	.094	103.49
3.00	.0950	.097	99.49
3.50	.1000	.100	100.00
4.00	.1000	.104	98.72
4.50	.1150	.106	103.16
5.00	.0875	.108	92.24
5.50	.1050	.109	98.38
6.00	.1100	.112	99.14
6.50	.0850	.114	86.94
7.00	.0825	.116	84.24
7.50	.1100	.118	96.09
8.00	.0650	.119	72.62
8.50	.0875	.120	82.97
9.00	.1300	.122	104.30
9.50	.1150	.124	95.06
10.00	.1250	.125	100.00

We can now solve for the theoretical 1.5-year spot as follows:

$$99.45 = 4.08654 + 3.91805 + \frac{104.25}{(1 + y_3)^3}$$

$$91.4451 = \frac{104.25}{(1 + y_3)^3}$$

$$(1 + y_3)^3 = 1.140024$$

$$y_3 = .04465$$

Doubling this yield, we obtain the bond-equivalent yield of .0893 or 8.93%, which is the theoretical 1.5-year spot rate.

Given the theoretical 1.5-year spot rate, we can obtain the theoretical two-year spot rate. The cash flow for the two-year coupon Treasury in Exhibit 13-2 is given below:

0.5 years	.090 × $100 × .5	=	$4.50
1.0 year	.090 × $100 × .5	=	$4.50
1.5 years	.090 × $100 × .5	=	$4.50
2.0 years	.090 × $100 × .5 + 100	=	$104.50

The present value of the cash flow is as follows:

$$\frac{4.50}{(1+y_1)^1} + \frac{4.50}{(1+y_2)^2} + \frac{4.50}{(1+y_3)^3} + \frac{4.50}{(1+y_4)^4}$$

where

y_4 = one-half the two-year theoretical spot rate

The six-month spot rate, one-year spot rate, and 1.5-year spot rate are 8.0%, 8.3%, and 8.93%, respectively, so:

$$y_1 = .04 \quad y_2 = .0415 \quad \text{and } y_3 = .04465$$

Therefore the present value of the two-year coupon Treasury security is:

$$\frac{4.50}{(1.0400)^1} + \frac{4.50}{(1.0415)^2} + \frac{4.50}{(1.04465)^3} + \frac{104.50}{(1+y_4)^4}$$

Because the price of the two-year coupon Treasury security is $99.64, the following relationship must hold:

$$99.64 = \frac{4.50}{(1.0400)^1} + \frac{4.50}{(1.0415)^2} + \frac{4.50}{(1.04465)^3} + \frac{104.50}{(1+y_4)^4}$$

We can now solve for the theoretical two-year spot rate as follows:

$$99.64 = 4.32692 + 4.14853 + 3.94730 + \frac{104.50}{(1+y_4)^4}$$

$$87.21725 = \frac{104.50}{(1+y_4)^4}$$

$$(1+y_4)^4 = 1.198158$$

$$y_4 = .046235$$

Doubling this yield, we obtain the theoretical two-year spot rate bond-equivalent yield of 9.247%.

We can then use the theoretical two-year spot rate and the 2.5-year coupon Treasury in Exhibit 13-2 to compute the 2.5-year theoretical spot rate. In general, to compute the theoretical spot rate for the nth six-month period, the following equation must be solved:

$$P_n = \frac{C^*}{(1+y_1)^1} + \frac{C^*}{(1+y_2)^2} + \frac{C^*}{(1+y_3)^3} + \ldots + \frac{C^*+100}{(1+y_n)^n}$$

where

P_n = Price of the coupon Treasury with n periods to maturity (per \$100 of par value),

C^* = Semiannual coupon interest for the coupon Treasury with n periods to maturity per \$100 of par value

y_t for $t = 1, 2, \ldots, n\text{-}1$ are the theoretical spot rates that are known

This expression can be rewritten as follows:

$$P_n = C^* \sum_{t=1}^{n-1} \frac{1}{(1+y_t)^t} + \frac{C^*+100}{(1+y_n)^n}$$

Solving for y_n, we get:

$$y_n = \left[\frac{C^*+100}{P_n - C^* \displaystyle\sum_{t=1}^{n-1} \frac{1}{(1+y_t)^t}} \right]^{1/n} - 1$$

Doubling y_n gives the theoretical spot rate on a bond-equivalent basis.

The equation above is used to determine the theoretical spot rates for each hypothetical Treasury security shown in Exhibit 13-2. The theoretical spot rates are presented in Exhibit 13-3. *It is this yield/maturity structure that would be used to construct the theoretical spot rate curve that is referred to as the term structure of interest rates.* The methodology described above for deriving the spot rate curve is called *bootstrapping*.[2]

Pricing a Bond

Given the cash flows of a bond and the Treasury spot rate curve, we can determine the price of a Treasury security by discounting each cash flow by the corresponding spot rate and adding up the present value of the cash flows. For example, consider an 8.8% coupon Treasury bond with 25 years to maturity. Exhibit 13-4 shows the cash flow for this bond

---

[2] The bootstrapping methodology for constructing the theoretical spot rate curve, although useful, is in practice more complex for several reasons. First, there may be more than one Treasury issue with the same maturity selling at different yields. This reflects other factors that affect yield: difference in coupon and the presence of a call feature. Second, there is not a current Treasury issue for every possible maturity, so a continuous yield curve cannot be constructed using this procedure.

Exhibit 13-3

Theoretical Spot Rates

Maturity	Yield to maturity	Theoretical spot rate
.50	.0800	.08000
1.00	.0830	.08300
1.50	.0890	.08930
2.00	.0920	.09247
2.50	.0940	.09468
3.00	.0970	.09787
3.50	.1000	.10129
4.00	.1040	.10592
4.50	.1060	.10850
5.00	.1080	.11021
5.50	.1090	.11175
6.00	.1120	.11584
6.50	.1140	.11744
7.00	.1160	.11991
7.50	.1180	.12405
8.00	.1190	.12278
8.50	.1200	.12546
9.00	.1220	.13152
9.50	.1240	.13377
10.00	.1250	.13623

per $100 of par value. Also shown in the exhibit are the assumed Treasury spot rates. The price of this Treasury bond is 96.6133.

Suppose instead that the 25-year bond is an option-free corporate bond rather than a Treasury. The corporate bond would trade at a lower price than the Treasury bond. The appropriate spot rate at which each cash flow will be discounted is the Treasury spot rate plus a premium to reflect the credit risk associated with investing in a corporate bond. For example, if an appropriate premium is 100 basis points, discounting the cash flows in Exhibit 13-4 by the assumed Treasury spot rate plus 100 basis points would give a price of 88.5473. While by that description we assume that the premium is the same for each period, a spot rate default spread curve can be developed and used to determine the spot rate at which to discount each cash flow.[3]

---

[3] See Robert Litterman and Thomas Iben, "Corporate Bond Valuation and the Term Structure of Credit Spreads," *Journal of Portfolio Management* (Spring 1991), pp. 52-64.

Exhibit 13-4

Calculation of Price of a 25-Year, 8.8% Coupon Bond Using Treasury Spot Rates

Period	Cash flow	Treasury spot rate	Present value
1	4.4	7.00000%	4.2512
2	4.4	7.04999	4.1055
3	4.4	7.09998	3.9628
4	4.4	7.12498	3.8251
5	4.4	7.13998	3.6922
6	4.4	7.16665	3.5622
7	4.4	7.19997	3.4351
8	4.4	7.26240	3.3077
9	4.4	7.33315	3.1820
10	4.4	7.38977	3.0611
11	4.4	7.44517	2.9434
12	4.4	7.49135	2.8302
13	4.4	7.53810	2.7200
14	4.4	7.57819	2.6141
15	4.4	7.61959	2.5112
16	4.4	7.66205	2.4111
17	4.4	7.70538	2.3139
18	4.4	7.74391	2.2207
19	4.4	7.78888	2.1291
20	4.4	7.83434	2.0404
21	4.4	8.22300	1.8879
22	4.4	8.33333	1.7923
23	4.4	8.40000	1.7080
24	4.4	8.50000	1.6204
25	4.4	8.54230	1.5465
26	4.4	8.72345	1.4500
27	4.4	8.90000	1.3581
28	4.4	9.00000	1.2829
29	4.4	9.01450	1.2252
30	4.4	9.23000	1.1367
31	4.4	9.39000	1.0611
32	4.4	9.44840	1.0045
33	4.4	9.50000	0.9514
34	4.4	9.50000	0.9083
35	4.4	9.50000	0.8671

Exhibit 13-4 continued.

Period	Cash flow	Treasury spot rate	Present value
36	4.4	9.50000	0.8278
37	4.4	9.55000	0.7833
38	4.4	9.56000	0.7462
39	4.4	9.58000	0.7095
40	4.4	9.58000	0.6671
41	4.4	9.60000	0.6436
42	4.4	9.70000	0.6020
43	4.4	9.80000	0.5625
44	4.4	9.90000	0.5251
45	4.4	10.00000	0.4897
46	4.4	10.10000	0.4563
47	4.4	10.30000	0.4154
48	4.4	10.50000	0.3774
49	4.4	10.60000	0.3503
50	104.4	10.80000	7.5278
		Theoretical price	96.6133

Drawback of Traditional Yield Spread Analysis

Traditional analysis of the yield premium for a non-Treasury bond involves calculating the difference between the yield to maturity (or yield to call) of the bond in question and the yield to maturity of a comparable-maturity coupon Treasury. The latter is obtained from the Treasury yield curve. For example, consider the following two 8.8% coupon, 25-year bonds:

Issue	Price	Yield to maturity
Treasury	96.6133	9.15%
Corporate	87.0798	10.24%

The yield spread for these two bonds as traditionally computed is 109 basis points (10.24% minus 9.15%). The drawbacks of this convention, however, are (1) for both bonds, the yield fails to take into consideration the yield curve or spot rate curves; and (2) in the case of callable and/or putable bonds, expected interest rate volatility may alter the cash flow of a bond. In this chapter, we focus only on the first problem: failure to consider the spot rate curve, which can be met by calculating a measure called *static spread*. We will deal with the second problem in the next section of this book.

Static Spread

In traditional yield spread analysis, the investor compares the yield to maturity of a particular bond with the yield to maturity of a similar maturity on-the-run Treasury security. This means that the yield to maturity of both a 25-year zero-coupon corporate bond and an 8.8% coupon 25-year corporate coupon bond would be compared to the on-the-run 25-year Treasury security. Such a comparison makes little sense, since the cash flow characteristics of the two corporate bonds will not be the same as that of the benchmark Treasury.

The proper way to compare non-Treasury bonds of the same maturity but with different coupon rates is to compare them to a portfolio of Treasury securities that have the same cash flows. For example, consider the 8.8%, 25-year corporate bond selling for 87.0798. The cash flow per $100 par value for this corporate bond, assuming that interest rates do not change (that is, assuming interest rates stay static) is 49 six-month payments of $4.40 and a payment in 25 years (at the end of 50 six-month periods) of $104.40. A portfolio that will replicate this cash flow would include 50 zero-coupon Treasury securities with maturities coinciding with the amounts and timing of the cash flows of the corporate bond.

The corporate bond's value is equal to the present value of all of its cash flows. Assuming the cash flows are riskless, the value will equal the present value of the replicating portfolio of Treasury securities. In turn, these cash flows are valued at the Treasury spot rates. The price of the risk-free 8.8%, 25-year bond assuming the Treasury spot rate curve shown in Exhibit 13-4, is 96.6133. The corporate bond's price is 87.0798, less than that package of zero-coupon Treasury securities, because investors in fact require a yield premium for the risk associated with holding a corporate bond rather than a riskless package of Treasury securities.

The *static spread* is a measure of the spread that the investor would realize over the entire Treasury spot rate curve if the bond is held to maturity. It is not a spread off one point on the Treasury yield curve, as is the traditional yield spread. The static spread, which is found by trial-and-error, is the spread that makes the present value of the cash flows from the corporate bond, when discounted at the Treasury spot rate plus the spread, equal to the corporate bond's price.

To illustrate the trial-and-error procedure, let's use the corporate bond in the previous illustration. Select some spread, say, 100 basis points, and add that to each Treasury spot rate shown in the third column in Exhibit 13-4. For example, the 14-year (period 28) spot rate becomes 10.0% (9% plus 1%). The spot rate plus 100 basis points is then used to calculate the present value of 88.5473. Because the present value is not equal to the corporate bond's price, which we know to be 87.0798, the static spread is not 100 basis points. If a spread of 110 basis points is tried, that results in a present value of 87.8031; again, because this is not equal to the corporate bond's price, 110 basis points is not the static spread. The last column of Exhibit 13-5 shows the present value when a 120-basis-point spread is tried. Here the present value is equal to the corporate bond price, 87.0798. Therefore 120 basis points is the static spread, in comparison with the traditional yield spread of 109 basis points.

Exhibit 13-5

Calculation of the Static Spread for a 25-Year, 8.8% Coupon Corporate Bond

Period	Cash flow	Treasury spot rate	Present value if spread used is		
			100 BP	110 BP	120 BP
1	4.4	7.00000%	4.2308	4.2287	4.2267
2	4.4	7.04999	4.0661	4.0622	4.0583
3	4.4	7.09998	3.9059	3.9003	3.8947
4	4.4	7.12498	3.7521	3.7449	3.7377
5	4.4	7.13998	3.6043	3.5957	3.5871
6	4.4	7.16665	3.4607	3.4508	3.4408
7	4.4	7.19997	3.3212	3.3101	3.2990
8	4.4	7.26240	3.1828	3.1706	3.1584
9	4.4	7.33315	3.0472	3.0340	3.0210
10	4.4	7.38977	2.9174	2.9034	2.8895
11	4.4	7.44517	2.7917	2.7770	2.7624
12	4.4	7.49135	2.6715	2.6562	2.6409
13	4.4	7.53810	2.5552	2.5394	2.5236
14	4.4	7.57819	2.4440	2.4277	2.4115
15	4.4	7.61959	2.3366	2.3198	2.3032
16	4.4	7.66205	2.2327	2.2157	2.1988
17	4.4	7.70538	2.1325	2.1152	2.0981
18	4.4	7.74391	2.0368	2.0193	2.0020
19	4.4	7.78888	1.9435	1.9259	1.9085
20	4.4	7.83434	1.8536	1.8359	1.8184
21	4.4	8.22300	1.7072	1.6902	1.6733
22	4.4	8.33333	1.6131	1.5963	1.5796
23	4.4	8.40000	1.5300	1.5132	1.4967
24	4.4	8.50000	1.4446	1.4282	1.4119
25	4.4	8.54230	1.3722	1.3559	1.3398
26	4.4	8.72345	1.2806	1.2648	1.2492
27	4.4	8.90000	1.1938	1.1785	1.1635
28	4.4	9.00000	1.1224	1.1075	1.0929
29	4.4	9.01450	1.0668	1.0522	1.0378
30	4.4	9.23000	0.9852	0.9712	0.9575
31	4.4	9.39000	0.9154	0.9020	0.8888
32	4.4	9.44840	0.8625	0.8495	0.8367
33	4.4	9.50000	0.8131	0.8004	0.7880
34	4.4	9.50000	0.7725	0.7601	0.7480
35	4.4	9.50000	0.7340	0.7219	0.7100

Period	Cash flow	Treasury spot rate	Present value if spread used is		
			100 BP	*110 BP*	*120 BP*
36	4.4	9.50000	0.6974	0.6855	0.6739
37	4.4	9.55000	0.6568	0.6453	0.6341
38	4.4	9.56000	0.6227	0.6116	0.6007
39	4.4	9.58000	0.5893	0.5785	0.5679
40	4.4	9.58000	0.5597	0.5492	0.5389
41	4.4	9.60000	0.5295	0.5193	0.5093
42	4.4	9.70000	0.4929	0.4832	0.4737
43	4.4	9.80000	0.4585	0.4492	0.4401
44	4.4	9.90000	0.4260	0.4172	0.4086
45	4.4	10.00000	0.3955	0.3871	0.3789
46	4.4	10.10000	0.3668	0.3588	0.3511
47	4.4	10.30000	0.3323	0.3250	0.3179
48	4.4	10.50000	0.3006	0.2939	0.2873
49	4.4	10.60000	0.2778	0.2714	0.2652
50	104.4	10.80000	5.9416	5.8030	5.6677
		Total present value	88.5473	87.8031	87.0798

Exhibit 13-6 shows the static spread and the traditional yield spread for bonds with various maturities and prices, assuming the Treasury spot rates shown in Exhibit 13-4. Notice that the shorter the maturity of the bond, the less the static spread differs from the traditional yield spread. The magnitude of the difference between the traditional yield spread and the static spread also depends on the shape of the yield curve. The steeper the yield curve, the more the difference for a given coupon and maturity.

The difference between the traditional yield spread and the static spread will be considerably greater for sinking fund bonds and mortgage-backed securities in a steep yield curve environment.

Forward Rates

We have seen how the theoretical spot rate curve can be constructed from the yield curve. But there may be more information contained in the yield curve. Specifically, can we use the yield curve to infer the market's expectations of future interest rates? Let's explore this possibility.

Suppose an investor with a one-year investment horizon is considering two alternatives:

Alternative 1: Buy a one-year Treasury bill
Alternative 2: Buy a six-month Treasury bill, and when it matures in six months buy another six-month Treasury bill

Exhibit 13-6

Comparison of Traditional Yield Spread
and Static Spread for Various Bonds(*)

Bond	Price	Yield to maturity	Spread (in basis points) Traditional	Static	Difference
		25-year, 8.8% coupon bond			
Treasury	96.6133	9.15%	—	—	—
A	88.5473	10.06%	91	100	9
B	87.8031	10.15%	100	110	10
C	87.0798	10.24%	109	120	11
		15-year, 8.8% coupon bond			
Treasury	101.9603	8.57%	—	—	—
D	94.1928	9.54%	97	100	3
E	93.4639	9.63%	106	110	4
F	92.7433	9.73%	116	120	4
		10-year, 8.8% coupon bond			
Treasury	107.4906	7.71%	—	—	—
G	100.6137	8.71%	100	100	0
H	99.9585	8.81%	110	110	0
I	99.3088	8.91%	120	120	0
		5-year, 8.8% coupon bond			
Treasury	105.9555	7.36%	—	—	—
J	101.7919	8.35%	99	100	1
K	101.3867	8.45%	109	110	1
L	100.9836	8.55%	119	120	1

*   Assumes Treasury spot rate curve given in Exhibit 13-4.

The investor will be indifferent between the two alternatives if they produce the same yield or the same number of dollars per dollar invested over the one-year investment horizon. The investor knows the spot rate on the six-month Treasury bill and the one-year Treasury bill, but not what yield will be available on a six-month Treasury bill purchased six months from now. The yield on a six-month Treasury bill six months from now is called the *forward rate*. Given the spot rate for the six-month Treasury bill and the one-year Treasury bill rate, it is possible to determine the forward rate on a six-month Treasury bill that will make investors indifferent to the two alternatives.

By investing in the one-year Treasury bill, the investor will receive the maturity value at the end of one year. Suppose that the maturity value of the one-year Treasury bill is $100. The price (cost) of the one-year Treasury bill would be as follows:

$$\frac{100}{(1 + y_2)^2}$$

where y_2 is one-half the bond-equivalent yield of the theoretical one-year spot rate.

Suppose that the investor purchases a six-month Treasury bill for P dollars. At the end of six months, the value of this investment would be

$$P(1+y_1)$$

where y_1 is one-half the bond-equivalent yield of the theoretical six-month spot rate.

Let f be one-half the forward rate on a six-month Treasury bill available six months from now. Then the future dollars available at the end of one year from the P dollars invested would be given by

$$P(1+y_1)(1+f)$$

Suppose that today we want to know how many P dollars the investor must invest in order to get \$100 one year from now. This can be found as follows:

$$P(1+y_1)(1+f) = 100$$

Solving, we get

$$P = \frac{100}{(1 + y_1)(1 + f)}$$

The investor will be indifferent between the two alternatives if the same dollar investment is made and \$100 is received from both investments at the end of one year. That is, the investor will be indifferent if

$$\frac{100}{(1 + y_2)^2} = \frac{100}{(1 + y_1)(1 + f)}$$

Solving for f, we get

$$f = \frac{(1 + y_2)^2}{(1 + y_1)} - 1$$

Doubling f gives the bond-equivalent yield for the six-month forward rate.

To illustrate application of this equation, we will use the theoretical spot rates shown in Exhibit 13.3. Because we use the theoretical spot rates to compute the forward rate, the resulting forward rate is called the *implied forward rate*. We know that:

Six-month bill rate = .080; therefore y_1 = .0400
One-year bill rate = .083; therefore y_2 = .0415

Substituting into the equation, we have

$$f = \frac{(1.0415)^2}{1.0400} - 1$$

$$= .043$$

The forward rate on a six-month security, quoted on a bond-equivalent basis, is 8.60% (.043 × 2).

We can confirm these results. The price of a one-year Treasury bill with a $100 maturity value is

$$\frac{100}{(1.0415)^2} = 92.19$$

If 92.19 is invested for six months at the six-month spot rate of 8%, the amount at the end of six months would be

$$92.19(1.0400) = 95.8776$$

If 95.8776 is reinvested for another six months in a six-month Treasury offering 4.3% for six months (8.6% annually), the amount at the end of one year is

$$95.8876(1.043) = 100$$

Each alternative has the same $100 payoff if the six-month Treasury bill yield six months from now is 4.3% (8.6% on a bond-equivalent basis). This means that if investors are guaranteed a 4.3% yield (8.6% bond-equivalent basis) on a six-month Treasury bill six months from now, they will be indifferent between the two alternatives.

While we have calculated only the implied six-month forward rate six months from now, we can follow the same methodology to determine the implied forward rate six months from now for an investment for a period longer than six months. That is, we can use the yield curve or, more specifically, the spot rate curve generated from the yield curve to construct an implied forward rate six months from now for one-year investments, 1.5-year investments, two-year investments, 2.5-year investments, and so on.

We can even take this one step farther. It is not necessary to limit ourselves to implied forward rates six months from now. The yield curve can be used to calculate the implied forward rate for any time into the future for any investment horizon. As examples, the following can be calculated:

■ The two-year implied forward rate five years from now

■ The six-year implied forward rate ten years from now

■ The seven-year implied forward rate three years from now

How is this done? To demonstrate how, we must introduce some notation. We will continue to let f represent the forward rate. But now we must identify two aspects of the forward rate. First, we want to denote when the forward rate begins. Second, we want to denote the length of time of the forward rate. To identify these two aspects of the forward rate, we use the following notation:

$_nf_t$ = The forward rate n periods from now for t periods

Remember that for our bond examples each period is equal to six months. Consider first the earlier example of the six-month forward rate six months from now. In this case, because we are looking at a forward rate six months from now, this is equal to one period from now. Thus n is 1. The length of the forward rate is six months, so t is equal to 1.

Consequently, the six-month forward rate six months from now is denoted by $_1f_1$. The six-month forward rates are then expressed as follows:

$_2f_1$ = Six-month forward rate one year (two periods) from now
$_3f_1$ = Six-month forward rate 1.5 years (three periods) from now
$_4f_1$ = Six-month forward rate two years (four periods) from now, etc.

For forward rates four years (eight periods) from now, we would have the following:

$_8f_1$ = Six-month forward rate four years (eight periods) from now
$_8f_2$ = One-year (two period) forward rate four years (eight periods) from now
$_8f_3$ = 1.5-year forward rate four years (eight periods) from now, etc.

Now let's see how the spot rates can be used to calculate the implied forward rate. We assume in the illustration that there are zero-coupon Treasury securities available.[4] Suppose that an investor with a five-year investment horizon is considering two alternatives:

Alternative 1:   Buy a five-year (ten period) zero-coupon Treasury security
Alternative 2:   Buy a three-year (six period) zero-coupon Treasury security, and when it matures in three years buy a two-year Treasury security.

The investor will be indifferent between the two alternatives if they produce the same yield or the same number of dollars per dollar invested over the five-year investment horizon. The spot rates on the five-year Treasury security and the three-year Treasury security are known, but the yield available on a two-year Treasury security purchased three years from now is not known. That is, the investor does not know the two-year forward rate three years from now. In terms of our notation that unknown is $_6f_4$.

The price of the five-year zero-coupon Treasury security with a maturity value of $100 would be

$$\frac{100}{(1 + y_{10})^{10}}$$

where y_{10} is one-half the bond-equivalent yield of the theoretical five-year spot rate.

Suppose that the investor purchases a three-year zero-coupon Treasury security for P dollars. At the end of three years, the value of this investment would be

$$P(1 + y_6)^6$$

where y_6 is one-half the bond-equivalent yield of the theoretical three-year spot rate. Let $_6f_4$ be the semiannual two-year forward rate three years from now. Then the future dollars available at the end of five years from the P dollars invested are

$$P(1 + y_6)^6 (1 + {_6f_4})^4$$

---

[4] The existence of zero-coupon Treasury securities is not necessary for determination of the implied forward rates. The assumption just simplifies the presentation.

Suppose that today we want to know how many P dollars the investor must invest in order to get \$100 one year from now. This can be found as follows:

$$P(1 + y_6)^6 (1 + {}_6f_4)^4 = 100$$

Solving for P,

$$P = \frac{100}{(1 + y_6)^6 (1 + {}_6f_4)^4}$$

Investors will be indifferent between the two alternatives if they make the same dollar investment and receive \$100 at the end of five years from both alternatives. That is, the investor will be indifferent if

$$\frac{100}{(1 + y_{10})^{10}} = \frac{100}{(1 + y_6)^6 (1 + {}_6f_4)^4}$$

Solving for ${}_6f_4$, we get

$$_6f_4 = \left[\frac{(1 + y_{10})^{10}}{(1 + y_6)^6} \right]^{1/4} - 1$$

Doubling ${}_6f_4$ gives the bond-equivalent yield for the two-year forward rate three years from now.

To illustrate this, we use the theoretical spot rates shown in Exhibit 13.3. We know that:

Three-year spot rate = .09787; therefore y_6 = .048935
Five-year spot rate   = .11021; therefore y_{10} = .055105

Substituting into the equation, we have

$$_6f_4 = \left[\frac{(1.055105)^{10}}{(1.048935)^6} \right]^{1/4} - 1$$

$$= \left[\frac{(1.709845)^{10}}{(1.331961)^6} \right]^{1/4} - 1$$

$$= .0644$$

The implied forward rate on a two-year Treasury security three years from now, quoted on a bond-equivalent basis, is calculated as 12.88% (.0644 × 2). Let's confirm our results. The price of a five-year zero-coupon Treasury security with a \$100 maturity value is

$$\frac{100}{(1.055105)^{10}} = 58.48$$

If 58.48 is invested for three years at the three-year spot rate of 9.787%, the amount at the end of six periods would be

$$58.48 \ (1.048935)^6 = 77.8931$$

If 77.8931 is reinvested for another two years (four periods) at 6.44% (12.88% annually), the amount at the end of the fifth year is

$$77.8931 \ (1.0644)^4 = 100$$

Each alternative does have the same $100 payoff if the two-year Treasury rate three years from now is 6.44% (12.88% on a bond-equivalent basis).

In general, the formula for the implied forward rate is:

$$_nf_t = \left[\frac{(1 + y_{n+t})^{n+t}}{(1 + y_n)^n} \right]^{1/t} - 1$$

where y_n is a semiannual spot rate. Doubling $_nf_t$ gives the implied forward rate on a bond-equivalent basis.

To illustrate application of the general equation, consider the earlier example where we sought the six-month forward rate six months from now. That is, we sought $_1f_1$. Because n is equal to 1 and t is equal to 1,

$$_1f_1 = \left[\frac{(1 + y_{1+1})^{1+1}}{(1 + y_1)^1} \right]^{1/1} - 1$$

or

$$= \frac{(1 + y_2)^2}{(1 + y_1)^1} - 1$$

This agrees with our earlier equation for a one-period spot rate one period from now.

Relationship Between Long Spot Rates and Short-Term Implied Forward Rates

Suppose our investor purchases a five-year zero-coupon Treasury security for $58.48 with a maturity value of $100. The investor instead could buy a six-month Treasury bill and reinvest the proceeds every six months for five years. The number of dollars that will be realized will depend on the six-month forward rates. If the investor can actually reinvest the proceeds maturing every six months at the implied six-month forward rates, let's see how many dollars would accumulate at the end of five years. The implied six-month forward rates were calculated for the yield curve given in Exhibit 13-2. The semiannual implied forward rates from Exhibit 13-3 are:

$$_1f_1 = .043000$$
$$_2f_1 = .050980$$
$$_3f_1 = .051005$$
$$_4f_1 = .051770$$
$$_5f_1 = .056945$$
$$_6f_1 = .060965$$
$$_7f_1 = .069310$$
$$_8f_1 = .064625$$
$$_9f_1 = .062830$$

By investing the $58.48 at the six-month spot rate of 4% (8% on a bond-equivalent basis) and reinvesting at the forward rates above, the number of dollars accumulated at the end of five years would be

$$\$54.48(1.04)(1.043)(1.05098)(1.051005)(1.05177)(1.056945)$$
$$(1.060965)(1.06931)(1.064625)(1.06283) = \$100$$

Therefore, we see that if the implied forward rates are realized, the $54.48 investment will produce the same number of dollars as an investment in a five-year zero-coupon Treasury security at the five-year spot rate. From this illustration, we can see that the five-year spot rate is related to the current six-month spot rate and the implied six-month forward rates.

In general the relationship among a t-period spot rate, the current six-month spot rate, and the implied six-month forward rates is as follows:

$$y_t = [(1 + y_1)(1 + {}_1f_1)(1 + {}_2f_1)(1 + {}_3f_1)\ldots(1 + f_1)]^{\frac{1}{t}} - 1$$

Arbitrage-Free Total Return

As we explain in Chapter 8, to compute a total return over some investment horizon, assumptions must be made about the reinvestment rate (or rates) and the yield of the bond at the end of the investment horizon for bonds with a maturity greater than the investment horizon. Money managers can use the implied forward rates for the market's expectations of future short-term rates for the reinvestment rate assumption and the yield on the bond at the end of the investment horizon.

Because we find the implied forward rates using arbitrage arguments, the total return calculated using the implied forward rates is called an *arbitrage-free total return*.

Summary

A bond should be viewed as a package of cash flows, with each cash flow representing nothing more than a zero-coupon instrument. The price of a bond is then the total value of all of the zero-coupon instruments. To determine the value of each cash flow/zero-coupon instrument, the starting point is the theoretical rate on Treasury zero-coupon instruments.

The yield curve shows the relationship between the yield on Treasury securities and maturity. From the yield curve, the theoretical Treasury spot rate curve can be derived through arbitrage arguments. The theoretical spot rates (or equivalently zero-coupon rates) are then used to calculate the price of a Treasury security. A non-Treasury security is priced by adding to the Treasury spot rate curve a premium to reflect credit and liquidity risks.

Traditional yield spread analysis fails to take into account (1) the yield curve or spot rate curve, and (2) any options embedded in the bond. We consider the first problem in this chapter and the second problem later on in this book. The static spread measures the spread over the Treasury spot rate curve assuming that interest rates will not change in the future.

14

Duration and the Yield Curve

As we explain in Chapter 13, the yield curve describes the relationship between maturity and yield on U.S. Treasury securities. The shape of the yield curve changes over time. Because a portfolio consists of bonds of different maturities, changes in the shape of the yield curve will have different effects on each bond's price.

Our objective in this chapter is threefold. First, we illustrate how the duration measure discussed in earlier chapters when applied to a portfolio of bonds does not capture the effect of changes in the shape of the yield curve. Second, we review the types of yield curve shifts that have been observed in the Treasury market. Finally, we provide duration measures that indicate the exposure of a portfolio to yield curve shifts.

Duration and Nonparallel Yield Curve Shifts

Two portfolios that have the same duration may perform quite differently if the yield curve does not shift in a parallel fashion. To illustrate this point, consider the three bonds in Illustration 12-4 of Chapter 12 and summarized in Exhibit 12-14.[1] Two portfolios were created from these three bonds: a bullet portfolio consisting of Bond C and a barbell portfolio consisting of roughly equal amounts of Bonds A and B. As explained in Chapter 12, both portfolios have the same dollar duration. However, the dollar convexity of the two portfolios is not equal. The dollar convexity of the bullet portfolio is less than that of the barbell portfolio. Also, the "yield" for the two portfolios is not the same. The yield for the bullet is simply the yield to maturity of Bond C, 9.25%. For the barbell portfolio, the traditional yield calculation is found by taking a weighted average of the yield to maturity of the two bonds included in the portfolio, which is 8.998%. Thus, the "yield" of the bullet portfolio is 25.2 basis points higher than that of the barbell portfolio.

Exhibit 14-1, column 2, shows the difference in the total return over a six-month investment horizon for the two portfolios, assuming that the yield curve shifts in a "parallel" fashion.[2] By parallel we mean that the yields for the short-term bond (A), the intermediate-term bond (C), and the long-term bond (B) change by the same number of basis points, as shown in the first column of the exhibit. The total return reported in the second column of Exhibit 14-1 is:

$$\text{Bullet portfolio's total return} - \text{Barbell portfolio's total return}$$

Thus a positive value in the second column means that the bullet portfolio outperforms the barbell portfolio, while a negative sign means that the barbell portfolio outperforms the bullet portfolio. As explained in Illustration 12-4, the better investment alternative depends on the amount by which yields change. If the yields change by less than 100 basis points, the bullet portfolio will outperform the barbell portfolio. The reverse is true if yields change by more than 100 basis points.

Now let's look at what happens if the yield curve does not shift in a parallel fashion. The third and fourth columns of Exhibit 14-1 show the relative performance of the two portfolios for a nonparallel shift of the yield curve. Specifically, the third column assumes that if the yield on Bond C (the intermediate-term bond) changes by the amount shown in the first column, the yield on Bond A (the short-term bond) will change by the same amount plus 25 basis points, while the yield on Bond B (the long-term bond) will change by the same amount shown in the first column less 25 basis points. In this case, the nonparallel shift assumed is a flattening of the yield curve. For this yield curve shift, the barbell will always outperform the bullet.

In the fourth column, the nonparallel shift assumes that for a change in Bond C's yield, the yield on Bond A will change by the same amount less 25 basis points, while that on Bond B will change by the same amount plus 25 points. That is, this nonparallel shift means that the yield curve will steepen. In this case, the bullet portfolio would

---

1   This illustration is adapted from Ravi E. Dattatreya and Frank J. Fabozzi, *Active Total Return Management of Fixed Income Portfolios* (Chicago: Probus Publishing, 1989).

2   Note that no assumption is needed for the reinvestment rate since the three bonds assumed to be trading right after a coupon payment has been made and therefore there is no accrued interest.

Exhibit 14-1

Relative Performance of Bullet Portfolio and Barbell Portfolio
Over a Six-Month Investment Horizon*

Yield change	Parallel shift	Nonparallel shift**	Nonparallel shift***
−5.000%	−7.19%	−10.69%	−3.89%
−4.750	−6.28	−9.61	−3.12
−4.500	−5.44	−8.62	−2.44
−4.250	−4.68	−7.71	−1.82
−4.000	−4.00	−6.88	−1.27
−3.750	−3.38	−6.13	−0.78
−3.500	−2.82	−5.44	−0.35
−3.250	−2.32	−4.82	0.03
−3.000	−1.88	−4.26	0.36
−2.750	−1.49	−3.75	0.65
−2.500	−1.15	−3.30	0.89
−2.250	−0.85	−2.90	1.09
−2.000	−0.59	−2.55	1.25
−1.750	−0.38	−2.24	1.37
−1.500	−0.20	−1.97	1.47
−1.250	−0.05	−1.74	1.53
−1.000	0.06	−1.54	1.57
−0.750	0.15	−1.38	1.58
−0.500	0.21	−1.24	1.57
−0.250	0.24	−1.14	1.53
0.000	0.25	−1.06	1.48
0.250	0.24	−1.01	1.41
0.500	0.21	−0.98	1.32
0.750	0.16	−0.97	1.21
1.000	0.09	−0.98	1.09
1.250	0.01	−1.00	0.96
1.500	−0.08	−1.05	0.81
1.750	−0.19	−1.10	0.66
2.000	−0.31	−1.18	0.49
2.250	−0.44	−1.26	0.32
2.500	−0.58	−1.36	0.14
2.750	−0.73	−1.46	−0.05
3.000	−0.88	−1.58	−0.24
3.250	−1.05	−1.70	−0.44
3.500	−1.21	−1.84	−0.64
3.750	−1.39	−1.98	−0.85

Exhibit 14-1 continued.

Yield change	Parallel shift	Nonparallel shift**	Nonparallel shift***
4.000	−1.57	−2.12	−1.06
4.250	−1.75	−2.27	−1.27
4.500	−1.93	−2.43	−1.48
4.750	−2.12	−2.58	−1.70
5.000	−2.31	−2.75	−1.92

* Performance is based on the difference in total return over a six-month investment horizon. Specifically:

Bullet portfolio's total return − Barbell portfolio's total return

Therefore a negative value means that the barbell portfolio outperformed the bullet portfolio.

** Change in yield for Bond C. Nonparallel shift as follows (flattening of yield curve):

Yield change Bond A = Yield change Bond C + 25 basis points
Yield change Bond B = Yield change Bond C − 25 basis points

*** Change in yield for Bond C. Nonparallel shift as follows (steepening of yield curve):

Yield change Bond A = Yield change Bond C − 25 basis points
Yield change Bond B = Yield change Bond C + 25 basis points

outperform the barbell portfolio so long as the yield on Bond C does not rise by more than 250 basis points or fall by more than 325 basis points.

The key point here is that measures such as yield (yield-to-maturity or some type of portfolio yield measure), duration, or convexity tell us little about performance over some investment horizon, because performance depends on the magnitude of the change in yields and how the yield curve shifts.

Types of Yield Curve Shifts

Frank Jones provides empirical evidence of the importance of changes in the yield curve in determining returns of Treasury securities for various maturity sectors from 1979 to 1990.[3] Historically, three basic yield curve shift patterns have been observed, each shown in Exhibit 14-2:

---

[3]   Frank J. Jones, "Yield Curve Strategies," *Journal of Fixed Income* (September 1991), pp. 33–41.

Exhibit 14-2

Types of Yield Curve Shifts

(a) Parallel shifts

(b) Twists

(c) Butterfly shifts

■   a parallel shift

■   a twist in the slope of the yield curve (i.e., a flattening or steepening of the yield curve)

■   a change in the humpedness of the yield curve (referred to as a *butterfly shift*)

Jones finds that parallel shifts and twists in the yield curve are responsible for 91.6% of Treasury returns, while 3.4% of changes are attributable to butterfly shifts, and the balance, 5%, to unexplained factor shifts.[4] The three types of yield curve shifts are not independent, but correlated. For example, an upward parallel shift in the yield curve and a flattening of the yield curve have a correlation of .41.[5] Jones's statistical analysis suggests that an upward shift of the yield curve by 10 basis points is consistent with a 2.5 basis point flattening of the yield curve. Moreover, he finds that an upward shift and flattening of the yield curve is correlated with a positive butterfly (less humpedness), while a downward shift and steepening of the yield curve is correlated with a negative butterfly (more humpedness). These two types of shifts in the yield curve are depicted in Exhibit 14-3.

Yield Curve Reshaping Durations

While the total return framework clearly demonstrates the performance potential of a bond portfolio, money managers still seek measures of the interest rate sensitivity of their portfolio, i.e., duration and convexity. The weakness of the traditional modified duration, as we have just illustrated, is that it assumes that yield curve changes shift in a parallel fashion.

The sensitivity of a portfolio to changes in the shape of the yield curve can be approximated. There have been several approaches suggested in the literature to accomplish this. The methodology described here is the one proposed by Klaffky, Ma, and Nozari.[6] We shall refer to the sensitivity of a portfolio to changes in the shape of the yield curve as *reshaping durations*.

To explain reshaping durations, we can use the illustration developed by Klaffky, Ma, and Nozari. Exhibit 14-4 shows two Treasury portfolios, Portfolio A and Portfolio B, constructed from three on-the-run Treasury securities: the two-year, ten-year, and 30-year. The analysis is based on the yield curve as of the close of May 29, 1992. The yield for each issue on that date was 5.18% for the two-year issue, 7.33% for the ten-year issue,

---

4 These findings are consistent with those reported in Robert Litterman and José Scheinkman, "Common Factors Affecting Bond Returns," *Journal of Fixed Income* (June 1991), pp. 54–61.

5 The meaning of correlation is explained in Chapter 24.

6 Thomas E. Klaffky, Y.Y. Ma, and Ardavan Nozari, "Managing Yield Curve Exposure: Introducing Reshaping Durations," *Journal of Fixed Income*, December 1992.

Exhibit 14-3

Combinations of Yield Curve Shifts

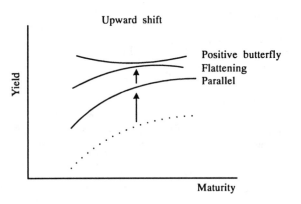

Upward shift

Positive butterfly
Flattening
Parallel

Yield

Maturity

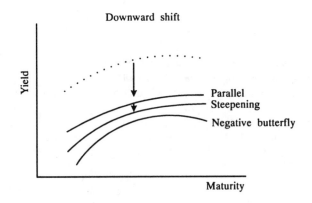

Downward shift

Parallel
Steepening
Negative butterfly

Yield

Maturity

Exhibit 14-4

Two Portfolios with Similar Durations
but Different Yield Curve Exposures

On-the-run Treasury Issue	Modified duration	Market weight Portfolio A	Portfolio B
5.125% of 5/31/94	1.9	20%	39%
7.50% of 5/12/02	7.1	60	20
8.0% of 11/15/21	11.1	20	41
Portfolio modified duration		7	7

Adapted from: Thomas E. Klaffky, Y.Y. Ma, and Ardavan Nozari, "Managing Yield Curve Exposure: Introducing Reshaping Durations," *Journal of Fixed Income*, December 1992.

and 7.84% for the 30-year issue. Also shown in the exhibit is the modified duration for each Treasury issue.[7] The modified duration for both portfolios is 7. Consequently, for a 50 basis point change for all three maturities of the yield curve, each portfolio should change by approximately 3.5%.

Let's look at the actual percentage price change for the two portfolios under three different yield curve scenarios. In the first scenario, suppose that the yield curve shifts in a parallel fashion so that the yield for all Treasury issues declines by 50 basis points. Under this scenario, the actual percentage price increase is 3.52% for Portfolio A and 3.56% for Portfolio B. Thus, the two portfolios would have similar performance. Note that the percentage price change is what would be projected using modified duration (3.5%).

In the next two scenarios, assume a reshaping of the yield curve. In the second scenario, suppose that the two-year yield declines by 50 basis points, while the ten-year and 30-year yields do not change (i.e., the yield curve steepens). In contrast to the first scenario, Portfolio A's price change will be .19%, while Portfolio B's will be .36%. Thus, Portfolio A will outperform Portfolio B by .17%. In the third scenario, assume that the two-year and ten-year yields do not change, but the 30-year yield declines by 50 basis

---

[7] Klaffky, Ma, and Nozari present a generalized approach in which Treasury and non-Treasury securities are included in the portfolio. The latter includes bonds with embedded options (i.e., callable and putable bonds). The valuation of these bonds is discussed in Part V of this book. As will be explained, for bonds with embedded options, a more appropriate measure of price sensitivity is effective duration, a measure we introduced in Chapter 11. Thus, in their paper, Klaffky, Ma, and Nozari refer to the effective duration rather than modified duration. For a noncallable Treasury issue, the two are almost identical, so the modified duration is used in our explanation of their methodology.

points (i.e., the yield curve flattens). In this scenario, Portfolio B will outperform Portfolio A by 1.25%, 2.42% versus 1.17%.

What we seek is a duration measure that takes into account how the reshaping of the yield curve affects price changes. In the measures discussed below, we focus on three points on the yield curve — two-year, ten-year, and 30-year — and the spread between the ten-year and two-year issue and between the 30-year and ten-year issue. The former spread is referred to as the *short-end of the yield curve,* and the latter spread as the *long-end of the yield curve.* Klaffky, Ma, and Nozari refer to the sensitivity of a portfolio to changes in the short end of the yield curve as *short-end duration* (SEDUR), and to changes in the long-end of the yield curve as *long-end duration* (LEDUR). These concepts, however, are applicable to other points on the yield curve.

Calculating Reshaping Duration

To calculate the SEDUR of each bond in the portfolio, the percentage change in the bond's price is calculated for (1) a steepening of the yield curve at the short end by 50 basis points, and (2) a flattening of the yield curve at the short end of the yield curve by 50 basis points. Then the bond's SEDUR is computed as follows:

$$\text{SEDUR} = \frac{P_s - P_f}{P_0} \times 100$$

where

P_s = Bond's price if the short end of the yield curve steepens by 50 basis points

P_f = Bond's price if the short end of the yield curve flattens by 50 basis points

P_0 = Bond's current market price

To calculate the LEDUR, we use the same procedure for each bond in the portfolio: calculate the price for (1) a flattening of the yield curve at the long end by 50 basis points, and (2) a steepening of the yield curve at the long end of the yield curve by 50 basis points. Then the bond's LEDUR is computed in the following manner:

$$\text{LEDUR} = \frac{P_f - P_s}{P_0} \times 100$$

The SEDUR and the LEDUR calculations are equivalent to the formula for approximating duration given in Chapter 11 when a 50 basis point change is used in the formula. Since in our illustration we are using Treasury issues, the modified duration for each bond is the appropriate measure. For example, the SEDUR for the two-year Treasury in Exhibit 14-4 is 1.9, and its LEDUR is zero. The SEDUR for the 30-year bond is zero, and its LEDUR is 11.1. The analysis proceeds from the shifting of the yield curve holding the ten-year yield constant, so the SEDUR and the LEDUR for the ten-year issue are zero.

The portfolio SEDUR and LEDUR are the weighted average of the corresponding durations for each bond in the portfolio. For example, the SEDUR for the two portfolios is calculated as follows:

Portfolio A: .2 (1.9) + .4 (0) + .2 (0) = 3.8
Portfolio B: .39 (1.9) + .2 (0) + .41 (0) = 7.4

A SEDUR of 3.8 means that if the short end of the yield curve shifts by 50 basis points, the portfolio value will change by approximately 1.9%. A similar shift for Portfolio B will result in a 3.7% change in the portfolio's value.

The LEDUR for the two portfolios is calculated in the following manner:

Portfolio A: .2 (0) + .4 (0) + .2 (11.1) = 2.2
Portfolio B: .39 (0) + .2 (0) + .41 (11.1) = 4.6

So far, we have looked at only bonds with maturities at the three points on the yield curve that are used to define the short end and long end. The methodology can be generalized to other maturities as follows.

(1) The shift in yields begins with the ten-year Treasury.

(2) At the short end, the steepening or flattening of the yield curve for any maturity other than two years is proportionate to the ten-year to two-year spread. For example, suppose that the ten-to-two-year spread is 200 basis points and that the ten-to-seven-year spread is 120 basis points. Assume that the yield spread widens by 50 basis points, a 25% increase in the spread. The yield spread for the ten-to-seven-year spread is then assumed to widen by 20 basis points (50 basis points − .25 × 120). The SEDUR for the 7-year is then calculated assuming a 20 basis point change in the spread, not 50 basis points.

(3) At the long end, the steepening or widening for any bond with a maturity of greater than ten years is assumed to be proportionate to the change in the 30-year-to-ten-year spread.

Summary

In this chapter the limitation of duration when the yield curve does not shift in a parallel fashion is illustrated. Three types of yield curve shifts have been observed: parallel shifts, a twist in the slope of the yield curve, and a change in the humpedness of the yield curve. To measure the exposure of a portfolio to yield curve shifts, yield curve reshaping durations can be calculated.

Part V

Analyzing Bonds with Embedded Call Options

15

Call Options: Investment and Price Characteristics

In previous chapters, we described the investment characteristics of option-free bonds. Most of the bonds that we encounter in the market, however, are not option-free. To establish a basis for understanding the price/yield relationship and price volatility characteristics of bonds with embedded options, we review the investment and price characteristics of options in this chapter. Our focus is on *call* options because most corporate bonds and municipal bonds and all mortgage pass-through securities have embedded call options.

What Is an Option?

An option is an agreement granting the buyer of the option the right to purchase from or sell to the writer of the option a designated instrument at a specified price within a specified period of time. The writer, also referred to as the seller, grants this right to the buyer in exchange for a sum of money called the *option price* or *option premium*. The price at which the instrument may be bought or sold is called the *exercise price* or *strike price*. The date after which an option is void is called the *expiration date* or *maturity date*. An option is called an *American option* if the buyer may exercise the option at any time up to and including the expiration date. An option is called a *European option* if the buyer may exercise the option on only the expiration date.

When an option grants the buyer the right to purchase the designated instrument from the writer, it is called a *call option*. When the option buyer has the right to sell the designated instrument to the writer (seller), the option is called a *put option*. The buyer of an option is said to be *long the option;* the writer (seller) is said to be *short the option.*

The most popular exchange-traded interest-rate options are options in which the designated instrument is an interest-rate futures contract. In this chapter we focus on options on cash market bonds because we will be applying the principles and concepts in this chapter to bonds with embedded options in which the cash market bond is the underlying instrument.

Payoffs from Buying and Selling Options

The maximum amount that an option buyer can lose is the option price. The maximum profit that the option writer (seller) can realize is the option price. The option buyer has substantial upside return potential while the option writer has substantial downside risk.

We describe the profit/loss or payoff profile for four basic option positions: (1) long call (buying a call option), (2) short call (selling or writing a call option), (3) long put (buying a put option), and (4) short put (selling or writing a put option). The discussion assumes that a position in only one option is taken. That is, no position is taken in another option or bond. *The profit/loss profiles presented assume that each option position is held to the expiration date and not exercised early.* Also, to simplify the illustrations we assume there are no transaction costs in implementing the position.

Long Call Position (Buying a Call Option)

An investor who purchases a call option is said to be in a *long call position*. This is the most straightforward option for allowing the investor to participate in an anticipated decrease in interest rates (increase in the price of bonds).

To illustrate this strategy, assume that there is a call option on a particular 10% coupon bond with a par value of $100 and 15 years and 2 months to maturity. The call option expires in two months, the strike price is $100, and the option price is $5.

Suppose that the current price of the bond is $100 (i.e., the bond is selling at par), which means that the yield on this bond is 10%. The payoff from this position will depend on the price of the bond at the expiration date. The price, in turn, will depend on the yield on 15-year bonds with 10% coupons, because in two months the bond will have only 15 years to maturity.

If the price of the bond at the expiration date is less than or equal to $100 (which means that the market yield is greater than or equal to 10%), then the investor would not exercise the option. The option buyer will lose the entire option price of $5. Notice, however, that this is the maximum loss that the option buyer will realize, no matter how far the price of the bond declines.

If the price of the bond is higher than $100 (that is, the market yield at expiration is less than 10%), the option buyer will exercise the option. To exercise, the option buyer purchases the bond for $100 (the strike price) and then can sell it in the market for a higher price. The option buyer will realize a loss at expiration if the price of the bond is more than $100 but less than $105 (which corresponds to a market yield at expiration of 10% and approximately 9.35%, respectively). The option buyer will break even if the price of the bond at expiration is $105. This is the break-even price because it costs the option buyer $5 to acquire the call option and $100 to exercise the option to purchase the bond. A profit will be realized if the price of the bond at expiration is more than $105 (that is, the market yield declines to at least 9.35%).

Exhibit 15-1 shows the profit/loss profile. While the break-even point and the loss will depend on the option price, the shape of the curve shown in the exhibit will hold for all buyers of call options. The shape indicates that the maximum loss is the option price and that there is substantial upside potential.

Exhibit 15-1

Profit/Loss for a Long Call Position

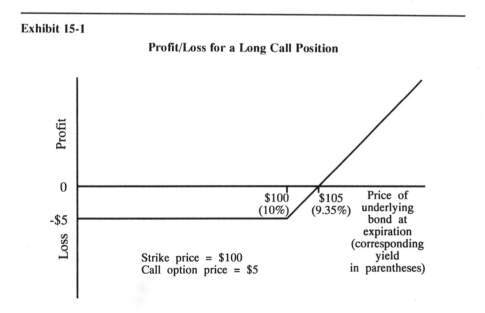

Short Call Position (Selling or Writing a Call Option)

An investor who sells or writes a call option is said to be in a *short call position.* Investors who believe that interest rates will rise or change very little can, if their expectations are correct, realize income by writing (selling) a call option.

To illustrate this option position we can use the call option used to illustrate the long call position. The profit/loss profile of the short call position is the mirror image of the payoff of the long call strategy. That is, the profit (loss) of the short call position for any given price of the bond at the expiration date is the same as the loss (profit) of the long call position. Consequently, the maximum profit that the short call position can produce is the option price; the maximum loss is limited only by how much the price of the bond can increase (i.e., how far the market yield can fall) by the expiration date, less the option price. This can be seen in Exhibit 15-2, which shows the profit/loss profile for this short call position.

Exhibit 15-2

Profit/Loss for a Short Call Position

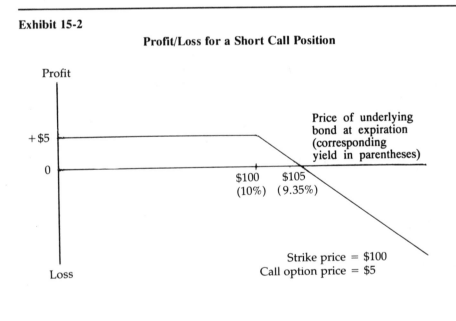

Long Put Position (Buying a Put Option)

The most straightforward option position an investor can take to benefit from an expected increase in interest rates is to buy a put option. This investment position is called a *long put position.*

To illustrate the payoff profile for this position, we'll assume a hypothetical put option for a 10% coupon bond with a par value of $100, 15 years and 2 months to maturity, and a strike price of $100, selling for $5.50. The current price of the bond is $100 (yield of 10%). The payoff for this strategy at the expiration date depends on the market yield at the time.

If the price of the bond is equal to or more than $100 because the market yield has fallen below 10%, the buyer of the put option will not exercise it, thereby incurring a loss of $5.50 (the option price). The investor will exercise the option when the price of the bond at expiration is less than $100 (the market yield at expiration is above 10%). If the market yield is higher than approximately 10.75%, the price of the bond will be lower than $94.50, resulting in a profit from the position. For market yields between 10% and about 10.75%, the investor will realize a loss but the loss is less than $5.50. The break-even market yield is approximately 10.75%, since this will result in a bond price of $94.50.

Exhibit 15-3 shows the profit/loss profile for this position. As with all long option positions, the loss is limited to the option price. The profit potential, however, is substantial; the theoretical maximum profit is generated if the bond price falls to zero.

Exhibit 15-3

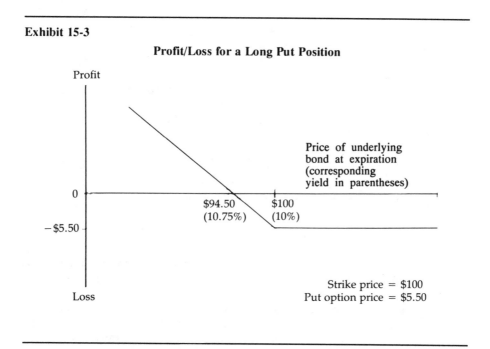

Profit/Loss for a Long Put Position

Profit

Price of underlying bond at expiration (corresponding yield in parentheses)

0

$94.50
(10.75%)

$100
(10%)

−$5.50

Loss

Strike price = $100
Put option price = $5.50

Short Put Position (Selling or Writing a Put Option)

The *short put position* involves the selling (writing) of a put option. This position is taken if the investor expects interest rates to fall or stay flat so that the price of the bond will increase or stay the same. The profit/loss profile for a short put position is the mirror image of the long put option. The maximum profit from this strategy is the option price. The maximum loss is limited only by how low the price of the bond can fall by the expiration date less the option price received for writing the option. Exhibit 15-4 graphically depicts the profit/loss profile.

Exhibit 15-4

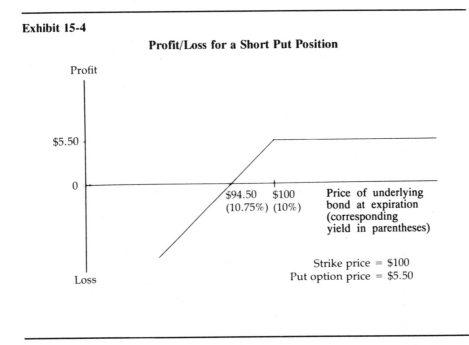

Profit/Loss for a Short Put Position

Considering the Time Value of Money

Our illustrations of the four basic option positions have neglected the time value of money. Specifically, the buyer of an option must pay the seller the option price at the time the option is purchased. Thus, the buyer must finance the purchase of the option or, if the funds do not have to be borrowed, the buyer loses the interest that could be earned by investing the option price. In contrast, assuming that the seller does not have to use the option price as margin for the short position, the seller has the opportunity to invest the option price.

The time value of money changes the profit profile of the option positions. The break-even price for the buyer and the seller of an option will not be the same as in our illustrations. The break-even price for the underlying instrument at the expiration date is higher for the buyer of the option; for the seller, it is lower.

The Intrinsic Value and Time Value of an Option

The cost to the buyer of an option is primarily a reflection of the option's *intrinsic* value and any additional amount over its intrinsic value. The premium over intrinsic value is often referred to as *time value*. This expression, "time value," should not be confused with our earlier use of the term to describe the valuation of cash flows.

Intrinsic Value of an Option

The intrinsic value of an option is the economic value of the option if it is exercised immediately. Since the buyer of an option need not exercise the option and, in fact, will not do so if no economic value will result from exercising, the intrinsic value cannot be less than zero.

The intrinsic value of a call option on a bond is the difference between the current bond price and the strike price. For example, if the *strike price* for a call option is $100 and the *current bond price* is $107, the intrinsic value is $7. That is, if the option buyer exercised the option and simultaneously sold the bond, the option buyer would realize $107 from the sale of the bond, which would be covered by acquiring the bond from the option writer for $100, thereby netting $7.

When a call option has intrinsic value, it is said to be "in the money." Our call option with a strike price of $100 is in the money when the price of the underlying bond is greater than $100. When the strike price of a call option exceeds the current bond price, the call option is said to be "out of the money" and has no intrinsic value. A call option for which the strike price is equal to the current bond price is said to be "at the money."

These relationships are summarized below for a call option:

If the current bond price is higher than the strike price, then the

(1) Intrinsic value is the difference between the current bond price and strike price;

(2) Option is said to be "in the money."

If the current bond price equals the strike price, then the

(1) Intrinsic value is zero;

(2) Option is said to be "at the money."

If the current bond price is lower than the strike price, then the

(1) Intrinsic value is zero;

(2) Option is said to be "out of the money."

For a put option, the intrinsic value is equal to the amount by which the current bond price is below the strike price. For example, if the strike price of a put option is $100, and the current bond price is $88, the intrinsic value is $12. That is, if the buyer of the put option exercises it and simultaneously buys the bond, he or she will net $12. The bond will be sold to the writer for $100 and purchased in the market for $88.

When the put option has intrinsic value, the option is said to be *in the money*. For our put option with a strike price of $100, the option will be in the money when the bond price is less than $100. A put option is *out of the money* when the current bond price exceeds the strike price. A put option is *at the money* when the strike price is equal to the current bond price.

These relationships are summarized below for a put option:

If the current bond price is lower than the strike price, then the

(1) Intrinsic value is the difference between the strike price and current bond price;

(2) Option is said to be "in the money."

If the current bond price equals the strike price, then the

(1) Intrinsic value is zero;

(2) Option is said to be "at the money."

If the current bond price is higher than the strike price, then

(1) Intrinsic value is zero;

(2) Option is said to be "out of the money."

Time Value of an Option

The time value of an option is the amount by which the option price exceeds the intrinsic value. That is,

$$\text{Time value of an option} = \text{Option price} - \text{Intrinsic value}.$$

For example, if the price of a call option with a strike price of $100 is $18 when the current bond price is $107, then for this option:

$$\text{Intrinsic value} = \$107 - \$100 = \$7;$$
$$\text{Time value of option} = \$18 - \$7 = \$11.$$

If the current bond price is $88 instead of $107, then the time value of this option is $18 since the option has no intrinsic value. Notice that for an at-the-money or out-of-the-money option, the time value of the option is equal to the option price because the intrinsic value is zero.

At the expiration date, the time value of the option will be zero. The option price at the expiration date will be equal to its intrinsic value.

Why would an option buyer be willing to pay a premium over the intrinsic value for an option? The reason is that the option buyer believes that at some time prior to expiration, changes in the market yield will increase the value of the rights conveyed by the option.

The Option Price

In the next two chapters we shall see that the price of a bond with an embedded option is determined by the price of the underlying bond and the value of the option. While we can easily determine the value of an option at the expiration date and the intrinsic value of an option at any time prior to the expiration date, the fair value or price of the option at any time prior to the expiration date must be estimated. In this section, we will discuss the factors that influence the fair or "theoretical" value of an option.[1]

Factors that Influence the Option Price

Six factors influence the option price:

(1) Current price of the underlying bond,

(2) Strike price,

(3) Time to expiration,

(4) Short-term risk-free interest rate over the life of the option,

(5) Coupon rate, and

(6) Expected interest rate volatility over the life of the option.

The effect of each of these factors depends on whether (1) the option is a call or a put and (2) the option is an American option (an option that may be exercised up to and including the expiration date) or a European option (an option that may be exercised only at the expiration date).[2]

Current Price of the Underlying Bond.   For a call option, as the current price of the underlying bond increases (decreases), the option price increases (decreases). For a put option, as the current price of the bond decreases (increases), the option price increases (decreases).

Strike Price.   All other factors constant, the higher the strike price, the lower the price of a call option. For a put option, the opposite is true: the higher the strike price, the higher the price of a put option.

---

[1] For a more detailed discussion of the impact of these factors on the price of an option, see Mark Pitts and Frank J. Fabozzi, *Interest Rate Futures and Options* (Chicago: Probus Publishing, 1989).

[2] The option price also will depend on whether the underlying instrument is a cash market bond or an interest rate futures contract. Our focus in this chapter is on options on cash market bonds.

Time to Expiration. For American options, all other factors constant, the longer the time to expiration, the higher the option price. No general statement can be made for European options.

Short-Term Risk-Free Interest Rate over the Life of the Option. Holding all other factors constant, the price of a call option on a bond will increase as the short-term risk-free interest rate rises. For a put option, the opposite is true: an increase in the short-term risk-free interest rate will reduce the price of a put option.

Coupon Rate. Coupons for options on bonds tend to reduce the price of a call option because the coupons make it more attractive to hold the bond than the option. Thus, call options on coupon-bearing bonds will tend to be priced lower than other similar call options on noncoupon-bearing bonds. For put options, coupons tend to increase their price.

Expected Interest Rate Volatility over the Life of the Option. As the expected interest rate volatility over the life of the option increases, the price of an option increases. The reason is that the more the expected volatility, as measured by the standard deviation or variance of interest rates,[3] the greater the probability that the price of the underlying bond will move in the direction that will benefit the option buyer.

Option Pricing Model

Several models have been developed to estimate the theoretical or fair price of an option. These models are based on an arbitrage or riskless hedge valuation model. Our purpose here is not to describe option pricing models, but instead, to mention some of the models that are commercially available from software vendors. Most of the dealer firms have developed their own option pricing models, which typically are not available to clients.

The most popular option pricing model for American call options on common stocks is the Black-Scholes option pricing model.[4] The key insight of the Black-Scholes option pricing model is that a synthetic option can be created by taking an appropriate position in the underlying common stock and borrowing or lending funds at the riskless interest rate.[5]

---

[3] These statistical measures are explained in Chapter 22.

[4] Fischer Black and Myron Scholes, "The Pricing of Corporate Liabilities," *Journal of Political Economy* (May-June 1973), pp. 637-659.

[5] The appropriate position in the underlying common stock depends on how the price of the option will change when the price of the stock changes. This relationship between the change in price of the option and the change in price of the underlying common stock is called the *delta* of the option and is discussed later in this chapter.

There are several problems in applying the Black-Scholes option pricing model to price interest rate options. To illustrate these problems, consider a three-month European call option on a three-year zero-coupon bond.[6] The maturity value of the underlying bond is $100, and the strike price is $120. Suppose further that the current price of the bond is $75.13, the three-year risk-free rate is 10% annually, and expected price volatility is 4%. What would be the fair value for this option? Do you really need an option pricing model to determine the value of this option?

Think about it. This zero-coupon bond will never have a price above $100 because that is the maturity value. As the strike price is $120, the option will never be exercised; its value is therefore zero. If you can get anyone to buy such as option, any price you obtain will be free money. Yet an option buyer armed with the Black-Scholes option pricing model will input the variables we assume above and come up with a value for this option of $5.60! Why is the Black-Scholes model off by so much? The answer lies in the underlying assumptions.

There are three assumptions underlying the Black-Scholes model that limit its use in pricing options on interest rate instruments. First, the probability distribution for the prices assumed by the Black-Scholes option pricing model is a lognormal distribution, which permits some probability — no matter how small — that the price can take on any positive value. In the case of the zero-coupon bond, that means the price can take on a value above $100. In the case of a coupon bond, we know that the price cannot exceed the sum of the coupon payments plus the maturity value. For example, for a five-year 10% coupon bond with a maturity value of $100, the price cannot be more than $150 (five coupon payments of $10 plus the maturity value of $100). The only way a bond's price can exceed the maximum value is if negative interest rates are permitted. This is not likely to occur, so any probability distribution for prices assumed by an option pricing model that permits bond prices to be more than the maximum bond value can generate nonsensical option prices. The Black-Scholes model does allow bond prices to exceed the maximum bond value (or, equivalently, allows negative interest rates). This is one of the reasons we obtained the nonsensical option price for the three-month European call option on the three-year zero-coupon bond.

The second assumption of the Black-Scholes option pricing model is that the short-term interest rate is constant over the life of the option. Yet the price of an interest rate option does change as interest rates change. A change in the short-term interest rate changes the rates along the yield curve. Therefore, to assume that the short-term rate will be constant is inappropriate for interest rate options.

The third assumption is that the variance of prices is constant over the life of the option. Recall from Chapter 5 that as a bond moves closer to maturity, its price volatility declines. Therefore, the assumption that price variance is constant over the life of the option is inappropriate.

---

[6] Lawrence Dyer and David Jacob, "Guide to Fixed Income Option Pricing Models," in Frank J. Fabozzi (ed.), *The Handbook of Fixed Income Options* (Chicago: Probus Publishing, 1989).

A binomial option pricing model based on the price distribution of the underlying bond suffers from the same problems as the Black-Scholes model. A way around the problem of negative interest rates is to use a model based on the distribution of yields rather than prices.

While the binomial option pricing model based on yields is superior to models based on prices, it still has a theoretical drawback. All option pricing models to be valid theoretically must satisfy the put-call parity relationship (explained later in the chapter). The problem with the binomial model based on yields is that it does not satisfy this relationship. It violates the relationship in that it fails to take into consideration the yield curve, thereby allowing arbitrage opportunities.

The most elaborate models that take the yield curve into consideration and as a result do not permit arbitrage opportunities are called *yield curve option pricing models* or *arbitrage-free option pricing models*. These models can incorporate different volatility assumptions along the yield curve. While they are theoretically superior to the other models we have described, they require extensive computer time to solve.[7]

Implied Interest Rate Volatility

Option pricing models provide a theoretical option price based on the six factors that we discussed earlier. Of the six factors, the only one that is not known and must be estimated is the expected interest rate volatility over the life of the option. A popular methodology for assessing whether an option is fairly priced is to assume that the option is priced correctly and to estimate the interest rate volatility that is implied by an option pricing model. Exhibit 15-5 describes the process for computing implied interest rate volatility.

For example, suppose that a money manager — using some option pricing model, the current price of the option, and the five factors that determine the price of an option — computes an implied interest rate volatility of 12%. If the money manager expects that the interest rate volatility over the life of the option will be greater than the implied interest rate volatility of 12%, the option is undervalued. If the money manager's expected interest rate volatility over the life of the option is less than the implied interest rate volatility, the option is overvalued.

While we have focused on the option price, the key to understanding the options market is that trading and investment strategies in this market involve buying and selling interest rate volatility. Looking at the implied interest rate volatility and comparing it to the trader's or money manager's expectations of future interest rate volatility is just another way of evaluating options.

---

[7] For a discussion of yield curve or arbitrage-free option pricing models see: Chapter 7 of Pitts and Fabozzi, *Interest Rate Futures and Options*; Dyer and Jacob, "Guide to Fixed Income Option Pricing Models," *The Handbook of Fixed Income Options*; and Ravi E. Dattatreya and Frank J. Fabozzi, "A Simplified Model for the Valuation of Debt Options," Chapter 4 in *The Handbook of Fixed Income Options*.

Exhibit 15-5

The Process of Obtaining Implied Interest Rate Volatility

A. To obtain theoretical option price

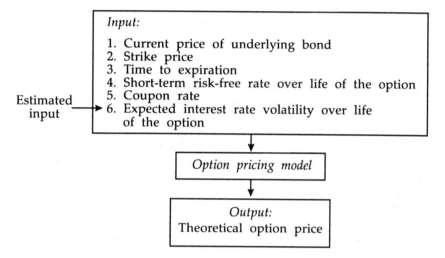

B. To obtain implied interest rate volatility

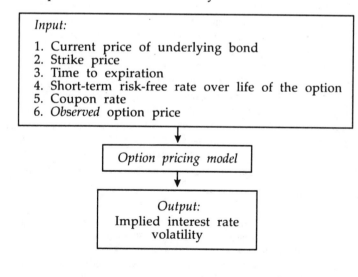

Sensitivity of the Theoretical Call Option Price to Changes in Factors

When any one of the six factors that affect the price of an option changes, the option price will change. Since the price of a bond with an embedded option will be affected by how the price of the embedded option changes, we will look at the sensitivity of the option price to three of the factors — the price of the underlying bond, time to expiration, and expected interest rate volatility. We focus our attention on call options.[8]

The Call Option Price and the Price of the Underlying Bond

Exhibit 15-6 shows the theoretical price of a call option based on the price of the underlying bond. The horizontal axis is the price of the underlying bond at any time. The vertical axis is the option price. The shape of the curve representing the theoretical price of a call option, given the price of the underlying bond, would be the same regardless of the actual option pricing model used. Specifically, the relationship between the price of the underlying bond and the theoretical call option price is convex. Thus, option prices also exhibit convexity.

The line from the origin to the strike price on the horizontal axis in Exhibit 15-6 is the intrinsic value of the call option when the price of the underlying bond is less than the strike price, since the intrinsic value is zero. The 45-degree line extending from the horizontal axis is the intrinsic value of the call option once the price of the underlying bond exceeds the strike price. The reason is that the intrinsic value of the call option will increase by the same amount as the increase in the price of the underlying bond. For example, if the exercise price is $100, and the price of the underlying bond increases from $100 to $101, the intrinsic value will increase by $1. If the price of the bond increases from $101 to $110, the intrinsic value of the option will increase from $1 to $10. Thus, the slope of the line representing the intrinsic value after the strike price is reached is 1.

Since the theoretical call option price is shown by the convex line, the difference between the theoretical call option price and the intrinsic value at any given price for the underlying bond is the time value of the option.

Exhibit 15-7 shows the theoretical call option price, but with a tangent line drawn at the price of p^*. Recall from the Chapter 12 that the tangent line was used to estimate the new price of a bond at a new yield level. Here we have an analogous situation. The tangent line in Exhibit 15-7 can be used to estimate what the new option price will be (and therefore what the change in the option price will be) if the price of the underlying bond changes. Once again, because of the convexity of the relationship between the

---

[8] For a detailed discussion of the role of these measures in option strategies, see Pitts and Fabozzi, *Interest Rate Futures and Options;* Richard M. Bookstaber, *Option Pricing and Investment Strategies* (Chicago: Probus Publishing, 1987), Chapter 4; and James F. Meisner and John A. Richards, "Option Premium Dynamics: With Applications to Fixed Income Portfolio Analysis," in *Advances in Bond Analysis and Portfolio Strategies*, Frank J. Fabozzi and T. Dessa Garlicki, eds. (Chicago: Probus Publishing, 1987).

Exhibit 15-6

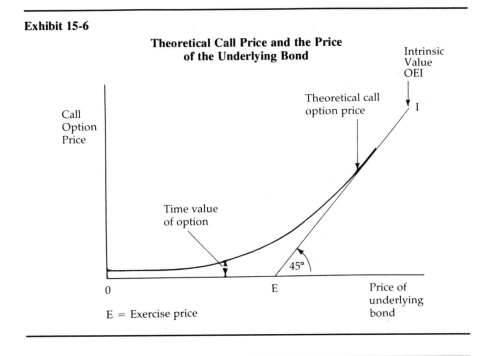

**Theoretical Call Price and the Price
of the Underlying Bond**

Intrinsic
Value
OEI

Theoretical call
option price

Call
Option
Price

I

Time value
of option

45°

0

E

Price of
underlying
bond

E = Exercise price

Exhibit 15-7

Delta of a Call Option

Intrinsic
value
OEI

Theoretical call
option price

I

Call
Option
Price

Tangent line
(delta) at p^*

45°

0

p^* E

Price of
underlying
bond

E = Exercise price

option price and the price of the underlying bond, the tangent line closely approximates the new option price for a small change in the price of the underlying bond. For large changes, however, the tangent line does not provide as good an approximation of the new option price.

The slope of the tangent line shows how the theoretical call option price will change for small changes in the price of the underlying bond. The slope of the tangent line is commonly referred to as the "delta" of the option.[9] Specifically,

$$\text{Delta} = \frac{\text{Change in price of call option}}{\text{Change in price of underlying bond}}.$$

For example, a delta of .5 means that a $1 change in the price of the underlying bond will change the price of the call option by $.50.

Exhibit 15-8 shows the curve of the theoretical call option price with three tangent lines drawn. The steeper the slope of the tangent line, the greater the delta. When an option is deep out of the money (that is, the price of the underlying bond is substantially below the strike price), the tangent line is nearly flat (see Line 1 in Exhibit 15-8). This means that the delta is close to zero. To understand why, consider a call option with a strike price of $100 and two months to expiration. If the price of the underlying bond is $20, the option price would not increase by much if the price of the underlying bond increased by $1, from $20 to $21.

For a call option that is deep in the money, the delta will be close to one. That is, the call option price will increase almost dollar for dollar with an increase in the price of the underlying bond. In terms of Exhibit 15-8, the slope of the tangent line approaches the slope of the intrinsic value line after the strike price. As we stated earlier, the slope of that line is 1.

Thus, the delta for a call option varies from zero (for call options deep out of the money) to one (for call options deep in the money). The delta for a call option at the money is approximately .5.

Related to the delta is the *lambda* of an option, which measures the percentage change in the price of the option for a 1% change in the price of the underlying bond. That is,

$$\text{Lambda} = \frac{\text{Percentage change in the price of the call option}}{\begin{array}{c}\text{Percentage change in}\\ \text{the price of the underlying bond}\end{array}}.$$

For example, a lambda of 1.5 indicates that if the price of the call option changes by 1%, the call option's price will change by 1.5%. The lambda of a call option will be greater than 1 because of the leverage offered by an option. As the price of the underlying bond increases, the option's lambda decreases.

---

[9] The delta is also referred to as the *hedge ratio*.

Exhibit 15-8

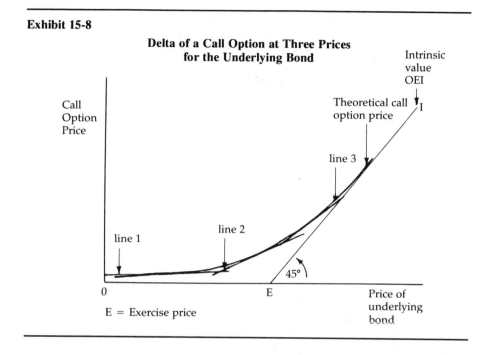

**Delta of a Call Option at Three Prices
for the Underlying Bond**

In the previous chapter, we measured the convexity of an option-free bond. We also can measure the convexity of a call option. Recall from the previous chapter that the convexity of a bond measures the rate of change in dollar duration. For call options, convexity measures the rate of change in delta. The measure of convexity for options is commonly referred to as *gamma,* defined as follows:

$$\text{Gamma} = \frac{\text{Change in delta}}{\text{Change in price of underlying bond}}.$$

The Call Option Price and Time to Expiration

All other factors constant, the longer the time to expiration, the higher the option price. Since each day the option moves to the expiration date, the time to expiration decreases. The *theta* of an option measures the change in the option price as the time to expiration decreases. That is,

$$\text{Theta} = \frac{\text{Change in price of option}}{\text{Decrease in time to expiration}}.$$

Assuming that the price of the underlying bond does not change so that the intrinsic value of the option does not change, theta measures how quickly the time value of the option changes as the option moves toward expiration.

The Call Option Price and Expected Interest Rate Volatility

All other factors constant, a change in the expected interest rate volatility will change the option price. The *kappa* (or *vega*) of an option measures the dollar price change in the price of the option for a 1% change in the expected interest rate volatility. That is,

$$\frac{\text{Kappa}}{(\text{Vega})} = \frac{\text{Change in option price}}{1\% \text{ change in expected interest rate volatility}}.$$

Duration of an Option

The modified duration of a bond is an indicator of its price sensitivity to changes in interest rates. We can similarly define a modified duration for an option as follows:

$$\text{Modified duration for an option} =$$
$$\left(\begin{array}{c}\text{Modified duration of the}\\ \text{underlying instrument}\end{array}\right) \times \text{delta} \times \left(\frac{\text{Price of underlying instrument}}{\text{Price of option}}\right)$$

Therefore, the modified duration for an option depends on three factors: (1) the modified duration of the underlying instrument, (2) the delta of the option and, (3) the ratio of the price of the underlying instrument to the price of the option. This last factor can be thought of as a measure of the "leverage" in the option.

Put-Call Parity Relationship

There is a relationship between the price of a call option and the price of a put option on the same underlying bond, with the same strike price and the same expiration date. This relationship is commonly referred to as the *put-call parity relationship*. For coupon bearing bonds it is

$$\text{Put price} = \text{Call price} + \text{Present value of strike price}$$
$$+ \text{Present value of coupon} - \text{Price of underlying bond}$$

This relationship is one form of the put-call parity relationship for European options. It is approximately true for American options. The relationship is based on arbitrage arguments.[10]

---

[10] Robert Jarrow and Andrew Rudd, *Option Pricing* (Homewood, Ill: Dow Jones-Irwin, 1983), Chapters 4 and 6.

Summary

In this chapter we have explained the investment and price characteristics of options, focusing on call options because they are the most common type of option embedded in bonds. The key concepts to be understood are as follows. First, the maximum profit that an option writer (seller) can realize is the option price; the option writer, however, is exposed to substantial downside risk. For an option buyer, the maximum loss is the option price. The option buyer retains all the upside potential (reduced by the option price).

Second, there are six factors that influence an option's price: current price of the underlying bond, strike price, time to expiration, short-term risk-free interest rate over the life of the option, coupon rate, and expected interest rate volatility over the life of the option. Option pricing models attempt to estimate the theoretical price of an option.

Third, buying and selling of options involves buying and selling expected interest rate volatility. Recall that we said the same thing in Chapter 12 when we explained that the value of convexity depends on expected interest rate volatility over some investment horizon. Rather than looking at the value of an option in terms of price, it is common for investors to compute the implied interest rate volatility of an option and compare it to expected interest rate volatility.

Fourth, there are measures used to assess the sensitivity of the option price to a change in factors such as the price of the underlying bond (delta and lambda), time (theta), and expected interest rate volatility (kappa or vega). A graph of the relationship between the theoretical call price and the price of the underlying bond is convex. Gamma measures the convexity (that is, how the delta changes). A duration for an option can be calculated.

Finally, the put-call parity relationship defines the relationships among the prices of a put option, a call option, and the underlying bond.

16

Price and Performance Characteristics of Callable Corporate Bonds

Most corporate bonds are callable to maturity.[1] As explained in Chapter 6, the traditional procedure for assessing the relative value of callable bonds is to compute first the yield to

---

[1] For a complete explanation of the various terms and conditions for the early redemption of a corporate bond, see Chapter 5 in Richard W. Wilson and Frank J. Fabozzi, *The New Corporate Bond Market* (Chicago: Probus Publishing, 1990).

call for a bond and then, using that measure (assuming it is less than the yield to maturity), compare it to various callable bonds. As we explained in the same chapter, however, this procedure will not permit evaluation of the relative performance of callable bonds over a predetermined investment horizon. In this chapter, a conceptual framework for evaluating corporate callable bonds is presented. Basically, the conceptual framework presented here assumes that an option pricing model can be used to value the embedded option or options in a bond. The following two chapters provide valuation approaches that do not rely on such a model.

Price/Yield Relationship for a Callable Corporate Bond

As we demonstrated in previous chapters, the price/yield relationship for an option-free (i.e., noncallable) bond is convex. Exhibit 16-1 shows the price/yield relationship for a noncallable bond and for the same bond if it is callable. The convex curve a-a' is the price/yield relationship for the noncallable (option-free) bond. The unusually shaped curve a-b is the price/yield relationship for the callable bond.

The reason for the shape of the price/yield relationship for the callable bond is as follows: When the prevailing market yield for comparable bonds is higher than the coupon rate on the bond, it is unlikely that the corporate issuer will call the bond. For example, if the coupon rate on a bond is 8% and the prevailing yield on comparable bonds is 16%, it is highly improbable that the corporate issuer will call in an 8% bond so that it

---

Exhibit 16-1

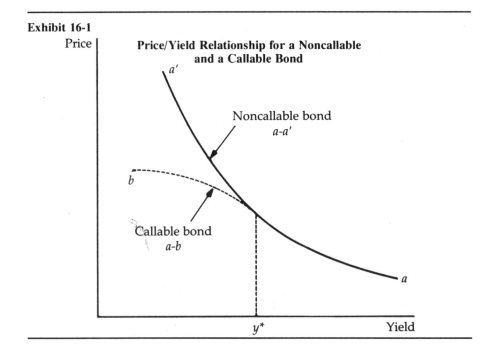

Price/Yield Relationship for a Noncallable and a Callable Bond

can issue a 16% bond. In option terminology, the call option is deep out of the money. Since the bond is unlikely to be called when it is deep out of the money, a callable bond will have the same price/yield relationship as a noncallable bond. However, even when the option is near the money (the coupon rate is just below the market yield), investors may not pay the same price for the bond had it been not callable because there is still the chance the market yield may drop further so that it would become beneficial for the issuer to call the bond.

As yields in the market decline, the likelihood that yields will decline further — so that the issuer will benefit from calling the bond — increases. We may not know the exact yield at which investors begin to view the issue as likely to be called, but we do know that there is some level. In Exhibit 16-1, at yields below y^*, the price/yield relationship for the callable bond departs from the price/yield relationship for the noncallable bond. If, for example, the market yield is such that a noncallable bond would be selling for 109 but, since it is callable, would be called at 104, investors would not pay 109. If they did and the bond is called, investors would receive 104 (the call price) for a bond they purchased for 109. Notice that for a range of yields below y^*, there is price compression — that is, there is limited price appreciation as yields decline.

Illustration 16-1. To illustrate the difference between the price/yield relationship for a noncallable and that for a callable corporate bond, consider a 12% coupon bond maturing in 17 years and callable in two years at 102.[2] Exhibit 16-2 shows the price/yield relationship for this bond assuming it is noncallable. Also shown in Exhibit 16-2 is the theoretical price for the callable bond. The computation of the *theoretical* price requires that certain assumptions be made. We discuss these assumptions in later illustrations. The price/yield relationship is graphed in Exhibit 16-3.

Notice the following in Exhibits 16-2 and 16-3. As the (noncallable) yield rises above approximately 14.5%, the price of the noncallable bond approaches the price of the callable bond. This is consistent with what we observe in Exhibit 16-1. In contrast, when the yield falls below 14.5%, the difference between the price of the noncallable bond and that of the callable bond increases. Once again, this is consistent with Exhibit 16-1. The price/yield relationship flattens as the yield moves deep in the money.

Breaking a Callable Corporate Bond into its Component Parts

To develop an analytical framework for assessing relative value and evaluating the potential performance of callable bonds over some investment horizon, it is necessary to understand what the components of the bond are. A callable corporate bond is a bond whose holder has sold the issuing corporation a call option that allows the issuer to

---

[2] The numerical values for this illustration and the others in this chapter were provided by Mark Dunetz and James Mahoney when they were employed by Kidder Peabody's Fixed Income Research Group. The illustration was based on GMAC 12% of June 2005 callable at 102 and a settlement date of June 1, 1998.

Exhibit 16-2

Price/Yield Relationship for a 12%, 17-Year Bond Callable at 102 in Two Years

Yield	Noncallable bond price	Theoretical callable bond price
20.51	60	60.000
20.18	61	61.000
19.86	62	62.000
19.55	63	63.000
19.24	64	64.000
18.95	65	65.000
18.66	66	66.000
18.39	67	67.000
18.11	68	68.000
17.85	69	68.999
17.59	70	69.999
17.34	71	70.999
17.10	72	71.998
16.86	73	72.998
16.63	74	73.997
16.40	75	74.995
16.18	76	75.994
15.96	77	76.992
15.75	78	77.988
15.54	79	78.984
15.33	80	79.980
15.13	81	80.973
14.94	82	81.964
14.75	83	82.954
14.56	84	83.943
14.38	85	84.925
14.20	86	85.905
14.02	87	86.884
13.85	88	87.854
13.68	89	88.817
13.51	90	89.777
13.35	91	90.735
13.19	92	91.670
13.03	93	92.602
12.87	94	93.531
12.72	95	94.443
12.57	96	95.333

Yield	Noncallable bond price	Theoretical callable bond price
12.42	97	96.217
12.28	98	97.096
12.00	100	98.765
11.73	102	100.384
11.46	104	101.888
11.33	105	102.620
11.20	106	103.339
11.07	107	103.988
10.95	108	104.627
10.83	109	105.258
10.71	110	105.866
10.59	111	106.404
10.47	112	106.933
10.35	113	107.452
10.24	114	107.944
10.13	115	108.369
10.02	116	108.785
9.91	117	109.192
9.80	118	109.571
9.69	119	109.889
9.59	120	110.199
9.48	121	110.501
9.38	122	110.780
9.28	123	111.004
9.18	124	111.222
9.08	125	111.433
8.98	126	111.628
8.89	127	111.776
8.79	128	111.920
8.60	130	112.187
8.42	132	112.368
8.24	134	112.534
8.07	136	112.638
7.90	138	112.733
7.73	140	112.790
7.24	146	112.894
6.79	152	112.925
6.36	158	112.934
5.96	164	112.936
5.57	170	112.936

Exhibit 16-3

Price/Yield Relationship for a 12%, 17-Year Corporate Bond Callable at 102 in Two Years

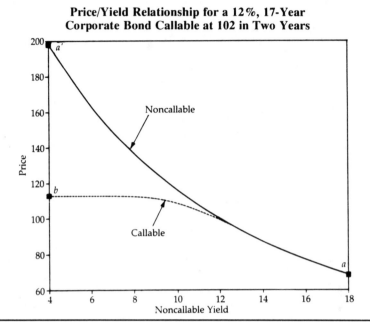

repurchase the contractual cash flow of the bond from the time the bond is first callable until the maturity date.

Illustration 16-2. Consider a callable corporate bond with an 8% coupon and 20 years to maturity that is callable in five years at 104. The bondholder then owns a five-year noncallable bond and has sold a call option granting the issuer the right to call away from the bondholder 15 years of cash flow five years from now. The exercise price is 104.

Illustration 16-3. Consider an investor who owns a 10-year, 9% corporate bond that is immediately callable at 100 (par). The investor owns a 10-year noncallable bond and has sold a call option granting the issuer the right immediately to call the entire 10-year contractual cash flow, or any cash flow remaining at the time the issue is called, for 100.

Illustration 16-4. Consider the 12%, 17-year corporate bond callable in two years at 102. A bondholder who owns this bond effectively owns a noncallable bond with two years to maturity (the first call date) and has sold a call option granting the issuer the right to call away from the bondholder 15 years of cash flows beginning two years from now. The exercise price for this call option is 102.

Effectively, the owner of a corporate callable bond is entering into two separate transactions. The first, is the purchase of a corporate noncallable bond from the issuer, for which some price is paid. The second is sale to the issuer of a call option, for which some option price is received from the issuer. Therefore, we can summarize the position of a corporate callable bondholder as follows:[3]

Long a callable bond
= Long a noncallable bond + Short a call option

In terms of price, the price of a callable corporate bond is therefore equal to a combination of the two component parts. That is,

Callable bond price = Noncallable bond price – Call option price.

The call option price is subtracted from the price of the noncallable bond. The reason is that when the bondholder sells a call option, he or she receives the option price. This is graphically demonstrated in Exhibit 16-1. The difference between the price of the noncallable bond and that of the callable bond is the price of the embedded call option.

Illustration 16-5. Returning to the 12%, 17-year callable bond in Illustration 16-1, the price of the noncallable bond and the theoretical price of the embedded call option are shown in Exhibit 16-4. The theoretical price of the call option is based on a binomial option pricing model.[4] Recall from the previous chapter that an assumption about future interest rate volatility is required as an input into the option pricing model to obtain the theoretical option price. The volatility assumption made to compute the theoretical call option price in Exhibit 16-4 is that it will be 12% per year. The difference between the price of the noncallable bond and the theoretical price of the call option is the price of the callable bond. Notice that the price of the callable bond is the same as that shown in Exhibit 16-2.

From the previous chapter we know that the price of a call option increases when expected interest rate volatility increases. Exhibit 16-5 shows the theoretical price of the call option when interest rate volatility is assumed to be 20% per year. The theoretical price of the call option is greater in Exhibit 16-5 than in Exhibit 16-4 because of the higher interest rate volatility assumed. Since the theoretical price of the call option is higher, the price of the callable bond is lower in Exhibit 16-5 than in Exhibit 16-4.

---

[3] Actually, the position is more complicated. The issuer may be entitled to call the bond at the first call date or any time thereafter, or at the first call date and any subsequent coupon anniversary. Thus the investor has effectively sold a strip of call options to the issuer. The exercise price is the call price, which may vary with the date the issue may be called. The cash flows of the underlying bond for the call option are the remaining coupon payments that would have been made by the issuer had the bond not been called. For exposition purposes, it is easier to understand the principles associated with the investment characteristics of callable corporate bonds by describing the investor's position as long a noncallable bond and short a call option.

[4] The theoretical option price for this illustration was provided by Andrew Ho of Kidder Peabody.

Exhibit 16-4

Price/Yield Relationship and Theoretical Option Price for a 12%,
17-Year Bond Callable at 102 in Two Years
(12% Interest Rate Volatility Assumption)

Assumptions to compute theoretical call option price:
Binomial option pricing model
Interest rate volatility: 12%
Short-term interest rate: 6%

Yield	Noncallable bond price	Theoretical option price	Theoretical callable bond price
20.51	60	.000	60.000
20.18	61	.000	61.000
19.86	62	.000	62.000
19.55	63	.000	63.000
19.24	64	.000	64.000
18.95	65	.000	65.000
18.66	66	.000	66.000
18.39	67	.000	67.000
18.11	68	.000	68.000
17.85	69	.001	68.999
17.59	70	.001	69.999
17.34	71	.001	70.999
17.10	72	.002	71.998
16.86	73	.002	72.998
16.63	74	.003	73.997
16.40	75	.005	74.995
16.18	76	.006	75.994
15.96	77	.008	76.992
15.75	78	.012	77.988
15.54	79	.016	78.984
15.33	80	.020	79.980
15.13	81	.027	80.973
14.94	82	.036	81.964
14.75	83	.046	82.954
14.56	84	.057	83.943
14.38	85	.075	84.925
14.20	86	.095	85.905
14.02	87	.116	86.884
13.85	88	.146	87.854
13.68	89	.183	88.817

Yield	Noncallable bond price	Theoretical option price	Theoretical callable bond price
13.51	90	.223	89.777
13.35	91	.265	90.735
13.19	92	.330	91.670
13.03	93	.398	92.602
12.87	94	.469	93.531
12.72	95	.557	94.443
12.57	96	.667	95.333
12.42	97	.783	96.217
12.28	98	.904	97.096
12.00	100	1.235	98.765
11.73	102	1.606	100.394
11.46	104	2.112	101.888
11.33	105	2.380	102.620
11.20	106	2.661	103.339
11.07	107	3.012	103.988
10.95	108	3.373	104.627
10.83	109	3.742	105.258
10.71	110	4.134	105.866
10.59	111	4.596	106.404
10.47	112	5.067	106.933
10.35	113	5.548	107.452
10.24	114	6.056	107.944
10.13	115	6.631	108.369
10.02	116	7.215	108.785
9.91	117	7.808	109.192
9.80	118	8.429	109.571
9.69	119	9.111	109.889
9.59	120	9.801	110.199
9.48	121	10.499	110.501
9.38	122	11.220	110.780
9.28	123	11.996	111.004
9.18	124	12.778	111.222
9.08	125	13.567	111.433
8.98	126	14.372	111.628
8.89	127	15.224	111.776
8.79	128	16.080	111.920
8.60	130	17.813	112.187
8.42	132	19.632	112.368
8.24	134	21.466	112.534

Exhibit 16-4 continued.

Yield	Noncallable bond price	Theoretical option price	Theoretical callable bond price
8.07	136	23.362	112.638
7.90	138	25.267	112.733
7.73	140	27.210	112.790
7.24	146	33.106	112.894
6.79	152	39.075	112.925
6.36	158	45.066	112.934
5.96	164	51.064	112.936
5.57	170	57.064	112.936

Exhibit 16-5

Price/Yield Relationship and Theoretical Option Price for a 12%, 17-Year Bond Callable at 102 in Two Years (20% Interest Rate Volatility Assumption)

Assumptions to compute theoretical call option price:
Binomial option pricing model
Interest rate volatility: 20%
Short-term interest rate: 6%

Yield	Noncallable bond price	Theoretical option price	Theoretical callable bond price
20.51	60	.019	59.981
20.18	61	.024	60.976
19.86	62	.029	61.971
19.55	63	.035	62.965
19.24	64	.044	63.956
18.95	65	.055	64.945
18.66	66	.066	65.934
18.39	67	.078	66.922
18.11	68	.092	67.908
17.85	69	.112	68.888
17.59	70	.134	69.866
17.34	71	.158	70.842
17.10	72	.182	71.818
16.86	73	.208	72.792

Yield	Noncallable bond price	Theoretical option price	Theoretical callable bond price
16.63	74	.248	73.752
16.40	75	.290	74.710
16.18	76	.334	75.666
15.96	77	.379	76.621
15.75	78	.427	77.573
15.54	79	.491	78.509
15.33	80	.564	79.436
15.13	81	.640	80.360
14.94	82	.718	81.282
14.75	83	.800	82.200
14.56	84	.887	83.113
14.38	85	1.006	83.994
14.20	86	1.128	84.872
14.02	87	1.254	85.746
13.85	88	1.384	86.616
13.68	89	1.518	87.482
13.51	90	1.665	88.335
13.35	91	1.851	89.149
13.19	92	2.041	89.959
13.03	93	2.235	90.765
12.87	94	2.434	91.566
12.72	95	2.637	92.363
12.57	96	2.855	93.145
12.42	97	3.125	93.875
12.28	98	3.399	94.601
12.00	100	3.964	96.036
11.73	102	4.550	97.450
11.46	104	5.285	98.715
11.33	105	5.664	99.336
11.20	106	6.049	99.951
11.07	107	6.439	100.561
10.95	108	6.835	101.165
10.83	109	7.272	101.728
10.71	110	7.752	102.248
10.59	111	8.238	102.762
10.47	112	8.730	103.270
10.35	113	9.228	103.772
10.24	114	9.731	104.269
10.13	115	10.240	104.760

Exhibit 16-5 continued.

Yield	Noncallable bond price	Theoretical option price	Theoretical callable bond price
10.02	116	10.821	105.179
9.91	117	11.414	105.586
9.80	118	12.013	105.987
9.69	119	12.618	106.382
9.59	120	13.227	106.773
9.48	121	13.842	107.158
9.38	122	14.479	107.521
9.28	123	15.172	107.828
9.18	124	15.871	108.129
9.08	125	16.575	108.425
8.98	126	17.283	108.717
8.89	127	17.996	109.004
8.79	128	18.713	109.287
8.60	130	20.250	109.750
8.42	132	21.832	110.168
8.24	134	23.431	110.569
8.07	136	25.076	110.924
7.90	138	26.797	111.203
7.73	140	28.529	111.471
7.24	146	33.925	112.075
6.79	152	39.541	112.459
6.36	158	45.311	112.689
5.96	164	51.183	112.817
5.57	170	57.117	112.883

This also can be seen in Exhibit 16-6, which shows the price/yield relationship assuming (1) the issue is not callable, (2) the issue is callable and interest rate volatility is assumed to be 12% per year, and (3) the issue is callable and interest rate volatility is assumed to be 20% per year. Notice that the price/yield relationship for the callable bond assuming a 20% interest rate volatility begins to depart from the price/yield relationship for the noncallable bond at a higher yield than the price/yield relationship for the callable bond with a 12% interest rate volatility. When the market yield is deep in the money, the price/yield relationship for the callable bond is the same regardless of the interest rate volatility assumption.

Exhibit 16-6

**Price/Yield Relationship for a Callable Bond
Based on Two Interest Rate Volatility Assumptions**

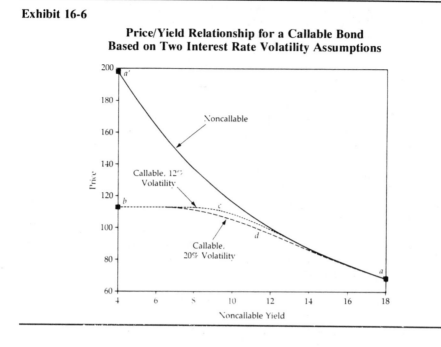

Call-Adjusted Yield for a Callable Corporate Bond

Given such a relationship for the callable bond, an investor wants to know if the noncall-able bond is correctly priced, in the sense that there is adequate reward for the credit risk associated with owning the bond. Although in our previous illustrations we have started with the price of the noncallable bond and computed the theoretical price of the callable bond by subtracting the theoretical price of the call option, the price that the noncallable bond will sell at in the market is not directly observable. It can be estimated by rewriting the relationship as

Noncallable bond price = Callable bond price + Call option price.

Can we estimate the price of the noncallable bond? Yes, if we can determine the price of the callable bond and the call option price. The price of the callable bond can be observed in the market. The price of the call option can be estimated using an option pricing model. Adding the two prices gives the implied price of the noncallable bond.

Given the implied price of the noncallable bond, it is then simple to compute the yield on this bond if it is not called but held to maturity. Recall from Chapter 6 that yield is the interest rate that will make the present value of the cash flows for the bond if held to maturity equal to the price. The yield computed is referred to as the *call-adjusted yield.*

Illustration 16-6. Suppose an investor is considering an 8% coupon callable corporate bond selling at 102 with 20 years to maturity and callable at 104. Suppose also that an option pricing model estimates the call option price at 4.21. Then the call-adjusted yield is found as follows.

First the implied price for the noncallable bond is computed as:

$$\text{Observed callable bond price} = 102;$$
$$\text{Theoretical call option price} = 4.21;$$
$$\text{Noncallable bond price} = 102 + 4.21 = 106.21.$$

The call-adjusted yield is computed by finding the interest rate that will make the present value of 40 coupon payments of $4 every six months plus $100 at the end of 40 six-month periods equal to $106.21. The calculated six-month interest rate that satisfies this is 3.7%. Doubling this interest rate gives the call-adjusted yield of 7.4% on a bond equivalent yield basis.

Illustration 16-7. Consider once again the 12%, 17-year callable corporate bond. Suppose that the *observed* price for the bond is 106.933. Also suppose that, based on an option pricing model and a volatility assumption of 12% per year, the theoretical option price for the call option is 5.067. The implied noncallable bond price is found as follows:

$$\text{Observed callable bond price} = 106.933;$$
$$\text{Theoretical call option price} = 5.067;$$
$$\text{Noncallable bond price} = 106.933 + 5.067 = 112.$$

The call-adjusted yield is found by determining the interest rate that will make the present value of the cash flows if this bond is not called but held to maturity equal to the implied price of the noncallable bond (112). The semiannual interest rate that will make the present value of the cash flows equal to 112 is 5.237%. Doubling this interest rate gives the call-adjusted yield, computed on a bond equivalent basis. The call-adjusted yield is therefore 10.474%.

The call-adjusted yield is the implied yield on the noncallable bond. A noncallable bond is priced fairly if the call-adjusted yield for a callable bond is the proper yield for a noncallable bond with the same features and of the same issuer. A bond is rich or overvalued if the call-adjusted yield is less; it is cheap or undervalued if the call-adjusted yield is more.

Call-Adjusted Duration

As we have stressed throughout this book, yield is only one side of the valuation equation and, in fact, has limited value if a bond is not held to maturity. The other side of the equation is price volatility, which will determine the performance of a bond over an investment horizon less than the maturity. The two parameters of a bond that determine price volatility are duration and convexity. In Chapters 11 and 12 we illustrated how to compute the duration and convexity of an option-free bond, respectively. Here we explain how to compute the duration of a callable bond, and in the next section we explain how to compute the convexity of a callable bond.[5]

The duration of a callable bond after adjusting for the call option, commonly referred to as the *call-adjusted duration*, is:[6]

$$\text{Call-adjusted duration} = \frac{\text{Price}_{NCB}}{\text{Price}_{CB}} \times \text{Dur}_{NCB} \times (1 - \text{Delta}),$$

where

    Price$_{NCB}$ = Price of a noncallable bond;
    Price$_{CB}$ = Price of a callable bond;
    Dur$_{NCB}$ = Modified duration of the noncallable bond;
    Delta = Delta of the call option.

As can be seen, the call-adjusted duration depends on the following three elements:

(1) The ratio of the price of the noncallable bond to the price of the callable bond. Recall that the difference between the price of a noncallable bond and the price of a callable bond is equal to the price of the call option. The greater (smaller) the price of the call option, the higher (lower) the ratio. Thus we see that the call-adjusted duration will depend on the price of the call option.

(2) The duration of the corresponding noncallable (option-free) bond.

(3) The delta of the call option. In the previous chapter we discussed this delta, which measures the change in the price of the call option when the price of the underlying bond changes.

Let's apply the call-adjusted duration to two extreme cases — a deep-discount callable bond and a premium callable bond with a coupon rate substantially above the prevailing market yield. First consider the deep-discount bond.

For a deep-discount bond, the coupon rate is substantially below the current market yield. For example, a 20-year bond with a coupon rate of 5% will trade at a deep discount when the current market yield on comparable bonds is 15%. Since it would not be economic for the corporate issuer to call the 5% coupon bond and replace it with a 15% coupon bond, the call option is deep out of the money. The option price would be small for this bond, and therefore the ratio of the noncallable bond price to the callable bond

---

[5] The mathematical derivations are given in the appendix to Chapter 4 in Frank J. Fabozzi, *Bond Markets, Analysis and Strategies* (Englewood Cliffs, NJ: Prentice Hall, 1993, 2nd ed).

[6] A *synthetic maturity date* for a callable bond is the maturity of a noncallable bond with the same coupon rate that would give the same duration as the call-adjusted duration for the callable bond. The probability that the call will be exercised at each interest rate can be calculated. From the probability of exercise, an expected maturity can be estimated. See Ravi Dattatreya and Frank J. Fabozzi, *Active Total Return Management of Fixed Income Portfolios* (Chicago: Probus Publishing, 1989).

price would be close to one. From the previous chapter, recall our discussion of the delta of a call option. When the option is deep out of the money, the delta is close to zero. Therefore,

$$\frac{Price_{NCB}}{Price_{CB}} = 1;$$
$$Delta = 0$$

Substituting into the formula for the call-adjusted duration, we have

$$Call\text{-}adjusted\ duration = 1 \times Dur_{NCB} \times (1 - 0)$$
$$= Dur_{NCB}$$

Thus, the call-adjusted duration of a deep-discount callable bond will be the same as its duration, assuming it is noncallable.

Now let's consider the duration of a premium callable bond with a coupon rate substantially higher than the current market yield. As an example, consider a 20-year bond with a coupon rate of 16% when the current market yield is 6% (the bond would sell at a premium). The call option would be deep in the money since it would be highly beneficial for the corporate issuer to call the issue and issue new bonds with a coupon rate of 6%. Once again, recall from the previous chapter that the delta of a deep in the money call option is 1. Substituting 1 for delta into the formula for the call-adjusted duration, we have

$$Call\text{-}adjusted\ duration = \frac{Price_{NCB}}{Price_{CB}} \times Dur_{NCB} \times (1 - 1)$$
$$= 0$$

Thus, the call-adjusted duration for a premium callable bond for which the coupon rate is substantially higher than the current market yield would be zero.

Anywhere in between a deep-discount bond and a premium bond with a high coupon rate relative to the prevailing market yield, the call-adjusted duration of a callable bond will be less than the duration of a noncallable bond.

Illustration 16-8. As in Illustration 16-7, suppose that for the 12%, 17-year callable bond the observed price is 106.933 and the theoretical call option price is 5.067. The implied price of the noncallable bond is 112, and the call-adjusted yield is 10.474%. The modified duration of the noncallable bond selling for 112 and with a yield of 10.474% would be 7.67. On the basis of the same option pricing model that generated the theoretical call option price of 5.067, the delta for the call option would be 0.486. The call-adjusted duration for this callable bond according to the information above would be

Price$_{NCB}$ = Implied price of noncallable bond = 112;
   Price$_{CB}$ = Observed price of callable bond = 106.933;
   Dur$_{NCB}$ = Duration of noncallable bond = 7.67;
      Delta = Delta of call option = 0.486;

$$\text{Call-adjusted duration} = \frac{112}{106.933} \times 7.67 \times (1 - 0.486)$$
$$= 4.13.$$

Call-Adjusted Convexity

Convexity measures how the duration of a bond changes as yield changes. Let's look at the convexity of a callable bond.

Exhibit 16-7 blows up the portion of the price/yield relationship in Exhibit 16-1 below y^*. Two tangent lines are shown. Recall from Chapter 12 that the duration of a bond is related to the slope of the tangent line — the steeper the tangent line, the greater the duration. A property of an option-free bond is that the duration changes in the desired direction as interest rates change: that is, the duration increases (decreases) as the interest rate decreases (increases).

This is not true for the portion of the callable bond's price/yield relationship shown in Exhibit 16-7. As the yield declines, the tangent line flattens. That is, the duration gets smaller as the yield declines. This is exactly what an investor who is long a bond does not want to happen. In fact, there is a range of yields at which the duration is zero (between y_1 and y_2). For this range, a decline in yield will not change the price of the bond. In contrast, as yields increase, the duration gets larger — the tangent line becomes steeper. Once again, this is not what an investor wants. Because of this feature — duration chang-

---

Exhibit 16-7

**Blow-up of Negative Convexity Portion of
Price/Yield Relationship for a Callable Bond**

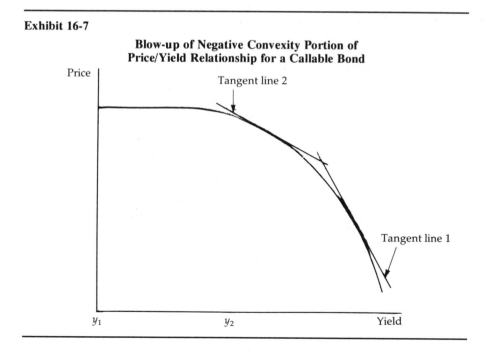

ing in the wrong direction—the shape of the price/yield relationship shown in Exhibit 16-7 is referred to as *negative convexity*.[7]

Negative convexity means that the price appreciation will be less than the price depreciation for a large change in yield of a given number of basis points. For a bond that is option-free and exhibits positive convexity, the price appreciation will be greater than the price depreciation for a large change in yield of a given number of basis points.

All of this agrees with our earlier observation that the duration of a callable bond ranges between zero and the duration of the noncallable bond. When the bond is deep in the money, the call-adjusted duration is zero. When it is deep out of the money, the call-adjusted duration is equal to the duration of the noncallable bond.

The call-adjusted convexity can be found as follows:

$$\text{Call-adjusted convexity} =$$

$$\frac{\text{Price}_{NCB}}{\text{Price}_{CB}} \left[\text{Con}_{NCB} \times (1 - \text{Delta}) - \text{Price}_{NCB} \times \text{Gamma} \times (\text{Dur}_{NCB})^2 \right]$$

where

Con_{NCB} = Convexity of the noncallable bond;
Gamma = Gamma of the call option.

The call-adjusted duration depends on the price of the call option (i.e., the ratio of the price of the noncallable bond to the price of the callable bond), the duration of the noncallable bond, and the delta. The call-adjusted convexity depends on the same three factors plus the convexity of the noncallable bond and the gamma of the call option. Recall from the previous chapter that the gamma of the call option measures the convexity of the call option.

Since the gamma of a call option is positive and the delta is between 0 and 1, call-adjusted convexity will be less than the convexity of the noncallable bond. Unlike the convexity for an option-free bond, which is always positive, the call-adjusted convexity may be negative. This occurs when the term in the brackets is negative. That is, when

$$\text{Con}_{NCB} \times (1 - \text{Delta}) < \text{Price}_{NCB} \times \text{Gamma} \times (\text{Dur}_{NCB})^2.$$

When will this condition result? When the yield falls such that the call option moves deep in the money, the delta will approach 1. The term on the left hand side will approach zero, and the term on the right hand side will be positive, resulting in a negative value for the term in the brackets in the formula for call-adjusted convexity.

Illustration 16-9. Continuing with our examination of the 12%, 17-year callable bond, assume the same information as in Illustration 16-8. The convexity of the noncallable bond is 91.82. The gamma for the call option (according to the option pricing model used to calculate the theoretical call option price) is .02878. The call-adjusted convexity is then:

---

[7] Mathematicians refer to the shape in Exhibit 16-7 as *concave*.

Price_{NCB} = Implied price of noncallable bond = 112;
Price_{CB} = Observed price of callable bond = 106.933;
Dur_{NCB} = Duration of noncallable bond = 7.67;
Con_{NCB} = Convexity of noncallable bond = 91.82;
Delta = Delta of call option = .486;
Gamma = .02878;

$$\text{Call-adjusted convexity} =$$
$$\frac{112}{106.933} \, [91.82 \times (1 - .486) - 112 \times .02878 \times (7.67)^2]$$
$$= -149.$$

The call-adjusted convexity is negative in this example because the call-adjusted yield is 10.474%, which is less than the coupon rate of 12%. The call option is therefore in the money.

Exhibits 16-8 and 16-9 show the price/yield relationship for this callable bond, the duration for the noncallable bond, the call-adjusted duration, the convexity of the noncallable bond, the delta of the call option, the gamma of the call option, and the call-adjusted convexity. Exhibits 16-8 and 16-9 assume that interest rate volatility will be 12% and 20%, respectively. (It is from Exhibits 16-8 and 16-9 that we constructed Exhibits 16-2 and 16-3.) Note in both Exhibits 16-8 and 16-9 that the duration for the callable bond approaches the duration of the noncallable bond as the yield rises above the coupon rate of 12%. As yields decline below 12%, the difference between the duration of the callable bond and that of the noncallable bond increases.

Total Return

The call-adjusted yield suffers from the same drawbacks as the yield to maturity: it assumes that the bond will be held until the maturity date and the coupon payments can be reinvested at an interest rate equal to the call-adjusted yield. In Chapter 8, we explained how the total return framework should be used to determine the performance of a bond. To compute the total return for a bond over some investment horizon, the following must be determined:

(1) The coupon interest;

(2) Interest on interest from reinvesting the coupon payments;

(3) Any capital gain or loss from disposal of the bond at the end of the investment horizon.

The last element depends on the duration and convexity of the bond. For an option-free bond, total return analysis is simple to conduct because the price of the bond at some specified investment horizon can be easily computed, given the projected yield to maturity offered on comparable bonds. For a callable bond, total return analysis requires that more assumptions be made. Specifically, because the price of the callable bond at the horizon date will depend on the option price, factors that determine the option price must

Exhibit 16-8

Call-Adjusted Duration and Call-Adjusted Convexity for a 12%, 17-Year Bond Callable in Two Years at 102 (12% Interest Rate Volatility Assumption)

Assumptions to compute theoretical call option price:
Binomial option pricing model
Interest rate volatility: 12%
Short-term interest rate: 6%

Yield	Noncallable bond			Call option			Callable bond		
	Price	Dur.	Con.	Price	Delta	Gamma	Price	Dur.	Con.
20.51	60	4.96	45.4	.000	.00	.000001	60.000	4.9	45.4
20.18	61	5.03	46.5	.000	.00	.000003	61.000	5.0	46.5
19.86	62	5.10	47.6	.000	.00	.000004	62.000	5.1	47.6
19.55	63	5.17	48.7	.000	.00	.000007	63.000	5.1	48.7
19.24	64	5.24	49.7	.000	.00	.000011	64.000	5.2	49.7
18.95	65	5.30	50.8	.000	.00	.000016	65.000	5.3	50.8
18.66	66	5.37	51.8	.000	.00	.000026	66.000	5.3	51.8
18.39	67	5.43	52.9	.000	.00	.000037	67.000	5.4	52.8
18.11	68	5.49	53.9	.000	.00	.000051	68.000	5.4	53.8
17.85	69	5.56	54.9	.001	.00	.000077	68.999	5.5	54.8
17.59	70	5.62	55.9	.001	.00	.000105	69.999	5.6	55.7
17.34	71	5.68	57.0	.001	.00	.000139	70.999	5.6	56.6
17.10	72	5.74	58.0	.002	.00	.000198	71.998	5.7	57.5

Exhibit 16-8 continued.

Yield	Noncallable bond Price	Dur.	Con.	Call option Price	Delta	Gamma	Callable bond Price	Dur.	Con.
16.86	73	5.80	59.0	.002	.00	.000262	72,998	5.8	58.3
16.63	74	5.86	59.9	.003	.00	.000331	73,997	5.8	59.0
16.40	75	5.92	60.9	.005	.00	.000455	74.995	5.9	59.6
16.18	76	5.98	61.9	.006	.00	.000587	75.994	5.9	60.2
15.96	77	6.04	62.8	.008	.00	.000725	76.992	6.0	60.7
15.75	78	6.09	63.8	.012	.00	.000942	77.988	6.0	60.9
15.54	79	6.15	64.7	.016	.00	.001187	78.984	6.1	60.9
15.33	80	6.20	65.7	.020	.00	.001441	79.980	6.1	60.9
15.13	81	6.26	66.6	.027	.00	.001775	80.973	6.2	60.5
14.94	82	6.31	67.5	.036	.01	.002191	81.964	6.2	59.7
14.75	83	6.36	68.4	.046	.01	.002620	82.954	6.2	58.9
14.56	84	6.42	69.4	.057	.01	.003079	83.943	6.3	57.7
14.38	85	6.47	70.3	.075	.01	.003725	84.925	6.3	55.8
14.20	86	6.52	71.1	.095	.02	.004383	85.905	6.3	53.6
14.02	87	6.57	72.0	.116	.02	.005054	86.884	6.4	51.2
13.85	88	6.62	72.9	.146	.03	.005875	87.854	6.4	48.0
13.68	89	6.67	73.8	.183	.03	.006795	88.817	6.4	44.1
13.51	90	6.72	74.6	.223	.04	.007724	89.777	6.4	39.9
13.35	91	6.77	75.5	.265	.05	.008673	90.735	6.4	35.4
13.19	92	6.82	76.3	.330	.06	.009839	91.670	6.4	29.5
13.03	93	6.86	77.2	.398	.07	.011006	92.602	6.3	23.3
12.87	94	6.91	78.0	.469	.08	.012174	93.531	6.3	16.8

Exhibit 16-8 continued.

	Noncallable bond			Call option			Callable bond		
Yield	Price	Dur.	Con.	Price	Delta	Gamma	Price	Dur.	Con.
12.72	95	6.96	78.8	.557	.09	.013406	94.443	6.3	9.5
12.57	96	7.00	79.6	.667	.11	.014725	95.333	6.2	1.4
12.42	97	7.05	80.4	.783	.12	.016032	96.217	6.2	−7.0
12.28	98	7.09	81.2	.904	.14	.017327	97.096	6.1	−15.8
12.00	100	7.18	82.8	1.235	.18	.019921	98.765	5.9	−35.2
11.73	102	7.27	84.4	1.606	.22	.022422	100.394	5.8	−55.9
11.46	104	7.35	85.9	2.112	.26	.024551	101.888	5.4	−76.7
11.33	105	7.39	86.7	2.380	.29	.025551	102.620	5.3	−87.4
11.20	106	7.43	87.4	2.661	.31	.026493	103.339	5.2	−98.1
11.07	107	7.47	88.2	3.012	.34	.027128	103.988	5.0	−107.5
10.95	108	7.51	88.9	3.373	.37	.027716	104.627	4.8	−117.0
10.83	109	7.55	89.6	3.742	.40	.028259	105.258	4.6	−126.4
10.71	110	7.59	90.3	4.134	.42	.028689	105.866	4.5	−135.5
10.59	111	7.63	91.1	4.596	.45	.028756	106.404	4.3	−142.5
10.47	112	7.67	91.8	5.067	.48	.028778	106.933	4.1	−149.3
10.35	113	7.71	92.5	5.548	.51	.028757	107.452	3.9	−155.9
10.24	114	7.75	93.2	6.056	.54	.028601	107.944	3.7	−161.7
10.13	115	7.78	93.9	6.631	.57	.028099	108.369	3.5	−165.1
10.02	116	7.82	94.6	7.215	.59	.027564	108.785	3.3	−168.2
9.91	117	7.86	95.2	7.808	.62	.026997	109.192	3.1	−170.9
9.80	118	7.89	95.9	8.429	.65	.026317	109.571	2.9	−172.7
9.69	119	7.93	96.6	9.111	.67	.025370	109.889	2.7	−172.0

Exhibit 16–8 continued.

	Noncallable bond			Call option			Callable bond		
Yield	Price	Dur.	Con.	Price	Delta	Gamma	Price	Dur.	Con.
9.59	120	7.96	97.2	9.801	.70	.024405	110.199	2.5	-171.0
9.48	121	8.00	97.9	10.499	.72	.023425	110.501	2.3	-169.6
9.38	122	8.03	98.6	11.220	.75	.022384	110.780	2.2	-167.3
9.28	123	8.07	99.2	11.996	.77	.021192	111.004	2.0	-163.1
9.18	124	8.10	99.9	12.778	.79	.020000	111.222	1.8	-158.6
9.08	125	8.14	100.5	13.567	.81	.018809	111.433	1.7	-153.6
8.98	126	8.17	101.1	14.372	.83	.017610	111.628	1.5	-148.1
8.89	127	8.20	101.8	15.224	.84	.016387	111.776	1.4	-141.7
8.79	128	8.24	102.4	16.080	.86	.015178	111.920	1.2	-134.9
8.60	130	8.30	103.6	17.813	.89	.012809	112.187	1.0	-120.3
8.42	132	8.36	104.8	19.632	.91	.010663	112.368	0.8	-105.4
8.24	134	8.43	106.0	21.466	.93	.008606	112.534	0.6	-89.6
8.07	136	8.49	107.2	23.362	.95	.006928	112.638	0.4	-75.7
7.90	138	8.55	108.4	25.267	.96	.005337	112.733	0.3	-61.3
7.73	140	8.61	109.5	27.210	.97	.004155	112.790	0.2	-50.0
7.24	146	8.78	112.8	33.106	.99	.001608	112.894	0.0	-22.1
6.79	152	8.94	116.0	39.075	.99	.000538	112.925	0.0	-8.4
6.36	158	9.10	119.1	45.066	.99	.000135	112.934	0.0	-2.3
5.96	164	9.25	122.0	51.064	1.00	.000029	112.936	0.0	-.5
5.57	170	9.39	124.8	57.064	1.00	.000004	112.936	0.0	-.0

Exhibit 16–9

Call–Adjusted Duration and Call-Adjusted Convexity for a 17-Year Bond Callable in Two Years at 102
(20% Interest Rate Volatility Assumption)

Assumptions to compute theoretical call option price:
Binomial option pricing model
Interest rate volatility: 20%
Short-term interest rate: 6%

Yield	Noncallable bond			Call option			Callable bond		
	Price	Dur.	Con.	Price	Delta	Gamma	Price	Dur.	Con.
20.51	60	4.96	45.4	.019	.00	.000845	59.981	4.9	44.0
20.18	61	5.03	46.5	.024	.00	.000987	60.976	5.0	44.8
19.86	62	5.10	47.6	.029	.00	.001130	61.971	5.0	45.5
19.55	63	5.17	48.7	.035	.00	.001274	62.965	5.1	46.2
19.24	64	5.24	49.7	.044	.00	.001493	63.956	5.1	46.7
18.95	65	5.30	50.8	.055	.01	.001716	64.945	5.2	47.1
18.66	66	5.37	51.8	.066	.01	.001939	65.934	5.3	47.5
18.39	67	5.43	52.9	.078	.01	.002161	66.922	5.3	47.9
18.11	68	5.49	53.9	.092	.01	.002397	67.908	5.4	48.2
17.85	69	5.56	54.9	.112	.01	.002718	68.888	5.4	48.1
17.59	70	5.62	55.9	.134	.02	.003036	69.866	5.5	48.1
17.34	71	5.68	57.0	.158	.02	.003352	70.842	5.5	47.9
17.10	72	5.74	58.0	.182	.02	.003665	71.818	5.5	47.7
16.86	73	5.80	59.0	.208	.03	.003982	72.792	5.6	47.4
16.63	74	5.86	59.9	.248	.03	.004400	73.752	5.6	46.7

Exhibit 16-9 continued.

	Noncallable bond			Call option			Callable bond		
Yield	Price	Dur.	Con.	Price	Delta	Gamma	Price	Dur.	Con.
16.40	75	5.92	60.9	.290	.04	.004812	74.710	5.7	45.9
16.18	76	5.98	61.9	.334	.04	.005218	75.666	5.7	45.0
15.96	77	6.04	62.8	.379	.05	.005621	76.621	5.7	44.0
15.75	78	6.09	63.8	.427	.05	.006018	77.573	5.7	43.0
15.54	79	6.15	64.7	.491	.06	.006480	78.509	5.7	41.5
15.33	80	6.20	65.7	.564	.07	.006963	79.436	5.8	39.8
15.13	81	6.26	66.6	.640	.07	.007438	80.360	5.8	38.1
14.94	82	6.31	67.5	.718	.08	.007906	81.282	5.8	36.2
14.75	83	6.36	68.4	.800	.09	.008367	82.200	5.8	34.2
14.56	84	6.42	69.4	.887	.10	.008828	83.113	5.8	32.1
14.38	85	6.47	70.3	1.006	.11	.009336	83.994	5.8	29.6
14.20	86	6.52	71.1	1.128	.12	.009835	84.872	5.8	26.9
14.02	87	6.57	72.0	1.254	.13	.010323	85.746	5.7	24.1
13.85	88	6.62	72.9	1.384	.14	.010803	86.616	5.7	21.2
13.68	89	6.67	73.8	1.518	.15	.011274	87.482	5.7	18.2
13.51	90	6.72	74.6	1.665	.16	.011739	88.335	5.7	15.0
13.35	91	6.77	75.5	1.851	.17	.012198	89.149	5.7	11.6
13.19	92	6.82	76.3	2.041	.18	.012646	89.959	5.6	8.0
13.03	93	6.86	77.2	2.235	.20	.013084	90.765	5.6	4.4
12.87	94	6.91	78.0	2.434	.21	.013511	91.566	5.5	0.6
12.72	95	6.96	78.8	2.637	.22	.013929	92.363	5.5	-3.2

Exhibit 16-9 continued.

Yield	Noncallable bond			Call option			Callable bond		
	Price	Dur.	Con.	Price	Delta	Gamma	Price	Dur.	Con.
12.57	96	7.00	79.6	2.855	.24	.014328	93.145	5.4	−7.2
12.42	97	7.05	80.4	3.125	.25	.014669	93.875	5.4	−11.1
12.28	98	7.09	81.2	3.399	.27	.015000	94.601	5.3	−15.2
12.00	100	7.18	82.8	3.964	.30	.015630	96.036	5.2	−23.7
11.72	102	7.27	84.4	4.550	.33	.016222	97.450	5.1	−32.5
11.46	104	7.35	85.9	5.285	.36	.016563	98.715	4.9	−40.6
11.33	105	7.39	86.7	5.664	.38	.016714	99.336	4.8	−44.8
11.20	106	7.43	87.4	6.049	.39	.016857	99.951	4.7	−49.0
11.07	107	7.47	88.2	6.439	.41	.016991	100.561	4.6	−53.2
10.95	108	7.51	88.9	6.835	.43	.017117	101.165	4.5	−57.5
10.83	109	7.55	89.6	7.272	.44	.017167	101.728	4.4	−61.5
10.71	110	7.59	90.3	7.752	.46	.017135	102.248	4.3	−65.1
10.59	111	7.63	91.1	8.238	.48	.017097	102.762	4.2	−68.6
10.47	112	7.67	91.8	8.730	.50	.017051	103.270	4.1	−72.2
10.35	113	7.71	92.5	9.228	.51	.017000	103.772	4.0	−75.7
10.24	114	7.75	93.2	9.731	.53	.016942	104.269	3.9	−79.3
10.13	115	7.78	93.9	10.240	.55	.016879	104.760	3.8	−82.9
10.02	116	7.82	94.6	10.821	.56	.016680	105.179	3.7	−85.5
9.91	117	7.86	95.2	11.414	.58	.016465	105.586	3.6	−87.9
9.80	118	7.89	95.9	12.013	.60	.016246	105.987	3.5	−90.3
9.69	119	7.93	96.6	12.618	.61	.016023	106.382	3.4	−92.7

Exhibit 16-9 continued.

Yield	Noncallable bond			Call option			Callable bond		
	Price	Dur.	Con.	Price	Delta	Gamma	Price	Dur.	Con.
9.59	120	7.96	97.2	13.227	.63	.015797	106.773	3.2	-95.0
9.48	121	8.00	97.9	13.842	.64	.015568	107.158	3.1	-97.3
9.38	122	8.03	98.6	14.479	.66	.015308	107.521	3.0	-99.3
9.28	123	8.07	99.2	15.172	.67	.014961	107.828	2.9	-100.4
9.18	124	8.10	99.9	15.871	.69	.014613	108.129	2.8	-101.4
9.08	125	8.14	100.5	16.575	.70	.014265	108.425	2.7	-102.3
8.98	126	8.17	101.1	17.283	.72	.013915	108.717	2.6	-103.1
8.89	127	8.20	101.8	17.996	.73	.013564	109.004	2.5	-103.8
8.79	128	8.24	102.4	18.713	.75	.013212	109.287	2.4	-104.4
8.60	130	8.30	103.6	20.250	.77	.012414	109.750	2.2	-104.1
8.42	132	8.36	104.8	21.832	.79	.011589	110.168	2.0	-103.0
8.24	134	8.43	106.0	23.431	.82	.010769	110.569	1.8	-101.3
8.07	136	8.49	107.2	25.076	.84	.009946	110.924	1.6	-98.9
7.90	138	8.55	108.4	26.797	.86	.009118	111.203	1.4	-95.4
7.73	140	8.61	109.5	28.529	.87	.008301	111.471	1.3	-91.5
7.24	146	8.78	112.8	33.925	.92	.006038	112.075	0.8	-77.0
6.79	152	8.94	116.0	39.541	.95	.004126	112.459	0.5	-60.3
6.36	158	9.10	119.1	45.311	.97	.002635	112.689	0.3	-43.8
5.96	164	9.25	122.0	51.183	.98	.001563	112.817	0.1	-29.3
5.57	170	9.39	124.8	57.117	.99	.000854	112.883	0.1	-17.9

be considered. The factor that will influence the option price that is difficult to assess in total return analysis is the expected interest rate volatility at the end of the investment horizon. Thus, total return analysis requires not only assumptions about the yield at the investment horizon date and the reinvestment rate but also the expected interest rate volatility at the end of the investment horizon.

Summary

The owner of a callable corporate bond is effectively long a noncallable bond and short a call option on that noncallable bond. The price and price performance of the callable corporate bond will therefore depend on the price characteristics of both the noncallable bond and the call option. In this chapter we have presented formulas to determine the call-adjusted yield, the call-adjusted duration, and the call-adjusted convexity of a callable bond.

Unlike that of an option-free bond, the duration of a callable bond may not increase as interest rates decline. At some yield level, the duration of a callable bond may exhibit negative convexity. The convexity of the callable bond will depend on the price of the call option, the delta of the call option, and the gamma of the call option.

While call-adjusted yield measures the yield after adjusting for the call option, the portfolio manager should use the total return framework to determine the potential return over some investment horizon. The total return will depend on how the price of the embedded call option changes. To determine how the price of the call option changes, assumptions must be made about expected interest rate volatility at the end of the investment horizon.

17

Valuation of Callable Bonds*

In the previous chapter, we described a conceptual approach to the valuation of a callable bond. That is, the value of a callable bond is equal to the value of a comparable noncallable bond minus the value of the call option. This insight is the basis for the first generation of valuation models that sought to value a callable bond by estimating the value of the call option. While the theory sounds straightforward, determining the call option embedded in callable bonds is not that simple. Suppose a 20-year bond is noncallable for five years, and then callable at any time on 30-days' notice. Suppose also that the schedule for the call price begins at 105 and declines to par by the 15th year. This is an extremely complicated call option. It is a deferred American option for the first five years. The strike or exercise price—which is the call price in the case of a callable bond—is not

---

* This chapter is adapted from Andrew Kalotay, George O. Williams, and Frank J. Fabozzi, "A Model for the Valuation of Bonds and Embedded Options," forthcoming in the *Financial Analysts Journal*.

constant but declines over time. Another example is a corporate bond with a sinking fund requirement that grants the issuer the right to accelerate the repayment of the principal. This is also a call option but one that is extremely difficult to value with an option pricing model. For a bond with multiple or interrelated embedded options — a bond that may be callable and putable, for example — valuation becomes complicated.

The valuation model presented in this chapter does not rely on an option pricing model. Rather, it is based on a consistent framework for valuing both option-free bonds and bonds with embedded options. If we can value an option-free bond and a bond with any embedded options, the value of the options can be determined.

The valuation principles that we have discussed so far in this book are assumed to apply here. Specifically, we demonstrated in Chapter 13 two important concepts. First, it is inappropriate to use a single rate to discount all the cash flows of a bond. Second, the correct rate to use to discount each cash flow is the spot rate. This is equivalent to discounting at a series of forward rates.

What we have to add to the valuation process is how interest rate volatility affects the value of a bond through its effects on the embedded options. We begin this chapter with a review of the valuation technique for bonds without any embedded options.

Valuation of Option-Free Bonds

In Chapter 13 we showed how the price of an option-free bond is the present value of the cash flows discounted at the spot rates. To illustrate this, let's use a hypothetical yield curve based on three on-the-run issues:

Maturity	Yield to Maturity	Market Value
1 year	3.50%	100
2 years	4.00%	100
3 years	4.50%	100

We simplify the illustration by assuming annual-pay bonds. Using the bootstrapping methodology described in Chapter 13, we obtain the spot rates and the one-year forward rates:

Year	Spot Rate	One-Year Forward Rate
1	3.500%	3.500%
2	4.010%	4.523%
3	4.541%	5.580%

Now consider an option-free bond with three years remaining to maturity and a coupon rate of 5.25%. The price of this bond can be calculated in one of two ways, each producing the same result. First, the coupon payments can be discounted at the zero-coupon rates as shown below:

$$\frac{\$5.25}{(1.035)} + \frac{\$5.25}{(1.0401)^2} + \frac{\$100 + \$5.25}{(1.04541)^3} = 102.075$$

The second way is to discount by the one-year forward rates as shown below:

$$\frac{\$5.25}{(1.035)} + \frac{\$5.25}{(1.035)\,(1.0401)} + \frac{\$100 + \$5.25}{(1.035)\,(1.0401)\,(1.04541)} = 102.075$$

Introducing Interest-Rate Volatility

We can account for interest rate volatility by introducing a *binomial interest rate tree*. This tree is nothing more than a graphical depiction of the one-period forward rates over time, based on some assumption about interest rate volatility.

Binomial Interest Rate Tree

Exhibit 17-1 shows an example of a binomial interest rate tree. In this tree, each node (bold circle) represents a time period that is equal to one year from the node to its left. Each node is labeled with an N, representing node, and a subscript that indicates the path that one-year forward rates took to get to that node. U denotes a rise in the forward rate and D a decline in the forward rate from the previous year. For example, node N_{UU} means that the one-year forward rate increased in the first year and then increased again in the second year.[1]

Look first at the point denoted by just N in Exhibit 17-1. This is the root of the tree and is simply the current one-year rate, or equivalently the one-year forward rate, which we denote by r_0. What we have assumed in creating this tree is that the one-year forward rate can take on two possible values the next period, and the two rates have the same probability of occurring. One rate will be higher than the other. For convenience, we refer to the higher of the two rates in the next period as resulting from a "rise" in rates and the lower as resulting from a "fall" in rates. More specifically, we assume that the one-year forward rate evolves over time according to a random process called a lognormal random walk with a certain volatility.

We will use some notation to describe the tree in the first year. Let

σ = assumed volatility of the one-year forward rate
$r_{1,D}$ = one-year forward rate one year from now if rates decline
$r_{1,U}$ = one-year forward rate one year from now if rates rise

The relationship between $r_{1,D}$ and $r_{1,U}$ is as follows:

$$r_{1,U} = r_{1,D}\,(e^{2\sigma})$$

---

[1] Note that N_{UD} is equivalent to N_{DU} in the second year and that in the third year N_{UUD} is equivalent to N_{UDU} and N_{DUU} and that N_{UDD} is equivalent to N_{DDU}. We have simply selected one label for a node rather than clutter up the exhibit with unnecessary information.

where e is the base of the natural logarithm 2.71828.

For example, suppose that $r_{1,D}$ is 4.074% and σ is 10% per year, then:

$$r_{1,U} = 4.074\% \ (e^{2 \times .10}) = 4.976\%$$

In the second year, there are three possible values for the one-year forward rate, which we denote as follows:

$r_{2,DD}$ = one-year forward rate in second year assuming rates fall in the first and second years

$r_{2,UU}$ = one-year forward rate in second year assuming rates rise in the first and second years

$r_{2,UD}$ = one-year forward rate in second year assuming rates either rise in the first year and fall in the second year *or* they fall in the first year and rise in the second year.

The relationship between $r_{2,DD}$ and the other two forward rates is as follows:

$$r_{2,UU} = r_{2,DD}(e^{4\sigma})$$

and

$$r_{2,UD} = r_{2,DD}(e^{2\sigma})$$

So, for example, if $r_{2,DD}$ is 4.53%, and assuming once again that σ is 10%, then

$$r_{2,UU} = 4.53\% \ (e^{4 \times .10}) = 6.757\%$$

and

$$r_{2,UD} = 4.53\% \ (e^{2 \times .10}) = 5.532\%$$

Exhibit 17-1 shows the notation for the binomial interest rate tree in the third year. We can simplify the notation by letting r_t be the one-year forward rate t years from now if interest rates decline because all the other forward rates t years from now depend on that rate. Exhibit 17-2 shows the interest rate tree using this simplified notation.

Before we go on to show how to use this binomial interest rate tree to value bonds, let's focus on two issues here. First, what does the volatility measure σ in the expression $e^{2\sigma}$ represent? Second, how do we find the value of the bond at each node?

Volatility and the Standard Deviation

It can be shown that the standard deviation of the one-year forward rate is equal to $r_0\sigma$.[2] As will be explained in Chapter 22, the standard deviation is a statistical measure of

---

[2] This can be seen by noting that $e^{2\sigma} \approx 1 + 2\sigma$. Then the standard deviation of one-period forward rates is

$$\frac{re^{2\sigma} - r}{2} \approx \frac{r + 2\sigma r - r}{2} = \sigma r$$

Exhibit 17-1

Three-Year Binomial Interest Rate Tree

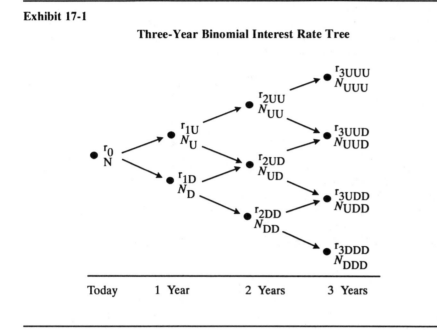

| Today | 1 Year | 2 Years | 3 Years |

Figure 17-2

Three-Year Binomial Interest Rate Tree
with One-Year Forward Rates

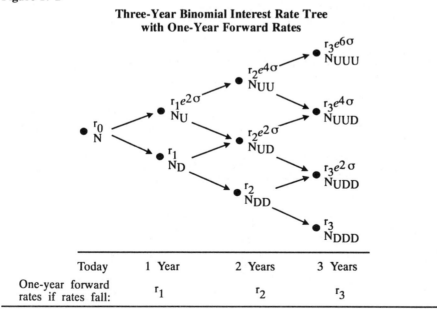

| | Today | 1 Year | 2 Years | 3 Years |
| One-year forward rates if rates fall: | | r_1 | r_2 | r_3 |

volatility. In that chapter we show how to estimate the standard deviation of interest rates. For now, it is important merely to see that the process that generates the binomial interest rate tree (or equivalently the forward rates) implies that volatility is measured relative to the current level of rates. For example, if σ is 10%, and the one-year rate (r_0) is 4%, then the standard deviation of the one-year forward rate is 4% × 10% = .4% or 40 basis points. If the current one-year rate is 12%, the standard deviation of the one-year forward rate would be 12% × 10% or 120 basis points.

Determining the Value at a Node

To find the value of the bond at a node, first calculate the bond's value at the two nodes to the immediate right of the node where we want to obtain the bond's value. For example, in Exhibit 17-2, suppose we want to determine the bond's value at node N_U. The bond's value at nodes N_{UU} and N_{UD} must first be determined. Hold aside for now how we get these two values, because, as we will see, the process involves starting from the last year in the tree and working backward to get the final solution we want, so these two values will be known.

Effectively, at a given node, the value will depend on the future cash flows. The future cash flows depend in turn on (1) the bond's value one year from now, and (2) the coupon payment one year from now. The coupon payment is known. The value one year ahead depends on whether the one-year forward rate rises or falls. The bond's value if the rate rises or falls is reported at the two nodes to the right of the node that is the focus of our attention. So, the cash flow at a node will be either (1) the bond's value if rates rise plus the coupon payment, or (2) the bond's value if rates fall plus the coupon payment. Again, if we are interested in the bond's value at N_U, the cash flow is either the bond's value at N_{UU} plus the coupon payment, or the bond's value at N_{UD} plus the coupon payment.

To get the bond's value at a node we follow the fundamental rule for valuation: the value is the present value of the expected cash flows. The appropriate discount rate to use is the one-year forward rate at the node. Of course there are two present values in this case: the present value if the one-year forward rate rises, and the present value if it falls. We assume that the probability of both outcomes is equal, so we compute the average of the two present values. This is illustrated in Exhibit 17-3 for any node, assuming that the one-year forward rate is r_* at the node where the valuation is sought. The notation is:

V_U = the bond's value if the one-year forward rate rises
V_D = the bond's value if the one-year forward rate falls
C = coupon payment

The cash flow at a node is then either:

$$V_U + C \text{ if the one-year forward rate rises}$$
$$V_D + C \text{ if the one-year forward rate falls}$$

The present value of these two cash flows using the one-year forward rate at the node, r_*, is:

Exhibit 17-3

Calculating a Value at a Node

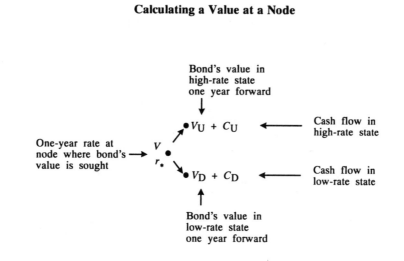

$$\frac{V_U + C}{(1 + r_*)} \quad \text{present value if the one-year rate rises}$$

$$\frac{V_D + C}{(1 + r_*)} \quad \text{present value if the one-year rate falls}$$

Then, the value of the bond at the node is found as follows:

$$\text{Value at a node} = \frac{1}{2}\left[\frac{V_U + C}{(1 + r_*)} + \frac{V_D + C}{(1 + r_*)}\right]$$

Constructing the Binomial Interest Rate Tree

To see how to construct the binomial interest rate tree, let's use the assumed current on-the-run yields we used earlier. We will assume that volatility, σ, is 10% and construct a two-year model using the two-year bond with a coupon rate of 4%.

Exhibit 17-4 gives a more detailed binomial interest rate tree showing the cash flow at each node. We'll see how all the values reported in the exhibit are obtained. The root rate for the tree, r_0, is simply the current one-year rate, 3.5%.

In the first year there are two possible one-year forward rates: one if rates fall, and one if rates rise. What we want to find is the two forward rates that are consistent with the

Exhibit 17-4

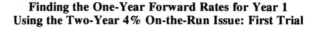

**Finding the One-Year Forward Rates for Year 1
Using the Two-Year 4% On-the-Run Issue: First Trial**

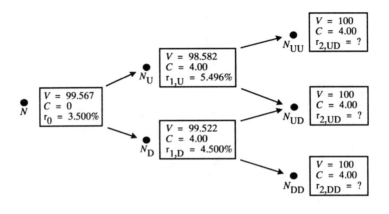

volatility assumption, the process that is assumed to generate the forward rates, and the observed market value of the bond. There is no simple formula for this and therefore requires an iterative process.

Step 1: Select a value for r_1. Recall that r_1 is the one-year forward rate one year from now if rates fall. In this first trial we *arbitrarily* select a value of 4.5%.

Step 2: Determine the corresponding value for the one-year forward rate if rates rise. As explained earlier, this rate is related to the one-year forward rate if rates fall as follows: $r_1\,e^{2\sigma}$. With r_1 at 4.5%, the one-year forward rate if rates rise is 5.496% (= 4.5% $e^{2\times.10}$). This value is reported in Exhibit 17-4 at node N_U.

Step 3: Compute the bond's value one year from now. This value is determined as follows:

3a. For a two-year bond, the bond's value is its maturity value ($100) plus its final coupon payment ($4). Thus, it is $104.

3b. Calculate the present value of the bond's value found in 3a, assuming rates rise. The appropriate discount rate is the one-year forward rate assuming rates rise, 5.496% in the example. The present value (V_U) is $98.582 (= $104/1.05496).

3c. Calculate the present value of the bond's value found in 3a, assuming rates fall. The discount rate in this case is the one-year forward rate assuming rates fall, 4.5%. The present value (V_D) is $99.522 (= $104/1.045).

3d. Add the coupon to these two values to get the cash flow at N_U and N_D, respectively. This makes $102.582 if rates rise and $103.522 if rates fall.

3e. Calculate the present value of the two values according to the one-year forward rate using r_*. At this point in the valuation, r_* , is the root rate, 3.50%. Therefore,

$$\frac{V_U + C}{1 + r_*} = \frac{\$102.582}{1.035} = \$99.113$$

and

$$\frac{V_D + C}{1 + r_*} = \frac{\$103.522}{1.035} = \$100.021$$

Step 4: Calculate the average present value of the two cash flows in Step 3. This is the value we referred to earlier as

$$\text{Value at a node} = \frac{1}{2}\left[\frac{V_U + C}{(1 + r_*)} + \frac{V_D + C}{(1 + r_*)}\right]$$

In our example, we have

$$\text{Value at a node} = \frac{1}{2}\ [\$99.113 + \$100.021] = \$99.567$$

Step 5: Compare the value calculated in Step 4 to the bond's market value. If the two are the same, then the r_1 used in the trial will have been the correct one: the one-year forward rate that is then used in the binomial interest rate tree for a decline in rates and from which we can figure the corresponding rate to use if rates rise. If the value calculated in Step 4 is not equal to the market value of the bond, then the value r_1 in this trial is not the correct one-period forward rate that is consistent with (1) the volatility assumption of 10%, (2) the process assumed to generate the one-year forward rate, and (3) the observed market value of the bond. In this case, the five steps are repeated with a different value for r_1.

In this example, when r_1 is 4.5%, we get a value of $99.567 in Step 4, which is less than the observed market value of $100. Therefore, 4.5% is too high a rate, and the five steps must be repeated trying a lower value for r_1.

Let's jump right to the correct value for r_1 in this example — 4.074% — then rework steps 1 through 5. The corresponding binomial interest rate tree is shown in Exhibit 17-5.

Step 1: In this trial we select a value of 4.074% for r_1.

Exhibit 17-5

The One-Year Forward Rates for Year 1
Using the Two-Year 4% On-the-Run Issue

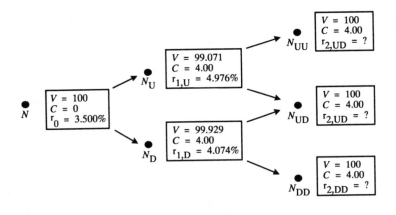

Step 2: The corresponding value for the one-year forward rate if rates rise is 4.976%
(= 4.074% $e^{2 \times .10}$).

Step 3: The bond's value one year from now is determined as follows:

    3a. The maturity value plus the coupon two years from now is $104, just as in the first trial.

    3b. The present value of $104, assuming rates rise, V_U, is $99.071 (= $104/1.04976).

    3c. The present value of $104, assuming rates fall, V_D, is $99.929 (= $104/1.04074).

    3d. Adding the coupon to V_U and V_D, we get $103.071 as the cash flow if rates rise, and $103.929 as the cash flow if rates fall.

    3e. The present value of the two cash flows using the one-year forward rate at the node to the left, 3.5%, gives

$$\frac{V_U + C}{1 + r_*} = \frac{\$103.071}{1.035} = \$99.586$$

and

$$\frac{V_D + C}{1 + r_*} = \frac{\$103.929}{1.035} = \$100.414$$

Step 4: The average present value is $100, which is the value at the node.

Step 5: Since the average present value is equal to the observed market value of $100, r_1 is 4.074%.

We're not done. Suppose that we want to "grow" this tree for one more year — that is, we want to determine r_2. Now we will use the three-year on-the-run issue, the 4.5% coupon bond, to get r_2. The same five steps are used in an iterative process to find the one-year forward rate two years from now. But now our objective is as follows: find the value for r_2 that will produce an average present value at node N_U equal to the bond value at that node ($98.074) and will also produce an average present value at node N_D equal to the bond value at that node ($99.926). Once this value is found, we know that given the forward rate we found for r_1, the bond's value at the root — the value of ultimate interest to us — will be 100, the observed market price.

It can be demonstrated that the value of r_2 that will produce that desired outcome is 4.530%. Exhibit 17-6 shows the completed binomial interest rate tree. It is this tree that we can use to value any option-free bond or any bond with embedded options.

Exhibit 17-6

**The One-Year Forward Rates for Year 2
Using the Three-Year 4.5% On-the-run Issue**

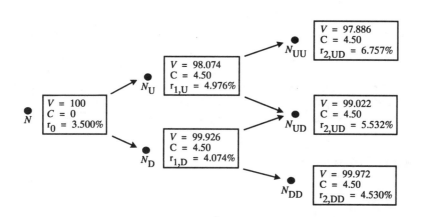

Valuing an Option-Free Bond

We can use the binomial interest rate tree further to evaluate a 5.25% option-free corporate bond with three years remaining to maturity. Assume that the issuer's on-the-run yield curve is the one given earlier, on page 300, and hence the appropriate binomial interest rate tree is the one in Exhibit 17-6. Exhibit 17-7 shows the various values in the discounting process, and produces a bond value of $102.075.

Exhibit 17-7

**Valuing an Option-Free Corporate Bond
with Three Years to Maturity
and a Coupon Rate of 5.25%**

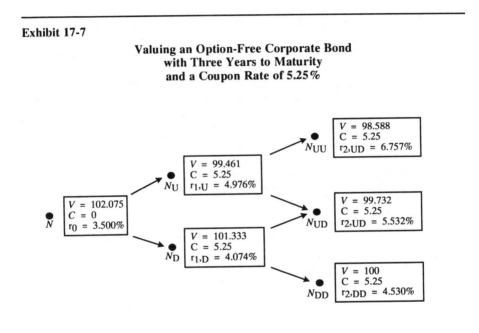

It is important to note that this value is identical to the bond value found at the very beginning of the chapter when we discounted at either the zero-coupon rates or the one-year forward rates. We should expect to find this result as long as the bond is option-free. This clearly demonstrates that the interest rate tree valuation model is consistent with the standard valuation model for an option-free bond.

Valuing a Callable Corporate Bond

Next we demonstrate how to apply the binomial interest rate tree to value a callable corporate bond. Valuation follows the same sort of steps as for an option-free bond, but with one exception. At the time that the call option can be exercised by the issuer, the bond value at a node must be changed to reflect the smaller of two values: the value if it is not called (i.e., the value obtained by applying the recursive valuation formula described above), or the call price.

For example, consider a 5.25% corporate bond with three years remaining to maturity that is callable in one year at $100. Exhibit 17-8 shows the values at each node of the binomial interest rate tree. The discounting process is identical to that shown in Exhibit 17-7 except that at two nodes, N_D and N_{DD}, the values reached through the recursive valuation formula ($101.002 at N_D and $100.689 at N_{DD}) exceed the $100 call price, so in the exhibit they have been struck out and replaced with $100, the lower of the values. Each time a value derived through the recursive valuation formula is replaced, the process for finding the values at that node is reworked, starting with the period to the right. The value for this callable bond is $101.432.

One issue not specifically addressed in the illustrations is the circumstances under which an issuer will call a bond. A discussion of the call rule is beyond the scope of this chapter, but basically the decision to call involves determining when it is economic on an after-tax basis for the issuer to call the bond.

Exhibit 17-8

**Valuing a Callable Corporate Bond
with Three Years to Maturity, a Coupon Rate of 5.25%,
and Callable in One Year at 100**

Determining the Call Option Value

The value of a callable bond, once again, can be expressed as:

Value of a callable bond =

Value of a noncallable bond − Value of the call option

This relationship can also be expressed as follows:

Value of a call option =
Value of a noncallable bond − Value of a callable bond

The binomial interest rate tree allows determination of the value of a noncallable bond and the value of a callable bond. The difference between the two values is therefore the value of the embedded call option.

In the last illustration, the value of the noncallable bond is $102.075 and the value of the callable bond is $101.432, so the value of the embedded call option is the difference: $0.643.

Extension to Other Embedded Options

The bond valuation framework that we describe can be used to analyze put options and option-like features such as caps and floors on floating-rate notes and the optional accelerated redemption available to an issuer to fulfill its sinking fund requirement.[3] For example, let's consider a putable bond. Suppose that a 5.25% corporate bond with three years remaining to maturity is putable in one year at par ($100). Also assume that the appropriate binomial interest rate tree for this issuer is the one in Exhibit 17-7. Exhibit 17-9 shows the binomial interest rate tree with the bond values altered at two nodes (N_{UU} and N_{UD}) because the bond values at these two nodes exceed $100, the value at which the bond can be put. The value of this putable bond is calculated as $102.523.

As in the case of a callable bond, the value of a nonputable bond can be expressed as the value of a putable bond minus the value of a put option on that bond. This means that:

Value of a put option =
Value of a nonputable bond − Value of a putable bond

In the example, because the value of the putable bond is $102.523, and the value of the corresponding nonputable (option-free) bond is $102.075, the value of the put option is −$0.448. The negative sign indicates the issuer has sold the option; the option is of value to the investor purchasing it.

The valuation framework can be extended to value bonds with multiple or interrelated embedded options. In each case the bond values at each node are altered, depending on whether one of the options is exercised.

---

[3] For a discussion of these options in a sinking fund provision, see Richard S. Wilson and Frank J. Fabozzi, *The New Corporate Bond Market* (Chicago: Probus Publishing, 1991), pp. 188-197. The valuation of these options is explained further in Andrew Kalotay and George O. Williams,"The Valuation and Management of Bonds with Sinking Fund Provisions," *Financial Analysts Journal* (March-April 1992), pp. 59-67.

Exhibit 17-9

**Valuing a Putable Corporate Bond
with Three Years to Maturity, a Coupon Rate of 5.25%,
and Putable in One Year at 100**

Summary

In this chapter we have presented a valuation framework that can be used to value any bond. It involves generating a binomial interest rate tree based on (1) an issuer's yield curve, (2) an assumed interest rate generation process, and (3) an assumed interest rate volatility. The binomial interest rate tree yields the appropriate volatility-dependent one-period forward rates that should be used to discount the expected cash flows of a bond.

18

Option-Adjusted Spread

We explain in Chapter 13 that traditional analysis of the yield premium for a non-Treasury bond requires calculating the difference between the yield of the bond in question and the yield to maturity of a comparable-maturity coupon Treasury. The drawbacks of this approach are (1) for both bonds, the yield as traditionally calculated fails to consider the yield curve and the spot rate curve, and (2) in the case of callable and/or putable bonds, expected interest rate volatility can change the cash flow of a bond. In Chapter 13, we addressed the first problem by introducing the concept of a static spread. In Chapter 16 we addressed the volatility issue by valuing the embedded call option using an option pricing model.

This chapter presents another analytical approach to valuing bonds with embedded options: the option-adjusted spread framework. Although we use corporate bonds in our examples, this framework is equally applicable to agency securities, municipal securities, and mortgage-backed securities. In Chapter 21, for example, we apply the option-adjusted spread framework to mortgage-backed securities.

Determining the Option-Adjusted Spread

To clarify the failure to consider interest rate volatility of the traditional yield spread analysis and calculation of the option-adjusted spread, assume an 8.8%, 10-year corporate bond that is immediately callable, and assume also that current interest rates are 8.8%. The likelihood that the issuer will call the bond increases as interest rates decline. If interest rates do fall and the bond is called, the investor's cash flows will change. A small drop in rates, of course, will not be sufficient to justify the issuer's calling the bond. The rate must drop enough so that it will be economic for the issuer to call the bond. For example, a decline of interest rates from 8.8% to 8.5% six months from now may not make it attractive to call the issue, given the cost of refunding or refinancing. Refunding costs are a function of (1) the remaining maturity on the bond, (2) the call price, and (3) fees associated with registering and underwriting the new issue, besides the interest rate.

The refinancing opportunities will depend on how interest rates change over the life of the bond. The possibilities are myriad. For example, suppose that six-month interest rates are now 7%. Exhibit 18-1 shows only 10 of the possible interest rate paths from that level for six-month forward rates for the subsequent 19 six-month periods shown in Exhibit 18-1, if six-month forward interest rates rise or fall by 10% every six months.

Refinancing will be based not on the short-term forward rate but on a longer-term rate that reflects how much the corporation would have to pay to refund a bond issue. Let's make a simple assumption that the refinancing rate for the corporation is 100 basis points higher than the short-term forward rate. Exhibit 18-2 shows the 10 possible paths for the refinancing rate, with each rate in the exhibit 100 basis points higher than in Exhibit 18-1.

For the purpose of illustration suppose that a rule is established for calling of the bond: If the refinancing rate is below 5.8% with at least three years remaining to maturity, then the bond will be called. Given this rule for calling, the bond would not be called if five of the paths in Exhibit 18-2 are realized (paths 1, 2, 4, 8, and 10). In this case, the cash flow for the bond at each six-month period is no different from that of a noncallable bond. For the other paths, the bond would be called.

Exhibit 18-3 shows the cash flow for this corporate bond given the call rule, and assuming that the bond has a call price of 103 whenever it is called. In the period a bond is called, the cash flow is 107.40 (the call price of 103 plus the semiannual coupon interest of 4.40). After the call period, the cash flow is zero.

There are obviously an enormous number of interest rate paths. Let's imagine for the moment that we could analyze each path. For each one, we would first calculate the present value of the cash flow of the bond using as a discount rate the Treasury spot rate at each period plus a spread. Recall from Chapter 13 that the forward rates can be calculated from the spot rates. Similarly, the spot rates can be calculated from the forward rates. Exhibit 18-4 shows the spot rates for each period given the short-term forward rates in Exhibit 18-1.

So, for each path we calculate a present value by using the spot rate plus some assumed spread. Then we compute an average of all the present values for all the paths. If the average present value is equal to the market price of the bond, then the spread added to the Treasury spot rates is called the *option-adjusted spread*. If the average present

Exhibit 18-1

Ten Possible Paths for Six-Month Forward Rates
Assuming an Initial Forward Rate of 7% and 10% Volatility

Period	Path of short-term forward rates									
	1	2	3	4	5	6	7	8	9	10
1	7.0%	7.0%	7.0%	7.0%	7.0%	7.0%	7.0%	7.0%	7.0%	7.0%
2	7.7%	7.7%	7.7%	6.3%	6.3%	6.3%	7.7%	6.3%	7.7%	7.7%
3	8.5%	6.9%	6.9%	6.9%	5.7%	5.7%	8.5%	5.7%	8.5%	8.5%
4	7.6%	6.2%	6.2%	7.6%	5.1%	6.2%	9.3%	6.2%	9.3%	9.3%
5	6.9%	6.9%	5.6%	8.4%	4.6%	6.9%	8.4%	6.9%	8.4%	8.4%
6	7.5%	7.5%	5.1%	9.2%	4.1%	6.2%	7.5%	7.5%	7.5%	7.5%
7	8.3%	8.3%	4.5%	10.1%	4.5%	5.6%	6.8%	8.3%	6.8%	6.8%
8	9.1%	9.1%	5.0%	11.2%	5.0%	5.0%	6.1%	9.1%	6.1%	6.1%
9	10.0%	10.0%	5.5%	12.3%	5.5%	4.5%	5.5%	8.2%	6.7%	6.7%
10	9.0%	9.0%	6.1%	13.5%	6.1%	4.1%	5.0%	7.4%	6.1%	7.4%
11	9.9%	8.1%	6.7%	12.2%	6.7%	4.5%	4.5%	8.1%	5.4%	6.7%
12	8.9%	8.9%	7.3%	10.9%	7.3%	4.0%	4.0%	8.9%	4.9%	6.0%
13	8.1%	9.8%	8.1%	9.8%	8.1%	4.4%	3.6%	9.8%	4.4%	5.4%
14	8.9%	8.9%	7.2%	8.9%	7.2%	4.0%	3.2%	10.8%	4.0%	4.9%
15	9.7%	8.0%	6.5%	8.0%	6.5%	4.4%	2.9%	9.7%	4.4%	5.3%
16	8.8%	7.2%	7.2%	8.8%	7.2%	3.9%	3.2%	10.7%	4.8%	4.8%
17	7.9%	6.5%	7.9%	9.6%	7.9%	3.5%	3.5%	9.6%	5.3%	4.3%
18	7.1%	7.1%	8.7%	10.6%	8.7%	3.2%	3.9%	10.6%	5.8%	4.8%
19	7.8%	7.8%	7.8%	11.7%	9.6%	2.9%	4.3%	11.7%	6.4%	5.2%
20	8.6%	7.0%	8.6%	10.5%	8.6%	3.2%	4.7%	12.8%	7.0%	4.7%

Exhibit 18-2

Ten Possible Paths for the Refinancing Rate Assuming It Is 100 Basis Points Higher than the Short-term Forward Rate

Period	\multicolumn{10}{c}{Path of refinancing rates}									
	1	2	3	4	5	6	7	8	9	10
1	8.0%	8.0%	8.0%	8.0%	8.0%	8.0%	8.0%	8.0%	8.0%	8.0%
2	8.7%	8.7%	8.7%	7.3%	7.3%	7.3%	8.7%	7.3%	8.7%	8.7%
3	9.5%	7.9%	7.9%	7.9%	6.7%	6.7%	9.5%	6.7%	9.5%	9.5%
4	8.6%	7.2%	7.2%	8.6%	6.1%	7.2%	10.3%	7.2%	10.3%	10.3%
5	7.9%	7.9%	6.6%	9.4%	5.6%	7.9%	9.4%	7.9%	9.4%	9.4%
6	8.5%	8.5%	6.1%	10.2%	5.1%	7.2%	8.5%	8.5%	8.5%	8.5%
7	9.3%	9.3%	5.5%	11.1%	5.5%	6.6%	7.8%	9.3%	7.8%	7.8%
8	10.1%	10.1%	6.0%	12.2%	6.0%	6.0%	7.1%	10.1%	7.1%	7.1%
9	11.0%	11.0%	6.5%	13.3%	6.5%	5.5%	6.5%	9.2%	7.7%	7.7%
10	10.0%	10.0%	7.1%	14.5%	7.1%	5.1%	6.0%	8.4%	7.1%	8.4%
11	10.9%	9.1%	7.7%	13.2%	7.7%	5.5%	5.5%	9.1%	6.4%	7.7%
12	9.9%	9.9%	8.3%	11.9%	8.3%	5.0%	5.0%	9.9%	5.9%	7.0%
13	9.1%	10.8%	9.1%	10.8%	9.1%	5.4%	4.6%	10.8%	5.4%	6.4%
14	9.9%	9.9%	8.2%	9.9%	8.2%	5.0%	4.2%	11.8%	5.0%	5.9%
15	10.7%	9.0%	7.5%	9.0%	7.5%	5.4%	3.9%	10.7%	5.4%	6.3%
16	9.8%	8.2%	8.2%	9.8%	8.2%	4.9%	4.2%	11.7%	5.8%	5.8%
17	8.9%	7.5%	8.9%	10.6%	8.9%	4.5%	4.5%	10.6%	6.3%	5.3%
18	8.1%	8.1%	9.7%	11.6%	9.7%	4.2%	4.9%	11.6%	6.8%	5.8%
19	8.8%	8.8%	8.8%	12.7%	10.6%	3.9%	5.3%	12.7%	7.4%	6.2%
20	9.6%	8.0%	9.6%	11.5%	9.6%	4.2%	5.7%	13.8%	8.0%	5.7%

Exhibit 18–3

Cash Flow for Each Refinancing Path of an 8.8%, 10-Year Corporate Bond Callable at 103

Call Rule: Call if refinancing rate falls to 5.8% or less and the bond has at least three years to maturity

Period	1	2	3	4	5	6	7	8	9	10
1	4.4	4.4	4.4	4.4	4.4	4.4	4.4	4.4	4.4	4.4
2	4.4	4.4	4.4	4.4	4.4	4.4	4.4	4.4	4.4	4.4
3	4.4	4.4	4.4	4.4	4.4	4.4	4.4	4.4	4.4	4.4
4	4.4	4.4	4.4	4.4	4.4	4.4	4.4	4.4	4.4	4.4
5	4.4	4.4	4.4	4.4	107.4	4.4	4.4	4.4	4.4	4.4
6	4.4	4.4	4.4	4.4	0.0	4.4	4.4	4.4	4.4	4.4
7	4.4	4.4	107.4	4.4	0.0	4.4	4.4	4.4	4.4	4.4
8	4.4	4.4	0.0	4.4	0.0	4.4	4.4	4.4	4.4	4.4
9	4.4	4.4	0.0	4.4	0.0	107.4	4.4	4.4	4.4	4.4
10	4.4	4.4	0.0	4.4	0.0	0.0	4.4	4.4	107.4	4.4
11	4.4	4.4	0.0	4.4	0.0	0.0	4.4	4.4	0.0	4.4
12	4.4	4.4	0.0	4.4	0.0	0.0	107.4	4.4	0.0	4.4
13	4.4	4.4	0.0	4.4	0.0	0.0	0.0	4.4	0.0	4.4
14	4.4	4.4	0.0	4.4	0.0	0.0	0.0	4.4	0.0	4.4
15	4.4	4.4	0.0	4.4	0.0	0.0	0.0	4.4	0.0	4.4
16	4.4	4.4	0.0	4.4	0.0	0.0	0.0	4.4	0.0	4.4
17	4.4	4.4	0.0	4.4	0.0	0.0	0.0	4.4	0.0	4.4
18	4.4	4.4	0.0	4.4	0.0	0.0	0.0	4.4	0.0	4.4
19	4.4	4.4	0.0	4.4	0.0	0.0	0.0	4.4	0.0	4.4
20	104.4	104.4	0.0	104.4	0.0	0.0	0.0	104.4	0.0	104.4

value is different, the present value along each path is calculated again at a different spread. Once again, if the average present value is equal to the market price of the bond, this new spread is the option-adjusted spread. If not, the process continues until a spread is found that satisfies this condition.

This is illustrated in Exhibit 18-5. The first column specifies the basis point spread added to each Treasury spot rate in Exhibit 18-4. The next ten columns show the present value for each path based on that spread. The last column shows the average present value. For example, if the market price of the particular corporate bond is 105.4, then the option-adjusted spread is 40 basis points.

The option-adjusted spread can be interpreted as the *average* spread over the Treasury spot rate curve based on potential paths that can be realized in the future for interest rates. The spread is called "option-adjusted" because the potential paths of the cash flows are adjusted to reflect the options embedded in the bond.

Taking Into Consideration Credit Risk

The spread over the Treasury spot rate curve as described above also reflects credit risk. The way we incorporate credit risk is to add a generic zero credit spread to the Treasury spot rate curve so that the cash flows on a path are then discounted at this combined rate.

The amount of the generic zero credit spread will depend on the quality rating of the particular issue, although there is no reason to expect that the zero credit spread should be the same for each period. While it is theoretically correct to incorporate a maturity structure of credit risk into an option-adjusted spread model, there are models in current use that assume a constant credit risk spread.

Some Technical Issues

There are several technical issues to address in developing an option-adjusted spread model. First, in the simplified illustration, we use only ten possible paths. This is much too small a sample to represent the entire range of potential cash flows that could result. In practice, paths can be generated using Monte Carlo simulation.[1] To do this, it is necessary to specify how the term structure will shift each period. This is accomplished by specifying a probability distribution for the short-term Treasury rate. A change in the short-term Treasury rate will determine how the entire term structure will shift.

A second technical consideration is to ensure that the assumed probability distribution is consistent with the existing term structure of interest rates. This means that when the on-the-run Treasury securities are evaluated, their option-adjusted spread should be zero. This is accomplished by adding a drift term to the short-term return generating process.[2]

---

[1] Monte Carlo simulation is explained in Chapter 22.

[2] For an explanation of how this is done, see Lakhbir S. Hayre and Kenneth Lauterbach, "Stochastic Valuation of Debt Securities," in Frank J. Fabozzi (ed.), *Managing Institutional Assets* (New York: Harper & Row, 1990), pp. 321-364.

Exhibit 18–4

Treasury Spot Rate on Each Path Constructed from Six–Month Forward Rates

Period	1	2	3	4	5	6	7	8	9	10
1	7.00%	7.00%	7.00%	7.00%	7.00%	7.00%	7.00%	7.00%	7.00%	7.00%
2	7.35%	7.35%	7.35%	6.65%	6.65%	6.65%	7.35%	6.65%	7.35%	7.35%
3	7.72%	7.21%	7.21%	6.74%	6.32%	6.32%	7.72%	6.32%	7.72%	7.72%
4	7.70%	6.97%	6.97%	6.96%	6.02%	6.30%	8.12%	6.30%	8.12%	8.12%
5	7.53%	6.95%	6.69%	7.25%	5.73%	6.41%	8.17%	6.41%	8.17%	8.17%
6	7.53%	7.05%	6.42%	7.57%	5.46%	6.37%	8.07%	6.60%	8.07%	8.07%
7	7.64%	7.22%	6.15%	7.94%	5.33%	6.26%	7.89%	6.84%	7.89%	7.89%
8	7.83%	7.46%	6.01%	8.34%	5.29%	6.10%	7.66%	7.13%	7.66%	7.66%
9	8.07%	7.75%	5.95%	8.77%	5.31%	5.92%	7.42%	7.25%	7.56%	7.56%
10	8.17%	7.88%	5.96%	9.24%	5.39%	5.73%	7.17%	7.26%	7.41%	7.54%
11	8.33%	7.90%	6.02%	9.51%	5.50%	5.62%	6.93%	7.34%	7.23%	7.46%
12	8.38%	7.99%	6.13%	9.62%	5.65%	5.48%	6.68%	7.48%	7.03%	7.34%
13	8.36%	8.13%	6.28%	9.64%	5.84%	5.40%	6.44%	7.66%	6.83%	7.19%
14	8.39%	8.18%	6.35%	9.59%	5.94%	5.30%	6.21%	7.88%	6.63%	7.02%
15	8.48%	8.17%	6.36%	9.48%	5.98%	5.24%	5.99%	8.01%	6.47%	6.91%
16	8.50%	8.11%	6.41%	9.43%	6.05%	5.15%	5.82%	8.17%	6.37%	6.78%
17	8.46%	8.01%	6.50%	9.45%	6.16%	5.06%	5.68%	8.26%	6.31%	6.63%
18	8.39%	7.96%	6.62%	9.51%	6.30%	4.95%	5.58%	8.39%	6.28%	6.53%
19	8.36%	7.95%	6.68%	9.62%	6.47%	4.84%	5.51%	8.56%	6.28%	6.46%
20	8.37%	7.90%	6.78%	9.67%	6.58%	4.76%	5.47%	8.77%	6.32%	6.37%

Exhibit 18–5

Present Value of Each Path and Average Present Value Using Various Spreads

	Present Value of Path										Average
Spread	1	2	3	4	5	6	7	8	9	10	Present value
40 bp	100.6	103.5	107.5	93.73	108.5	111.5	107.9	100.4	107.7	112.4	105.4
50 bp	100.0	102.9	107.3	93.14	108.3	111.1	107.4	99.77	107.2	111.6	104.9
60 bp	99.35	102.2	107.0	92.55	108.0	110.7	106.9	99.13	106.7	110.8	104.3
70 bp	98.70	101.5	106.7	91.97	107.8	110.3	106.5	98.49	106.2	110.1	103.8
80 bp	98.06	100.8	106.4	91.40	107.5	109.9	106.0	97.86	105.7	109.3	103.3
90 bp	97.43	100.2	106.1	90.83	107.3	109.5	105.5	97.24	105.3	108.6	102.8
100 bp	96.80	99.58	105.9	90.26	107.1	109.1	105.1	96.62	104.8	107.9	102.3
110 bp	96.18	98.93	105.6	89.70	106.8	108.7	104.6	96.00	104.3	107.1	101.8
120 bp	95.56	98.29	105.3	89.14	106.6	108.3	104.2	95.39	103.8	106.4	101.3

A third technical issue is determination of the relationship between short-term rates and refinancing rates. In our simplified illustration, we conveniently assume that the spread between the two is 100 basis points. Empirical evidence in fact is necessary to determine the relationship.

The call rule, that is, the conditions that must exist for the corporation to call the bond, must be specified. In our simplified illustration, we assumed only that the refinancing rate must be 5.8% or less, and there must be at least three years remaining to maturity. In practice, a call rule will be more complex. Establishment of a call rule requires consideration of the after-tax interest cost savings, the call premium (which declines over time), the legal and underwriting fees, and the time remaining to maturity.

The last technical issue involves estimation of interest rate volatility, which will have an impact on the option-adjusted spread. Volatility is a factor in selection of a probability distribution for the short-term Treasury rate. One of the parameters that must be specified in selecting a probability distribution is the variance (or standard deviation). The larger the variance assumed, the greater the volatility assumed for interest rates.

Our illustration assumes a constant volatility of 10% per period for the short-term forward rate. Instead of assuming a constant volatility, however, we can develop a model that takes the short-term forward rate as a random variable[3] or in which volatility is different for different periods. The volatility assumption for the option-adjusted spread is an important issue, as we see later in this section.

Because of the number of technical issues involved, the option-adjusted spread that dealers report for the same corporate bond can differ by 20 basis points.[4] For mortgage-backed securities, the differences in reported option-adjusted spreads can be considerably greater.

Summary of Option-Adjusted Spread Calculation

We can summarize the procedure to calculate the option-adjusted spread as follows:

(1) From the Treasury yield curve estimate the spot rates and the implied forward rates.

(2) Select a probability distribution[5] for short-term Treasury spot rates. The probability distribution should be selected so that it is consistent with (a) the current spot rate curve, and (b) the historical behavior of interest rates. This will prevent the possibility of arbitrage along the yield curve.

---

[3] The meaning of a random variable is explained in Chapter 21.

[4] John D. Finnerty and Michael Rose, "Arbitrage-Free Spread: A Consistent Measure of Relative Value," *Journal of Portfolio Management* (Spring 1991), p. 77.

[5] Probability distributions are explained in Chapter 21.

(3) Use the probability distribution and Monte Carlo simulation to determine randomly a large number of interest rate paths (say, 1,500).[6] The determination of the number of paths is based on a method from operations research called the variance reduction method.

(4) For bonds with embedded options (such as callable or putable bonds), develop rules for determining the exercise of an option.

(5) For each path found in (3), determine the cash flows, given (a) information about the bond issue (e.g., call provisions), and (b) the rules established in (4).

(6) For an assumed spread and the term structure along a path, calculate a present value for each path.

(7) Calculate the average present value for all paths.

(8) Compare the average present value to the market price of the bond. If they are equal, the assumed spread used in (6) is the option-adjusted spread. If the values are not equal, try another spread and repeat (7) and (8).

Valuing the Embedded Option

In the previous chapter, we found that the price of a callable bond is equal to the price of a noncallable bond minus the value of the embedded call option. A by-product of option-adjusted spread analysis provides the implied value of the embedded call option.

The procedure for obtaining this value after estimating an option-adjusted spread is as follows. First, use the option-adjusted spread to determine what a noncallable bond would sell for. This price, which is called the implied noncallable bond price, is determined by adding the option-adjusted spread to the Treasury spot rates and calculating the present value of the cash flows to maturity. Next, subtract the callable bond's market price from the implied noncallable bond price. The difference is the value of the embedded call option.

The value of the embedded call option (or option cost) can be measured in terms of yield as follows:

$$\text{Option cost} = \text{Static spread} - \text{Option-adjusted spread}$$

Effectively, this says that if the issuer did not have the option to call the bond, the bondholder would realize the static spread. Because of the issuer's option, however, the investor will realize a reduced spread.

---

[6] The determination of the number of paths is based on a method from operations research called the variance reduction method.

Application to Other Bond Structures with Embedded Options

While we have focused here on callable corporate bonds, option-adjusted spread analysis is applicable to any corporate bond structure such as putable bonds, floating-rate notes, and sinking fund bonds. It can easily accommodate more than one embedded option simultaneously. For example, if a corporate bond is both callable and putable, estimation of the cash flow along a path can take into account the fact that the bond may be called before it is put if interest rates fall sufficiently (depending on the call rule), or be put before it is called if interest rates rise (according to some specified put rule). In the case of floating-rate notes, the presence of any interest rate cap or floor can be easily accommodated.

High-yield ("junk") bond structures typically have multiple embedded options. Consider, for example, the payment-in-kind bond. If rates decline sufficiently, the bond may be called; if interest rates rise, however, the issuer has the option of putting to the bondholder another bond with the same coupon as the issue. The option-adjusted spread approach can handle this structure.

Effective or Option-Adjusted Duration and Convexity

In the previous chapter, we describe the price performance characteristics of callable bonds. Modified duration and convexity measures for option-free bonds are inappropriate for callable bonds. In Chapter 11 we presented a measure called effective duration, which we repeat below:

$$\text{Effective duration} = \frac{P_- - P_+}{(P_0)\,(y_+ - y_-)}$$

where

P_- = price if yield is decreased by × basis points

P_+ = price if yield is increased by × basis points

P_0 = initial price (per \$100 of par value)

y_+ = initial yield plus × basis points

y_- = initial yield minus × basis points

The formula for effective convexity is:

$$\text{Effective convexity} = \frac{P_+ + P_- - 2\,(P_0)}{(P_0)\,[.5\,(\,y_+ - y_-)]^2}$$

Application of these two measures to callable bonds allows the price of the callable bond in question to be calculated on the basis of the revised expected cash flows that would occur with a change in interest rates. Within the option-adjusted spread framework, effective duration and convexity can be computed by increasing and decreasing short-term Treasury rates by a small amount, while keeping the option-adjusted spread constant. This will produce two average prices: one when short-term interest rates are increased, and one when short-term interest rates are decreased. The average prices are then substituted into the formula for effective duration and convexity.

The Limitations of Option-Adjusted Spread Analysis

While the option-adjusted spread analysis framework is clearly superior to traditional yield spread analysis, it does not have its limitations. The key components in an OAS model are (1) a probability distribution for the short-term forward rates, (2) expected interest rate volatility, and (3) a rule for determining when an embedded option will be exercised. If any of the components of the model is incorrectly specified, the results of the analysis will be misleading.[7] This risk is referred to as *modeling risk.*

A more appropriate approach to evaluate the investment merits of a bond with an embedded option to accomplish an investment objective over some horizon is the total return framework. The option-adjusted spread analysis is used in the total return framework to compute the price at the end of the investment horizon. If a total return is calculated assuming the OAS at the end of the investment horizon is the same as at the beginning, a common industry practice, then the total return is said to be calculated on a constant OAS basis.

Summary

This chapter has explained the option-adjusted spread approach to valuing a bond with an embedded option(s). This approach takes into account (1) the yield curve and spot rate curves, (2) the options embedded in the bond, and (3) the expected volatility of interest rates. The traditional yield spread approach does not account for such factors.

The option-adjusted spread is the spread over the Treasury spot rate curve that results because the embedded option(s) will cause the cash flow of the bond to change as interest rates change. It is an average spread in that it is based on a large number of potential paths for interest rates. The cost of the embedded option is a by-product of the model and is not estimated directly using an option pricing model.

Because there are many technical details in developing an option-adjusted spread model, there can be considerable differences in the values reported by dealer firms. A money manager using an option-adjusted spread reported by a dealer or one from a model developed by a vendor firm must recognize why these differences may occur.

---

[7] For a more detailed criticism of the option-adjusted spread methodology, see Finnerty and Rose, "Arbitrage-Free Spread: A Consistent Measure of Relative Value." See also the response by Lakhbir S. Hayre in the same issue.

VI

Analyzing Mortgage-Backed Securities

19

Cash Flow
Characteristics
of Mortgages

A mortgage is a pledge of real estate to secure the payment of the loan originated for the purchase of that real property. The mortgage gives the lender (*mortgagee*) the right to foreclose on the loan and seize the property in order to ensure that the loan is paid off if the borrower (*mortgagor*) fails to make the contracted payments.

A mortgage loan specifies the interest rate of the loan, the frequency of payment, and the number of years to maturity. In this chapter we show how to compute the cash flow of mortgages. While there are many types of mortgages, we focus in this chapter on level-payment fixed-rate mortgages. A level-payment fixed-rate mortgage has the following features: (1) the term of the loan is fixed, (2) the interest rate is fixed, and (3) the amount of the monthly mortgage payment is fixed for the entire term of the loan (i.e., the mortgage is "level-pay").

A characteristic that mortgages share with callable corporate bonds is that their cash flow is not known with certainty. For callable corporate bonds, this happens because the bondholder has effectively granted the corporate issuer the option to call the issue. For mortgages, the lender has effectively granted the homeowner the right to repay *all* or *any* *part* of the mortgage balance at any time.

Mortgages are the underlying collateral for mortgage-backed securities.[1] In the next chapter we describe the cash flow characteristics of mortgage-backed securities, along with the effect of prepayments.

Determining the Monthly Mortgage Payment

In Chapter 3 we explained calculation of the present value of an ordinary annuity. To compute the monthly mortgage payment for a level-payment fixed-rate mortgage requires application of the formula for the present value of an ordinary annuity formula, which is

$$PV = A \left[\frac{1 - \left[\frac{1}{(1+i)^n} \right]}{i} \right],$$

where
PV = Present value of an annuity ($);
A = Amount of the annuity ($);
i = Periodic interest rate;
n = Number of periods.

We can redefine these terms to yield a formula for a level-payment fixed-rate mortgage as follows:

$$MB_0 = MP \left[\frac{1 - \left[\frac{1}{(1+i)^n} \right]}{i} \right],$$

where
MB_0 = Original mortgage balance ($);
MP = Monthly mortgage payment ($);
i = Simple monthly interest rate (annual interest rate/12);
n = Number of months.

Solving for the monthly mortgage payment (MP) gives

---

[1] Other types of mortgages can serve as the underlying collateral for mortgage-backed securities. These include adjustable-rate mortgages and balloon/reset mortgages. For a discussion of the characteristics of these mortgages, see Frank J. Fabozzi and Franco Modigliani, *Mortgage and Mortgage-Backed Securities* (Boston: Harvard Business School Press, 1992).

$$MP = \cfrac{MB_0}{\left[\cfrac{1 - \left[\cfrac{1}{(1 + i)^n} \right]}{i} \right]}$$

This can be expressed in a simplified form as follows:

$$MP = MB_0 \left[\frac{i(1 + i)^n}{[(1 + i)^n - 1]} \right].$$

Illustration 19-1. Suppose a homeowner enters into a mortgage for $100,000 for 360 months (30 years), at a mortgage rate of 9.5%. The monthly mortgage payment is determined as follows:

$MB_0 = \$100,000;$
$\quad i = .0079167\ (= .095/12);$
$\quad n = 360.$

The monthly mortgage payment is then

$$MP = \$100,000 \left[\frac{.0079167\,(1.0079167)^{360}}{[(1.0079167)^{360} - 1]} \right]$$

$$= \$100,000\ \frac{[.0079167\,(17.095)]}{[17.095 - 1]}$$

$$= \$840.85.$$

Cash Flow of a Level-Payment Fixed-Rate Mortgage

Each monthly mortgage payment for a level-payment fixed-rate mortgage due on the first of each month consists of:

(1) Interest of 1/12th of the fixed annual interest rate times the amount of the outstanding mortgage balance at the beginning of the previous month (interest "in arrears"), and

(2) Repayment of a portion of the outstanding mortgage balance (principal).

The difference between the monthly mortgage payment and the portion of the payment that represents interest equals the amount that is applied to reduce the outstanding mortgage balance. The monthly mortgage payment is designed so that after the last scheduled monthly payment of the loan is made, the amount of the outstanding mortgage balance is zero (i.e., the mortgage is fully repaid).

Illustration 19-2. Consider the mortgage in Illustration 19-1. Exhibit 19-1 shows how each monthly mortgage payment is divided between interest and repayment of principal. At the beginning of month 1, the mortgage balance is $100,000, the amount of the original loan. The mortgage payment for month 1 includes interest for the month on the $100,000 borrowed. Since the interest rate is 9.5%, the monthly interest rate is .0079167 (.095 divided by 12). Interest for month 1 is therefore $791.67 ($100,000 times .0079167). The portion of the monthly mortgage payment that represents repayment of principal is the difference between the monthly mortgage payment of $840.85 and the interest of $791.67. Thus, the scheduled principal repayment is $49.18, and the mortgage balance is reduced by this amount.[2]

The mortgage balance at the end of month 1 (beginning of month 2) is then $99,950.81 ($100,00 minus $49.19). The interest for the second month is $791.28, the monthly interest rate (.0079167) times the mortgage balance at the end of month 1 ($99,950.81). The difference between the $840.85 monthly mortgage payment and the $791.28 interest is $49.57, representing the amount of the mortgage balance paid off with that monthly mortgage payment.

The last line of Exhibit 19-1 shows the last monthly mortgage payment is sufficient to pay off the remaining mortgage balance. When a loan repayment schedule is structured so that the payments made by the borrower will completely pay off the interest and principal, the loan is said to be *self-amortizing.* Exhibit 19-1 is thus referred to as an amortization schedule.

As Exhibit 19-1 clearly shows, *the portion of the monthly mortgage payment applied to interest declines each month, and the portion that goes to reducing the mortgage balance increases.* The reason for this is that as the mortgage balance is reduced with each monthly mortgage payment, the interest on the mortgage balance declines. Since the monthly mortgage payment is fixed, a larger part of the monthly payment is applied to reduce the principal each month.

It is not necessary to construct an amortization schedule such as Exhibit 19-1 in order to determine the remaining mortgage balance for any month. The following formula can be used:

$$MB_t = MB_0 \left[\frac{[(1 + i)^n - (1 + i)^t]}{[(1 + i)^n - 1]} \right],$$

where

MB_t = Mortgage balance after t months ($);
MB_0 = The original mortgage balance ($);
  i = Simple monthly interest rate (annual interest rate/12);
  n = Original number of months of mortgage.

---

[2] Because Exhibit 19-1 is computer-generated, rounding resulted in the values of $49.19 and $49.18 shown in the exhibit.

Exhibit 19-1

Amortization Schedule for a Level-Payment Fixed-Rate Mortgage

Mortgage loan: $100,000
Mortgage rate: 9.5%
Monthly payment: $840.85
Term of loan: 30 years (360 months)

Month	Beginning mortgage balance	Monthly mortgage payment	Interest for month	Principal repayment	Ending mortgage balance
1	$100,000.00	$840.85	$791.67	$49.19	$99,950.81
2	99,950.81	840.85	791.28	49.58	99,901.24
3	99,901.24	840.85	790.88	49.97	99,851.27
4	99,851.27	840.85	790.49	50.37	99,800.90
5	99,800.90	840.85	790.09	50.76	99,750.14
6	99,750.14	840.85	789.69	51.10	99,698.97
7	99,698.97	840.85	789.28	51.57	99,647.40
8	99,647.40	840.85	788.88	51.90	99,595.42
9	99,595.42	840.85	788.46	52.39	99,543.03
10	99,543.03	840.85	788.05	52.81	99,490.23
11	99,490.23	840.85	787.63	53.22	99,437.00
12	99,437.00	840.85	787.21	53.64	99,383.36
13	99,383.36	840.85	786.78	54.07	99,329.29
14	99,329.29	840.85	786.36	54.50	99,274.79
15	99,274.79	840.85	785.93	54.93	99,219.86

Exhibit 19-1 continued.

Month	Beginning mortgage balance	Monthly mortgage payment	Interest for month	Principal repayment	Ending mortgage balance
16	99,219.86	840.85	785.49	55.36	99,164.50
17	99,164.50	840.85	785.05	55.80	99,108.70
18	99,108.70	840.85	784.61	56.24	99,052.45
19	99,052.45	840.85	784.17	56.69	98,995.77
20	98,995.77	840.85	783.72	57.14	98,938.63
21	98,938.63	840.85	783.26	57.59	98,881.04
22	98,881.04	840.85	782.81	58.05	98,822.99
23	98,822.99	840.85	782.35	58.51	98,764.49
24	98,764.49	840.85	781.89	58.97	98,705.52
25	98,705.52	840.85	781.42	59.44	98,646.08
26	98,646.08	840.85	780.95	59.91	98,586.18
27	98,586.18	840.85	780.47	60.38	98,525.80
28	98,525.80	840.85	780.00	60.86	98,464.94
29	98,464.94	840.85	779.51	61.34	98,403.60
30	98,403.60	840.85	779.03	61.83	98,341.77
31	98,341.77	840.85	778.54	62.32	98,279.46
32	98,279.46	840.85	778.05	62.81	98,216.65
33	98,216.65	840.85	777.55	63.31	98,153.34
34	98,153.34	840.85	777.05	63.81	98,089.53
35	98,089.53	840.85	776.54	64.31	98,025.22

Exhibit 19-1 continued.

Month	Beginning mortgage balance	Monthly mortgage payment	Interest for month	Principal repayment	Ending mortgage balance
36	98,025.22	840.85	776.03	64.82	97,960.40
:	......	......	......	......	......
:	......	......	......	......	......
:	......	......	......	......	......
98	92,862.54	840.85	735.16	105.69	92,756.85
99	92,756.85	840.85	734.33	106.53	92,650.32
100	92,650.32	840.85	733.48	107.37	92,542.95
101	92,542.95	840.85	732.63	108.22	92,434.72
102	92,434.72	840.85	731.77	109.08	92,325.64
103	92,325.64	840.85	730.91	109.94	92,215.70
104	92,215.70	840.85	730.04	110.81	92,104.89
105	92,104.89	840.85	729.16	111.69	91,993.20
106	91,993.20	840.85	728.28	112.57	91,880.62
107	91,880.62	840.85	727.39	113.47	91,767.16
108	91,767.16	840.85	726.49	114.36	91,652.79
109	91,652.79	840.85	725.58	115.27	91,537.52
110	91,537.52	840.85	724.67	116.18	91,421.34
111	91,421.34	840.85	723.75	117.10	91,304.24
112	91,304.24	840.85	722.83	118.03	91,186.21
113	91,186.21	840.85	721.89	118.96	91,067.25

Exhibit 19-1 continued.

Month	Beginning mortgage balance	Monthly mortgage payment	Interest for month	Principal repayment	Ending mortgage balance
114	91,067.25	840.85	720.95	119.91	90,947.34
115	90,947.34	840.85	720.00	120.85	90,826.49
...	......	......	......	......	......
...	......	......	......	......	......
...	......	......	......	......	......
201	76,135.92	840.85	602.74	238.11	75,897.80
202	75,897.80	840.85	600.86	240.00	75,657.81
203	75,657.81	840.85	598.96	241.90	75,415.91
204	75,415.91	840.85	597.04	243.81	75,172.10
205	75,172.10	840.85	595.11	245.74	74,926.36
206	74,926.36	840.85	593.17	247.69	74,678.67
207	74,678.67	840.85	591.21	249.65	74,429.02
208	74,429.02	840.85	589.23	251.62	74,177.40
209	74,177.40	840.85	587.24	253.62	73,923.78
210	73,923.78	840.85	585.23	255.62	73,668.16
211	73,668.16	840.85	583.21	257.65	73,410.51
212	73,410.51	840.85	581.17	259.69	73,150.82
213	73,150.82	840.85	579.11	261.74	72,889.08
214	72,889.08	840.85	577.04	263.82	72,625.26
215	72,625.26	840.85	574.95	265.90	72,359.36

Exhibit 19-1 continued.

Month	Beginning mortgage balance	Monthly mortgage payment	Interest for month	Principal repayment	Ending mortgage balance
216	72,359.36	840.85	572.84	268.01	72,091.35
217	72,091.35	840.85	570.72	270.13	71,821.22
218	71,821.22	840.85	568.58	272.27	71,548.95
219	71,548.95	840.85	566.43	274.43	71,274.52
220	71,274.52	840.85	564.26	276.60	70,997.93
⋯	⋯⋯	⋯⋯	⋯⋯	⋯⋯	⋯⋯
⋯	⋯⋯	⋯⋯	⋯⋯	⋯⋯	⋯⋯
⋯	⋯⋯	⋯⋯	⋯⋯	⋯⋯	⋯⋯
342	14,778.59	840.85	117.00	723.86	14,054.73
343	14,054.73	840.85	111.27	729.59	13,325.15
344	13,325.15	840.85	105.49	735.36	12,589.78
345	12,589.78	840.85	99.67	741.19	11,848.60
346	11,848.60	840.85	93.80	747.05	11,101.55
347	11,101.55	840.85	87.89	752.97	10,348.58
348	10,348.58	840.85	81.93	758.93	9,589.65
349	9,589.65	840.85	75.92	764.94	8,824.71
350	8,824.71	840.85	69.86	770.99	8,053.72
351	8,053.72	840.85	63.76	777.10	7,276.63
352	7,276.63	840.85	57.61	783.25	6,493.38
353	6,493.38	840.85	51.41	789.45	5,703.93

Exhibit 19-1 continued.

Month	Beginning mortgage balance	Monthly mortgage payment	Interest for month	Principal repayment	Ending mortgage balance
354	5,703.93	840.85	45.16	795.70	4,908.23
355	4,908.23	840.85	38.86	802.00	4,106.24
356	4,106.24	840.85	32.51	808.35	3,297.89
357	3,297.89	840.85	26.11	814.75	2,483.14
358	2,483.14	840.85	19.66	821.20	1,661.95
359	1,661.95	840.85	13.16	827.70	834.25
360	834.25	840.85	6.60	834.25	0.00

Illustration 19-3. For the mortgage in Illustration 19-1, the mortgage balance after the 210th month is:

$$t = 210;$$
$$MB_0 = \$100,000;$$
$$i = .0079167;$$
$$n = 360.$$

$$MB_{210} = \$100,000 \left[\frac{[(1.0079167)^{360} - (1.0079167)^{210}]}{[(1.0079167)^{360} - 1]} \right]$$

$$= \$100,000 \left[\frac{(17.095 - 5.2381)}{(17.095 - 1)} \right]$$

$$= \$73,668.$$

This agrees with the ending mortgage balance for month 210 shown in Exhibit 19-1.

Another formula can be used to determine the amount of the scheduled principal repayment in month t:

$$P_t = MB_0 \left[\frac{[i(1 + i)^{t-1}]}{[(1 + i)^n - 1]} \right],$$

where

P_t = Scheduled principal repayment for month t.

Illustration 19-4. The scheduled principal repayment for the 210th month for the mortgage in Illustration 19-1 is

$$\$100,000 \left[\frac{[.0079167 (1.0079167)^{210 - 1}]}{[(1.0079167)^{360} - 1]} \right]$$

$$= \$100,000 \left[\frac{[.0079167 (5.19696)]}{[17.095 - 1]} \right]$$

$$= \$255.62.$$

Once again, this agrees with Exhibit 19-1.

To compute the interest paid for month t, a final formula can be used:

$$I_t = MB_0 \left[\frac{i[(1 + i)^n - (1 + i)^{t-1}]}{[(1 + i)^n - 1]} \right],$$

where

I_t = Interest for month t.

Illustration 19-5. For the 210th month, the interest for the mortgage in Illustration 19-1 is

$$I_{210} = \$100,000 \left[\frac{.0079167 \left[(1.0079167)^{360} - (1.0079167)^{210-1} \right]}{[(1.0079167)^{360} - 1]} \right]$$

$$= \$100,000 \left[\frac{.0079167 \, (17.095 - 5.19696)}{(17.095 - 1)} \right]$$

$$= \$585.23.$$

This result can be confirmed by examination of Exhibit 19-1.

Cash Flow and Servicing Fee

An investor who owns a mortgage receives the monthly mortgage payment as the *scheduled* cash flow. A mortgage, however, requires monitoring to ensure that the borrower complies with the terms of the mortgage. In addition, the investor must periodically supply certain information to the borrower. These activities are referred to as *servicing* the mortgage. More specifically, servicing of the mortgage involves collecting monthly payments from mortgagors, sending payment notices to mortgagors, reminding mortgagors when payments are overdue, maintaining records of mortgage balances, furnishing tax information to mortgagors, administering an escrow account for real estate taxes and insurance purposes, and, if necessary, initiating foreclosure proceedings. Part of the mortgage rate includes the cost of servicing the mortgage. The servicing fee is a fixed percentage of the outstanding mortgage balance.

An investor who acquires a mortgage may either service the mortgage or sell the right to service the mortgage. In the former case, the investor's cash flow is the entire cash flow from the mortgage. In the latter case it is the cash flow net of the servicing fee.

The monthly cash flow from the mortgage can therefore be decomposed into three parts:

(1) The amount to service the mortgage;

(2) The interest payment net of the servicing fee;

(3) The scheduled principal repayment.

Illustration 19-6. Consider once again the 30-year mortgage loan for $100,000 with a mortgage rate of 9.5%. Suppose the servicing fee is .5% per year. Exhibit 19-2 shows the cash flow for the mortgage assuming this servicing fee. The monthly mortgage payment is unchanged from Exhibit 19-1, and so is the amount of the principal repayment. The difference is that the interest is reduced by the amount of the servicing fee. The servicing fee, just like the interest, declines each month because the mortgage balance declines.

Exhibit 19-2

Cash Flow for a Mortgage with Servicing Fee

Mortgage loan: $100,000
Mortgage rate: 9.5%
Servicing fee: 0.5%
Monthly payment: $840.85
Term of loan: 30 years (360 months)

Month	Beginning mortgage balance	Monthly mortgage payment	Net interest for month	Servicing fee	Principal repayment	Ending mortgage balance
1	$100,000.00	$840.85	$750.00	$41.67	$49.19	$99,950.81
2	99,950.81	840.85	749.63	41.65	49.58	99,901.24
3	99,901.24	840.85	749.26	41.63	49.97	99,851.27
4	99,851.27	840.85	748.88	41.60	50.37	99,800.90
5	99,800.90	840.85	748.51	41.58	50.76	99,750.14
6	99,750.14	840.85	748.13	41.56	51.17	99,698.97
7	99,698.97	840.85	747.74	41.54	51.57	99,647.40
8	99,647.40	840.85	747.36	41.52	51.98	99,595.42
9	99,595.42	840.85	746.97	41.50	52.39	99,543.03
10	99,543.03	840.85	746.57	41.48	52.81	99,490.23
11	99,490.23	840.85	746.18	41.45	53.22	99,437.00
12	99,437.00	840.85	745.78	41.43	53.64	99,383.36
13	99,383.36	840.85	745.38	41.41	54.07	99,329.29

Exhibit 19-2 continued.

Month	Beginning mortgage balance	Monthly mortgage payment	Net interest for month	Servicing fee	Principal repayment	Ending mortgage balance
14	99,329.29	840.85	744.97	41.39	54.50	99,274.79
15	99,274.79	840.85	744.56	41.36	54.93	99,219.86
16	99,219.86	840.85	744.15	41.34	55.36	99,164.50
17	99,164.50	840.85	743.73	41.32	55.80	99,108.70
18	99,108.70	840.85	743.32	41.30	56.24	99,052.45
19	99,052.45	840.85	742.89	41.27	56.69	98,995.77
20	98,995.77	840.85	742.47	41.25	57.14	98,938.63
21	98,938.63	840.85	742.04	41.22	57.59	98,881.04
22	98,881.04	840.85	741.61	41.20	58.05	98,822.99
23	98,822.99	840.85	741.17	41.18	58.51	98,764.49
24	98,764.49	840.85	740.73	41.15	58.97	98,705.52
25	98,705.52	840.85	740.29	41.13	59.44	98,646.08
26	98,646.08	840.85	739.85	41.10	59.91	98,586.18
27	98,586.18	840.85	739.40	41.08	60.38	98,525.80
28	98,525.80	840.85	738.94	41.05	60.86	98,464.94
29	98,464.94	840.85	738.49	41.03	61.34	98,403.60
30	98,403.60	840.85	738.03	41.00	61.83	98,341.77
31	98,341.77	840.85	737.56	40.98	62.32	98,279.46
32	98,279.46	840.85	737.10	40.95	62.81	98,216.65
33	98,216.65	840.85	736.62	40.92	63.31	98,153.34

Exhibit 19-2 continued.

Month	Beginning mortgage balance	Monthly mortgage payment	Net interest for month	Servicing fee	Principal repayment	Ending mortgage balance
34	98,153.34	840.85	736.15	40.90	63.81	98,089.53
35	98,089.53	840.85	735.67	40.87	64.31	98,025.22
36	98,025.22	840.85	735.19	40.84	64.82	97,960.40
:	....	....	....	....	....	....
:	....	....	....	....	....	....
:	....	....	....	....	....	....
98	92,862.54	840.85	696.47	38.69	105.69	92,756.85
99	92,756.85	840.85	695.68	38.65	106.53	92,650.32
100	92,650.32	840.85	694.88	38.60	107.37	92,542.95
101	92,542.95	840.85	694.07	38.56	108.22	92,434.72
102	92,434.72	840.85	693.26	38.51	109.08	92,325.64
103	92,325.64	840.85	692.44	38.47	109.94	92,215.70
104	92,215.70	840.85	691.62	38.42	110.81	92,104.89
105	92,104.89	840.85	690.79	38.38	111.69	91,993.20
106	91,993.20	840.85	689.95	38.33	112.57	91,880.62
107	91,880.62	840.85	689.10	38.28	113.47	91,767.16
108	91,767.16	840.85	688.25	38.24	114.36	91,652.79
109	91,652.79	840.85	687.40	38.19	115.27	91,537.52
110	91,537.52	840.85	686.53	38.14	116.18	91,421.34
111	91,421.34	840.85	685.66	38.09	117.10	91,304.24

Exhibit 19-2 continued.

Month	Beginning mortgage balance	Monthly mortgage payment	Net interest for month	Servicing fee	Principal repayment	Ending mortgage balance
112	91,304.24	840.85	684.78	38.04	118.03	91,186.21
113	91,186.21	840.85	683.90	37.99	118.96	91,067.25
114	91,067.25	840.85	683.00	37.94	119.91	90,947.34
115	90,947.34	840.85	682.11	37.89	120.85	90,826.49
:	......	......	......	......	......	......
:	......	......	......	......	......	......
::	......	......	......	......	......	......
201	76,135.92	840.85	571.02	31.72	238.11	75,897.80
202	75,897.80	840.85	569.23	31.62	240.00	75,657.81
203	75,657.81	840.85	567.43	31.52	241.90	75,415.91
204	75,415.91	840.85	565.62	31.42	243.81	75,172.10
205	75,172.10	840.85	563.79	31.32	245.74	74,926.36
206	74,926.36	840.85	561.95	31.22	247.69	74,678.67
207	74,678.67	840.85	560.09	31.12	249.65	74,429.02
208	74,429.02	840.85	558.22	31.01	251.62	74,177.40
209	74,177.40	840.85	556.33	30.91	253.62	73,923.78
210	73,923.78	840.85	554.43	30.80	255.62	73,668.16
211	73,668.16	840.85	552.51	30.70	257.65	73,410.51
212	73,410.51	840.85	550.58	30.59	259.69	73,150.82
213	73,150.82	840.85	548.63	30.48	261.74	72,889.08
214	72,889,08	840.85	546.67	30.37	263.82	72,625.26

Exhibit 19-2 continued.

Month	Beginning mortgage balance	Monthly mortgage payment	Net interest for month	Servicing fee	Principal repayment	Ending mortgage balance
215	72,625.26	840.85	544.69	30.26	265.90	72,359.36
216	72,359.36	840.85	542.70	30.15	268.01	72,091.35
217	72,091,35	840.85	540.69	30.04	270.13	71,821.22
218	71,821.22	840.85	538.66	29.93	272.27	71,548.95
219	71,548.95	840.85	536.62	29.81	274.43	71,274.52
220	71,274.52	840.85	534.56	29.70	276.60	70,997.93
:	....	....	....	....	....	....
:	....	....	....	....	....	....
:	....	....	....	....	....	....
342	14,778.59	840.85	110.84	6.16	723.86	14,054.73
343	14,054.73	840.85	105.41	5.86	729.59	13,325.15
344	13,325.15	840.85	99.94	5.55	735.36	12,589.78
345	12,589.78	840.85	94.42	5.25	741.19	11,848.60
346	11,848.60	840.85	88.86	4.94	747.05	11,101.55
347	11,101.55	840.85	83.26	4.63	752.97	10,348.58
348	10,348.58	840.85	77.61	4.31	758.93	9,589.65
349	9,589.65	840.85	71.92	4.00	764.94	8,824.71
350	8,824.71	840.85	66.19	3.68	770.99	8,053.72
351	8,053.72	840.85	60.40	3.36	777.10	7,276.63
352	7,276.63	840.85	54.57	3.03	783.25	6,493.38
353	6,493.38	840.85	48.70	2.71	789.45	5,703.93

Exhibit 19-2 continued.

Month	Beginning mortgage balance	Monthly mortgage payment	Net interest for month	Servicing fee	Principal repayment	Ending mortgage balance
354	5,703.93	840.85	42.78	2.38	795.70	4,908.23
355	4,908.23	840.85	36.81	2.05	802.00	4,106.24
356	4,106.24	840.85	30.80	1.71	808.35	3,297.89
357	3,297.89	840.85	24.73	1.37	814.75	2,483.14
358	2,483.14	840.85	18.62	1.03	821.20	1,661.95
359	1,661.95	840.85	12.46	0.69	827.70	834.25
360	834.25	840.85	6.60	0.38	834.25	0

Summary

In this chapter we have shown how to determine the cash flow of a level-payment fixed-rate mortgage. The cash flow of a mortgage consists of the monthly interest plus the scheduled principal repayment. Each month, the mortgage balance declines, resulting in a lower monthly dollar interest than in the previous month, with more of the fixed monthly mortgage payment applied to reduction of the mortgage balance. The cash flow can be partitioned further by dividing the interest into (1) a servicing fee and (2) interest net of the servicing fee. Exhibit 19-3 summarizes the formulas presented in the chapter.

Exhibit 19-3

Summary of Formulas for Cash Flow of Level-Payment Fixed-Rate Mortgages (Assuming No Prepayments)

(1) The monthly mortgage payment:

$$MP = MB_0 \left[\frac{[i(1+i)^n]}{[(1+i)^n - 1]} \right],$$

where

MP = Monthly mortgage payment ($);
MB_0 = Original mortgage balance ($);
i = Simple monthly interest rate (annual interest rate/12);
n = Number of months.

(2) The remaining mortgage balance at the end of month t:

$$MB_t = MB_0 \left[\frac{[(1+i)^n - (1+i)^t]}{[(1+i)^n - 1]} \right],$$

where

MB_t = Mortgage balance after t months ($);
n = Original number of months of mortgage.

(3) The scheduled principal repayments in month t:

$$P_t = MB_0 \left[\frac{[(i(+i)^{t-1}]}{[(1+i)^n - 1]} \right],$$

where

P_t = Scheduled principal repayment for month t.

(4) The interest for month t:

$$I_t = MB_0 \left[\frac{i[(1+i)^n - (1+i)^{t-1}]}{[(1+i)^n - 1]} \right],$$

where

I_t = Interest for month t.

20

Cash Flow Characteristics of Mortgage-Backed Securities

A mortgage-backed security (MBS) is created by pooling mortgage loans and using this pool of mortgage loans as collateral for the security. There are three types of mortgage-backed securities: a mortgage pass-through security, a collateralized mortgage obligation, and a stripped MBS. The cash flow of any MBS depends on the cash flow of the underlying mortgage pool. Since the cash flow of an individual mortgage loan is uncertain because of the potential of prepayments, the same is true for MBSs.

In this chapter we focus on the various conventions for projecting the cash flow of an MBS. We show how to project the cash flow for a mortgage pass-through security as well as for the other products, collateralized mortgage obligations and stripped MBS.

The Prepayment Option and the Cash Flow

In our illustration of the cash flow from a level-payment fixed-rate mortgage in the previous chapter, we assumed that the homeowner would not pay any portion of the mortgage balance off prior to the scheduled due date. But homeowners do pay off some or all of their mortgage balance prior to the maturity date. Payments made in excess of the scheduled principal repayments are called *prepayments*.

Prepayments occur for one of several reasons. First, homeowners pay off the entire mortgage when they sell their home. The sale of a home may be due to (1) a change of employment that necessitates moving, (2) the purchase of a more expensive home ("trading up"), or (3) a divorce settlement requiring sale of the marital residence. Second, borrowers have an incentive to prepay a mortgage loan as mortgage rates in the market fall below the specified rate on their mortgage loan. Third, in the case of homeowners who cannot meet their mortgage obligations, the property may be repossessed and sold, with the proceeds from the sale used to pay off the mortgage loan. Finally, if property is destroyed by fire or another insured catastrophe occurs, the insurance proceeds are used to pay off the mortgage.

The effect of the right to prepay is that the cash flow from a mortgage is not known with certainty. This is true for all mortgage loans, not just level-payment fixed-rate mortgages.

Overview of Mortgage-Backed Securities

We illustrate the creation of mortgage-backed securities using Exhibits 20-1 through 20-14. Exhibit 20-1 shows ten mortgage loans (each loan depicted as a home) and the cash flows from these loans. For the sake of simplicity, we assume that the amount of each loan is $100,000 so that the aggregate value of all ten loans is $1 million. The cash flows are monthly and consist of three components:

(1) interest

(2) scheduled principal repayment

(3) payments in excess of the regularly scheduled principal repayment.

How (1) and (2) are determined is explained in Chapter 19. The third component, payments in excess of the scheduled principal payment, is what we said is a prepayment. It is the amount and timing of this component of the cash flow from a mortgage that makes the entire cash flow (and therefore analysis of mortgages and mortgage-backed securities) complicated. This is referred to as *prepayment risk*. Creation of mortgage-backed securities does not alter the total amount of prepayment risk. The distribution of that risk among investors, however, can be altered.

An investor who owns any one of the mortgage loans shown in Exhibit 20-1 faces prepayment risk. For an individual loan, it may be difficult to predict prepayments, but if an individual investor purchased all ten loans, there could be a way to predict prepayments better. In fact, if there were 500 mortgage loans in Exhibit 20-1 rather than ten, we could use historical prepayment experience to improve predictions about prepayments.

Exhibit 20-1

Ten Mortgage Loans

Monthly cash flow

| | Interest
Scheduled principal repayment
Prepayments |
Loan #1

Loan #2 → Interest / Scheduled principal repayment / Prepayments

Loan #3 → Interest / Scheduled principal repayment / Prepayments

Loan #4 → Interest / Scheduled principal repayment / Prepayments

Loan #5 → Interest / Scheduled principal repayment / Prepayments

Loan #6 → Interest / Scheduled principal repayment / Prepayments

Loan #7 → Interest / Scheduled principal repayment / Prepayments

Loan #8 → Interest / Scheduled principal repayment / Prepayments

Loan #9 → Interest / Scheduled principal repayment / Prepayments

Loan #10 → Interest / Scheduled principal repayment / Prepayments

Each loan is for $100,000
Total loans: $1 million

But an investor would have to invest $1 million to buy ten loans and $50 million to buy 500 loans assuming each loan is for $100,000.

Mortgage Pass-through Securities

Suppose, instead, that some entity purchases all ten loans in Exhibit 20-1 and pools them. The ten loans can be used as collateral for the issuance of a security, whose cash flow would reflect the cash flow from the ten loans, as depicted in Exhibit 20-2. Suppose there are 40 units of this security issued. Thus, each unit is initially worth $25,000 ($1 million divided by 40). Each unit would be entitled to 2.5% (1/40) of the cash flow. The security created is called a *mortgage pass-through security*, or simply, a *pass-through*. The majority of pass-throughs are guaranteed by a government-related entity, the Government National Mortgage Association (GNMA, nicknamed "Ginnie Mae"), and two government-sponsored entities, the Federal National Mortgage Association (FNMA, nicknamed "Fannie Mae") and the Federal Home Loan Mortgage Corporation (FHLMC, nicknamed "Freddie Mac"). Pass-throughs are also issued by private entities; these securities are referred to as *conventional pass-throughs* or *private label pass-throughs*.

Let's see what has been accomplished by creating the pass-through. The total amount of prepayment risk has not changed. Instead, with an investment of less than $1 million, the investor is now exposed to the total prepayment risk of all ten loans rather than facing the risk of an individual mortgage loan.

So far, this financial "engineering" has not resulted in creation of a totally new instrument, as an individual investor could have achieved the same outcome by purchasing all ten loans. The pass-through does reduce the $1 million requirement and increases the liquidity of the security. Moreover, by selling a pass-through the investor can dispose of all ten loans rather than having to dispose of each loan one by one. Thus, a pass-through can be viewed as a more transactionally efficient vehicle for investing in mortgages than the purchase of individual mortgages would be.

Mortgage loans that are included in a pool to create a pass-through are said to be *securitized*. The process of creating a pass-through is referred to as the securitization of mortgage loans.

Collateralized Mortgage Obligations

An investor in a pass-through is still exposed to the total prepayment risk associated with the pool of mortgage loans underlying the security. A way to change this is instead of distributing the monthly cash flow on a pro rata basis, as in the case of a pass-through, to distribute the principal (both scheduled and prepayments) on some prioritized basis. How this may be done is illustrated in Exhibit 20-3.

Exhibit 20-3 shows the cash flow of our original ten mortgage loans and the pass-through. Also shown are three classes of bonds of different par values, with a set of rules indicating how the principal from the pass-through is to be distributed to each. The sum of the par value of the three classes is equal to $1 million. While it is not shown in the exhibit, for each of the three classes there are units representing a proportionate interest in the class. Each unit then receives a proportionate share of what is received by the class.

Exhibit 20-2

Creation of a Pass-Through Security

Each loan is for $100,000
Total loans: $1 million

For example, suppose that for Class A, which has a par value of $400,000, there are 50 units issued. Class A holders then receive proportionate shares of 2% of the distribution of principal.

The rule for the distribution of principal shown in Exhibit 20-3 is that Class A will receive all principal (both scheduled and prepayments) until that class receives its entire par value of $400,000. Then, Class B receives all principal payments until it receives its par value of $350,000. Finally, after Class B is completely paid off, Class C receives principal payments. The rule for the distribution of interest in Exhibit 20-3 indicates that each of the three classes will receive interest based on the amount of par value outstanding.

The mortgage-backed security that has been created is called a *collateralized mortgage obligation* (CMO). The collateral for a loan may be either one or more pass-throughs or a pool of mortgage loans that have not been securitized. The ultimate source for the CMO's cash flow is the pool of mortgage loans.

Let's evaluate what has been accomplished. Once again, the total prepayment risk for the CMO remains the same as the total prepayment risk for the ten mortgage loans. Creation of three classes, however, means that the prepayment risk is distributed differently among the three classes of the CMO. Class A absorbs prepayments first, next Class B, and last of all Class C. The result is that Class A effectively holds a shorter-term security than the other two classes; Class C has the longest maturity. Institutional investors will be attracted to the different classes given the varying nature of their liability structure and the effective maturity of the CMO class. Moreover, the cash flow distribution rules mitigate the uncertainty about the maturity of each class of the CMO.

Thus, redirection of the cash flow from the underlying mortgage pool creates classes of bonds that may be more attractive to institutional investors to satisfy asset/liability objectives than a pass-through.

The CMO we depict in Exhibit 20-3 has a simple set of rules for prioritizing the distribution of principal. Today, much more complicated CMO structures exist, such as *planned amortization class (PAC) bonds, targeted amortization class (TAC) bonds,* and *very accurately determined maturity (VADM) bonds.* These CMO structures are intended to expose certain CMO classes to less prepayment risk. Note, however, that this can occur only if the reduction in prepayment risk for some classes is absorbed by other classes in the CMO structure, which are referred to as *support bonds* or *companion bonds.*

Stripped MBS

The CMO in Exhibit 20-3 specified a set of rules for prioritizing the distribution of the principal payments among the various classes. A stripped MBS calls for dividing all the principal and all the interest between two bond classes. One class is entitled to receive all the principal, the other class all the interest. The former class is called the *principal-only* or *PO* class, and the latter the *interest-only* or *IO* class. This is depicted in Exhibit 20-4.

It may be less clear why stripped mortgage-backed securities are created. Suffice it to say that the risk/return characteristics of stripped MBSs make them attractive for purposes of hedging a portfolio of pass-throughs, creating synthetic securities, and hedging a portfolio of a mortgage-related product, mortgage servicing rights.

Exhibit 20-3

Creation of a Collateralized Mortgage Obligation

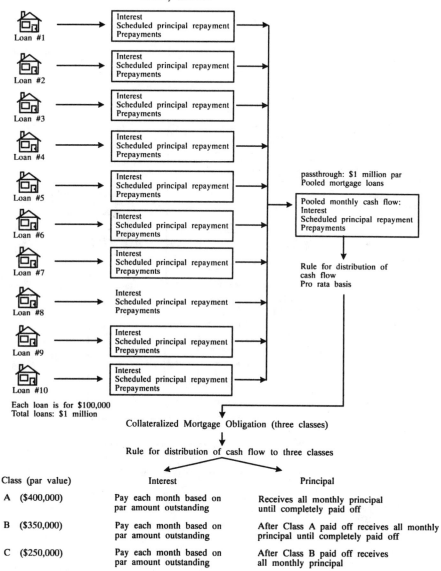

Monthly cash flow

Each loan is for $100,000
Total loans: $1 million

passthrough: $1 million par
Pooled mortgage loans

Pooled monthly cash flow:
Interest
Scheduled principal repayment
Prepayments

Rule for distribution of
cash flow
Pro rata basis

Collateralized Mortgage Obligation (three classes)

Rule for distribution of cash flow to three classes

Class (par value)	Interest	Principal
A ($400,000)	Pay each month based on par amount outstanding	Receives all monthly principal until completely paid off
B ($350,000)	Pay each month based on par amount outstanding	After Class A paid off receives all monthly principal until completely paid off
C ($250,000)	Pay each month based on par amount outstanding	After Class B paid off receives all monthly principal

Exhibit 20-4

Creation of a Stripped Mortgage-Backed Security

Monthly cash flow

Loan #1 → Interest / Scheduled principal repayment / Prepayments

Loan #2 → Interest / Scheduled principal repayment / Prepayments

Loan #3 → Interest / Scheduled principal repayment / Prepayments

Loan #4 → Interest / Scheduled principal repayment / Prepayments

Loan #5 → Interest / Scheduled principal repayment / Prepayments

Loan #6 → Interest / Scheduled principal repayment / Prepayments

Loan #7 → Interest / Scheduled principal repayment / Prepayments

Loan #8 → Interest / Scheduled principal repayment / Prepayments

Loan #9 → Interest / Scheduled principal repayment / Prepayments

Loan #10 → Interest / Scheduled principal repayment / Prepayments

Each loan is for $100,000
Total loans: $1 million

passthrough: $1 million par
Pooled mortgage loans

Pooled monthly cash flow:
Interest
Scheduled principal repayment
Prepayments

Rule for distribution of
cash flow
Pro rata basis

Stripped Mortgage-Backed Securities (two classes)

Rule for distribution of cash flow to two classes

Class (par value)	Interest	Principal
X ($0)	All	None
Y ($1,000,000)	None	All

Mortgage Servicing Rights

There is yet another asset whose value depends on the cash flow of a mortgage pool. Consider that the cash flow to investors in Exhibits 20-1 to 20-4 omits an important component: a fee paid to service a mortgage loan. If an investor in a mortgage-backed security were forced to maintain staff to service the underlying pool of mortgage loans, these securities would have much less appeal to institutional investors.

Fortunately, the servicing of mortgage loans can be separated from the investment in those loans. This is depicted in Exhibit 20-5, which is similar to Exhibit 20-2 but now shows that the cash flow is separated into two parts: (1) a servicing fee (which is a fixed percentage of the outstanding mortgage balance), and (2) the cash flow minus the servicing fee. The right to service the mortgage loans is an asset whose cash flow is uncertain because of the uncertainty about prepayments, as well as the future costs associated with servicing the mortgages.

Cash Flow for a Pass-Through

A pass-through is commonly used as collateral for a CMO and a stripped MBS. Given the estimated cash flow of the pass-through, the cash flow of CMO bond classes and PO and IO classes can then be estimated.

The cash flow of a pass-through depends on the cash flow of the underlying mortgages. It consists of monthly mortgage payments representing interest, the scheduled repayment of principal, and any prepayments. Payments are made to security holders each month. Neither the amount nor the timing, however, of the cash flow from the pool of mortgages is identical to that of the cash flow passed through to investors. The monthly cash flow for a pass-through is less than the monthly cash flow of the underlying mortgages by an amount equal to servicing and other fees. The other fees are those charged by the issuer or guarantor of the pass-through for guaranteeing the issue.[1] The coupon rate on a pass-through, called the *pass-through rate*, is less than the contract rate on the underlying pool of mortgage loans by an amount equal to the servicing and guaranteeing fees.

The timing of the cash flow is also different. The monthly mortgage payment is due from each mortgagor on the first day of each month. There is a delay in passing through the corresponding monthly cash flow to the security holders, which varies by the type of pass-through. Because of prepayments, the cash flow of a pass-through is not known with certainty.

---

[1] Actually, the servicer pays the guarantee fee to the issuer or guarantor.

Exhibit 20-5

Cash Flow When Servicing Is Considered

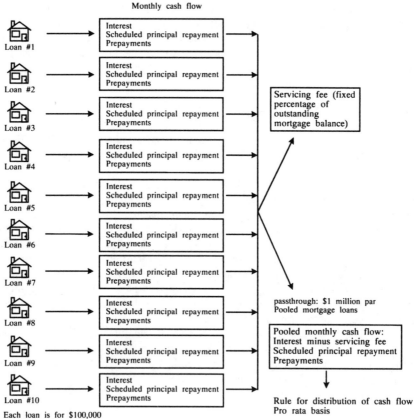

Monthly cash flow

Loan #1 → Interest / Scheduled principal repayment / Prepayments

Loan #2 → Interest / Scheduled principal repayment / Prepayments

Loan #3 → Interest / Scheduled principal repayment / Prepayments

Loan #4 → Interest / Scheduled principal repayment / Prepayments

Loan #5 → Interest / Scheduled principal repayment / Prepayments

Loan #6 → Interest / Scheduled principal repayment / Prepayments

Loan #7 → Interest / Scheduled principal repayment / Prepayments

Loan #8 → Interest / Scheduled principal repayment / Prepayments

Loan #9 → Interest / Scheduled principal repayment / Prepayments

Loan #10 → Interest / Scheduled principal repayment / Prepayments

Servicing fee (fixed percentage of outstanding mortgage balance)

passthrough: $1 million par
Pooled mortgage loans

Pooled monthly cash flow:
Interest minus servicing fee
Scheduled principal repayment
Prepayments

Rule for distribution of cash flow
Pro rata basis

Each loan is for $100,000
Total loans: $1 million

Prepayment Benchmark Conventions

Estimating the cash flow from a pass-through requires forecasting prepayments. Current practice is to use the Public Securities Association (PSA) prepayment benchmark. This benchmark is based on a series of constant prepayment rates.[2]

Constant Prepayment Rate: One way to project prepayments and cash flow is to assume that some fraction of the remaining principal in the pool is prepaid *each* month for the remaining term of the mortgages. The prepayment rate assumed for a pool, called the *constant prepayment rate (CPR)*, is based on the characteristics of the pool (including its historical prepayment experience) and the current and expected economic environment.

The CPR is an annual prepayment rate. To estimate monthly prepayments, the CPR must be converted into a monthly prepayment rate, commonly referred to as the *single monthly mortality rate* (SMM). The following formula can be used to determine the SMM for a given CPR:

$$SMM = 1 - (1 - CPR)^{1/12}$$

Illustration 20-1:   Suppose that the CPR used to project prepayments is 6%. The corresponding SMM is:

$$SMM = 1 - (1 - .06)^{1/12}$$

$$= 1 - (.94)^{.083333} = .005143$$

An SMM of $w\%$ means that approximately $w\%$ of the remaining mortgage balance at the beginning of the month after subtracting the scheduled principal payment will prepay that month. That is,

---

[2] In the early stages of the development of the pass-through market, cash flows were calculated assuming no prepayments for 12 years. In the twelfth year, all the mortgages in the pool would prepay. This naive approach was replaced by the "FHA prepayment experience" for 30-year mortgages derived from an FHA probability table on mortgage survivals. On the basis of FHA experience, the cash flow is projected for a mortgage pool, assuming that the prepayment rate is the same as the FHA experience ("100% FHA") or some multiple of FHA experience (faster than FHA experience or slower than FHA experience).

Despite its popularity at one time, prepayment projections based on FHA experience were not necessarily indicative of the prepayment rate for a particular pool. This is so because FHA experience represents an estimate of prepayments on all FHA-insured mortgages originated *over various interest rate periods.* Prepayment rates, of course, are tied to interest rate cycles, so an average prepayment rate over various cycles is not of much value for estimating prepayments. In addition, new FHA tables are published periodically, leading to confusion as to which FHA table prepayments should be based on. Consequently, as estimated prepayments using FHA experience may be misleading, the resulting cash flow is not meaningful for valuing pass-throughs.

$$\text{prepayment for month} = \text{SMM} \times$$
$$\text{(beginning mortgage balance} - \text{scheduled principal for month)}$$

Illustration 20-2:   Suppose that an investor owns a pass-through whose remaining mortgage balance at the beginning of some month is $50,525. Assuming that the SMM is .5143% and the scheduled principal payment is $67, the estimated prepayment for the month is:

$$.005143 \times (\$50,525 - \$67) = \$260$$

PSA Standard Prepayment Benchmark: The Public Securities Association (PSA) standard prepayment benchmark[3] is expressed as a monthly series of annual CPRs. The benchmark PSA model assumes that prepayment rates will be low for newly originated mortgages, and then will speed up as the mortgages become seasoned.

More specifically, the PSA standard benchmark assumes the following prepayment rates for 30-year mortgages:

(1) a CPR of .2% for the first month, increased by .2% per month for the next 30 months, when it reaches 6% per year, and

(2) a 6% CPR for the remaining years.

This benchmark is referred to as "100% PSA" and can be expressed as follows:

$$\text{if } t \leq 30 \text{ then CPR} = \frac{6\% \, t}{30}$$

$$\text{if } t > 30 \text{ then CPR} = 6\%$$

where t is the number of months since the mortgage originated. Exhibit 20-6 illustrates this benchmark.

Slower or faster speeds than the benchmark are then referred to as some percentage of PSA. For example, 50% PSA means one-half the CPR of the PSA prepayment rate; 150% PSA means one-and-a-half the CPR of the PSA prepayment rate. This is illustrated in Exhibit 20-7. The CPR is converted to an SMM using the formula presented earlier.

Illustration 20-3:   The SMM for month 5, month 20, and months 31 through 360, assuming 100% PSA, are calculated as follows:

For month 5:

$$\text{CPR} = \frac{6\% \, (5)}{30} = 1\% = .01$$

---

3 This benchmark is commonly referred to as a prepayment model, suggesting that it can be used to estimate prepayments. In fact, this is an inappropriate characterization.

Exhibit 20-6

100% PSA

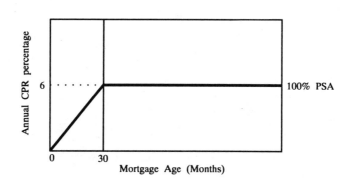

Exhibit 20-7

Multiples of PSA

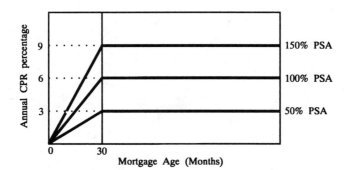

$$SMM = 1 - (1 - .01)^{1/12}$$
$$= 1 - (.99)^{.083333} = .000837$$

For month 20:

$$CPR = \frac{6\% (20)}{30} = 4\% = .04$$
$$SMM = 1 - (1 - .04)^{1/12}$$
$$= 1 - (.96)^{.083333} = .003396$$

For months 31–360:

$$CPR = 6\%$$
$$SMM = 1 - (1 - .06)^{1/12}$$
$$= 1 - (.94)^{.083333} = .005143$$

Illustration 20-4: The SMM for month 5, month 20, and months 31 through 360, assuming 150% PSA, are computed as follows:

For month 5:

$$CPR = \frac{6\% (5)}{30} = 1\% = .01$$
$$150\% \ PSA = 1.5 \ (.01) = .015$$
$$SMM = 1 - (1 - .015)^{1/12}$$
$$= 1 - (.985)^{.083333} = .001259$$

For month 20:

$$CPR = \frac{6\%(20)}{30} = 4\% = .04$$
$$150\% \ PSA = 1.5 \ (.04) = .06$$
$$SMM = 1 - (1 - .06)^{1/12}$$
$$= 1 - (.94)^{.083333} = .005143$$

For months 31–360:

$$CPR = 6\% = .06$$
$$150\% \ PSA = 1.5 \ (.06) = .09$$
$$SMM = 1 - (1 - .09)^{1/12}$$
$$= 1 - (.91)^{.083333} = .007828$$

Notice that the SMM assuming 150% PSA is not just 1.5 times the SMM assuming 100% PSA. It is the CPR that is a multiple of the CPR assuming 100% PSA.

Illustration 20.5: The SMM for month 5, month 20, and months 31 through 360, assuming 50% PSA, are as follows:

For month 5:

$$CPR = \frac{6\% \, (5)}{30} = 1\% = .01$$
$$50\% \text{ PSA} = .5 \, (.01) = .005$$
$$SMM = 1 - (1 - .005)^{1/12}$$
$$= 1 - (.995)^{.083333}$$
$$= .000418.$$

For month 20:

$$CPR = \frac{6\% \, (20)}{30} = 4\% = .04$$
$$50\% \text{ PSA} = .5 \, (.04) = .02$$
$$SMM = 1 - (1 - .02)^{1/12}$$
$$= 1 - (.98)^{.083333}$$
$$= .001682.$$

For months 31–360:

$$CPR = 6\% = .06$$
$$50\% \text{ PSA} = .5 \, (.06) = .03$$
$$SMM = 1 - (1 - .03)^{1/12}$$
$$= 1 - (.97)^{.083333}$$
$$= .002535.$$

Once again, notice that the SMM assuming 50% PSA is not just half the SMM assuming 100% PSA. It is the CPR that is a multiple of the CPR assuming 100% PSA.

Constructing the Projected Cash Flow

We can construct a cash flow schedule for a mortgage pass-through security on the basis of some assumed prepayment rate (or rates), using several formulas. First, the formula to obtain the projected monthly mortgage payment for any month is

$$\overline{MP}_t = \overline{MB}_{t-1} \left[\frac{i(1 + i)^{n-t+1}}{(1 + i)^{n-t+1} - 1} \right],$$

where
   $\overline{MP}_t$ = Projected monthly mortgage payment for month t;
   $\overline{MB}_{t-1}$ = Projected mortgage balance at the end of month t given prepayments have occurred in the past (which is the projected mortgage balance at the beginning of month t);
   i = Simple monthly interest rate (annual interest rate/12);
   n = Original number of months of mortgage.

Second, to compute the portion of the projected monthly mortgage payment that is interest, the formula is:

$$\overline{I}_t = \overline{MB}_{t-1}\, i\, ,$$

where
$\overline{I}_t$ = Projected monthly interest for month t.

This formula states that the projected monthly interest is found by multiplying the mortgage balance at the end of the previous month by the monthly interest rate. The projected monthly interest rate can be divided into two parts: (1) the projected net monthly interest rate after the servicing fee, and (2) the servicing fee. The formulas are as follows:

$$\overline{NI}_t = \overline{MB}_{t-1}\, (i - s)\, ,$$

$$\overline{S}_t = \overline{MB}_{t-1}\, s\ \ ,$$

where
$\overline{NI}_t$ = Projected interest net of servicing fee for month t;
s = Servicing fee rate;
$\overline{S}_t$ = Projected servicing fee for month t.

The projected monthly scheduled principal payment is found by subtracting from the projected monthly mortgage payment the projected monthly interest. In terms of our notation,

$$\overline{SP}_t = \overline{MP}_t - \overline{I}_t\, ,$$

where
$\overline{SP}_t$ = Projected monthly scheduled principal payment for month t.

As explained earlier, the projected monthly principal prepayment is found by multiplying the SMM by the difference between the outstanding balance at the beginning of the month (the ending balance in the previous month) and the projected scheduled principal payment for the month. That is,

$$\overline{PR}_t = SMM_t\, (\overline{MB}_{t-1} - \overline{SP}_t)\, ,$$

where
$\overline{PR}_t$ = Projected monthly principal prepayment for month t
SMM_t = Assumed single monthly mortality rate for month t.

The cash flow to the investor is then the sum of (1) the projected monthly interest net of the servicing fee, (2) the projected monthly scheduled principal payment, and (3) the projected monthly principal prepayment. That is,

$$\overline{CF}_t = \overline{NI}_t + \overline{SP}_t + \overline{PR}_t,$$

where
$\overline{CF}_t$ = Projected cash flow for month t.

Alternatively, this can be expressed as

$$\overline{CF}_t = \overline{I}_t + \overline{SP}_t + \overline{PR}_t - \overline{S}_t\, .$$

The next three illustrations demonstrate application of these formulas.

Illustration 20.6. Suppose that an investor owns a pass-through with an original mortgage balance of $100 million, mortgage rate of 9.5%, a .5% servicing fee, and 360 months to maturity. The pass-through rate is therefore 9%. Suppose that the PSA prepayment benchmark is used to project prepayments for the pass-through. In particular, assume that the investor believes that the mortgages will prepay at 100% PSA.

Using our notation:

MB_0 = $100,000,000;

n = 360;

i = .0079167 (.095/12);

s = .0004167 (.005/12);

Exhibit 20-8 shows the cash flow for the pass-through for selected months. The SMMs shown in the third column agree with those computed earlier.

Let's look at the components of the cash flow for the first month. The initial monthly mortgage payment for this pass-through, shown in Column (5), is $841,000. The monthly interest is the monthly interest rate of .0079167 (.095 divided by 12) multiplied by the original mortgage balance, $100 million. The regularly scheduled principal is the difference between the monthly mortgage payment for the month, $841,000 in the first month, and the monthly interest of $792,000. The difference, $49,000, is shown in Column (6).

The prepayment for the month is found by multiplying the SMM for the month by the difference between the mortgage balance at the beginning of the month and the regularly scheduled principal repayment. In the first month, since the SMM is .000166, and the difference between the beginning mortgage balance of $1,000,000 and the projected scheduled principal payment of $49,000 is $9,951,000, the projected prepayment for the month is $17,000, shown in Column (8).

The amount of the monthly servicing fee is found by multiplying the mortgage balance at the beginning of the month by the servicing fee. For the first month, in our illustration it is .0004166 (.005 divided by 12) multiplied by $100 million. The product is $42,000, which is shown in Column (9).

The monthly cash flow is then the projected monthly mortgage payment ($841,000) plus the projected monthly prepayment ($17,000) minus the amount of the servicing fee ($42,000). Alternatively, the monthly cash flow is the monthly interest net of servicing ($792,000 minus $42,000) plus the projected principal repayment, which consists of the projected monthly regularly scheduled principal repayment ($49,000) and the monthly projected prepayment ($17,000). The projected monthly cash flow of $816,000 is shown in Column (10).

Finally, the last column shows the end of month mortgage balance, found by subtracting the projected principal repayment from the mortgage balance at the beginning of the month. In the first month, the ending mortgage balance is $100,000,000 minus $66,000 ($49,000 + $17,000), or $99,934,000. This amount is then the beginning mortgage balance for month 2. From this amount, the cash flow can be calculated for the second month.

Exhibit 20-8

Projected Cash Flow Assuming 100% PSA*

Original balance $100 million
Mortgage rate 9.5%
Servicing fee 0.5%
Term 360 months

(1) t	(2) $\overline{MB}_{t-1}$	(3) SMM_t	(4) $\bar{b}_{t-1}$	(5) $\overline{MP}_t$	(6) $\overline{SP}_t$	(7) $\bar{I}_t$	(8) $\overline{PR}_t$	(9) $\bar{S}_t$	(10) $\overline{CF}_t$	(11) $\overline{MB}_t$
1	100,000	0.000166	1.00000	841	49	792	17	42	816	99,934
2	99,934	0.000333	0.99983	841	50	791	33	42	832	99,851
3	99,851	0.000501	0.99950	840	50	790	50	42	849	99,751
4	99,751	0.000669	0.99900	840	50	790	67	42	865	99,634
5	99,634	0.000837	0.99833	839	51	789	83	42	881	99,500
6	99,500	0.001005	0.99749	839	51	788	100	41	897	99,349
7	99,349	0.001174	0.99649	838	51	787	117	41	913	99,181
8	99,181	0.001343	0.99532	837	52	785	133	41	929	98,996
9	98,996	0.001512	0.99398	836	52	784	150	41	944	98,795
10	98,795	0.001682	0.99248	835	52	782	166	41	959	98,576
11	98,576	0.001852	0.99081	833	53	780	182	41	975	98,341
12	98,341	0.002022	0.98898	832	53	779	199	41	989	98,089
13	98,089	0.002192	0.98698	830	53	777	215	41	1,004	97,821
14	97,821	0.002363	0.98481	828	54	774	231	41	1,018	97,536
15	97,536	0.002535	0.98248	826	54	772	247	41	1,033	97,235

Exhibit 20-8 continued.

(1) t	(2) $\overline{MB}_{t-1}$	(3) SMM_t	(4) $\overline{b}_{t-1}$	(5) $\overline{MP}_t$	(6) $\overline{SP}_t$	(7) $\overline{I}_t$	(8) $\overline{PR}_t$	(9) $\overline{S}_t$	(10) $\overline{CF}_t$	(11) $\overline{MB}_t$
16	97,235	0.002706	0.97999	824	54	770	263	41	1,047	96,917
17	96,917	0.002878	0.97734	822	55	767	279	40	1,060	96,584
18	96,584	0.003050	0.97453	819	55	765	294	40	1,074	96,235
19	96,235	0.003223	0.97155	817	55	762	310	40	1,087	95,870
20	95,870	0.003396	0.96842	814	55	759	325	40	1,100	95,489
21	95,489	0.003569	0.96513	812	56	756	341	40	1,113	95,093
.	.	.	.	.	.	.	.	.	.	.
31	90,860	0.005143	0.92392	777	58	719	467	38	1,206	90,336
32	90,336	0.005143	0.91917	773	58	715	464	38	1,200	89,814
33	89,814	0.005143	0.91444	769	58	711	462	37	1,193	89,294
34	89,294	0.005143	0.90974	765	58	707	459	37	1,187	88,777
35	88,777	0.005143	0.90506	761	58	703	456	37	1,180	88,263
36	88,263	0.005143	0.90041	757	58	699	454	37	1,174	87,751
.	.	.	.	.	.	.	.	.	.	.
98	60,735	0.005143	0.65403	550	69	481	312	25	837	60,354
99	60,354	0.005143	0.65067	547	69	478	310	25	832	59,975
100	59,975	0.005143	0.64732	544	70	475	308	25	827	59,597
.	.	.	.	.	.	.	.	.	.	.
209	27,372	0.005143	0.36901	310	94	217	140	11	439	27,138
210	27,138	0.005143	0.36711	309	94	215	139	11	436	26,905

Exhibit 20-8 continued.

(1) t	(2) $\overline{MB}_{t-1}$	(3) SMM_t	(4) $\overline{b}_{t-1}$	(5) $\overline{MP}_t$	(6) $\overline{SP}_t$	(7) $\overline{I}_t$	(8) $\overline{PR}_t$	(9) $\overline{S}_t$	(10) $\overline{CF}_t$	(11) $\overline{MB}_t$
211	26,905	0.005143	0.36522	307	94	213	138	11	434	26,673
. . .	. . .	. . .	. . .	. . .	. . .	. . .	. . .	. . .	. . .	. . .
357	567	0.005143	0.17203	145	140	4	1	0	147	425
358	425	0.005143	0.17115	144	141	3	1	0	145	283
359	283	0.005143	0.17027	143	141	2	1	0	144	141
360	141	0.005143	0.16939	142	141	1	0	0	142	0

Key:

$\overline{MB}_{t-1}$ = Projected mortgage balance at the end of month $t-1$

SMM_t = Single monthly mortality

$\overline{b}_{t-1}$ = $(1 - SMM_{t-1})(1 - SMM_{t-2}) \ldots (1 - SMM_2)(1 - SMM_1)$

$\overline{MP}_t$ = Projected monthly mortgage payment for month t

$\overline{SP}_t$ = Projected monthly scheduled principal payment for month t

$\overline{I}_t$ = Projected monthly interest for month t

$\overline{PR}_t$ = Projected monthly principal prepayment for month t

$\overline{S}_t$ = Projected servicing fee for month t

$\overline{CF}_t$ = Projected cash flow for month t

Notice that the monthly mortgage payment declines over time. This is because mortgages in the pool are assumed to be prepaying.

Illustration 20-7. Now suppose that instead of 100% PSA, 150% PSA is assumed. Exhibit 20-9 shows the cash flow for the mortgage pass-through security for selected months. The SMMs shown in Column (3) are the same as those computed in Illustration 20-6.

Illustration 20-8. Suppose the prepayment rate is assumed to be 50% PSA. For selected months, Exhibit 20-10 shows the cash flow.

In the formulas we develop above, the process begins with determination of the mortgage balance at the beginning of the month, given prepayments that have occurred in the past. While this balance can be determined by using the procedure shown in Exhibits 20-8 to 20-10, there are formulas that can be used to compute the projected cash flow without knowing the mortgage balance at the beginning of the month. First, it is necessary to introduce the following concept.[4]

Let
$$\bar{b}_t = (1 - SMM_t)(1 - SMM_{t-1}) \ldots (1 - SMM_2)(1 - SMM_1),$$

where

$\bar{b}_t$ = Projected mortgage balance in month t per \$1 of the original mortgage, given prepayments through month t.

Then, the projected monthly mortgage payment in month t is

$$\overline{MP}_t = \bar{b}_{t-1}MP,$$

where

MP = Monthly mortgage payment on the original principal, assuming no prepayments.

The projected scheduled principal payment is found as follows:

$$\overline{SP}_t = \bar{b}_{t-1}P_t,$$

where

P_t = Scheduled principal payment on the original balance, assuming no prepayments.

Once MP and P_t are computed, the other values necessary to compute the projected cash flow can be easily determined.

---

[4] See the appendix to Lakhbir S. Hayre and Cyrus Mohebbi, "Mortgage Pass-Through Securities," in Frank J. Fabozzi (ed.) *Advances and Innovations in the Bond and Mortgage Markets* (Chicago: Probus Publishing, 1989), pp. 259–304.

Exhibit 20–9

Projected Cash Flow Assuming 150% PSA*

Original balance $100 million
Mortgage rate 9.5%
Servicing fee 0.5%
Term 360 months

(1) t	(2) $\overline{MB}_{t-1}$	(3) SMM_t	(4) $\overline{b}_{t-1}$	(5) $\overline{MP}_t$	(6) $\overline{SP}_t$	(7) $\overline{I}_t$	(8) $\overline{PR}_t$	(9) $\overline{S}_t$	(10) $\overline{CF}_t$	(11) $\overline{MB}_t$
1	100,000	0.000250	1.00000	841	49	792	25	42	824	99,926
2	99,926	0.000501	0.99975	841	50	791	50	42	849	99,826
3	99,826	0.000753	0.99925	840	50	790	75	42	874	99,701
4	99,701	0.001005	0.99850	840	50	789	100	42	898	99,551
5	99,551	0.001258	0.99749	839	51	788	125	41	923	99,375
6	99,375	0.001512	0.99624	838	51	787	150	41	947	99,174
7	99,174	0.001767	0.99473	836	51	785	175	41	970	98,947
8	98,947	0.002022	0.99297	835	52	783	200	41	994	98,695
9	98,695	0.002278	0.99096	833	52	781	225	41	1,017	98,419
10	98,419	0.002535	0.98871	831	52	799	249	41	1,040	98,117
11	98,117	0.002792	0.98620	829	52	777	274	41	1,062	97,791
12	97,791	0.003050	0.98345	827	53	774	298	41	1,084	97,440
13	97,440	0.003309	0.98045	824	53	771	322	41	1,106	97,065

*See the key in Exhibit 20-8

Exhibit 20-9 continued.

(1) t	(2) $\overline{MB}_{t-1}$	(3) SMM_t	(4) $\overline{b}_{t-1}$	(5) $\overline{MP}_t$	(6) $\overline{SP}_t$	(7) $\overline{I}_t$	(8) $\overline{PR}_t$	(9) $\overline{S}_t$	(10) $\overline{CF}_t$	(11) $\overline{MB}_t$
14	97,065	0.003569	0.97720	822	53	768	346	40	1,127	96,665
15	96,665	0.003829	0.97371	819	53	765	370	40	1,148	96,242
16	96,242	0.004090	0.96998	816	54	762	393	40	1,169	95,794
17	95,794	0.004352	0.96602	812	54	758	417	40	1,189	95,324
18	95,324	0.004615	0.96181	809	54	755	440	40	1,209	94,830
19	94,830	0.004878	0.95737	805	54	751	462	40	1,228	94,313
20	94,313	0.005143	0.95270	801	54	747	485	39	1,247	93,774
21	93,774	0.005407	0.94780	797	55	742	507	39	1,266	93,213
. . .										. . .
31	87,224	0.007828	0.88695	746	55	691	682	36	1,392	86,487
32	86,487	0.007828	0.88001	740	55	685	677	36	1,381	85,755
33	85,755	0.007828	0.87312	734	55	679	671	36	1,369	85,028
34	85,028	0.007828	0.86628	728	55	673	665	35	1,358	84,308
35	84,308	0.007828	0.85950	723	55	667	660	35	1,347	83,593
36	83,593	0.007828	0.85277	717	55	662	654	35	1,335	82,884
. . .										. . .
98	48,647	0.007828	0.52386	400	55	385	380	20	801	48,211
99	48,211	0.007828	0.51976	437	55	382	377	20	794	47,779
100	47,779	0.007828	0.51569	434	55	378	374	20	787	47,350
. . .										. . .

Exhibit 20-9 continued.

(1) t	(2) $\overline{MB}_{t-1}$	(3) SMM_t	(4) $\overline{b}_{t-1}$	(5) $\overline{MP}_t$	(6) $\overline{SP}_t$	(7) $\overline{I}_t$	(8) $\overline{PR}_t$	(9) $\overline{S}_t$	(10) $\overline{CF}_t$	(11) $\overline{MB}_t$
209	16,241	0.007828	0.21895	184	56	129	127	7	304	16,059
210	16,059	0.007828	0.21724	183	56	127	125	7	301	15,878
211	15,878	0.007828	0.21554	181	56	126	124	7	299	15,699
⋮										
357	226	0.007828	0.06842	58	56	1	1	0	58	169
358	169	0.007828	0.06789	57	56	1	1	0	58	112
359	112	0.007828	0.06735	57	56	1	0	0	57	56
360	56	0.007828	0.06683	56	56	0	0	0	56	0

Exhibit 20-10

Projected Cash Flow Assuming 50% PSA*

Original balance $100 million
Mortgage rate 9.5%
Servicing fee 0.5%
Term 360 months

(1)	(2)	(3)	(4)	(5)	(6)	(7)	(8)	(9)	(10)	(11)
t	$\overline{MB}_{t-1}$	SMM_t	$\overline{b}_{t-1}$	$\overline{MP}_t$	$\overline{SP}_t$	$\overline{I}_t$	$\overline{PR}_t$	$\overline{S}_t$	$\overline{CF}_t$	$\overline{MB}_t$
1	100,000	0.000083	1.00000	841	49	792	8	42	808	99,942
2	99,942	0.000166	0.99992	841	50	791	17	42	816	99,876
3	99,876	0.000250	0.99975	841	50	791	25	42	824	99,801
4	99,801	0.000333	0.99950	840	50	790	33	42	832	99,718
5	99,718	0.000417	0.99917	840	51	789	42	42	840	99,625
6	99,625	0.000501	0.99875	840	51	789	50	42	848	99,524
7	99,524	0.000585	0.99825	839	51	788	58	41	856	99,415
8	99,415	0.000669	0.99766	839	52	787	66	41	864	99,296
9	99,296	0.000753	0.99700	838	52	786	75	41	872	99,169
10	99,169	0.000837	0.99625	838	53	785	83	41	879	99,034
11	99,034	0.000921	0.99541	837	53	784	91	41	887	98,890
12	98,890	0.001005	0.99449	836	53	783	99	41	894	98,737
13	98,737	0.001089	0.99349	835	54	782	108	41	902	98,576

*See the key in Exhibit 20-8

Exhibit 20-10 continued.

(1) t	(2) $\overline{MB}_{t-1}$	(3) SMM_t	(4) $\overline{b}_{t-1}$	(5) $\overline{MP}_t$	(6) $\overline{SP}_t$	(7) $\overline{I}_t$	(8) $\overline{PR}_t$	(9) $\overline{S}_t$	(10) $\overline{CF}_t$	(11) $\overline{MB}_t$
14	98,576	0.001174	0.99241	834	54	780	116	41	909	98,406
15	98,406	0.001258	0.99125	833	54	779	124	41	916	98,227
16	98,227	0.001343	0.99000	832	55	778	132	41	923	98,041
17	98,041	0.001427	0.98867	831	55	776	140	41	930	97,846
18	97,846	0.001512	0.98726	830	56	775	148	41	937	97,642
19	97,642	0.001597	0.98576	829	56	773	156	41	944	97,431
20	97,431	0.001682	0.98419	828	56	771	164	41	951	97,211
21	97,211	0.001767	0.98253	826	57	770	172	41	957	96,982
. . .										
31	94,566	0.002535	0.96161	809	60	749	240	39	1,009	94,267
32	94,267	0.002535	0.95917	807	60	746	239	39	1,006	93,968
33	93,968	0.002535	0.95674	804	61	744	238	39	1,003	93,669
34	93,669	0.002535	0.95431	802	61	742	237	39	1,001	93,371
35	93,371	0.002535	0.95189	800	61	739	237	39	998	93,073
36	93,073	0.002535	0.94948	798	62	737	236	39	995	92,776
. . .										
98	75,332	0.002535	0.81122	682	86	596	191	31	841	75,056
99	75,056	0.002535	0.80917	680	86	594	190	31	839	74,779
100	74,779	0.002535	0.80711	679	87	592	189	31	837	74,503

Exhibit 20-10 continued.

(1) t	(2) $\overline{MB}_{t-1}$	(3) SMM_t	(4) $\overline{b}_{t-1}$	(5) $\overline{MP}_t$	(6) $\overline{SP}_t$	(7) $\overline{I}_t$	(8) $\overline{PR}_t$	(9) $\overline{S}_t$	(10) $\overline{CF}_t$	(11) $\overline{MB}_t$
209	45,399	0.002535	0.61204	515	155	359	115	19	610	45,129
210	45,129	0.002535	0.61049	513	156	357	114	19	609	44,859
211	44,859	0.002535	0.60894	512	157	355	113	19	607	44,589
. . . .										
357	1,386	0.002535	0.42037	353	342	11	3	1	356	1,041
358	1,041	0.002535	0.41930	353	344	8	2	0	354	695
359	695	0.002535	0.41824	352	346	6	1	0	352	348
360	348	0.002535	0.41718	351	348	3	0	0	351	0

(The formulas for obtaining MP and P_t were given in the previous chapter.)

Illustration 20-9. Consider the pass-through we have been using in all previous illustrations. Assuming a prepayment speed of 100% PSA, the projected monthly mortgage payment for month 8 is

$$\overline{MP}_8 = \overline{b}_7 MP.$$

The monthly mortgage payment assuming no principal prepayments is $840,850. The SMM for each month is shown in Column (3) of Exhibit 20-8. Then

$$\overline{b}_8 = (1 - .000166)(1 - .000333)(1 - .000501)(1 - .000669)$$
$$(1 - .000837)(1 - .001005)(1 - .001174) = .99532$$

So,

$$\overline{MP}_8 = (.99532)\ \$840,850 = \$836,915$$

The projected scheduled principal payment is

$$\overline{SP}_8 = \overline{b}_7 P_8 .$$

The scheduled principal payment in month 8 assuming no prepayments is $52,000. The projected scheduled principal payment is then

$$\overline{SP}_8 = (.99532)\ \$52,000 = \$51,757$$

Notice that both of the values computed here agree with the values for month 8 shown in Exhibit 20-8 ($837 for $\overline{MP}_8$ and $52 for $\overline{SP}_8$).

WACs and WAMs

Our illustrations have assumed that all the mortgage loans in the pool have the same mortgage rate (9.5%), the same servicing fee (.5%), and the same number of months remaining to maturity (360). In practice, mortgage loans within a pool can have different mortgage rates, servicing fees, and remaining months to maturity.

To construct the cash flow for a pass-through, the measures we use for the mortgage rate and the remaining months to maturity are the weighted average coupon rate (WAC) and the weighted average maturity (WAM), respectively. The WAC is the weighted average of all the mortgage rates in the pool, where the weight used for each mortgage loan is the amount of the balance outstanding. The WAM is the weighted average of the number of months to maturity of all the mortgage loans in the pool, where the weight for each mortgage loan is the amount of the balance outstanding.

Beware of Prepayment Conventions

We must emphasize that the PSA prepayment benchmark is simply a market convention. It is a product of a study by the PSA based on FHA prepayment data. Data that the PSA committee examined seemed to suggest that mortgages became "seasoned" (i.e., prepayment rates tended to level off) after 30 months, and the CPR tended to be 6%. How did the PSA come up with the CPRs used for months 1 through 29? Not on the basis of empirical evidence. Instead, the committee selected a linear increase from month 1 to month 30 such that at month 30 the CPR is 6%. Moreover, the same benchmark or seasoning process is used in quoting pass-throughs regardless of the collateral — 30- and 15-year loans, fixed- and adjustable-rate loans, and conventional and VA/FHA-insured loans. Consequently, care must be taken in using any measure that is based on the PSA prepayment benchmark.

Vector Analysis

One approach market participants take to overcome the limitations of the PSA benchmark is to assume that the PSA speed can change over time. This technique is referred to as *vector analysis*. A "vector" is simply a set of numbers. In the case of prepayments, it is a vector of prepayment speeds.

In Illustrations 20-6 to 20-8, this would be done by replacing the SMMs in the relevant exhibits with the appropriate values based on the vector of PSA prepayment speeds. Specifically, consider Illustration 20-6, where it is assumed that the prepayment speed is 100% PSA for the entire life of the pass-through. Suppose instead that the following vector of prepayment speeds is assumed:

> months   1–43 100% PSA
> months   44–204 150% PSA
> months 205–360 50% PSA

To construct the cash flow given this vector of prepayment speeds, the SMMs would be as follows. For months 1–43, the SMM would be the same as in Exhibit 20-8. The SMM for months 44–204 would be the SMM given in Exhibit 20-9 for the same months. Finally, for months 205–360, the SMM would be the same as for the corresponding months in Exhibit 20-10.

Obtaining Prepayment Estimates

The major dealers in pass-throughs and independent vendors have developed statistical models that estimate prepayment rates. These models take into account the factors that are expected to influence prepayment rates. The prepayment rates of dealer firms are reported on financial information services.

In actuality, the dealer firms do not project a PSA speed directly. Instead, a firm projects monthly prepayment rates from its statistical model, and then converts them to a PSA speed. This is often done as follows. Given the price of a pass-through and the monthly prepayment rates (and hence monthly cash flow), the equivalent PSA is the rate that will produce the same cash flow yield. (We explain how to calculate the cash flow yield in the next chapter.)

Cash Flow for a CMO, a Stripped MBS, and Mortgage Servicing Rights

Given the cash flow for a pass-through, we can determine the cash flow for any derivative of a pass-through such as a CMO bond class and a stripped MBS.

Illustration 20-10. Consider a stripped MBS whose collateral is the pass-through in Illustrations 20-6 through 20-8. Then for a principal-only security with this collateral, the cash flow assuming 100% PSA can be determined from Exhibit 20-8. The cash flow is only the principal. Since the principal is equal to the sum of the regularly scheduled principal repayment and prepayments, the cash flow for this PO security is the sum of Columns (6) and (8) in the exhibit. The cash flow for the corresponding interest-only security assuming the same prepayment speed of 100% PSA is the net interest. In Exhibit 20-8, this is the difference between the gross interest reported in Column (7) and the servicing fee in Column (9).

Illustration 20-11. Suppose that the same pass-through is used as collateral for a CMO with two bond classes, A and B. Suppose further that the coupon rate for both bond classes is 9.0% (the same as the pass-through in our illustration), and the par value for Class A is $54,333,000, for Class B $45,667,000. The rules for distributing the cash flow to the two bond classes are as follows.

For the principal:

> Pay all principal to Class A until it is fully paid off, then
> pay Class B all the principal

For the interest:

> Pay interest to both classes based on the balance outstanding
> at the beginning of the month.

According to these disbursement rules, and assuming a prepayment speed of 150% PSA, the cash flow for each bond class can be determined from Exhibit 20-9. At the end of month 104 (not shown in the exhibit), the remaining mortgage balance is $45,667,000. This means that $54,333,000 of principal has been repaid. Since this is the amount of the par value assumed for Class A, the principal payments to this bond class will be paid off by month 104. The principal payments for Class A are therefore those shown in months 1 through 104 in Exhibit 20-9. The principal payment in each month is the sum of Columns (6) and (8).

The interest payment is determined by first calculating the balance for Class A at the beginning of the month and then multiplying by the pass-through rate, .75% (9%/12). For example, at the beginning of month 1, the balance for Class A is $54,333,000. The principal payment to Class A in month 1 is $74,000 ($49,000 + $25,000). The monthly interest for Class A is then $407,498 ($54,333,000 times .75%). The balance at the beginning of month 2 is then $54,259,000 ($54,333,000 − $74,000). In month 2, the interest for Class A is then $406,943 ($54,259,000 times .75). The cash flow for Class A is then the principal payments and monthly interest for months 1 through 104.

For Class B, the principal payments are as shown in Exhibit 20-9 for months 105 through 360. For months 1 through 104, the monthly interest is simply the difference between the interest to Class A and the net interest shown in the exhibit. For months 105 through 360, the interest is the net interest in the exhibit.

Illustration 20-12. For the same pass-through as in the two previous illustrations, the cash flow for a servicer who purchased the right to service all the mortgages in the pool would depend on the prepayment speed assumed. Assuming a prepayment speed of 150% PSA, the cash flow that would be expected is shown in Column (9) of Exhibit 20-9.

Summary

In this chapter we showed how to construct the projected cash flow for any mortgage-backed security (pass-through, CMO, and stripped MBS), as well as a mortgage-related product such as a portfolio of servicing rights. The cash flow depends on the cash flow of the underlying pool of mortgage loans, which in turn depends on prepayments. The market convention to determine prepayment speed is the PSA benchmark, which is simply a series of constant prepayment rates. Once prepayments are determined for a pass-through, the cash flow for any other MBS can be determined according to the rules for allocating principal and interest payments.

Exhibit 20-11 summarizes the formulas presented in this chapter.

Exhibit 20-11

Summary of Formulas

To convert from CPR to SMM:

$$SMM = 1 - (1 - CPR)^{1/12}.$$

Benchmark PSA prepayment model:

$$\text{if } t < 30 \text{ then CPR} = \frac{6\% \, t}{30} \, ,$$
$$\text{if } t > 30 \text{ then CPR} = 6\%,$$

where t is the number of months since the mortgage originated.

Constructing the Cash Flow:

Let

$\overline{MP}_t$ = Projected monthly mortgage payment for month t;

$\overline{MB}_{t-1}$ = Projected mortgage balance at the end of month $t - 1$, given prepayments that have occurred in the past (which is the projected mortgage balance at the beginning of month t);

i = Simple monthly interest rate (annual interest rate/12);

n = Original number of months of mortgage;

$\overline{I}_t$ = Projected monthly interest for month t;

$\overline{NI}_t$ = Projected interest, net of servicing fee, for month t;

s = Servicing fee rate;

$\overline{S}_t$ = Projected servicing fee for month t;

$\overline{SP}_t$ = Projected monthly scheduled principal payment for month t;

$\overline{PR}_t$ = Projected monthly principal prepayment for month t;

$\overline{CF}_t$ = Projected cash flow for month t.

$$\overline{MP}_t = \overline{MB}_{t-1} \left[\frac{i(1 + i)^{n - t + 1}}{(1 + i)^{n - t + 1} - 1} \right],$$

then

$$\overline{I}_t = \overline{MB}_{t-1}\, i;$$
$$\overline{NI}_t = \overline{MB}_{t-1}\,(i - s)\;;$$
$$\overline{S}_t = \overline{MB}_{t-1}\, s\;;$$
$$\overline{SP}_t = \overline{MB}_t - \overline{I}_t\;;$$
$$\overline{PR}_t = SMM_t\,(\overline{MB}_{t-1} - \overline{SP}_t)\;;$$
$$\overline{CF}_t = \overline{NI}_t + \overline{SP}_t + \overline{PR}_t\;;$$
$$\text{or } \overline{CF}_t = \overline{I}_t + \overline{SP}_t + \overline{PR}_t - \overline{S}_t\;.$$

Alternatively, let

$\overline{b}_t$ = The projected mortgage balance in month t per \$1 of the original mortgage, given prepayments through month t;

SMM_t = Assumed single monthly mortality rate for month t;

MP = Monthly mortgage payment on the original principal, assuming no prepayments;

P_t = Scheduled principal payment on the original balance, assuming no prepayments.

Then,

$$\overline{b}_t = (1 - SMM_t)(1 - SMM_{t-1})\ \ldots\ (1 - SMM_2)(1 - SMM_1);$$
$$\overline{MP}_t = \overline{b}_{t-1}\, MP;$$
$$\overline{SP}_t = \overline{b}_{t-1}\, P_t.$$

21

Techniques for Evaluating Mortgage-Backed Securities

Once the cash flow is determined for a mortgage-backed security (pass-throughs, collateralized mortgage obligations, and stripped mortgage-backed securities), the next step is to evaluate a bond with respect to its potential return and volatility characteristics. Two approaches are used: (1) static cash flow yield methodology, and (2) the option-adjusted spread methodology.

Static Cash Flow Yield Methodology

The static cash flow yield methodology is the simplest to use, but it offers little insight into the relative value of an MBS.

Cash Flow Yield

Recall from Chapter 4 that the yield is the interest rate that will make the present value of the expected cash flows equal to the price (plus accrued interest if any). A yield computed in this manner is called a *cash flow yield*.

The cash flow for an MBS may be monthly (as in the case of pass-throughs, most CMO bond classes, and stripped MBS) or quarterly or semiannually for some CMO bond classes. Thus, the cash flow yield as just described must be annualized. The convention is to compare the yield on an MBS with that of Treasury coupon securities and corporate bonds by calculating the bond equivalent yield of the MBS. Recall that the bond equivalent yield for a Treasury coupon security and a corporate bond is found by doubling the semiannual yield. It is not correct to do this for MBSs that pay more than semiannually. The reason is that since such an MBS pays more frequently than semiannually, the investor has the opportunity to generate greater interest by reinvesting the cash flows.

The market practice is to calculate a yield so as to make it comparable to the yield to maturity on a bond equivalent yield basis. The formula for annualizing the periodic cash flow yield on an MBS is as follows:

For a monthly-pay MBS:

$$\text{Bond equivalent yield} = 2\left[(1 + i_M)^6 - 1\right]$$

where i_M is the interest rate that will equate the present value of the projected monthly cash flows to the price of the MBS. The bond equivalent semiannual yield for a monthly-pay MBS is

$$(1 + i_M)^6 - 1$$

For a quarterly-pay MBS:

$$\text{Bond equivalent yield} = 2\left[(1 + i_Q)^2 - 1\right]$$

where i_Q is the interest rate that will equate the present value of the projected quarterly cash flows to the price of the MBS. The bond equivalent semiannual yield for a quarterly-pay MBS is

$$(1 + i_Q)^2 - 1$$

Illustration 21-1. Suppose that a pass-through with a mortgage rate of 9.5%, a servicing fee of 0.5%, 360 months remaining to maturity (new pass-through), and an original mortgage balance of $100,000 can be purchased for $94,521. To compute the cash flow yield, a prepayment assumption must be made. Assuming that the prepayment rate is 100% PSA, the cash flows would be as shown in Exhibit 20-8 of Chapter 20.

Assuming that the first monthly cash flow will occur 30 days from now, the interest rate that will make the present value of the cash flows, assuming 100% PSA, equal to the price of $94,521 is .8333% (.008333). The bond equivalent yield is then 10.21%, as shown below:

$$i_M = .008333$$

Bond equivalent yield $= 2[(1.008333)^6 - 1] = .1021 = 10.21\%$.

Illustration 21-2. Suppose that the pass-through in the previous illustration can be purchased for $105,985. Assuming a prepayment rate of 200% PSA, the interest rate that will make the present value of the cash flows equal to $105,985 is .006667 (.6667%). The bond equivalent yield is found as follows:

$$i_M = .006667$$

Bond equivalent yield $= 2[(1.006667)^6 - 1] = .0813 = 8.13\%$.

Drawbacks of the Cash Flow Yield Measure

As we note several times throughout this book, the yield to maturity has two shortcomings as a measure of a bond's potential return: (1) the coupon payments must be reinvested at a rate equal to the yield to maturity, and (2) the bond must be held to maturity. These shortcomings are equally applicable to the cash flow yield measure: (1) the projected cash flows are assumed to be reinvested at the cash flow yield, and (2) the mortgage-backed security is assumed to be held until the final payout based on some prepayment assumption.

The importance of reinvestment risk, the risk that the cash flows must be reinvested at a rate below the cash flow yield, is particularly important for most mortgage-backed securities because payments are monthly or quarterly. In addition, the cash flow yield is dependent on realization of the projected cash flows according to some prepayment rate. If the prepayment experience is different from the prepayment rate assumed, the cash flow yield will not be realized.

Spread to Treasuries

It should be clear that at the time of purchase it is not possible to determine an exact yield for a mortgage-backed security; the yield depends on the actual prepayment experience of the mortgages in the pool. Nevertheless, the convention in all fixed-income markets is to measure the yield on a non-Treasury security to that of a "comparable" Treasury security.

In comparing the yield of a mortgage-backed security to a comparable Treasury, it is inappropriate to use the stated maturity of the MBS because of the potential for prepayments. Instead, market participants have used two measures: Macaulay duration and average life.

Macaulay Duration: Calculating Macaulay duration requires a projection of the cash flows, which, in turn, requires a prepayment rate assumption. We can then use the projected cash flows, the price of the MBS, and the periodic interest rate (computed from the yield on a bond equivalent basis) to compute Macaulay duration, as illustrated in Chapter 11. Macaulay duration is converted into years by dividing the periodic Macaulay duration by 12 in the case of a monthly-pay MBS or by 4 in the case of a quarterly-pay MBS.

Illustration 21-3.   For the pass-through in Illustration 21-1, selling for $94,521 and yielding 10.21% (assuming 100% PSA), Macaulay duration is 6.17, as shown below.

The numerator of the Macaulay duration is the present value of the projected cash flows using a monthly interest rate of 0.8333% times the time period (the month). For our pass-through, the numerator is $6,998,347. Macaulay duration is then found by dividing by the price of the pass-through.

Thus,

$$\text{Macaulay duration (in months)} = \frac{\$6,998,347}{\$94,521} = 74.04 .$$

To convert the Macaulay duration in months to Macaulay duration in years:

$$\text{Macaulay duration (in years)} = \frac{74.04}{12} = 6.17 .$$

Average Life: A second measure commonly used to compare Treasury securities and MBSs is the average life, which is the average time to receipt of principal payments (projected scheduled principal and projected principal prepayments), weighted by the amount of principal expected divided by the total principal to be repaid.

Mathematically, the average life is expressed as follows:

$$\text{Average life} = \frac{1}{12} \sum_{t=1}^{n} \frac{t \, (\text{Principal received at time } t)}{\text{Total principal received}} ,$$

where n is the number of months remaining.

Illustration 21-4.   For the pass-through in the previous illustration, assuming the same prepayment rate (100% PSA), the principal payments are shown in Columns (6) and (8) of Exhibit 20-8 of Chapter 20. Adding the principal payments in these two columns and applying the formula above, the average life is 12.18 years.

Price

Given the required yield for an MBS, the price is simply the present value of the projected cash flows. Care must be taken, however, in determining the monthly interest rate that should be used to compute the present value of each cash flow.

To convert a bond equivalent yield to a monthly interest rate, we can use the formula:

$$i_M = [1 + (.5) \text{ Bond equivalent yield}]^{1/6} - 1.$$

For a quarterly interest rate, the formula is:

$$i_Q = [1 + (.5) \text{ Bond equivalent yield}]^{1/2} - 1.$$

Illustration 21-5. Once again, consider the pass-through in Illustration 21-1. Suppose that the investor (1) requires an 8.13% yield on a bond equivalent basis, and (2) assumes a prepayment rate of 150% PSA. The corresponding monthly interest rate for a bond equivalent yield of 8.13% is .6667% (.006667), as shown below:

$$i_M = [1 + (.5) .0813]^{1/6} - 1$$
$$= [1.04065]^{.16667} - 1$$
$$= .006667.$$

The projected cash flows, based on 150% PSA, would be the same as Exhibit 20-9 in Chapter 20. Discounting the projected cash flow at .6667% gives a price of $106,710.

Illustration 21-6. Suppose that instead of 8.13%, the investor wants a yield of 12.30%. Also assume that the investor believes that a 25% PSA rate is appropriate to project the cash flow. The monthly interest rate is determined as follows:

$$i_M = [1 + (.5) .1230]^{1/6} - 1$$
$$= [1.0615]^{.16667} - 1$$
$$= .01.$$

Discounting the cash flows projected on the basis of 25% PSA would give a price of $79,976.

The cash flows of IO and PO securities depend on the cash flows of the underlying pass-through, which, in turn, depends on the cash flows of the underlying pool of mortgages. Thus, to determine the price of an IO or PO, a prepayment rate must be assumed. The price of an IO is the present value of the projected interest payments net of the servicing fee. The price of a PO is the present value of the projected principal payments (projected scheduled principal payments and projected principal prepayments).

Illustration 21-7. For the 9.5% pass-through with a .5% servicing fee and 360 months to maturity, the projected interest payments net of the servicing fee and the projected principal payments assuming 100% PSA are shown in Exhibit 20-8 of Chapter 20 for selected months. Assuming a required yield of 10.21%, then:

Price of pass-through	$94,521
Price of IO	55,548
Price of PO	38,973

Illustration 21-8. Assuming that the required yield is 12.30% rather than 10.21%, and the prepayment rate is 25% PSA rather than 100% PSA, then:

Price of pass-through	$79,976
Price of IO	61,010
Price of PO	18,966

Notice what has happened to the price of the IO security in Illustration 21-7 compared to Illustration 21-8. As interest rates increased from 10.21% to 12.30%, the price of the IO increased. This is to be expected, as the holder of an IO security benefits when prepayments slow — that is, the longer the mortgages are outstanding because of fewer prepayments, the longer the IO receives interest. The PO portion decreases as interest rates increase.

Illustration 21-9.   Assuming that the required yield is 8.14% rather than 10.21% and the prepayment rate is 200% PSA rather than 100% PSA, then:

Price of pass-through	$105,985
Price of IO	47,875
Price of PO	58,110

The price of the IO in Illustration 21-9 has decreased as a result of both a lower required yield and a higher prepayment rate compared to Illustration 21-7. The opposite is true for the PO.

From the last two illustrations we can see that IOs move in the same direction as interest rates, while POs move inversely with interest rates.

Total Return

The total return framework can be used to assess the relative attractiveness of an MBS over some investment horizon. The total receipts resulting from investing in an MBS consist of:

(1) The projected cash flows of the MBS from:

   (a) the projected interest payments (net of servicing fee),

   (b) the projected principal repayment (scheduled plus prepayments),

(2) The interest earned on the reinvestment of the projected interest payments and the projected principal repayments, and

(3) The projected price of the MBS at the end of the investment horizon.

To obtain (1), a prepayment rate over the investment horizon must be assumed. To calculate (2), a reinvestment rate must be assumed. Finally, to calculate (3) the investor must make two assumptions. First, the investor must project what the bond equivalent yield will be for the MBS at the end of the investment horizon. Second, the investor must project what prepayment rate the market will assume at the end of the investment horizon. Obviously, the first and second assumptions are not independent. The projected prepayment rate will depend on the projected yield in the market.

As we have stressed throughout this book, an investor should not use one set of projections to determine the total return. Instead, an investor should assess the performance of a security over a range of likely assumptions.

The monthly total return is then found by using the formula:

$$\left[\frac{\text{Total future amount}}{\text{Price of the MBS}} \right]^{1/\text{Number of months}} - 1$$

The monthly total return can be annualized on the basis of the bond equivalent yield given earlier or by computing the effective annual yield as follows:

$$(1 + \text{Monthly total return})^{12} - 1$$

Illustration 21-10. Suppose a portfolio manager is considering investing in a pass-through with a 9.5% mortgage rate, .5% servicing fee, 360 months remaining to maturity, and an original mortgage balance of $100,000. The price of this security is $94,521. The cash flow yield, assuming 100% PSA, is 10.21% (see Illustration 21-1). The portfolio manager has a six-month investment horizon and believes the following:

(1) For the next six months the prepayment rate will be 100% PSA,

(2) The projected cash flows can be reinvested at .5% per month,

(3) The pass-through will sell to yield 7.62% at the end of the investment horizon, and

(4) The projected PSA prepayment rate at the end of the investment horizon will be 185% PSA.

On the basis of the first assumption, the projected cash flows (projected interest net of servicing fee, projected scheduled principal, and projected principal prepayment) for the first six months is:

End of month	Projected cash flow
1	$816
2	832
3	849
4	865
5	881
6	897

The projected cash flow is obtained from Exhibit 20-8 of Chapter 20.

The projected cash flow, plus interest from reinvesting the cash flow at .5% per month, is:

End of month	Projected cash flow	Projected cash flows plus reinvestment income
1	$816	$837
2	832	849
3	849	862
4	865	874
5	881	885
6	897	897
	Total	$5,204

At the end of the investment horizon, our original pass-through would have a remaining mortgage balance of $99,379 (see Exhibit 20-8 of Chapter 20) and remaining maturity of 354 months. Assuming a required yield of 7.62% and a prepayment rate of 185% PSA, the projected price of this pass-through would be $106,210.

The total future amount is then:

Projected cash flows plus reinvestment income	$5,204
Projected price	106,210
Total	$111,414

The monthly total return is

$$\left[\frac{\$111,414}{\$94,521}\right]^{\frac{1}{6}} - 1 = .02778 \ .$$

On a bond equivalent basis, the total return is

$$2[(1.02778)^6 - 1] = .3574 = 35.74\%.$$

On an effective annual yield basis, the total return is

$$(1.02778)^{12} - 1 = .3893 = 38.93\%.$$

Illustration 21-11. Suppose that a portfolio manager wants to assess the performance of the pass-through in the previous illustration over a six-month investment horizon on the basis of the following assumptions.

(1) For the next six months the prepayment rate will be 100% PSA,

(2) The projected cash flow can be reinvested at .75% per month,

(3) The pass-through will sell to yield 12.30% at the end of the investment horizon, and

(4) The projected PSA prepayment rate at the end of the investment horizon will be 50% PSA.

On the basis of the first assumption, the projected cash flows for the first six months are the same as in the previous illustration. The projected cash flows plus interest from reinvesting the cash flow at 0.75% per month are computed below:

End of month	Projected cash flow	Projected cash flow plus reinvestment income
1	$816	$847
2	832	857
3	849	868
4	865	878
5	881	888
6	897	897
	Total	$5,235

At the end of the investment horizon, our original pass-through would have a remaining balance of $99,174 and remaining maturity of 354 months. Assuming a required yield of 12.30% and a prepayment rate of 50% PSA, the projected price of this pass-through would be $78,757.

The total future amount is then

Projected cash flows plus reinvestment income	$5,235
Projected price	78,757
Total	$83,992

The monthly total return is

$$\left[\frac{\$83,992}{\$94,521}\right]^{\frac{1}{6}} -1 = -.019491 .$$

On a bond equivalent basis, the total return is

$$2[(0.98051)^6 - 1] = -.2228 = -22.28\%.$$

On an effective annual yield basis, the total return is

$$(0.98051)^{12} - 1 = -.2104 = -21.04\%.$$

Effective Duration and Convexity

Duration is a measure of the relationship of a bond's price to interest rate changes, assuming that the expected cash flows do not change with interest rates. Consequently, Macaulay duration is not an appropriate measure for mortgage-backed securities, because mortgage prepayments mean that the projected cash flows change as interest rates change. When interest rates decline (rise), prepayments are expected to rise (fall). As a result, when interest rates decline (increase), duration may decline (increase) rather than increase (decline). This property, as we explained in Chapter 16, is referred to as negative convexity.

To see this effect, consider the Macaulay duration for the 9.5% pass-through (assuming 100% PSA) selling to yield 10.21%. If the required yield decreases to 8.14% instantaneously, and the prepayment rate is assumed not to change, Macaulay duration would increase from 6.17 to 6.80. Suppose, however, that when the yield declines to 8.14%, the assumed prepayment rate changes to 150% PSA. The Macaulay duration would decline to 5.91 rather than increase.

Negative convexity has the same impact on the price performance of a mortgage-backed security as it does for a callable bond (discussed in Chapter 16). When interest rates decline, a bond with an embedded call option such as a mortgage-backed security will not perform as well as an option-free bond.

For example, if the required yield decreases instantaneously from 10.21% to 8.14%, the price would increase from $94,521 to $107,596. If the prepayment rate increases to 150% PSA, however, the price will rise to only $106,710.

While Macaulay duration and modified duration are inappropriate as measures of interest rate sensitivity, there are ways to adjust these measures to allow for changing prepayment rates as interest rates change. This can be done by calculating the effective duration and convexity that was presented in Chapter 11.

Effective Duration: The formula for effective duration is:

$$\text{effective duration} = \frac{P_- - P_+}{(P_0)(y_+ - y_-)}$$

where

P_- = Price if yield is decreased by x basis points

P_+ = Price if yield is increased by x basis points

P_0 = Initial price (per \$100 of par value)

y_+ = Initial yield plus x basis points

y_- = initial yield minus x basis points

In the effective duration calculation, the price at the higher and the lower yields will depend on the prepayment rate assumed. A higher prepayment rate is typically assumed at a lower yield level than at a higher yield level. Thus, calculation of effective duration requires a prepayment model to determine how prepayments are expected to change as interest rates change.

Illustration 21-12.   To illustrate the calculation of effective duration, consider the pass-through in Exhibit 20-8 of Chapter 20. The price assuming 100% PSA and a yield of 10.21% is \$94,521, or 94.521 per \$100 of par value. Let's look at what would happen to the price if the yield changes by 50 basis points. Suppose that if the yield decreases by 50 basis points to 9.71%, the prepayment rate is assumed to be unchanged at 100% PSA. If the yield increases by 50 basis points to 10.71%, however, the prepayment rate is assumed to decrease to 75% PSA. The price at 9.71% and 10.71% would be \$97,520 (97.520 per \$100 of par value) and \$90,992 (90.992 per \$100 of par value), respectively. Therefore,

P_- = 97.520

P_+ = 90.992

P_0 = 94.521

y_+ = .1071 (.1021 + .50)

y_- = .0971 (.1021 - .50)

$$\text{Effective duration} = \frac{97.520 - 90.992}{94.521 \ (.1071 - .0971 \ )} = 6.91$$

Effective convexity: The formula for effective convexity is:

$$\text{Effective convexity} = \frac{P_+ + P_- - 2 \ (P_0)}{(P_0) \ [5 \ (y_+ - y_-)]^2}$$

Illustration 21-13. For the pass-through in the previous illustration:

$$\text{Effective convexity} = \frac{90.992 + 97.520 - 2(94.521)}{(94.521)\,[.5\,(.1071 - .0971)]^2}$$

$$= \frac{-.530}{94.521\,(.005)^2} = -224.29$$

Notice that the convexity of this pass-through is negative.

Option-Adjusted Spread Methodology

For the static cash flow yield methodology, the yield spread for a mortgage-backed security is the difference between the cash flow yield and the yield to maturity of a comparable Treasury. The latter is obtained from the yield curve. The drawback of this procedure is that the cash flow yield for neither the mortgage-backed security nor Treasury security is calculated properly, because the calculation fails to take into consideration (1) the term structure of interest rates for Treasuries (i.e., the theoretical spot rate curve), and (2) interest rate volatility that will alter the expected cash flows for the pass-through through changes in prepayments. Application of the option-adjusted spread methodology addresses this drawback.

Static Spread

As we explain in Chapter 17, the proper way to evaluate mortgage-backed securities of the same duration but with different coupon rates is to compare them with a portfolio of zero-coupon Treasury securities that have the same cash flow stream as projected for the mortgage-backed security. Assuming the mortgage-backed security's cash flows are riskless, its value is equal to the portfolio value of all of the zero-coupon Treasuries, with cash flows valued at the spot rates. A mortgage-backed security's value will be less than the portfolio of zero-coupon Treasury securities because investors demand a spread for the risk associated with holding a mortgage-backed security rather than a riskless package (in the sense of default risk and certainty of the cash flows) of Treasury securities.

The static spread to Treasuries is determined as follows. It is the spread that will make the present value of the projected cash flows from the mortgage-backed security when discounted at the spot rate plus a spread equal to its market price. A trial-and-error procedure is required to determine this spread.

Option Cost

Using the decomposition principle for a callable bond discussed in Chapter 16, we can obtain the implied cost of the option embedded in a mortgage-backed security by calculating the difference between the option-adjusted spread at the assumed volatility of interest rates and the static spread. That is,

Option cost = Static spread − Option-adjusted spread

The option cost measures the prepayment (or option) risk embedded in the security.

Effective Duration and Convexity

Within the option-adjusted spread methodology, effective duration and convexity can be computed by increasing and decreasing short-term Treasury rates by a small amount. When these interest rates are changed, the option-adjusted spread is kept constant. This will produce two average total present values: one when short-term interest rates increase, and one when short-term interest rates decrease. These average total present values can be viewed as the theoretical prices under small interest rate changes. These prices are then substituted into the formula for effective duration and convexity given earlier in this chapter.

When effective duration is calculated using the OAS methodology to produce the two prices for a higher and lower yield, the result is commonly referred to as an *OAS-duration*. Thus, effective duration means in general that the duration is calculated after allowing for the cash flows to change as yields change. The OAS-duration is a special case where price sensitivity is determined within an OAS framework.

Summary

There are two methodologies commonly used to value mortgage-backed securities: static cash flow yield and option-adjusted spread. The static cash flow yield is the yield that will make the present value of the cash flows, given some prepayment assumption, equal to the market price of the mortgage-backed security. An effective duration and convexity can also be computed. The drawback of this framework is the difficulty of selecting an appropriate benchmark Treasury security.

The option-adjusted spread methodology may be applied to mortgage-backed securities, in which case the cash flow on the generated paths is based on a prepayment model. This methodology can be used to determine the option-adjusted spread and option cost of mortgage-backed securities.

Exhibit 21-1 summarizes the formulas introduced in this chapter.

Exhibit 21-1

Summary of Formulas

Bond equivalent yield for a monthly-pay MBS:

$$\text{Bond equivalent yield} = 2\left[(1 + i_M)^6 - 1\right]$$

where i_M is the interest rate that will equate the present value of the projected monthly cash flows to the price of the MBS.

Bond equivalent yield for a quarterly-pay MBS:

$$\text{Bond equivalent yield} = 2\left[(1 + i_Q)^2 - 1\right]$$

where i_Q is the interest rate that will equate the present value of the projected quarterly cash flows to the price of the MBS.

Conversion of a bond equivalent yield for a monthly-pay MBS to a monthly interest rate:

$$i_M = \left[1 + (.5)\text{ Bond equivalent yield}\right]^{1/6} - 1$$

Conversion of a bond equivalent yield for a quarterly-pay MBS to a quarterly interest rate:

$$i_Q = \left[1 + (.5)\text{ Bond equivalent yield}\right]^{1/2} - 1$$

Average Life:

$$\text{Average life} = \frac{1}{12}\sum_{t=1}^{n}\frac{t\,(\text{Principal received at time }t)}{\text{Total principal received}},$$

where n is the number of months remaining.

VII

Statistical and Optimization Techniques

22

Probability Theory

In most instances of fixed income analysis or fixed income portfolio management, a decision's outcome depends on variables that are not known with certainty at the time the decision is made. Stochastic or probabilistic analysis is often used in these circumstances to aid in making such decisions. This involves estimating probabilities of the various outcomes that may result from a decision. In this chapter, we establish the fundamentals of probability theory and show some applications. One particularly important application is estimation of interest rate volatility from historical data.

Objective versus Subjective Probabilities

Probabilities can be determined through objective or subjective analysis. The *objective approach* to probability theory basically asserts that probabilities relate to long-run frequencies of occurrence. That is, the objective probability of an outcome or event can be defined as the relative frequency with which an event would occur, given a large number of observations. An objectivist would assign a probability of 1/6 (one in six), for example, to the outcome or event that a value of "1" would appear if a fair die is rolled and a probability of 4/52 to the outcome or event that an ace of any suit would be drawn from a fair deck of 52 cards.

The *subjective approach* basically maintains that probabilities measure the decision maker's degree of belief in the likelihood of a given outcome. It is a broad and flexible approach, allowing assignment of probabilities to outcomes for which no objective data

399

may exist, or in circumstances where there may be a combination of objective data and subjective belief.

Basic Concepts in Probability Theory

Some basic concepts in probability theory hold true whether the objective or the subjective approach is taken.

Simple and Compound Events

Suppose an experiment is performed that involves tossing a fair die. There are then six possible outcomes: 1,2,3,4,5, or 6. Each of these outcomes is referred to as a *simple event*. The characteristic of a simple event is that it cannot be decomposed into other events. A *compound event* is one that can be decomposed into simple events. For example, an outcome that an even number will occur when a fair die is tossed is a compound event, because it can be decomposed into three simple events: getting a 2, 4, or 6.

Illustration 22-1. Suppose that a portfolio manager is considering buying a 20.5-year bond with a coupon rate of 10% and selling at par to yield 10%. The next coupon payment is exactly six months from now. Suppose also that the portfolio manager has a six-month investment horizon. The portfolio's total return will depend only on the yield for 20-year bonds six months from now. We refer to this yield as the *horizon yield*. The portfolio manager believes that only the following nine possible horizon yields for 20-year bonds six months from now will result:

Possible horizon yields

12.0%

11.5%

11.0%

10.5%

10.0%

9.5%

9.0%

8.5%

8.0%

Each of these horizon yields is a simple event. The event that the horizon yield will be less than the yield today (10%) is a compound event. It can be decomposed into four simple events: 8.0%, 8.5%, 9.0%, and 9.5%.

Mutually Exclusive Events

If two events or outcomes have nothing in common, they are referred to as *mutually exclusive events*. That is, if an experiment can result in only one of the two events occurring, then the events are mutually exclusive. For example, in the tossing of a die, the probability of a 1 and a 2 occurring is zero. Both cannot appear simultaneously. Hence the events defining an outcome of 1 and an outcome of 2 are mutually exclusive.

Conditional Probabilities

Conditional probabilities are probabilities obtained after the initial conditions have changed. For example, the probability of picking an ace with one draw of a card from the deck of 52 cards is 4/52. Suppose that the card drawn is not an ace. If you then pick another card without replacing the original card in the deck, the probability of drawing an ace is now 4/51. This probability is a conditional probability because it is conditional on the withdrawal and nonreplacement of a card that is not an ace. In probability notation, the probability of some event E_i conditional on the occurrence of some other event E_j is denoted by $P(E_i \backslash E_j)$.

As another example of a conditional probability, suppose that an investor is trying to estimate the probability that an issuer will default on a five-year debt instrument. Today, the investor assigns a probability that the issuer will default two years from now. A conditional probability would be the probability that the issuer does not default two years from now, given that the issuer does not default in the first year.

Joint Probabilities

Joint probabilities refer to the probability that more than one event will occur simultaneously. For example, suppose a single card selection experiment defines one outcome as selecting an ace and a second outcome as selecting a card that is a heart. The joint event of the two events defined above would be selecting the ace of hearts. The probability of this joint event is 1/52. In probability notation, the joint probability of two events E_i and E_j is denoted by $P(E_i \& E_j)$.

Basic Rules of Probability Theory

From the concepts of probability theory described above, we can state four basic rules of probability theory.

Rule 1: Given an experiment with n possible simple events or outcomes denoted by $E_1, E_2, \ldots, E_n$, a nonnegative number is assigned to each outcome. This is denoted mathematically by

$$P(E_i) \geq 0$$

Rule 2: The sum of the probabilities of all possible simple events is one; that is

$$P(E_1) + P(E_2) + \ldots + P(E_n) = 1$$

Rule 3:   For two mutually exclusive events, E_i and E_j, the probability of either occurring is the sum of the two probabilities. That is,

$$P(E_i \text{ or } E_j) = P(E_i) + P(E_j)$$

Rule 4:   Two events are *statistically independent* if the occurrence of one does not affect the probability of the other. When two events E_i and E_k are statistically independent, then[1]

$$P(E_i \backslash E_k) = P(E_i) \text{ or } P(E_k \backslash E_i) = P(E_k)$$

Alternatively, two events are statistically independent if the following holds:

$$P(E_i \text{ \& } E_k) = P(E_i) \, P(E_k)$$

That is, if two events are statistically independent, the joint probability can be obtained by multiplying the probabilities of the two events.

To illustrate statistical independence, suppose a fair coin is tossed twice. Define the first event as a head appearing on the first toss, and the second event as a head appearing on the second toss. If a head in fact does turn up on the first toss, how does this affect the probability of obtaining a head on the second toss? It does not, as a probability of 1/2 is still correct for a head occurring on the second toss. Hence, the two events are statistically independent.

Random Variable and Probability Distribution

A *random variable* is a variable for which a probability can be assigned to each possible result (value) that the variable can take. A *probability distribution* or *probability function* is a function that describes all the values that the random variable can take and the probability associated with each. For example, suppose that two dice are rolled. There are 36 possible outcomes. The pairs of values in each parenthesis represent the value appearing on the first and second die.

---

[1] In the notation of probability theory, a backslash (\) means "given." For example, $P(E_i \backslash E_k)$ means the probability of event i occurring *given* that event k occurs.

(1,1)	(2,1)	(3,1)	(4,1)	(5,1)	(6,1)
(1,2)	(2,2)	(3,2)	(4,2)	(5,2)	(6,2)
(1,3)	(2,3)	(3,3)	(4,3)	(5,3)	(6,3)
(1,4)	(2,4)	(3,4)	(4,4)	(5,4)	(6,4)
(1,5)	(2,5)	(3,5)	(4,5)	(5,5)	(6,5)
(1,6)	(2,6)	(3,6)	(4,6)	(5,6)	(6,6)

If X represents the sum of the two values appearing on the two dice, then X can take on integer values from 2 to 12. The probability distribution for X is shown in Exhibit 22-1. For example, the outcomes that result in a value of 5 for the random variable X are (1,4), (2,3), (3,2), and (4,1). Thus 4 of the 36 possible outcomes will sum to 5. The probability of this is therefore 4/36 or 1/9.

A *cumulative probability distribution* is a function that shows the probability that the random variable will attain a value less than or equal to each value that the random variable can take on. For the dice rolling experiment, for example, the probability that X will realize a value less than or equal to 5 is equal to the sum of the probabilities associated with X realizing a value of 2, 3, 4, and 5, which is 10/36 or 5/18. The cumulative probability distribution is also shown in Exhibit 22-1.

A subscript is used to denote specific values of the random variable. For example, in the dice-rolling experiment, there are 11 possible values that can occur for the random variable X, as follows:

i	1	2	3	4	5	6	7	8	9	10	11
X	2	3	4	5	6	7	8	9	10	11	12

These possible values can be denoted as X_i where i refers to the ith value for the random variable X. Thus, X_4 is the fourth value for the random variable X, which is the value 5, expressed as follows:

$$X_4 = 5$$

The probability that X will be equal to 5 can be expressed as follows:

$$P(X = 5) = P(X_4)$$

In the examples in this chapter, we denote the probability of a specific value for the random variable X by stating the specific value [i.e., P(X = specific value)] or by using the subscript notation [i.e., $P(X_i)$].

Illustration 22-2. To illustrate these basic rules, we continue the bond return problem in Illustration 22-1. Exhibit 22-2 shows the nine possible horizon yields and the assumed

Exhibit 22-1

Probability Distribution and Cumulative Probability Distribution for the Sum of the Values Appearing when Two Dice Are Tossed

Sum of values (X)	No. of outcomes that will result in X	Probability distribution	Cumulative probability
2	1	$\frac{1}{36}$	$\frac{1}{36}$
3	2	$\frac{2}{36} = \frac{1}{18}$	$\frac{3}{36} = \frac{1}{12}$
4	3	$\frac{2}{36} = \frac{1}{12}$	$\frac{6}{36} = \frac{1}{6}$
5	4	$\frac{4}{36} = \frac{1}{9}$	$\frac{10}{36} = \frac{5}{18}$
6	5	$\frac{5}{36}$	$\frac{15}{36} = \frac{5}{12}$
7	6	$\frac{6}{36} = \frac{1}{6}$	$\frac{21}{36} = \frac{7}{12}$
8	5	$\frac{5}{36}$	$\frac{26}{36} = \frac{13}{18}$
9	4	$\frac{4}{36} = \frac{1}{9}$	$\frac{30}{36} = \frac{5}{6}$
10	3	$\frac{3}{36} = \frac{1}{12}$	$\frac{33}{36} = \frac{11}{12}$
11	2	$\frac{2}{36} = \frac{1}{18}$	$\frac{35}{36}$
12	1	$\frac{1}{36}$	$\frac{36}{36} = 1$

probability that each horizon yield will occur. Notice that the sum of the probabilities is one. The random variable in this illustration is the horizon yield, which can take on nine possible outcomes, but the total return can also be considered the random variable. A total return corresponds to each horizon yield, with the probability distribution for the total return the same as the probability distribution for the horizon yield.

The probability that the total return will be 14.2% is 10%. That is, $P(X = 14.2\%)$ or $P(X_7)$ is 10%. The probability that the total return will be less than 14.2% is the cumulative probability shown in the fourth column of Exhibit 22-2. The probability is 77%.

Exhibit 22-2

Probability Distribution for the Six-Month Total Return for a 20.5 Year, 10% Coupon Bond Selling Initially at Par

i	*Horizon yield*	*Probability*	*Cumulative probability*	*Price at horizon*	*Total return*
1	12.0%	.05	.05	84.85	–10.15%
2	11.5	.08	.13	88.35	–6.65
3	11.0	.10	.23	91.98	–3.02
4	10.5	.16	.39	95.85	0.85
5	10.0	.22	.61	100.00	5.00
6	9.5	.16	.77	104.44	9.44
7	9.0	.10	.87	109.20	14.20
8	8.5	.08	.95	114.31	19.31
9	8.0	.05	1.00	119.79	24.79

* Since the initial price is 100 and the six-month coupon is 5 per 100 of par value, the six-month total return is found as follows:

$$(100 - \text{Price at Horizon} + 5)/100$$

Statistical Measures of a Probability Distribution

Various measures are used to summarize the probability distribution of a random variable. The two most often used measures are the expected value and the variance (or standard deviation).

Expected Value

The *expected value* of a probability distribution is the weighted average of the distribution. The weights in this case are the probabilities associated with the random variable X. The expected value of a random variable is denoted by E(X) and is computed using the following expression:

$$E(X) = P_1 X_1 + P_2 X_2 + \ldots + P_n X_n$$

where P_i is the probability associated with the outcome X_i.

Illustration 22-3. The expected value for the six-month total return for the probability distribution in Exhibit 22-2 is found as follows:

$$E(X) = .05 \,(-10.15) + .08 \,(-6.65) + .10 \,(-3.02) +$$
$$.16 \,(0.85) + .22 \,(5.00) + .16 \,(9.44) + .10 \,(14.20)$$
$$+ .08 \,(19.31) + .05 \,(24.79) = 5.61\%$$

The expected value for the six-month total return is 5.61%.

Variance

A portfolio manager is interested not only in the expected value of a probability distribution but also in the dispersion of the random variable around the expected value. A measure of dispersion of the probability distribution is the *variance* of the distribution. The variance of a random variable X, denoted by var(X), is computed as:

$$var(X) = [X_1 - E(X)]^2 \, P_1 + [X_2 - E(X)]^2 \, P_2 + \ldots + [X_n - E(X)]^2 \, P_n$$

Notice that the variance is simply a weighted average of the deviations of each possible outcome from the expected value, where the weight is the probability of an outcome occurring. The greater the variance, the wider the distribution of the possible outcomes for the random variable. The reason that the deviations from the expected value are squared is so that outcomes above and below the expected value will not cancel each other out.

The problem with using the variance as a measure of dispersion is that it is expressed in terms of squared units of the random variable. Consequently, we use the square root of the variance, called the *standard deviation*, as a better measure of the degree of dispersion. Mathematically this can be expressed as follows:

$$std(X) = \sqrt{var(X)}$$

where std(X) denotes the standard deviation of the random variable X.

Illustration 22-4.   The variance for the six-month total return whose probability distribution is given in Exhibit 22-2 is calculated as follows:

$$var(X) = (-10.15 - 5.61)^2 \,.05 + (-6.65 - 5.61)^2 \,.08 + (-3.02 - 5.61)^2$$
$$.10 + (0.85 - 5.61)^2 \,.16 + (5.00 - 5.61)^2 \,.22 + (9.44 - 5.61)^2$$
$$.16 + (14.20 - 5.61)^2 \,.10 + (19.31 - 5.61)^2 \,.08 + (24.79 - 5.61)^2$$
$$.05 = 78.73\%$$

The standard deviation is 8.87%, which is the square root of the variance, 78.73%.

Normal Probability Distribution

In many applications involving probability distributions, it is assumed that the underlying probability distribution is a *normal distribution*. An example of a normal distribution is shown in Exhibit 22-3.

The area under the normal distribution (or normal curve) between any two points on a horizontal axis represents the probability of obtaining a value between those two values.

Exhibit 22-3

Normal Distribution (or Normal Curve)

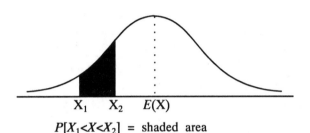

$$P[X_1 < X < X_2] = \text{shaded area}$$

For example, the probability of realizing a value for the random variable X that is between X_1 and X_2 in Exhibit 22-3 is shown by the shaded area. Mathematically, the probability of realizing a value for X between these two variables can be written as follows:

$$P(X_1 < X < X_2)$$

The entire area under the normal curve is equal to 1. This follows from the second rule of probability theory, which states that the sum of the probabilities of all possible simple events is 1.

Properties of the Normal Distribution

The normal distribution has the following properties:

(1) The point in the middle of the normal curve is the expected value for the distribution.

(2) The distribution is symmetric around the expected value. That is, half of the distribution is to the left of the expected value, and the other half is to the right. Thus, the probability of obtaining a value less than the expected value is 50%.

The probability of obtaining a value greater than the expected value is also 50%. Mathematically, this is expressed as follows:

$$P[X < E(X)] = .5 \text{ and } P[X > E(X)] = .5$$

(3) The probability that the actual outcome will be within a range of one standard deviation above the expected value and one standard deviation below the expected value is 68.26%, rounded to 68.3%.

(4) The probability that the actual outcome will be within a range of two standard deviations above the expected value and two standard deviations below the expected value is 95.46%, rounded to 95.5%.

(5) The probability that the actual outcome will be within a range of three standard deviations above the expected value and three standard deviations below the expected value is 99.74%, rounded to 99.7%.

Illustration 22-5. Suppose that the one-year total return for a portfolio has an expected value of 7% and a standard deviation of 4%, and that the probability distribution is a normal distribution. The probability is 68.3% that the one-year total return will be between 3% (the expected value of 7% minus one standard deviation of 4%) and 11% (the expected value of 7% plus one standard deviation of 4%). The probability is 95.5% that the one-year total return will be between -1% (the expected value minus two standard deviations) and 15% (the expected value plus two standard deviations).

Illustration 22-6. Suppose that the standard deviation for the one-year total return in the previous illustration is 2% rather than 4%. Then the probability is 68.3% that the one-year total return will be between 5% and 9%; the probability is 95.5% that the one-year total return will be between 3% and 11%.

Notice that the smaller the standard deviation, the narrower the range of the possible outcome for a given probability.

Using Normal Distribution Tables

Tables are available that give the probability of obtaining a value between any two values of a normal probability distribution. All that must be known in order to determine the probability is the expected value and the standard deviation. However, the normal distribution table is constructed for a normal distribution that has an expected value of 0 and a standard deviation of 1. In order to use the table, therefore, it is necessary to convert the normal distribution under consideration into a distribution that has an expected value of 0 and standard deviation of 1. This is done by standardizing the values of the distribution under consideration.

The procedure is as follows. Suppose that a normal distribution for some random variable X has an expected value $E(X)$ and a standard deviation denoted by $std(X)$. To standardize any particular value, say X_1, the following is computed:

$$z_1 = \frac{X_1 - E(X)}{std(X)}$$

where z_1 is the *standardized value* for X_1. The standardized value is also called the *normal deviate*.

Exhibit 22-4 is an abridged normal distribution table that shows the area under the normal curve, which, as stated before, represents probability. This particular table shows the probability of obtaining a value greater than some specified value in standardized form in the right-hand tail of the distribution. This is the shaded area shown in the normal curve at the top of Exhibit 22-4.

We demonstrate how to use the table in the next nine illustrations. In Illustrations 22-7 to 22-13 it is assumed that a life insurance company has estimated that the value of one of its long-term Treasury bond portfolios is normally distributed with an expected value of $10 million and a standard deviation of $2 million.

Illustration 22-7. Suppose that the portfolio manager wants to know the probability of realizing a portfolio value greater than $14 million. The standardized value corresponding to $14 million in this case is 2, as shown below:

$$\frac{\$14 \text{ million} - \$10 \text{ million}}{\$2 \text{ million}} = 2$$

The probability of obtaining a value greater than $14 million is the same as a standardized value greater than 2. (See Exhibit 22-5.) From Exhibit 22-4, the probability of obtaining a value greater than 2 is .0228 or 2.28%, expressed as follows:

$$P(X > \$14 \text{ million}) = P(z > 2) = .0228$$

Illustration 22-8. Suppose the probability of obtaining a value greater than $11 million is wanted. The standardized value is .5, as shown below:

$$\frac{\$11 \text{ million} - \$10 \text{ million}}{\$2 \text{ million}} = .5$$

From Exhibit 22-4, the probability of obtaining a value greater than .5 is .3085 or 30.85%, expressed as follows:

$$P(X > \$11 \text{ million}) = P(z > .5) = .3085$$

Illustration 22-9. Suppose that the probability of obtaining a value less than $14 million is wanted. This is simple, because the entire area under the normal curve is equal to 1. If the probability of obtaining a value greater than $14 million is .0228, the probability of obtaining a portfolio value less than $14 million is $1 - .0228$, or 97.72%. This is expressed as follows:

$$P(X < \$14 \text{ million}) = P(z < 2) = 1 - P(z > 2) = 1 - .0228 = .9772$$

Illustration 22-10. Let's look now at how to obtain the probability of obtaining some value between the expected value and a value to the right of the expected value. Suppose

Exhibit 22-4

Normal Distribution Table for Standardized Value (or Normal Deviate) z

z	.00	.01	.02	.03	.04	.05	.06	.07	.08	.09
0.0	.5000	.4960	.4920	.4880	.4840	.4801	.4761	.4721	.4681	.4641
0.1	.4602	.4562	.4522	.4483	.4443	.4404	.4364	.4325	.4286	.4247
0.2	.4207	.4168	.4129	.4090	.4052	.4013	.3974	.3936	.3897	.3859
0.3	.3821	.3783	.3745	.3707	.3669	.3632	.3594	.3557	.3520	.3483
0.4	.3446	.3409	.3372	.3336	.3300	.3264	.3228	.3192	.3156	.3121
0.5	.3085	.3050	.3015	.2981	.2946	.2912	.2877	.2843	.2810	.2776
0.6	.2743	.2709	.2676	.2643	.2611	.2578	.2546	.2514	.2483	.2451
0.7	.2420	.2389	.2358	.2327	.2296	.2266	.2236	.2206	.2177	.2148
0.8	.2110	.2090	.2061	.2033	.2005	.1977	.1949	.1922	.1894	.1867
0.9	.1841	.1814	.1788	.1762	.1736	.1711	.1685	.1660	.1635	.1611
1.0	.1587	.1562	.1539	.1515	.1492	.1469	.1449	.1423	.1401	.1379
1.1	.1357	.1335	.1314	.1292	.1271	.1251	.1230	.1210	.1190	.1170
1.2	.1151	.1131	.1112	.1093	.1075	.1056	.1038	.1020	.1003	.0985
1.3	.0968	.0951	.0934	.0918	.0901	.0885	.0869	.0853	.0838	.0823
1.4	.0808	.0793	.0778	.0764	.0749	.0735	.0721	.0708	.0694	.0681
1.5	.0668	.0655	.0643	.0630	.0618	.0606	.0594	.0582	.0571	.0559
1.6	.0548	.0537	.0526	.0516	.0505	.0495	.0485	.0475	.0465	.0455
1.7	.0446	.0436	.0427	.0418	.0409	.0401	.0392	.0384	.0375	.0367
1.8	.0359	.0351	.0344	.0336	.0329	.0322	.0314	.0307	.0301	.0294
1.9	.0287	.0281	.0274	.0268	.0262	.0256	.0250	.0244	.0239	.0233
2.0	.0228	.0222	.0217	.0212	.0207	.0202	.0197	.0192	.0188	.0183
2.1	.0179	.0174	.0170	.0166	.0162	.0158	.0154	.0150	.0146	.0143
2.2	.0139	.0136	.0132	.0129	.0125	.0122	.0119	.0116	.0113	.0110
2.3	.0107	.0104	.0102	.0099	.0096	.0094	.0091	.0089	.0087	.0084
2.4	.0082	.0080	.0078	.0075	.0073	.0071	.0069	.0068	.0066	.0064
2.5	.0062	.0060	.0059	.0057	.0055	.0054	.0052	.0051	.0049	.0048
2.6	.0047	.0045	.0044	.0043	.0041	.0040	.0039	.0038	.0037	.0036
2.7	.0035	.0034	.0033	.0032	.0031	.0030	.0029	.0028	.0027	.0026
2.8	.0026	.0025	.0024	.0023	.0023	.0022	.0021	.0021	.0020	.0019
2.9	.0019	.0018	.0018	.0017	.0016	.0016	.0015	.0015	.0014	.0014
3.0	.0013	.0013	.0013	.0012	.0012	.0011	.0011	.0011	.0010	.0010

Exhibit 22-5

Relationship Between Normal Distribution of X
and Standardized Value of z

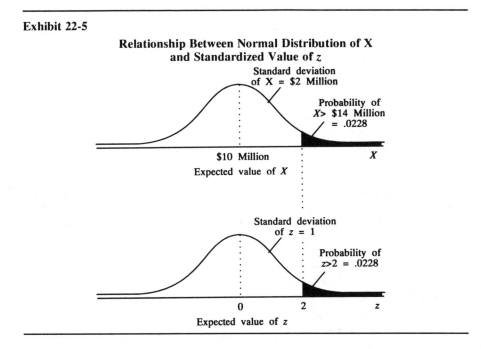

the portfolio manager wants to know what the probability of obtaining a portfolio value between $10 million (the expected value) and $14 million. From the second property of the normal curve explained above, the probability of obtaining a value greater than the expected value is 50%. Since the shaded area to the right of the standardized value 2, which corresponds to a portfolio value of $14 million, is .0228, the probability of obtaining a portfolio value between $10 million and $14 million must be equal to the difference between the entire area to the right of the expected value, which is .5, and the area to the right of 2, which is .0228. Therefore, the probability of obtaining a value between $10 million and $14 million is .4772 or 47.72%. This is expressed as follows:

$$P(\$10 \text{ million} < X < \$14 \text{ million}) = .5 - .0228 = .4772$$

Illustration 22-11. Suppose that instead of determining the probability of obtaining a value between the expected value and some value to its right, the probability of obtaining a portfolio value between $11 million and $14 million is desired. This corresponds to the probability of obtaining a standardized value between 5 and 2. Thus, the probability can be found by subtracting the two probabilities. The probability of obtaining a portfolio value between $11 million and $14 million is 30.85% − 2.28% or 28.57%.

Illustration 22-12. The tricky aspect of using the normal distribution table is dealing with values that are less than the expected value; i.e., values that are to the left of the expected value. For example, suppose the probability of obtaining a portfolio value less than $6 million is desired. The standardized value corresponding to $6 million is −2.

There is no –2 in Exhibit 22-4; the table gives only positive values for the standardized value, because the distribution is symmetric around the expected value. The symmetric distribution means that the area in the tail of the distribution corresponding to a standardized value of 2 can be used. Hence, the probability of obtaining a portfolio value less than $6 million is 2.28%.

Illustration 22-13.   Suppose the portfolio manager wants to know the probability of obtaining a portfolio value between $6 million and $11 million. Note that the expected value ($10 million) is between these two values. The probability can be found as follows (see Exhibit 22-6). First, the probability of obtaining a portfolio value greater than $10 million and $11 million is calculated by finding the probability of obtaining a portfolio value greater than $11 million and subtracting it from 50%. According to Illustration 22-11, the probability of obtaining a portfolio value greater than $11 million is 30.85%. Hence, the probability of obtaining a portfolio value between $10 million and $11 million is 19.15% (.5 – .3085). Next, the probability of obtaining a portfolio value between $6 million and $10 million must be determined. This is accomplished by subtracting the probability of obtaining a portfolio value less than $6 million from 50%. Since the probability of obtaining a portfolio value less than $6 million is 2.28% (according to Illustration 22-12), the probability of obtaining a portfolio value between $6 million and $10 million is 47.72% (.5 – .0228). The probability of obtaining a portfolio value between $6 million and $11 million is then the sum of the probabilities of obtaining a value between $6 million and $10 million and $10 million and $11 million: 66.87% (47.72% + 19.15%).

Exhibit 22-6

Illustration of Determining How to Find the Probability of X between $6 Million and $11 Million

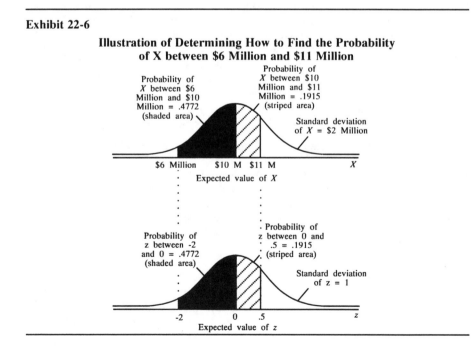

Illustration 22-14. Consider once again the probability distribution for the one-year total return for a portfolio with an expected value of 7% and a standard deviation of 4% in Illustration 22-5. Suppose that one-year Treasury bills are offering a total return of 4%. Assuming that the probability distribution is normal, the investor wants to know the probability that the return will be less than the one-year Treasury bill rate of 4%. If R is a random variable representing the one-year total return, then:

$$E(R) = 7\% \text{ and } std(R) = 4\%$$

The investor wants to know the probability that R is less than 4%; that is, $P(R < 4\%)$. The standardized value corresponding to R equal to 4% is

$$z = \frac{4\% - 7\%}{4\%} = -.75$$

Therefore, the investor wants to know the:

$$P(R < 4\%) = P(z < -.75) = P(z > .75) = 22.66\%$$

Illustration 22-15. Suppose the portfolio manager in the previous illustration will receive a bonus if the portfolio's one-year return exceeds the one-year Treasury return by 500 basis points. The probability that this will occur can be expressed as

$$P(R > 7\% + 5\%) \text{ or } P(R > 12\%)$$

The corresponding standardized value is:

$$z = \frac{12\% - 7\%}{4\%} = 1.25$$

Thus, the probability sought is:

$$P(R > 12\%) = P(z > 1.25) = 10.56\%.$$

Calculating Historical Interest Rate Volatility: An Application of the Standard Deviation

The standard deviation is a measure of the variation of a random variable around its mean or expected value. It is commonly used as a measure of the volatility of prices or yields. Because volatility plays such a key role in fixed income portfolio management and the valuation of fixed income options, we discuss how to calculate the standard deviation from historical data.[2]

---

[2] In addition to historical volatility, market participants calculate *implied volatility*. This value is estimated from the observed price of an option which is assumed to be fairly priced according to some assumed option pricing model and the other inputs in an option pricing model.

Calculating Standard Deviation from Historical Data

We have shown already how to calculate the standard deviation and variance of a random variable given a probability distribution. The variance of a random variable using historical data is calculated using the following formula:

$$\text{variance} = \sum_{t=1}^{T} \frac{(X_t - \overline{X})^2}{T-1}$$

and then

$$\text{standard deviation} = \sqrt{\text{variance}}$$

where

T = The number of observations in the sample

X_t = Observation t on variable X

$\overline{X}$ = The average sample value for variable X_t

Illustration 22-16. We can use the data in Exhibit 22-7 to illustrate how to calculate a standard deviation from historical data. The data reproduce the closing yield on the December 1992 Eurodollar CD futures contract for 31 days ending July 30, 1992. We use the 10 days ending July 30, 1992, to calculate the standard deviation of the 90-day Eurodollar CD rate.

Exhibit 22-8 shows the worksheet. There are ten observations, each one (X_t) the percentage change in yield from the previous day. For example, from July 23, 1992, to July 24, 1992, the yield increased from 3.83% to 3.85%, a change of .02/3.83, or .0052218. This is the value shown for the sixth observation (t = 6) in the third column in Exhibit 22-8.

The fourth column shows the average for the ten days. The last column gives the square of the difference between the observation and the average, and the sum of those values becomes the numerator for the variance formula. Dividing that number by T − 1, the number of observations minus one (9 in our illustration), gives the variance. The square root of the variance then gives the standard deviation, which is .86% in this illustration.

The calculation can be done easily using a spreadsheet with a built-in function. For example, in LOTUS 123, the function @STD calculates the standard deviation. You will want to know the precise way in which the standard deviation is calculated, however. Specifically, the denominator of the variance formula that we use is T − 1. The rationale behind this is that there is no deviation until there is more than one observation. Some spreadsheet developers divide by T rather than T − 1. Obviously, if T is large, there is little difference whether the numerator is divided by T − 1 or T. If T is small, however, the difference can be quite large. In our illustration, the standard deviation would be .81% if we divide the numerator by 10 rather than 9. If a spreadsheet is used that divides by T rather than T − 1, the value reported for the standard deviation on the spreadsheet can be corrected by multiplying by $[T/(T-1)]^{.5}$.

Exhibit 22-7

December 1992 Eurodollar Futures Closing Yield
from 6/17/92 to 7/30/92

Date	Closing yield
6/17/92	4.70%
6/18/92	4.63
6/19/92	4.71
6/22/92	4.67
6/23/92	4.71
6/24/92	4.56
6/25/92	4.48
6/26/92	4.48
6/29/92	4.41
6/30/92	4.41
7/01/92	4.37
7/02/92	4.06
7/06/92	4.02
7/07/92	3.98
7/08/92	4.01
7/09/92	3.98
7/10/92	3.97
7/13/92	3.97
7/14/92	3.94
7/15/92	3.88
7/16/92	3.88
7/17/92	3.90
7/20/92	3.91
7/21/92	3.93
7/22/92	3.90
7/23/92	3.83
7/24/92	3.85
7/27/92	3.85
7/28/92	3.81
7/29/92	3.83
7/30/92	3.86

Exhibit 22-8

Worksheet for the Calculation of 10-Day Interest Rate Volatility Based on December 1992 Eurodollar Futures Contract

Date	Observation	X_t	$\overline{X}$	$(X_t - \overline{X})^2$
7/17/92	1	.00515	−.00048	.0000317874
7/20/92	2	.00256	−.00048	.0000092872
7/21/92	3	.00512	−.00048	.0000313430
7/22/92	4	−.00763	−.00048	.0000511253
7/23/92	5	−.01795	−.00048	.0003050376
7/24/92	6	.00522	−.00048	.0000325507
7/27/92	7	.00000	−.00048	.0000002337
7/28/92	8	−.01039	−.00048	.0000981332
7/29/92	9	.00525	−.00048	.0000328642
7/30/92	10	.00783	−.00048	.0000691607
	Total	−.00483		.000661523

$$\overline{X} = \frac{-.00483}{10} = -.00048$$

$$\text{Var}(X) = \frac{.000661523}{10 - 1} = .0000735026$$

$$\text{Std}(X) = \sqrt{.0000735026} = .0085733633$$

Market practice with respect to the number of days that should be used to calculate the daily standard deviation varies. The number of days can be as small as 10 days or as long as 100 days.

Market participants are interested in annualized yield volatility, so the daily standard deviation is annualized as follows:

$$\text{daily standard deviation} \times \sqrt{\text{Number of days in a year}}$$

Market practice varies with respect to the number of days in the year that should be used in the annualizing formula above. Typically, 250 days, 260 days, or 365 days are used.

To calculate an annual standard deviation, the portfolio manager must decide on:

(1) the number of daily observations to use

(2) the number of days in the year to use to annualize the daily standard deviation.

Exhibit 22-9 shows the difference in the annual standard deviation assuming 10, 20, and 30 days are used to calculate the daily standard deviation, and 250, 260, and 365 days are used to annualize the daily standard deviation. Also shown in the exhibit are the annual standard deviations produced by dividing by the number of observations (T) and the number of observations minus one (T − 1). Notice that differences in the various assumptions cause the annual standard deviation to range from a low of 12.86% to a high of 32.71%.

Exhibit 22-9

**Calculated Annualized Interest Rate Volatility
Based on Various Assumptions**

No. of daily	*Number of days used for annualizing*		
observations	*250*	*260*	*365*
10 days			
T = 10	12.86%	13.11%	15.54%
T = 9	13.56%	13.82%	16.38%
20 days			
T = 20	26.39%	26.91%	31.88%
T = 19	27.07%	27.61%	32.71%
30 days			
T = 30	24.80%	25.29%	29.97%
T = 29	25.22%	25.72%	30.48%

Yield Volatility Versus Price Volatility

Market participants more commonly use yield volatility rather than price volatility because the latter is affected by the duration of a bond, and price volatility itself changes over time as duration changes. For example, daily price volatility for a long-term bond will be greater than that for a short-term bond. This is not surprising, because the duration of a long-term bond is greater than that of a short-term bond, so that for a given change in yield the long-term bond will exhibit greater price volatility. This does not mean that the yield volatility of a long-term bond is greater than that of a short-term bond. In fact, the opposite is true as can be seen from Exhibit 22-10, which shows the price volatility and yield volatility of the on-the-run Treasuries in 1987.

Once yield volatility is calculated, price volatility can be estimated using the following formula:

$$\text{Price volatility} = \frac{\text{Yield volatility} \times \text{PVBP} \times \text{Yield} \times 10{,}000}{\text{Price}}$$

where PVBP is the price value of a basis point.

Exhibit 22-10

Price and Yield Volatility for On-the-Run Treasuries in 1987

Treasury	Price volatility	Yield volatility
2-year	2.52%	19.99%
3-year	3.34	17.97
4-year	4.46	18.04
5-year	5.84	18.73
7-year	7.63	17.79
10-year	10.72	17.40
20-year	13.93	16.59
30-year	14.82	17.21

Source: Exhibit 4 in Keith Anderson and Scott Amero, "Measuring, Interpreting and Applying Volatility Within the Fixed Income Market," Chapter 6 in Frank J. Fabozzi (ed.), *The Handbook of Fixed Income Options* (Chicago: Probus Publishing, 1989).

Interpreting the Annualized Standard Deviation

What does it mean if the annual standard deviation or annual yield volatility for long-term bonds is, say, 15%? It means that if the prevailing yield on long-term bonds is 7%, the standard deviation of long-term yields in one year is 105 basis points (7% times 15%).

Assuming that the yield volatility is approximately normally distributed, this means there is a 68.3% probability that the yield on long-term bonds one year from now will be within one standard deviation below and above 7%. Thus, there is a 68.3% probability that the yield on long-term bonds one year from now will be between 5.95% and 8.05%. Similarly, from the properties of a normal distribution, we know that there is a 95.5% probability that the yield level on long-term bonds one year from now will be within a range of two standard deviations (between 4.9% and 9.10%); there is a 99.7% probability it will be within a range of three standard deviations (3.85% and 10.15%).

Notice that the higher the yield volatility, the wider the range of the yield level in the future. This means there is greater uncertainty about the future yield level. For example, if the yield volatility is 20% rather than 15%, this translates into a yield volatility of 140 basis points (20% times 7%). Assuming a normal distribution, there is a 68.3% probability that the yield one year from now will be between 5.6% and 8.4%; a 95.5% probability that it will be between 4.2% and 9.8%; and a 99.7% probability that it will be between 2.8% and 11.2%.

Empirical evidence suggests that daily percentage yield changes are approximately normally distributed. This can be seen in Exhibit 22-11, which shows the distribution of daily percentage yield changes for the 30-year Constant Maturity Treasury between January 1982 and January 1988.

23

Simulation

The performance of a fixed income portfolio depends on the outcome of many variables. These influences include the magnitude of the change in Treasury rates, the spread between non-Treasury and Treasury securities, changes in the shape of the yield curve, changes in the quality rating of individual corporate bond issues, and actual prepayment speeds in the case of mortgage-backed securities. Moreover, changes in every random variable may proceed along a substantial number of possible paths. These eventualities make it impractical to evaluate all possible combinations of outcomes in order to assess the risks associated with a portfolio.

In this chapter, we explain a technique called *simulation* for tackling such situations. We describe the steps in a simulation and use a hypothetical bond portfolio management example to illustrate the procedure. We also demonstrate an actual application to a mortgage-backed security problem.

Monte Carlo Simulation

Suppose that a portfolio manager wants to assess the performance of a portfolio over a one-year investment horizon. Suppose further that the portfolio's performance will be determined by the actual outcome for each of nine random variables and that each of the nine random variables has seven possible outcomes. There are thus 4,782,969 (9^7) possible outcomes, representing all possible combinations of the nine random variables. Furthermore, each of the 4,782,969 outcomes has a different probability of occurrence.

One approach for a portfolio manager is to take the "best guess" for each random variable and determine the impact on performance. The best-guess value for each random variable is usually the expected value of the random variable.[1] There are serious problems with this short-cut approach. To understand its shortcomings, suppose the probability associated with the best guess for each random variable is 75%. If the probability distribution for each random variable is independently distributed, the probability of occurrence for the best-guess result would be only 7.5%. At this level of probability, no portfolio manager would have a great deal of confidence in this best-guess result.

Between the extremes of enumerating and evaluating all possible combinations and the best-guess approach is the simulation approach. Simulation is less a model than a procedure or algorithm. The solutions obtained do not represent an optimal solution to a problem. Rather, simulation provides information about a problem so that a portfolio manager can assess the risks of a particular course of action. Because it offers a flexible approach to dealing with business problems, simulation is probably one of the tools most often used.

There are many types of simulation techniques. When probability distributions are assigned to the random variables, the simulation technique is known as a *Monte Carlo simulation* — named after the famous gambling spot on the French Riviera. Monte Carlo simulation enables portfolio managers to determine the statistical properties of a problem that they face. Armed with this information, a portfolio manager can select the most prudent course of action. Monte Carlo simulation is also used in the pricing of bonds with embedded options.

Steps for Monte Carlo Simulation

There are 12 steps in a Monte Carlo simulation:

Step 1. The performance measure must be specified. The performance measure may be, for example, total return over some investment horizon or net interest (spread) income.

Step 2. The problem under investigation must be expressed mathematically, including all important variables and their interactions. The variables in the mathematical model will be either *deterministic* or *random*. A deterministic variable can take on only one value; a random variable can take on more than one value.

Step 3. For those variables that are random variables, a probability distribution for each must be specified.

---

[1] The expected value of a random variable is explained in Chapter 22.

Step 4. For each variable whose probability distribution must be specified, the probability distribution must be converted into a cumulative probability distribution.

Step 5. For each random variable, representative numbers must be assigned on the basis of the cumulative probability distribution to each possible outcome specified.

Step 6. A random number must be obtained for each random variable.

Step 7. For each random number, the corresponding value of the random variable must be determined.

Step 8. The corresponding value of each random variable found in the previous step must be used to determine the value of the performance measure developed in step 2.

Step 9. The value of the performance measure found in step 8 must be recorded.

Step 10. Steps 6 through 9 must be repeated many times, say, 100 to 1,000 times. The repetition of steps 6 through 9 is known as a *trial*.

Step 11. The values for the performance measure for each trial recorded in step 9 become the basis for construction of a probability distribution and cumulative probability distribution.

Step 12. The cumulative probability distribution constructed in step 11 is analyzed. This is done by calculating summary statistics such as the mean, standard deviation, and the range.

Generating Random Numbers

Before we illustrate these steps, we need to explain how random numbers are obtained in step 6. Any procedure used must have the following property: for each number that may possibly be selected, the probability of selection must be equal.

There are several procedures that can be used to generate random numbers. First, suppose that two-digit random numbers from 00 to 99 are wanted. The portfolio manager could write each number on a piece of paper of equal size, put it in a bag, shake the bag, and then pick out one piece of paper. The number that turns up on that pick is the random number for the random variable. As long as each piece of paper has an equal chance of being selected, the procedure is acceptable for generating random numbers. For each trial, however, the paper picked in the previous trial must be put back into the bag. If it is not, each piece of paper would no longer have an equal chance of being selected in a subsequent trial.

Because there are many instances where random numbers are needed, *random number tables* have been prepared that provide them. Exhibit 23-1 is an example. To obtain random numbers from this table, the portfolio manager can start anywhere in the table (providing the starting point is selected at random) and move in any direction to obtain a subsequent number. Start right at the beginning of the table and select numbers moving down the rows. Suppose that the portfolio manager wants to select five two-digit random numbers between 0 and 99. The random numbers from Exhibit 23-1 would be 23,

Exhibit 23-1

Random Number Table (First and Second Thousands)

FIRST THOUSAND

	1–4	5–8	9–12	13–16	17–20	21–24	25–28	29–32	33–36	37–40
1	23 15	75 48	50 01	83 72	59 93	76 24	97 08	86 95	23 03	67 44
2	05 54	55 50	43 10	53 74	35 08	90 61	18 37	44 10	96 22	13 43
3	14 87	16 03	50 32	40 43	62 23	50 05	10 03	22 11	54 38	08 34
4	38 97	67 49	51 94	05 17	58 53	78 80	59 01	94 32	42 87	16 95
5	97 31	26 17	18 99	75 53	08 70	94 25	12 58	41 54	88 21	05 13
6	11 74	26 93	81 44	33 93	08 72	32 79	73 31	18 22	64 70	68 50
7	43 36	12 88	59 11	01 64	56 23	93 00	90 04	99 43	64 07	40 36
8	93 80	62 04	78 38	26 80	44 91	55 75	11 89	32 58	47 55	25 71
9	49 54	01 31	81 08	42 98	41 87	69 53	82 96	61 77	73 80	95 27
10	36 76	87 26	33 37	94 82	15 69	41 95	96 86	70 45	27 48	38 80
11	07 09	25 23	92 24	62 71	26 07	06 55	84 53	44 67	33 84	53 20
12	43 31	00 10	81 44	86 38	03 07	52 55	51 61	48 89	74 29	46 47
13	61 57	00 63	60 06	17 36	37 75	63 14	89 51	23 35	01 74	69 93
14	31 35	28 37	99 10	77 91	89 41	31 57	97 64	48 62	58 48	69 19
15	57 04	88 65	26 27	79 59	36 82	90 52	95 65	46 35	06 53	22 54
16	09 24	34 42	00 68	72 10	71 37	30 72	97 57	56 09	29 82	76 50
17	97 95	53 50	18 40	89 48	83 29	52 23	08 25	21 22	53 26	15 87
18	93 73	25 95	70 43	78 19	88 85	56 67	16 68	26 95	99 64	45 69
19	72 62	11 12	25 00	92 26	82 64	35 66	65 94	34 71	68 75	18 67
20	61 02	07 44	18 45	37 12	07 94	95 91	73 78	66 99	53 61	93 78
21	97 83	98 54	74 33	05 59	17 18	45 47	35 41	44 22	03 42	30 00
22	89 16	09 71	92 22	23 29	06 37	35 05	54 54	89 88	43 81	63 61
23	25 96	68 82	20 62	87 17	92 65	02 82	35 28	62 84	91 95	48 83
24	81 44	33 17	19 05	04 95	48 06	74 69	00 75	67 65	01 71	65 45
25	11 32	25 49	31 42	36 23	43 86	08 62	49 76	67 42	24 52	32 45

SECOND THOUSAND

1	64 75	58 38	85 84	12 22	59 20	17 69	61 56	55 95	04 59	59 47
2	10 30	25 22	89 77	43 63	44 30	38 11	24 90	67 07	34 82	33 28
3	71 01	79 84	95 51	30 85	03 74	66 59	10 28	87 53	76 56	91 49
4	60 01	25 56	05 88	41 03	48 79	79 65	59 01	69 78	80 00	36 66
5	37 33	09 46	56 49	16 14	28 02	48 27	45 47	55 44	55 36	50 90
6	47 86	98 70	01 31	59 11	22 73	60 62	61 28	22 34	69 16	12 12
7	38 04	04 27	37 64	16 78	95 78	39 32	34 93	24 88	43 43	87 06
8	73 50	83 09	03 83	05 48	00 78	36 66	93 02	95 56	46 04	53 36
9	32 62	34 64	74 84	06 10	43 24	20 62	83 73	19 32	35 64	39 69
10	97 59	19 95	49 36	63 03	51 06	62 06	99 29	75 95	32 05	77 34
11	74 01	23 19	55 59	79 09	69 82	66 22	42 40	15 96	74 90	75 89
12	56 75	42 64	57 13	35 10	50 14	90 96	63 36	74 69	09 63	34 88
13	49 80	04 99	08 54	83 12	19 98	08 52	82 63	72 92	92 36	50 26
14	43 58	48 96	47 24	87 85	66 70	00 22	15 01	93 99	59 16	23 77
15	16 65	37 96	64 60	32 57	13 01	35 74	28 36	36 73	05 88	72 29
16	48 50	26 90	55 65	32 25	87 48	31 44	68 02	37 31	25 29	63 67
17	96 76	55 46	92 36	31 68	62 30	48 29	63 83	52 23	81 66	40 94
18	38 92	36 15	50 80	35 78	17 84	23 44	41 24	63 33	99 22	81 28
19	77 95	88 16	94 25	·22 50	55 87	51 07	30 10	70 60	21 86	19 61
20	17 92	82 80	65 25	58 60	87 71	02 64	18 50	64 65	79 64	81 70
21	94 03	68 59	78 02	31 80	44 99	41 05	41 05	31 87	43 12	15 96
22	47 46	06 04	79 56	23 04	84 17	14 37	28 51	67 27	55 80	03·68
23	47 85	65 60	88 51	99 28	34 39	40 64	41 71	70 13	46 31	82 88
24	57 61	63 46	53 92	29 86	20 18	10 37	57 65	15 62	98 69	07 56
25	08 30	09 27	04 66	75 26	66 10	57 18	87 91	07 54	22 22	20 13

5, 14, 38, and 97. If five four-digit random numbers between 0 and 8000 are sought, the following random numbers would be selected from Exhibit 23-1: 2315, 554, 1487, 3897, and 1174. Notice that we skip the fifth random number in the table — 9731 — because this number is more than the upper limit of 8000.

Spreadsheets and other software include add-on features that can be used to generate random numbers. The function *@RAND*, for example, in LOTUS 123, will generate a random number between 0 and 1. To get a two-digit number the value generated by *@RAND* can be multiplied by 100.

Illustration of the Steps of Monte Carlo Simulation

Consider a portfolio manager who has invested $15 million in three bonds. Exhibit 23-2 specifies the three hypothetical bonds and the relevant information about each issue. For purposes of our illustration, each bond is assumed to pay its next coupon six months from now. The portfolio manager wants to simulate the six-month period total return assuming that the only two random variables are (1) the change in the level and shape of the Treasury yield curve, and (2) the change in the quality spread between Treasuries and BBB-corporates.

Exhibit 23-2

Hypothetical Three-Bond Portfolio for Simulation Illustration

Bond	Maturity	Coupon	Price	Par	YTM
Treasury	5.5 years	6.0%	100	$5 million	6.0%
BBB-corporate	15.5 years	9.0	100	4 million	9.0
BBB-corporate	25.5 years	10.5	100	6 million	10.5

Exhibit 23-3 gives six possible Treasury yield curves six months from now that the portfolio manager believes may occur. Exhibit 23-4 gives six possible Treasury/corporate spreads (i.e., quality spreads) assuming that spread is the same regardless of maturity.

Exhibit 23-3

Information for Monte Carlo Simulation of a Three-Bond Portfolio
Random Variable: Treasury Yield Curve

Years to maturity			Probability Distribution	Cumulative Probability Distribution	Representative Numbers Assigned
5	15	25			
4%	6%	7%	.20	.20	0 – 19
5	8	9	.15	.35	20 – 34
6	7	7	.10	.45	35 – 44
7	8	8	.10	.55	45 – 54
9	9	9	.20	.25	55 – 74
10	8	8	.25	1.00	75 – 99

Exhibit 23-4

Information for Monte Carlo Simulation of a Three-Bond Portfolio Random Variable: BBB Corporate/Treasury Yield Spread

BBB/Treasury Yield Spread	Probability Distribution	Cumulative Probability Distribution	Representative Numbers Assigned
75 bp	.10	.10	0 – 9
100	.20	.30	10 – 29
125	.25	.55	30 – 54
150	.25	.80	55 – 79
175	.15	.95	80 – 94
200	.05	1.00	95 – 99

We use all this information to describe each of the 12 steps of the Monte Carlo simulation technique.

Step 1. The performance measure must be specified. The performance measure is the annualized six-month total return for the three bond portfolio.

Step 2. The problem under investigation must be expressed mathematically. The six-month total return can be expressed as follows:

Let p_i = the price of bond i at the end of six months (i = 1, 2, and 3, where 1 is the Treasury, 2 is the shorter BBB-corporate bond, and 3 is the longer BBB corporate bond)

c_i = the six-month coupon payment for bond i.

The total future dollars from each bond at the end of the six-month horizon is then $p_i + c_i$. The six-month total return for the three-bond portfolio whose initial portfolio value is $15 million is then:

$$\text{Total return} = \frac{(p_1 + c_1) + (p_2 + c_2) + (p_3 + c_3)}{\$15,000,000}$$

Doubling the total return gives an annualized total return on a bond equivalent yield basis.

Step 3. For those variables that are random variables, a probability distribution for each must be specified. In this case there are two random variables — the Treasury yield curve and the yield spread — and a probability distribution must be specified for both. Assume that the probability distributions for these two random variables are as shown in Exhibits 23-3 and 23-4. The coupon payment is a deterministic variable.

Step 4. For each random variable whose probability distribution must be specified, the probability distribution must be converted into a cumulative probability distribution. As we explain in Chapter 22, the cumulative probability of attaining a value less than or equal to a specified value is computed by summing the probabilities over the range of outcomes up to the specified value. The cumulative probability distribution for the two random variables in this case is shown in Exhibits 23-3 and 23-4.

Step 5. For each random variable, representative numbers must be assigned on the basis of the cumulative probability distribution to each possible outcome specified by the probability distribution. The representative numbers assigned for the two random variables in this case are shown in the last column of Exhibits 23-3 and 23-4.

Note that there are 100 assigned two-digit numbers ranging from 0 to 99. Each possible outcome (value for the random variable) is assigned enough numbers so that the ratio of the total numbers assigned to 100 will equal the probability of the outcome. For example, for the Treasury yield curve (the first random variable), the first yield curve outcome in Exhibit 23-3 is assigned numbers from 0 to 19. There are 20 numbers in the range of 0 to 19, so 20 of the 100 numbers, or 20%, are assigned to the first possible Treasury yield curve shape to equal its probability of 20%. A similar choice applies for the fifth possible Treasury yield curve, which also has a probability of 20%. Here the 20 numbers assigned are 55 to 74; the numbers 0 to 19 are not assigned to this outcome because they were assigned at the outset to the first Treasury yield curve.

Step 6: first trial. Obtain a random number for each random variable. We can obtain a random number for a random variable either from a random number table or by computer generation. Here we use the random number function available in LOTUS 123.

The first random number selected in steps 6 through 9 will be for the random variable representing the Treasury yield curve. The second will be for the random variable representing the quality spread. The second and sixth columns of Exhibit 23-5 indicate the random numbers for these two random variables. In the first trial, the first random number is 91, and the second random number is 12.

Step 7: first trial. For each random number, determine the corresponding value of the random variable. Given the random number of 91 for the Treasury yield curve and 12 for the quality spread, the corresponding outcome for the two random variables can be determined with the information in Exhibits 23-3 and 23-4. The Treasury yield curve in this trial would be:

5-year Treasury = 10%
15-year Treasury = 8%
25-year Treasury = 8%

The quality spread in this trial would be 100 basis points. Therefore, the horizon yield for the three bonds in this trial is:

5-year Treasury = 10%
15-year BBB corporate bond = 9%
25-year BBB corporate bond = 9%

Step 8: first trial. Use the corresponding value of each random variable found in the previous step to determine the value of the performance measure developed in step 1. The total future dollars from each bond for the first trial are shown in the eighth, ninth, and tenth columns in Exhibit 23-5. The next-to-last column shows the total future dollars for the portfolio, and the last column shows the total return percentage for the first trial.

Step 9: first trial. Record the value for the performance measure found in step 8. The value of the performance measure for the first trial is 10.16%.

Step 10: first trial. Repeat steps 6 through 9. Here we describe repeating steps 6 through 9 for only one more trial.

Step 6: second trial. Obtain a random number for each random variable. Exhibit 23-5 shows the next two random numbers to be generated are 64 and 18.

Step 7: second trial. For each random number, determine the corresponding value of the random variable. Given the random number of 64 for the Treasury yield curve and 18 for the quality spread, we can determine the corresponding outcome for the two random variables with the information in Exhibits 23-3 and 23-4. The Treasury yield curve in this trial would be:

> 5-year Treasury = 9%
> 15-year Treasury = 9%
> 25-year Treasury = 9%

The quality spread in this trial would be 100 basis points. Therefore, the horizon yield for the three bonds in this trial is:

> 5-year Treasury = 9%
> 15-year BBB corporate bond = 10%
> 25-year BBB corporate bond = 10%

Step 8: second trial. Use the corresponding value of each random variable found in the previous step to determine the value of the performance measure. Future dollars for the portfolio produce the value shown in the last column of Exhibit 23-5, .24%.

Step 9: second trial. Record the .24% value for the performance measure found in step 8.

Steps 6 through 9 are then repeated 98 more times. The results of the first 20 trials are shown in Exhibit 23-5.

Step 11. On the basis of the value for the performance measure for each trial recorded in step 9, construct a probability distribution and a cumulative probability distribution. From the results of the 100 trials shown in Exhibit 23-5, we construct the probability distribution for the total return according to some arbitrary intervals as shown in Exhibit 23-6. The mean and standard deviation are indicated at the bottom of the exhibit.

Step 12: Analyze the cumulative probability distribution constructed in step 11. Exhibit 23-6, indicates that the cumulative probability of realizing a negative total return is 19%.

Exhibit 23-5

Results of First 20 Trials for Total Return Simulation Illustration

Trial	Rand. no.	Treasury yield curve 5-yr	15-yr	25-yr	Rand. no.	Quality spread	5.5 yr. Treasury	15.5-yr. BBB corp.	25.5-yr. BBB corp.	Portfolio	Total return
1	91	10%	8%	8%	12	100	4,377,827	4,180,000	7,204,290	15,762,117	10.16%
2	64	9%	9%	9%	18	100	4,556,546	3,872,551	6,588,839	15,017,936	0.24
3	48	7%	8%	8%	54	125	4,942,085	4,099,740	7,041,255	16,083,079	14.44
4	44	6%	7%	7%	20	100	5,150,000	4,525,841	7,926,164	17,602,005	34.69
5	85	10%	8%	8%	84	175	4,377,827	3,946,091	6,733,821	15,057,738	0.77
6	10	4%	6%	7%	76	150	5,599,129	4,714,877	7,550,584	17,864,590	38.19
7	66	9%	9%	9%	53	125	4,556,546	3,801,105	6,449,317	14,806,968	-2.57
8	38	6%	7%	7%	64	150	5,150,000	4,347,790	7,550,584	17,048,374	27.31
9	42	6%	7%	7%	14	100	5,150,000	4,525,841	7,926,164	17,602,005	34.69
10	23	5%	8%	9%	81	175	5,368,802	3,946,091	6,185,646	15,500,539	6.67
11	61	9%	9%	9%	62	150	4,556,546	3,731,683	6,315,000	14,603,229	-5.29
12	90	10%	8%	8%	5	75	4,377,827	4,262,656	7,373,955	16,014,438	13.53
13	57	9%	9%	9%	51	125	4,556,546	3,801,105	6,449,317	14,806,968	-2.57
14	29	5%	8%	9%	49	125	5,368,802	4,099,740	6,449,317	15,917,858	12.24
15	6	4%	6%	7%	18	100	5,599,129	4,915,682	7,926,164	18,440,975	45.88
16	67	9%	9%	9%	81	175	4,556,546	3,664,220	6,185,646	14,406,412	-7.91
17	38	6%	7%	7%	40	125	5,150,000	4,435,489	7,734,529	17,320,018	30.93
18	42	6%	7%	7%	8	75	5,150,000	4,618,938	8,125,883	17,894,822	38.60
19	68	9%	9%	9%	86	175	4,556,546	3,664,220	6,185,646	14,406,412	-7.91
20	86	10%	8%	8%	71	150	4,377,827	4,021,796	6,884,531	15,284,154	3.79

Additional outcomes can be found using this information. A portfolio manager can determine, for example, the probability of realizing a total return greater than the six-month Treasury bill rate (on an annual basis). Suppose that the six-month Treasury bill yield (on an annual basis) is 4.99%. The probability of realizing a total return of 5% is equal to one minus the probability of realizing a total return less than 5%. From Exhibit 23-6, the probability is thus 65%.

Exhibit 23-6

Probability Distribution for Total Return Simulation Illustration

Range		Number	Probability	Cumulative Prob.
lower	upper	of Trialsr	Distribution	Distribution
-7.91%	-3.99%	11	11%	11%
-4.00	-0.01	8	8	19
0.00	2.99	12	12	31
3.00	4.99	4	4	35
5.00	6.99	6	6	41
7.00	9.99	6	6	47
10.00	14.99	19	19	66
15.00	19.99	7	7	73
20.00	24.99	1	1	74
25.00	29.99	2	2	76
30.00	34.99	5	5	81
35.00	39.99	3	3	84
40.00	44.99	7	7	91
45.00	49.94	9	9	100

Summary Statistics for Portfolio

	Total future dollars	Total return
Mean	$16,091,200	14.55%
Standard deviation	1,290,702	17.21
Minimum	14,406,412	-7.91
Maximum	18,745,770	49.94

Application to a Mortgage-Backed Securities Portfolio

In Part VI of this book, we discuss mortgage-backed securities and the complexities of valuing those securities. Simulation is one technique available to identify the potential performance of a portfolio of mortgage-backed securities. We provide two illustrations to demonstrate this application of simulation.

The first illustration is based on an example developed by Lakhbir Hayre, Charles Huang, and Vincent Pica to show assessment of the six-month performance (as measured by total return) of an interest-only (IO) trust under various yield curve scenarios.[2] The IO examined is FNMA Trust 2 based on closing prices on August 11, 1992. Simulation of the yield curve requires that assumptions be made about:

■ the volatility of short-term Treasury rates

■ the volatility of long-term Treasury rates

■ the correlation between the movement in short-term and long-term Treasury rates

The projection of prepayments and therefore the interest from the IO requires assumptions about:

■ a prepayment model

■ the relationship between long-term Treasury rates and mortgage rates

Finally, the total return calculation requires assumptions about the horizon price of the IO, which is based on an assumed option-adjusted spread. Chapter 18 explains how to use an OAS model to obtain a price consistent with an OAS.

The specific assumptions for this simulation are as follows:

■ the annual volatility (standard deviation) for the six-month Treasury bill rate is 15%

■ the annual volatility for the 10-year Treasury rate is 10%

■ the correlation between the six-month Treasury rate and the 10-year Treasury rate is 75%

■ mortgage rates and the 10-year Treasury rate move together

The prepayment model used is the Prudential Securities Inc. Prepayment Model.

Exhibit 23-7 shows possible six-month total returns on the basis of 2,000 randomly generated yield curves. The first four columns give information about the possible outcomes for the yield curve. The first column shows the probability of a particular yield curve (as defined by the yield on the six-month Treasury bill and the 10-year Treasury rate).

The center five columns show the results for the Trust 2 IO. The assumed OAS at the horizon is 939 basis points. The horizon balance is the percentage of the collateral outstanding after six months, given the yield curve. Note that the horizon balance is not sensitive to the change in the level or shape of the yield curve. The six-month total return

---

[2] Lakhbir Hayre, Charles Huang, and Vincent Pica, *Realistic Holding-Period Analysis: Technology and Its Impact on Valuation Metrics*, Study #14, Financial Strategies Group, Prudential Securities, August 13, 1992.

Exhibit 23-7   Six-Month Total Returns based on 2,000 Randomly Generated Yield Curves

	Trust 2 IO:	Current Price = 21-00		Current OAS = 939		Effective Duration = -12.2
	10-Year Treasury:	Current Price = 107-08				Effective Duration = 6.9

Initial Yield Curve (%):	6-Month 3.31	1-Year 3.42	2-Year 4.11	3-Year 4.66	5-Year 5.48	7-Year 5.97	10-Year 6.48	30-Year 7.33

Hedged Combination: $100 par value of Trust 2 IO, $34.70 Par Value of Ten-Year Treasury

Trust 2IO

Probability (%)	6-MonthTsy (%)	10-Year Tsy. (%)	10-Yr./6-Mo. Spread (%)	Assumed Horizon OAS (BPs.)	Horizon Price	Horizon Balance	% Price Gain	6-Mo. Total Return	Total Return on 10-Yr. Tsy (%)	Tot. Return on Zero-Duration Tsy./IO Combo
0.70	2.70	5.45	2.75	939	22.258	0.7235	-22.40	-3.52	21.05	12.19
3.00	2.78	5.76	2.98	939	23.254	0.7250	-19.78	1.67	16.83	11.36
3.40	2.83	6.12	3.29	939	24.496	0.7281	-15.23	10.69	12.10	11.59
0.80	2.84	6.46	3.62	939	26.035	0.7312	-9.61	21.81	7.77	12.83
0.15	3.07	5.48	2.40	939	21.920	0.7278	-24.00	-6.64	20.48	10.70
4.90	3.07	5.81	2.74	939	22.703	0.7264	-21.50	-1.69	15.93	9.57
14.65	3.12	6.14	3.02	939	23.673	0.7289	-17.93	5.39	11.61	9.37
16.40	3.15	6.49	3.34	939	25.016	0.7316	-13.04	15.07	7.18	10.03
3.85	3.22	6.85	3.63	939	26.406	0.7365	-7.69	25.68	2.71	10.99
0.25	3.25	7.19	3.94	939	27.911	0.7393	-2.15	36.62	-1.39	12.32
0.30	3.40	5.88	2.48	939	22.407	0.7261	-22.53	-3.70	14.78	8.11
5.45	3.42	6.19	2.77	939	23.300	0.7288	-19.20	2.89	10.74	7.91
17.00	3.49	6.54	3.05	939	24.507	0.7324	-14.69	11.85	6.31	8.37
11.85	3.51	6.89	3.38	939	25.916	0.7355	-9.50	22.12	2.01	9.27
3.45	3.55	7.23	3.68	939	27.362	0.7379	-4.22	32.55	-2.07	10.42
0.30	3.60	7.58	3.98	939	28.916	0.7423	1.73	44.34	-6.14	12.07
0.10	3.78	6.15	2.37	939	22.877	0.7260	-20.95	-0.56	10.97	6.81
2.30	3.84	6.59	2.75	939	24.366	0.7337	-15.02	11.23	5.43	7.52
4.55	3.87	6.91	3.04	939	25.599	0.7359	-10.53	20.11	1.51	8.22
3.55	3.89	7.26	3.37	939	27.070	0.7394	-5.04	30.98	-2.66	9.48
1.40	3.95	7.63	3.68	939	28.686	0.7440	1.16	43.25	-6.95	11.16
0.10	3.97	7.95	3.98	939	30.118	0.7454	6.34	53.46	-10.56	12.54
0.25	4.20	6.90	2.70	939	25.352	0.7342	-11.58	18.06	1.39	7.40
0.75	4.28	7.32	3.04	939	27.055	0.7404	-4.95	31.19	-3.62	8.94
0.50	4.32	7.70	3.38	939	28.713	0.7433	1.16	43.28	-7.98	10.51
0.05	4.49	8.26	3.77	939	30.999	0.7417	8.85	58.45	-14.26	11.97

Note: 1. Based on closing prices on August 11, 1992.
2. For the IO, the "%Price Gain" factors in the decline in the principal balance.

Source: Lakhbir Hayre, Charles Huang and Vincent Pica, *Realistic Holding-Period Analysis, Technology and Its Impact on Valuation Metrics: Study #14*, Financial Strategies Group, Prudential Securities, August 13, 1992, p. 3.

rate, shown in the last of the five columns reporting the outcome for the IO, varies from a low of –6.64% to a high of 58.45%. The average total return for the Trust 2 IO is 14.31%. The standard deviation is 10.10%, indicating the substantial risk associated with the position.

The next-to-last column shows the total return for a 10-year Treasury for each yield curve environment. The last column shows the total return of a portfolio consisting of the Trust 2 IO and 10-year Treasuries. The amount of each security in the portfolio is such that the initial portfolio duration is zero (i.e., the portfolio is hedged).

Summary statistics for the three portfolios are:

	Trust 2 IO	*10-year Treasury*	*Zero-duration combination*
Average total return	14.31%	6.70%	9.44%
Standard deviation	10.10%	5.54%	1.11%
Low total return	–6.64%	–14.26%	6.81%
High total return	58.45%	21.05%	12.83%

This simulation procedure allows assessment of the risks and rewards of the three portfolios. While the summary statistics clearly indicate that the Trust 2 IO and 10-year Treasury as stand-alone investments have considerable risk as measured by the standard deviation, the combination produces average total return below that of the Trust 2 IO but higher than the 10-year Treasury, at considerably reduced standard deviation (risk).

Our second illustration uses a real-world application provided by David Canuel of Aetna Bond Investors. The simulation involves assessing the potential performance of a current portfolio of discount and current coupon pass-throughs over a one-year investment horizon. The performance is compared to a similar portfolio after addition of an interest-only (IO) stripped MBS position equivalent to about 3.5% of the fund on a market value basis. The IO position is composed of three trusts backed by 8.5%, 9.0%, and 9.5% collateral.

Generating the total returns requires a set of techniques to (1) model a large number of interest rate paths over the one-year investment horizon, and (2) compare individual returns over the horizon. The modeling of interest rate paths uses historical data on interest rate volatilities and correlations between movements of different points along the yield curve. This is necessary in order to constrain the range of allowable rate levels and yield curve shapes.

Computation of total returns requires models for generating cash flows over the course of the horizon, an assumption on reinvestment of those cash flows to the end of the horizon, and a technique to compute the horizon price. The horizon price and intra-horizon cash flows are sensitive to interest rate levels. For the pass-throughs, a prepayment function must be specified. As in the previous illustration, the prepayment function is typically "path sensitive": prepayments reflect not only the present level of interest rates, but also the path that rates have followed over time. The total returns for individual securities are weighted and aggregated to compute total returns for portfolios of securities and synthetic securities.

Exhibit 23-8 shows the relative frequency for the current portfolio and the same portfolio with IOs added. Statistics for the return distributions are as follows:

Distribution	Current	3.5% IO
Mean	5.28%	6.41%
Standard deviation	1.27%	1.99%
Range	–0.90% to 8.63%	–3.56% to 10.07%

Adding the IOs to the current portfolio shifts the distribution to the right. As the mean for the distribution increases, the riskiness measured in terms of the standard deviation and range also increases. The longer "tail" to the left of the distribution in Exhibit 23-8 reflects the negative convexity of the IO position.

Exhibit 23-8

Simulation of Total Returns for Current Portfolio and Addition of IOs

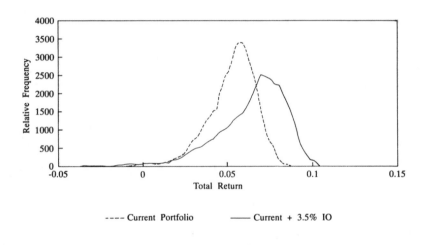

Summary

Simulation analysis is a valuable technique in fixed income portfolio management. Where there are a substantial number of random variables that will affect the total return of a portfolio, it is generally impractical to evaluate each possible outcome in order to determine the optimal solution or assess the risks associated with a portfolio. Simulation is more of a procedure than a model, and Monte Carlo simulation is a particular type of approach taking the probability distribution for each random variable into consideration.

24

Regression Analysis

Many applications in fixed income analysis require estimation of a relationship between two or more random variables. In cross-hedging applications, for example, the relationship between the yield on the instrument to be hedged and the instrument being used for hedging (a cash market instrument or a derivative security) must be estimated. Evaluation of mortgage-backed securities requires projection of prepayments. A prepayment model requires an analysis of the relationship between prepayment rates and the variables expected to affect prepayments.

This chapter shows how *regression analysis* can be used to estimate relationships between variables. An illustration clarifies the application.

The Simple Linear Regression Model

Suppose that a portfolio manager wants to estimate the relationship between the yield on new single-A rated medium-term industrial bonds and the yield on 10-year Treasuries. Assume that the portfolio manager believes the industrial/Treasury yield relationship can be expressed as:

$$\text{Industrial yield} = a + b \text{ (Treasury yield)}$$

If the values for *a* and *b* can be estimated, the portfolio manager can use the industrial/Treasury yield relationship to estimate the yield on new single-A rated medium-term industrial bonds for a given yield level of 10-year Treasuries. The values *a* and *b* are called the *parameters* of the model, and the objective of regression analysis is to estimate the parameters.

There are several points to understand about this relationship. First, there are only two variables in the relationship — the yield on new single-A rate medium-term industrials and the yield on 10-year Treasuries. Because there are only two variables and the relationship is linear, the regression model is called a *simple linear regression*. Because the yield on the industrials is assumed to depend on the yield on 10-year Treasuries, the former variable is referred to as the *dependent* variable. The yield on 10-year Treasuries is referred to as the *explanatory* or *independent* variable because it is what is taken to explain the yield on the industrial bonds. When there is more than one explanatory or independent variable, the regression model is called a *multiple regression model*.

Second, it is highly unlikely that the estimated industrial/Treasury yield relationship above will describe the true relationship between the two yields exactly, because other factors besides the level of 10-year Treasuries may influence the yield on new single-A rated medium-term industrial bonds. Consequently, this industrial/Treasury yield relationship may be described more accurately by adding a random error term to the relationship. That is, the industrial/Treasury yield relationship can be expressed as:

Industrial yield = *a* + *b* (Treasury yield) + Random error term

The expression can be simplified as follows:

$Y = a + bX + e$

where

Y = Yield on new single-A medium-term industrial bonds
X = Yield on 10-year Treasuries
e = Random error term

This expression is referred to as the *simple linear regression model*.

Procedure for Estimating the Parameters of the Simple Linear Regression

In order to estimate the parameters of the simple linear regression model, historical information is needed on the yield on new single-A rated medium-term industrial bonds and the yield on 10-year Treasuries. The third and fourth columns in Exhibit 24-1 give the yields for 45 months beginning on 11/30/88 and ending on 7/31/92.[1] Each pair of values for the two variables X and Y is referred to as an *observation*. The 45 observations shown

---

[1] The data are provided by Ardavan Nozari of Salomon Brothers Inc.

Exhibit 24-1

Worksheet for the Estimation of the Parameters of the Simple Linear Regression: Industrial/Corporate Yield Relationship

Date	Obser. *t*	Yield on Treasury *X*	Yield on Industrial *Y*	*XY*	X^2	Y^2
11/30/88	1	9.057%	9.900%	89.6643	82.0292	98.0100
12/30/88	2	9.140	10.000	91.4000	83.5396	100.0000
1/31/89	3	8.983	9.800	88.0334	80.6943	96.0400
2/28/89	4	9.298	10.250	95.3045	86.4528	105.0625
3/31/89	5	9.279	10.100	93.7179	86.0998	102.0100
4/28/89	6	9.057	9.950	90.1172	82.0292	99.0025
5/31/89	7	8.598	9.550	82.1109	73.9256	91.2025
6/30/89	8	8.079	9.000	72.7110	65.2702	81.0000
7/31/89	9	7.808	8.700	67.9296	60.9649	75.6900
8/31/89	10	8.256	9.150	75.5424	68.1615	83.7225
9/29/89	11	8.298	9.250	76.7565	68.8568	85.5625
10/31/89	12	7.913	9.000	71.2170	62.6156	81.0000
11/30/89	13	7.833	8.950	70.1054	61.3559	80.1025
12/29/89	14	7.924	9.100	72.1084	62.7898	82.8100
1/31/90	15	8.418	9.380	78.9608	70.8627	87.9844
2/28/90	16	8.518	9.550	81.3469	72.5563	91.2025
3/30/90	17	8.636	9.650	83.3374	74.5805	93.1225
4/30/90	18	9.028	10.050	90.7314	81.5048	101.0025
5/31/90	19	8.599	9.550	82.1205	73.9428	91.2025
6/29/90	20	8.414	9.400	79.0916	70.7954	88.3600
7/31/90	21	8.341	9.200	76.7372	69.5723	84.6400
8/31/90	22	8.854	9.875	87.4333	78.3933	97.5156
9/28/90	23	8.800	10.000	88.0000	77.4400	100.0000
10/31/90	24	8.620	9.850	84.9070	74.3044	97.0225
11/30/90	25	8.252	9.500	78.3940	68.0955	90.2500
12/31/90	26	8.069	9.350	75.4452	65.1088	87.4225
1/31/91	27	8.011	9.200	73.7012	64.1761	84.6400
2/28/91	28	8.036	9.100	73.1276	64.5773	82.8100
3/28/91	29	8.059	9.050	72.9340	64.9475	81.9025
4/30/91	30	8.013	8.900	71.3157	64.2082	79.2100
5/31/91	31	8.059	8.875	71.5236	64.9475	78.7656
6/28/91	32	8.227	9.050	74.4544	67.6835	81.9025
7/31/91	33	8.147	9.000	73.3230	66.3736	81.0000
8/30/91	34	7.814	8.600	67.2004	61.0586	73.9600
9/30/91	35	7.448	8.250	61.4460	55.4727	68.0625

Exhibit 24-1 continued.

10/31/91	36	7.462	8.250	61.5615	55.6814	68.0625
11/29/91	37	7.378	8.125	59.9463	54.4349	66.0156
12/31/91	38	6.700	7.600	50.9200	44.8900	57.7600
1/31/91	39	7.281	8.000	58.2480	53.0130	64.0000
2/28/92	40	7.257	8.050	58.4189	52.6640	64.8025
3/31/92	41	7.530	8.230	61.9719	56.7009	67.7329
4/30/92	42	7.583	8.300	62.9389	57.5019	68.8900
5/29/92	43	7.325	8.000	58.6000	53.6556	64.0000
6/30/92	44	7.123	7.750	55.2033	50.7371	60.0625
7/31/92	45	6.709	7.300	48.9757	45.0107	53.2900
Total		366.234	407.685	3,339.0338	2,999.6767	3,717.8092

in Exhibit 24-1 that are used to estimate the regression are plotted in Exhibit 24-2. When observations are plotted in this fashion, the resulting graph is called a *scatter diagram*.

Exhibit 24-2

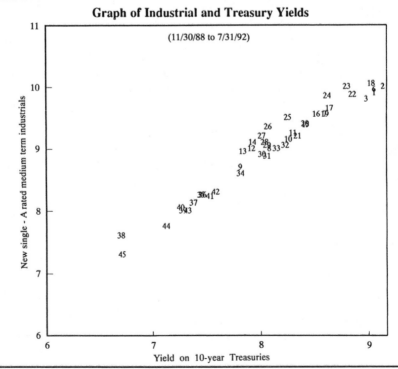

Graph of Industrial and Treasury Yields

(11/30/88 to 7/31/92)

One way to estimate the industrial/Treasury yield relationship is simply to draw a line through the observations that an observer believes best represent the relationship. Then two points on this line can be used to estimate the relationship. This method, sometimes referred to as the *free-hand method*, is a poor procedure for estimating a relationship. The obvious drawback is that there is no specified criterion for drawing the line; different observers are likely to obtain different estimates of the relationship from the same observations.

Another approach is the *high-low method*, where the two extreme observations for the explanatory variables are selected. These two points are then the basis for the line used to estimate the relationship. This is also a poor procedure, because it ignores all the other observations.

The *regression method*, unlike the free-hand method and the high-low method, does specify a logical criterion for estimating the relationship. To explain this criterion, we first rewrite the simple linear regression so that it shows the estimated relationship for each observation:

$$Y_t = a + bX_t + e_t$$

where the subscript t denotes the observation for the tth month. For example, for the third observation ($t = 3$), the expression becomes

$$9.800 = a + b\,(8.983) + e_3$$

For the sixth observation ($t = 6$), the expression is

$$9.950 = a + b\,(9.057) + e_6$$

The values for e_3 and e_6 are referred to as the *observed error term for the observation*. Note that the value of the observed error term for both observations will depend on the values selected for a and b. This suggests a criterion for selecting the two parameters: the parameters should be estimated so that the sum of the observed error terms for all observations is as small as possible.

Although this is a good standard, it presents one problem. Some observed error terms will be positive, and others will be negative. Consequently, positive and negative observed error terms will offset each other. To overcome this problem, each error term could be squared. On the basis of that criterion, the objective would then be to select parameters so as to minimize the sum of the square of the observed error terms. This is precisely the criterion used to estimate the parameters in regression analysis. Because of this property, regression analysis is sometimes referred to as the *method of least squares*.

This criterion is portrayed graphically in Exhibit 24-3, a generic scatter diagram with an estimated regression line drawn. Consider point L in Exhibit 24-3, which represents a specific observation. If a line is dropped from point L to the X axis at point N, then the observed value for Y is LN, and the estimated value of Y based on the estimated line is MN. The observed error term is the difference between the observed value for Y and the estimated value for Y. In Exhibit 24-3, the difference is the vertical difference LM.

The estimated line in Exhibit 24-3 overestimates the observed Y for all observed values below the line and underestimates all observed points above the estimated line. Squaring the observed error term removes the possibility that the underestimates and

Exhibit 24-3

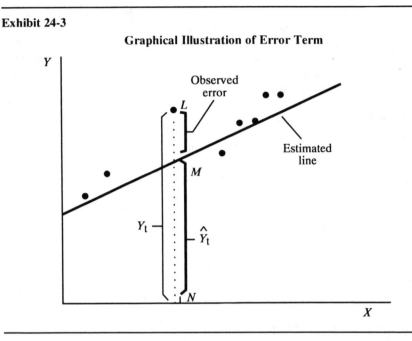

Graphical Illustration of Error Term

overestimates will offset each other. By squaring and summing the observed errors this cannot occur.

The objective in estimation of the regression line is to select a value for the parameters — a and b — so as to minimize the sum of the squares of the observed error terms. The formulas used to estimate the parameters on the basis of this criterion are derived using calculus.

If a hat ($\wedge$) over the parameter denotes the estimated value, and T denotes the total number of observations, the estimated parameters for a and b are computed from the observations using the formulas:

$$\hat{b} = \frac{\sum\limits_{t=1}^{T} X_t Y_t - \frac{1}{T}\sum\limits_{t=1}^{T} X_t \sum\limits_{t=1}^{T} Y_t}{\sum\limits_{t=1}^{T} X_t^2 - \frac{1}{T}\left(\sum\limits_{t=1}^{T} X_t\right)^2}$$

and

$$\hat{a} = \frac{1}{T}\sum\limits_{t=1}^{T} Y_t - \frac{1}{T}(\hat{b})\sum\limits_{t=1}^{T} X_t$$

where the Greek letter $\sum$ means to sum over the subscripted values.

Although the formulas may look complicated, they are easy to apply in practice. For actual problems with a large number of observations, we can use regression analysis programs that compute the value of the parameters using the appropriate formulas. Most electronic spread sheets are preprogrammed to perform simple linear regression analysis.

We can use the formulas to compute the estimated parameters on the basis of the observations given in Exhibit 24-1. The worksheet for the sums needed to apply the formula is shown as Exhibit 24-1 and summarized below.

$$\sum_{t=1}^{45} X_t = 366.234 \quad \sum_{t=1}^{45} Y_t = 407.685$$

$$\sum_{t=1}^{45} X_t Y_t = 3,339.0338 \quad \sum_{t=1}^{45} X_t^2 = 2,999.6767$$

Substituting into the formula for $\hat{b}$

$$\hat{b} = \frac{3,339.0338 - \dfrac{1}{45}(366.234)(407.685)}{2,999.6767 - \dfrac{1}{45}(366.234)^2}$$

$$= \frac{3,339.0338 - 3,317.9579}{2,999.6767 - 2,980.6076} = 1.1052$$

Substituting into the formula for $\hat{a}$

$$\hat{a} = \frac{1}{45}(407.685) - \frac{1}{45}(1.1052)(366.234)$$

$$= .0649$$

The industrial/Treasury yield relationship is then

$$Y = .0649 + 1.1052\,X$$

Goodness of Fit of the Relationship

A portfolio manager will want to know how "good" an estimated relationship is before relying on it for any investment strategy, so statistical tests are needed to determine in some sense how good the relationship is between the dependent variable and the explanatory variable. A measure of the "goodness of fit" of the relationship is the *coefficient of determination*.

Exhibit 24-4 demonstrates the meaning and measurement of the coefficient of determination. We know that the explanatory or independent variable X is being used to try

Exhibit 24-4

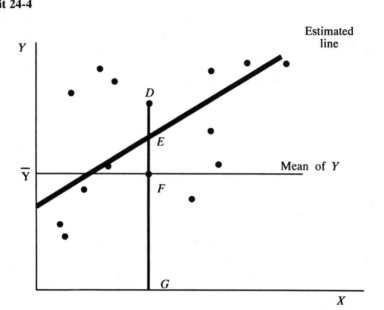

to explain movements in the dependent variable Y. That is, the variable X is trying to explain why the variable Y would deviate from its mean. If no explanatory variable is used to try to explain movements in Y, the method of least squares would give the mean of Y as its value estimate. Thus the ability of X to explain deviations of Y from its mean is the factor of interest.

In Exhibit 24-4, the observed value of Y at point D deviates from the mean of Y as measured by the vertical distance DF. It is the deviation of Y from its mean, i.e., DF, that the variable X must explain. This DF difference is made up of two components. The first component is EF, which is the difference between the value estimated by the regression line and the mean value of Y. This distance is the amount of the deviation from the mean of Y explained by X or, equivalently, explained by the regression line.

The second component is DE, which is the deviation of Y from its mean that is still unexplained. Consequently, the deviation of the observed Y from the mean of Y can be expressed as follows:

$$DF = EF + DE$$

where

DF = The deviation of the observed Y from the mean of Y

EF = The amount of the deviation of the observed Y from the mean of Y explained by X

DE = The amount of the deviation of Y from the mean of Y still unexplained

If the deviations of the observed Y from the mean of Y are squared and all these deviations are summed, for each observation the resulting value indicates the total deviations of the observed Y from the mean of Y. This is referred to as the *total sum of squares*. The second component is the deviations of the observed Y from the mean of Y that are still unexplained. This component is referred to as the *unexplained sum of squares*. Thus,

Total sum of squares =

Explained sum of squares + Unexplained sum of squares

How much of the total sum of squares is explained by X is the factor of interest. One way, therefore, to measure how good the relationship is is to determine what percent of the total sum of squares is explained by X. That is, how good the relationship is can be measured by dividing the explained sum of squares by the total sum of squares. This ratio is the *coefficient of determination*:

$$\text{Coefficient of determination} = \frac{\text{Explained sum of squares}}{\text{Total sum of squares}}$$

The coefficient of determination can take on a value between 0 and 1. If the total sum of squares is fully explained by X, the coefficient of determination is 1. When none of the total sum of squares is explained by X, the coefficient of determination is 0. Hence, the closer the coefficient of determination is to 1, the stronger the relationship between the variables.

Another interpretation of the coefficient of determination is that it measures how close the observed points are to the regression line. The nearer the observed points are to the regression line, the closer the coefficient of determination will be to 1. The farther the scatter of the observed points from the regression line, the closer the coefficient of determination will be to 0.

The coefficient of determination is commonly referred to as "R-squared" denoted by R^2. Computation of the coefficient of determination proceeds as follows: The total sum of squares is computed as:

$$\text{Total sum of squares} = \sum_{t=1}^{T} Y_t^2 - \frac{1}{T}\left(\sum_{t=1}^{T} Y_t\right)^2$$

The explained sum of squares is computed as:

$$\text{Explained sum of squares} = \hat{b}\left(\sum_{t=1}^{T} X_t Y_t - \frac{1}{T}\sum_{t=1}^{T} X_t \sum_{t=1}^{T} Y_t\right)$$

The coefficient of determination is then found by dividing the explained sum of squares by the total sum of squares.

From the worksheet shown as Exhibit 24-1,

$$\sum_{t=1}^{45} Y_t = 407.685 \quad \sum_{t=1}^{45} X_t = 366.234$$

$$\sum_{t=1}^{45} X_t Y_t = 3,339.0338 \quad \sum_{t=1}^{45} Y_t^2 = 3,717.8092$$

then

$$\text{Total sum of squares} = 3,717.8092 - \frac{1}{45}(407.685)^2$$
$$= 24.3191$$

and

Explained sum of squares

$$= (1.1052)[3,339.0338 - \frac{1}{45}(366.234)(407.685)]$$
$$= 23.2931$$

The coefficient of determination is therefore

$$\text{Coefficient of determination} = \frac{23.2931}{24.3191} = .96$$

A coefficient of determination of .96 indicates that approximately 96% of the total variation in the yield on new single-A medium-term industrial bonds is explained by the yield on 10-year Treasuries.

A warning is in order on the topic of the coefficient of determination. A coefficient of determination close to 0 does not necessarily imply that there is no relationship between the two variables. There may in fact be a strong relationship, but it will not be a linear relationship.

Correlation Coefficient and Covariance

The coefficient of determination is related to the correlation coefficient, which measures the association between two variables. No cause and effect are assumed in calculation of a correlation coefficient, so there is no assumption about which of two variables is the dependent variable and which is the explanatory variable. This is different from regression analysis, which assumes one variable is dependent on the other.

The coefficient of determination turns out to be equal to the square of the correlation coefficient. Thus, the square root of the coefficient of determination is the correlation coefficient. As the coefficient of determination can be between 0 and 1, the correlation coefficient will be between −1 and 1. The sign of the correlation coefficient is the same as the sign of the slope of the regression, b. In our illustration, because the coefficient of determination is .96, the correlation coefficient is .98.

The covariance measures how the two random variables vary together. It is related to the correlation coefficient as follows:

covariance = (std. of X) (std. of Y) (correlation coefficient)

where

std. = standard deviation

Standard Error of Estimate and Confidence Interval for Forecasted Value

Knowing how to assess the strength of the relationship between two variables, we can now show how to use the estimated regression model to obtain a forecasted value for the dependent variable Y. Continuing estimation of the relationship between the yield on 10-year Treasuries (X) and the yield on new single-A rated medium-term industrial bonds (Y), suppose that the portfolio manager believes that the yield on 10-year Treasuries next month will be 7%. X is therefore 7. The forecasted yield for new single-A rated medium-term industrial bonds (Y) is:

$$Y = .0649 + 1.1052 (7) = 7.801$$

The forecasted value of 7.801% is known as a *point estimate*, because only one value is forecasted. In practice, a portfolio manager would want a range for the dependent variable, along with a probability that the actual value will fall within the range. To accomplish this, it is necessary first to compute the *standard error of the estimate*, which is another measure of how good the regression relationship is. Three steps are required:

Step 1: Compute the unexplained sum of squares, which is just the total sum of squares that is not explained by the regression. The unexplained sum of squares is found as follows:

Unexplained sum of squares =
Total sum of squares – Explained sum of squares

Step 2: Divide the unexplained sum of squares by the number of observations minus 2. That is, if T represents the number of observations, then compute

$$\frac{\text{Unexplained sum of squares}}{T - 2}$$

Step 3: Take the square root of the quantity found in step 2 to get the standard error of the estimate.

According to the data for the regression estimated earlier:

Step 1: The total sum of squares is 24.3191 and the explained sum of squares is 23.2931, so the unexplained sum of squares is 1.026.

Step 2: There are 45 observations, so the unexplained sum of squares is divided by 43 to give .0239.

Step 3: The square root of .0239 is .1546.

Note that the larger the unexplained sum of squares, the greater the standard error of the estimate. Recall that the larger the unexplained sum of squares, the lower the coefficient of determination, which measures the goodness of fit of the regression relationship. Thus, the greater the standard error of the estimate, the poorer the regression relationship.

Once the standard error of the estimate is found, a range or interval estimate for a forecasted value of Y can be computed, given a value for the explanatory variable X, and a probability can be assigned that the actual value for Y will fall within the range or interval. The interval computed is known as a *confidence interval*, and the probability assigned to this interval is called a *confidence coefficient*.

To compute a confidence interval, nine steps are necessary:[2]

Step 1: Find the difference between the value for the explanatory variable X and the average value for X.

Step 2: Square the value in step 1.

Step 3: Divide the amount in step 2 by the value in the denominator of the formula used to find $\hat{b}$.

Step 4: Add to the amount in step 3 the value $1/T$.

Step 5: Take the square root of the amount in step 4.

Step 6: Multiply the amount in step 5 by the value below that corresponds to the confidence level selected:[3]

Confidence Level	Multiply by this
99%	2.57
95%	1.96
90%	1.65

Step 7: Multiply the amount in step 6 by the standard error of the estimate.

Step 8: Add the amount in step 7 to the forecasted value for Y to obtain the upper range of the confidence interval.

---

[2] This formula is given in J. Johnston, *Econometric Methods*, New York: McGraw-Hill, 1972, p. 41.

[3] These values are obtained from a normal distribution explained in the previous chapter. Technically, the values given above apply when there are at least 32 observations. For a smaller number of observations used to estimate the regression model, the values to be used are larger.

Step 9:   Subtract the amount in step 7 from the forecasted value for Y to obtain the lower range of the confidence interval.

To illustrate this process, we construct a confidence interval with a 95% confidence level for the industrial/Treasury yield relationship, assuming that the yield on 10-year Treasuries is expected to be 7%.

Step 1:   Find the difference between the value for the explanatory variable X of 7% and the average value for X of 8.135%. The difference is 1.135%.

Step 2:   Squaring 1.135% gives 1.2882.

Step 3:   The denominator of the formula used to find $\hat{b}$ is

$$3,339.0338 - \frac{1}{45}(366.234)(407.685) = 21.0759$$

Dividing 1.2882 by 21.0759 gives .0611.

Step 4:   Adding .0222 (1 divided by the number of observations, 45) to .0611 gives .0833.

Step 5:   The square root of .0833 is .2886.

Step 6:   As the confidence level is 95%, multiply .2886 by 1.96. The result is .5657.

Step 7:   Multiplying .5657 by the standard error of the estimate, .1546, gives .088.

Step 8:   The forecasted value of Y found earlier is 7.801. Adding .088 to 7.801 gives 7.889%, which is the upper limit of the confidence interval.

Step 9:   Subtracting .088 from 7.801 gives 7.713%, which is the lower limit of the confidence interval.

Thus a confidence interval for a 95% confidence level is 7.713% to 7.801%. This means there is a 95% probability that the yield on a new single-A rated medium-term industrial bond will be within this interval if the yield on 10-year Treasuries is 7%.

Extension of the Simple Linear Regression Model

In many applications, a dependent variable is best explained by more than one explanatory variable. Estimation of such a relationship is referred to as a *multiple regression*. The parameters of a multiple regression are difficult to compute by hand, but there are numerous commercial multiple regression analysis programs available for estimation.

Interpretation of the coefficient of determination is much the same for multiple regression as in simple linear regression. In the latter case, it is the total sum of squares explained by the explanatory variable X. In multiple regression, the coefficient of determination is the total sum of squares explained by all the explanatory variables. By adding an explanatory variable to a regression model, the belief is that the new explanatory variable will increase the explained sum of squares significantly.

For example, suppose that a simple linear regression is estimated, and that the total sum of squares is 1,000 and the explained sum of squares is 600. Suppose that another explanatory variable is added to the regression model, and that inclusion of this explanatory variable increases the explained sum of squares from 600 to 750. Thus, the coefficient of determination would rise from 60% to 75% (750/1,000). This new explanatory variable would appear to have contributed substantially to explaining the variation in the dependent variable. Had the explained sum of squares increased from 600 to 610, the coefficient of determination would increase from 60% to only 61%, in which case the new explanatory variable would not appear to do much to help explain the dependent variable.

To estimate a relationship, it is not necessary to restrict selection of explanatory variables to quantitative variables, that is, a variable that can be expressed numerically. Qualitative variables, those expressed by a nonnumerical property, can also be used. Suppose that the portfolio manager believes that the industrial/Treasury yield relationship differs in times of economic recession and of economic prosperity. Such an hypothesis can be tested by using a qualitative variable as follows. If the observation occurs in a period of economic recession, the value for the variable for the observation is equal to 1. If the observation occurs in a period of economic prosperity, the value for the variable for the observation is equal to 0. A qualitative variable used in regression analysis is commonly referred to as a *dummy variable*. In general, a dummy variable takes on a value of 1 if the observation has the attribute assumed by the qualitative variable, and a value of 0 otherwise.

We have discussed regression analysis in the form of simple linear regression analysis. A simple linear regression model takes the general form:

$$Y = a + bX + e$$

Consider the following relationship to be estimated using regression analysis:

$$Y = a + bZ^2 + e$$

Is the above relationship a simple linear regression model? If we let the variable X equal Z^2, then the relationship can be rewritten as $Y = a + bX + e$. This relationship is expressed in the same format as the simple linear regression model, and the parameters can be estimated using the formulas presented so far.

Consider next the equation:

$$V = cZ^b$$

Can this equation be converted into a simple linear regression model? The answer is that it can. If logarithms are taken of both sides of the equation, and an error term is added, the equation can be rewritten as

$$\log V = \log c + b \log Z + \text{Error term}$$

If we let Y equal $\log V$, X equal $\log Z$, and a equal $\log c$, then the relationship can be expressed in the format of a simple linear regression. The estimated value of b and a

can be obtained using regression analysis. To obtain the estimate of c, the antilog of a can be calculated.

Statistical Significance of Relationships

Statistical tests indicate whether a relationship estimated using regression analysis is statistically significant. There are also tests to determine whether an increase in the explained sum of squares attributable to the inclusion of an additional explanatory variable is statistically significant. Such tests are described in textbooks on regression analysis.[4]

Many statistical problems arise in estimating relationships through regression analysis. Some have to do with the assumptions underlying the regression model. Potential problems include *multicollinearity, autocorrelation,* and *heteroscedasticity.* Multicollinearity means that the explanatory variables themselves are highly correlated, so it becomes difficult to identify how a particular explanatory variable affects the dependent variable. Autocorrelation and heteroscedasticity have to do with the error term. It is assumed that (1) the error terms will be uncorrelated from observation to observation, and (2) the variance of the error term will be constant for all observations. Violation of the first assumption is referred to as autocorrelation; violation of the second assumption is referred to as heteroscedasticity.

Summary

Regression analysis is a technique for estimation of the relationship between variables. A simple linear regression includes one explanatory variable and a dependent variable. A multiple regression includes more than one explanatory variable. The method of least squares is used to estimate the parameters of the relationship.

The coefficient of determination is a measure of the goodness of fit of the linear relationship. The coefficient of determination is the ratio of the explained sum of squares to the total sum of squares, and consequently varies between 0 and 1. The larger the coefficient of determination, the better the relationship. The square root of the coefficient of determination is related to the correlation coefficient.

An estimated relationship can be used to forecast a value for the dependent variable. Either a point estimate or a confidence interval can be obtained.

---

[4] See, for example, J. Johnston, *ibid.*

25

Optimization Models

An optimization model prescribes the best course of action to be pursued in order to achieve an objective. The optimization models used in most fixed income portfolio management applications are mathematical programming models. We describe in this chapter how optimization models can be used in fixed income portfolio management, without delving into the nuances of these models or the algorithms for solving a mathematical programming problem. Any real-world problem confronting a portfolio manager will be complex enough to require the use of commercially available software to solve.

Optimization models are commonly used in structured portfolio strategies, which do not rely on expectations of interest rate movements or changes in yield spreads. Instead the objective is design of an optimal portfolio that will achieve the performance of a predetermined benchmark. The target could be: (1) the return on a specific benchmark index; (2) sufficient dollars to satisfy a future single liability; or (3) sufficient dollars to satisfy each liability of a future liability stream. The structured bond portfolio strategy used when the target to be achieved is replication of a predetermined benchmark index is called an *indexing strategy*. When the objective is to generate sufficient funds to pay off predetermined future liabilities, the strategy is called a *liability funding strategy*. Optimization models are also used in making asset allocation decisions (i.e., decisions on allocation of funds among major asset classes).

Mathematical Programming

Mathematical programming models are used to solve problems that involve the allocation of limited resources so as to optimize a quantitative goal. An allocation problem assumes there are many acceptable solutions that satisfy the decision maker's constraints or restrictions, but that there may be one best solution that optimizes the value of the specified goal.

Setting Up a Mathematical Programming Model

There are four steps in setting up a mathematical programming or optimization problem.

Step 1. Define the variables on which a decision must be made. These variables are called *decision variables*. In a structured portfolio problem, the decision variables are typically the amount of a security that should be purchased or sold. In an asset allocation problem, the decision variables are the amounts to be allocated to each major asset class.

Step 2. Specify mathematically the objective the decision maker seeks to optimize. This mathematical expression is called the *objective function*. The linear or nonlinear nature of the objective function is what distinguishes the different types of mathematical programming models.

Step 3. Specify mathematically the constraints under which the objective function is to be optimized. One constraint, for example, might be that the portfolio's duration be equal to 4. Or a constraint may specify that the amount allocated to one sector of the market may not exceed a certain percentage of the portfolio, or that the minimum amount allocated to liquid assets be a specified percentage. As with the objective function, the mathematical characterization of the constraints determines the type of mathematical programming problem.

Step 4. Solve for the optimal solution.

Types of Mathematical Programming Models

The most common types of mathematical programming models include: (1) linear programming; (2) mixed integer programming; (3) quadratic programming; (4) dynamic programming; and (5) goal programming.

Linear Programming

The objective function and all the constraints in a linear programming problem are linear. For example, a structured portfolio strategy may call for construction of a portfolio to satisfy a liability or set of liabilities at a minimum cost. Suppose that the acceptable universe of bonds is 500 issues made up of Treasuries, agencies, and all investment-grade corporate bonds. The decision variables are the percentage of the portfolio to be invested in an issue. There are then 500 decision variables, one representing each of the acceptable issues in the universe.

Let

w_i = the par amount to purchase of a particular issue ($i = 1, 2, \ldots ,500$), and

p_i = the price of issue i (as a percent of par value, e.g., .90, 1.00, 1.05).

Then the total cost of the portfolio is:

$$w_1 p_1 + w_2 p_2 + \ldots + w_{500} p_{500}$$

This expression represents the objective function. The objective function is linear, and the portfolio manager would seek to minimize the objective function subject to the constraints imposed.

Two examples of a linear constraint would be that a minimum of $10 million of the portfolio must be invested in Treasury issues, and that no more than $15 million may be invested in BBB-rated corporate bonds. Mathematically, assuming that issues 1, 2, . . . , 150 are the Treasury issues, the first constraint can be expressed as follows:

$$w_1 p_1 + w_2 p_2 + \ldots + w_{150} p_{150} \geq \$10,000,000$$

Assuming that issues 425 to 500 are triple-B rated corporate bonds, the second constraint can be expressed mathematically as follows:

$$w_{425} p_{425} + w_{426} p_{426} + \ldots + w_{500} p_{500} \leq \$15,000,000$$

One common linear constraint in structured portfolio strategies is a restriction on portfolio duration. For example, an immunization strategy (discussed in Chapter 12) would constrain portfolio duration to match the duration of the liability. Assuming no short selling, all the decision variables are then constrained to be greater than or equal to zero.

Mixed Integer Programming

Linear programming assumes that the decision variables are divisible and result in whole numbers. Suppose an automobile manufacturer uses a linear programming model to determine the optimal number of various car models to produce, given its resources (capital and labor). The solution might indicate that 555.6 of one type of car be produced and 442.7 of another type. So, is producing 556 of Model A and 443 of Model T the optimal solution? In fact, (1) the modified (rounded) optimal solution may no longer satisfy all the constraints, or (2) there may be another solution that is better than the modified optimal solution. To handle this type of problem, mixed integer programming is used.

Integer programming restricts the decision variables to take on integer values. Integer programming is used in structured portfolio applications when transaction sizes in round lots are sought, or where one of two issues but not both may be part of the optimal solution.

Quadratic Programming

The restriction imposed in employing linear programming is that both the objective function and the constraints be linear. It is common in structured portfolio strategies and asset allocation models, however, to have a quadratic objective function. For example, a common objective in constructing an indexed portfolio is to minimize tracking error. Tracking error is measured by the variance of the indexed portfolio's return from the benchmark (i.e., index) return. Solving this problem requires the use of a mathematical programming model that permits a quadratic objective function. In the case of asset allocation models, the objective is to allocate funds among asset classes to minimize portfolio risk. Portfolio risk is measured by the variance of the portfolio, which is expressed mathematically as a quadratic expression.

Linear programming is inappropriate in these applications. A special type of mathematical programming called quadratic programming does permit a quadratic objective function. Quadratic programming also permits the constraints to be a nonlinear expression.

Dynamic Programming

The mathematical programming models discussed so far deal with solving problems involving a single decision time. Dynamic programming is a mathematical programming model for solving sequential problems where parameters of the model vary from period to period. Although dynamic programming is more powerful than the other models discussed, its computational requirements are very involved and time-consuming, even for small-sized problems.

Goal Programming

A problem with the mathematical programming models discussed above is that they do not permit consideration of multiple objectives. That is, these mathematical programming models can find the optimal solution when a single objective is specified, but for multiple and perhaps conflicting objectives, a special type of mathematical programming model is needed. Goal programming calls for goals instead of constraints. That is, each constraint is expressed as a goal with a priority level specified in ordinal terms. Within a given priority level, there may be several goals.

While goal programming represents a potentially powerful technique for finding optimal solutions to fixed income portfolio management problems, no applications have been reported at the time of this writing.

Applications

Mathematical programming has been used to provide solutions for many types of fixed income portfolio problems, including immunization, dedicated portfolio strategies, indexing, optimized rebalancing, and asset allocation.

Immunization

Immunization is a structured portfolio strategy designed to protect against interest rate changes. A single-period immunization addresses one future liability when the objective is to construct a portfolio to minimize the risk that changes in interest rates will result in not satisfying the objective. Life insurance companies use single-period immunization in managing portfolios to satisfy their obligations of guaranteed investment contracts. A requirement for single-period immunization is that the duration of the portfolio be equal to the maturity of the liability.

Multi-period immunization is used in the case of more than one future liability. Examples of multiple liabilities are liabilities of a pension fund, liabilities of annuity policies issued by life insurance companies, and liabilities resulting from a state-sponsored lottery. Once again, the objective is to construct a minimum-cost portfolio designed to satisfy all the liabilities, however interest rates change. Two requirements of multi-period immunization are that (1) the duration of the portfolio be equal to the duration of the liabilities, and (2) the convexity of the portfolio be greater than or equal to the convexity of the liabilities.

Dedicated Portfolio Strategies

A dedicated portfolio strategy involves construction of a portfolio to satisfy multiple liabilities but without duration or convexity requirements. Instead, a minimum-cost portfolio is constructed so that the portfolio's cash flow matches as closely as possible the amount and the times when the liabilities must be paid. A dedicated portfolio strategy therefore is also referred to as a *cash flow matching strategy*.

A popular variation of the immunization and dedicated portfolio strategies is a *combination strategy*, also called a *horizon-matching strategy*. Here a portfolio is duration-matched, with the added constraint that it be cash-matched in the first few years, usually five years. The advantages of combination matching over immunization are that liquidity needs are provided for in the initial cash flow-matched period. Because most of the positive slope or inversion of a yield curve tends to take place in the first few years, cash flow-matching the initial portion minimizes the risk associated with nonparallel shifts of a sloped yield curve.

An extension of cash flow-matching is *symmetric cash matching*.[1] It allows the portfolio manager to construct an optimal portfolio that allows for borrowing to meet a particular liability.

---

[1] See T. Dessa Fabozzi, Tom Tong, and Yu Zhu, "Extensions of Dedicated Portfolio Techniques," Chapter 44 in Frank J. Fabozzi (ed.), *The Handbook of Fixed-Income Securities* (Homewood, IL: Richard D. Irwin, 1991).

Indexing

Indexing involves constructing a portfolio to match the performance of a specified index. There are three popular methodologies for designing a portfolio to replicate an index: (1) the cell approach, (2) the optimization approach, and (3) the variance minimization approach.

The cell approach divides the index into cells, each representing a different characteristic of the index. The most common characteristics used to distinguish a bond index are: (1) duration; (2) coupon; (3) maturity; (4) market sector (Treasury, corporate, mortgage-backed); (5) credit rating; (6) call factors; and (7) sinking fund features. The objective is to select from all of the issues in the index one or more issues in each cell that can be used to represent the entire cell. No optimization is involved with this methodology.

The optimization approach requires the portfolio manager to construct a portfolio that will match a cell breakdown and satisfy other constraints, but also optimize some objective.[2] An objective could be to maximize the yield to maturity or some other yield measure, to maximize convexity, or to maximize total return.[3] Constraints other than matching the cell breakdown might include not investing more than a specified amount in one issuer or group of issuers, and overweighting certain sectors for enhanced indexing. Depending on the mathematical characterization of the objective function and constraints, either linear or quadratic programming is used to solve for the optimal portfolio.

The variance minimization methodology is by far the most complex. It requires the use of historical data to estimate the variance of the tracking error. This is accomplished by statistically estimating a price function for every issue in the index on the basis of two sets of factors: (1) the cash flows from the issue discounted at theoretical spot rates,[4] and (2) other characteristics such as those described earlier. Once the price function for each issue is estimated, a variance equation for the tracking error is constructed. The objective then is to minimize the variance of the tracking error in constructing an indexed portfolio. Quadratic programming is used because the variance is a quadratic expression, and the objective is to minimize the variance.

Optimized Portfolio Rebalancing

Once the optimal solution or optimal portfolio is found in any particular application, the optimization process does not end. In most strategies, an initially optimal portfolio must

---

[2] For an illustration of this methodology, see Philip Galdi, "Indexing Fixed Income Portfolios," in Frank J. Fabozzi and Dessa Garlicki (eds.), *Advances in Bond Analysis and Portfolio Strategies* (Chicago: Probus Publishing, 1987).

[3] For a mathematical presentation of this methodology, as well as the variance minimization methodology, see Christina Seix and Ravi Akoury, "Bond Indexation: The Optimal Quantitative Approach," *Journal of Portfolio Management* (Spring 1986), pp. 50-53.

[4] Theoretical spot rates are explained in Chapter 13.

be rebalanced periodically as the characteristics of the portfolio change. For example, in an immunized portfolio, the duration for the individual issues changes over time as the issues approach maturity and as yields in the market change. Therefore the portfolio's duration will change or wander from its target.

Rebalancing requires the purchase of issues (either new issues not in the original optimal portfolio or additional amounts of issues included in the original portfolio) and the sale of some or all of the issues in the original optimal portfolio. An optimization model can be used to minimize the transactions costs associated with rebalancing a portfolio.

Asset Allocation

The objective of an asset allocation model is to divide funds among major asset classes so as either (1) to maximize expected return subject to a certain level of risk, or (2) to minimize risk subject to a certain level of expected return. The two are equivalent statements of the asset allocation problem.

The basic inputs for an asset allocation model are expected returns of the major asset classes, risk estimates, and correlations (or covariances) for each major asset class. The portfolio's expected return is simply the weighted average of the expected value of each asset class, where the weight is the proportion of the portfolio devoted to the asset class. That is, if X_i denotes the proportion of the portfolio allocated to asset class i and R_i the expected return for asset class i, the portfolio's expected return, assuming that there are M major asset classes, can be expressed as:

$$E(R_p) = X_1 R_1 + X_2 R_2 + \ldots + X_M R_M$$

where $E(R_p)$ is the expected return for the portfolio.

The expected risk of a portfolio is measured by the variance of the portfolio. Unlike the expected portfolio return, which is a weighted average of the expected return of each asset class, the portfolio variance also depends on the covariance (or correlation) between the asset classes. For example, if there are only two asset classes, the portfolio variance is calculated as follows:

$$Var(R_p) = X_1^2 \, Var(R_1) + X_2^2 \, Var(R_2) + 2 \, X_1 \, X_2 \, Covar(R_1, R_2)$$

where

$Var(R_p)$ = The portfolio variance;

$Var(R_i)$ = The variance of asset class i;

$Covar(R_1, R_2)$ = The covariance between the returns for asset classes 1 and 2.

Alternatively, the portfolio variance can be expressed as follows:

$$Var(R_p) = X_1 \, Var(R_1) + X_2 \, Var(R_2) \\ + 2 \, X_1^2 \, X_2^2 \, Std(R_1) \, Std(R_2) \, Corr(R_1, R_2)$$

where

Std(R_i) = Standard deviation of asset class i;

Corr(R_1,R_2) = The correlation between the returns for asset classes 1 and 2.

Because the portfolio variance is a quadratic expression (the decision variables — the X_i's — are squared), quadratic programming is used.

Given the portfolio expected return and variance, quadratic programming will yield a set of optimal or efficient portfolios. These are portfolios that will give the minimum portfolio variance for a given level of expected portfolio return.

The asset allocation model can be extended further. Beyond developing a model to minimize portfolio risk, the decision maker can determine the probability of not achieving a portfolio expected return. These probabilities are referred to as risk-of-loss probabilities.[5] The model can be extended further to provide an optimal asset allocation when short-term and long-term expectations are different.

Summary

Optimization models indicate the best solution to a problem, given some objective function and one or more constraints. Mathematical programming models are used in problems where an optimal solution is sought. Of the several types of mathematical programming models, the two most commonly used in fixed income portfolio management are linear programming and quadratic programming.

Optimization models are typically used in structured portfolio strategies, which include indexing and liability funding (immunization and dedicated portfolio strategies). Optimization models are also used in making asset allocation decisions.

---

[5] For a further explanation of risk of loss analysis, see H. Gifford Fong and Frank J. Fabozzi, "Asset Allocation Optimization Models," Chapter 8 in Robert D. Arnott and Frank J. Fabozzi (eds.), *Active Asset Allocation* (Chicago: Probus Publishing, 1992).

Index